DATE DUE

DEMCO 38-296

Historical Perspectives
on Business Enterprise
Series
▼

Letterhead from the Rhenish Railway in the 1830s
Courtesy Rheinisch-Westfälisches
Wirtschaftsarchiv, Cologne

Capitalism, Politics, and Railroads in Prussia, 1830–1870

▼

JAMES M. BROPHY

Ohio State University Press

Columbus

An earlier version of chapter 5 and part of chapter 8
originally appeared in *Central European History*.

Library of Congress Cataloging-in-Publication Data
Brophy, James M.
    Capitalism, politics, and railroads in Prussia, 1830–1870 / James
M. Brophy.
        p.   cm. — (Historical perspectives on business enterprise
series)
    Includes bibliographical references (p.   ) and index.
    ISBN 0-8142-0751-0 (cloth : alk. paper)
    1. Railroads and state—Germany—Prussia—History—19th century.
2. Business and politics—Germany—Prussia—History—19th century.
I. Title.   II. Series.
HE3079.P7B76   1998
385'.0943'09034—dc21   97-29251
                                                                     CIP

Text and jacket design by Nighthawk Design.
Type set in Times Roman by Tseng Information Systems.
Printed by McNaughton & Gunn, Inc.

The paper in this publication meets the minimum requirements
of American National Standard for Information Sciences—
Permanence of Paper for Printed Library Materials.
ANSI Z39 48–1992.
9   8   7   6   5   4   3   2   1

For Susan

CONTENTS

PREFACE

Anthony Trollope's biting satire of London's establishment, *The Way We Live Now* (1875), turns on a monstrous railroad scheme and a continental financier, allowing the author to display the layers of hypocrisy in the pretensions of birthright, capital wealth, and political power. The railroad world also acts as the mise-en-scène of Emile Zola's *La bête humaine* (1890), a setting that credibly intertwines murder, corrupt justice, and political manipulation. The final scene of a runaway train evinces Zola's view of humanity's helplessness in the face of vast industrial power. And when, in the aftermath of the 1873 stock-market crash, German politicians needed a figure to absorb the public fury over stock swindles, the preeminent choice was the German railroad magnate Bethel Henry Strousberg, whose collapsed railroad empire symbolized the unscrupulous greed of the modern age. Whether in fiction or in actual deed, the politics of building railroads gripped the minds of nineteenth-century Europeans. The unprecedented share capital, the magnitude of profit, and the interpenetration of railroad capitalism with state power and ruling elites did indeed change "the way we live now."

The current work, too, examines the politics of making money in the railroad industry. Centering on the relationship of railroad entrepreneurs with the Prussian state during the industry's critical phase of growth and consolidation, this study presents how a capitalist economy was established within a political system stamped by Prussian conservatism. It provides a new view of business politics by exploring the political practices of railroad businessmen, who, in their aim to profit from Germany's largest industrial sector, both struggled against and cooperated with the Prussian state. The business politics of the railroad industry played a critical role in German political culture, state building, and bourgeois civil society. For this reason, as the introductory chapter will make clear, this political history of business elites contributes to a number of current discussions. By cutting across the customary boundaries of business, economic, and political history, this book illuminates how business elites' search for a "mutual accommodation" between capital and political authority affected the political development of the Prussian-German nation-state.

This study consists of eight chapters. The opening chapter poses the problem and presents the historiographical context. I have endeavored to provide an informative overview for readers not conversant with the problem of German exceptionalism or with the influential works that have framed the discussions of nineteenth-century political economy. In providing access to this well-developed body of literature for scholars not specializing in German history, this study hopes to sharpen future comparative studies on entrepreneurs and statebuilding. Chapters 2, 3, and 7 are narrative chapters that provide a chronological analysis of government-business relations over forty years. Chapters 4, 5, and 6 are thematic chapters, focusing on specific issues of railroad politics regarding government regulation, joint-stock banking, and state railroad finance. The final chapter offers a synoptic conclusion, while briefly discussing the ramifications of railroad nationalization in 1879. The book surveys railroad politics throughout Prussia but devotes substantial attention to the Rhineland owing to available repositories of private railroad companies.

I have incurred numerous debts of gratitude while researching and writing this book, and it gives me great pleasure to acknowledge them. I am especially grateful to the German Academic Exchange Service (DAAD), which launched the project with a summer grant and subsequently provided a year-long research stipend. I also thank the International Research Exchange Board (IREX), which facilitated six months of research in the former German Democratic Republic, enabling me to mine systematically the files of the Prussian Trade Ministry. A generous research grant from the University of Delaware brought me back to German archives in 1993 and 1995, for which I am appreciative. The archivists at the former Zentrales Staatsarchiv in Merseburg were extremely accommodating during my long stay, and I further thank Dr. Eberhard Illner and the fine staff at the Historisches Archiv der Stadt Köln for their unstinting cooperation. Alfred and Irmgard Eschweiler, Ralph and Ulrike Verch, Dr. Jörg-Werner Kremp, Martina Frey, Dr. Gerhard Eschweiler, Professor Silke von der Emde, Professor Bert Wachsmuth, Herr Doktor and Frau Doktor von der Emde, and Horst and Margret Wachsmuth were all instrumental with their assistance and friendship during my research visits. The cooperation that numerous librarians extended to me at the Berlin Staatsbibliothek, Cologne's Universitätsbibliothek, Indiana University, and the University of Delaware is also cordially acknowledged.

There are a number of individual historians whom I wish to thank. At every stage of this project Otto Pflanze provided indispensable advice, editing, and criticism. Over the last twelve years, it has been a pleasure and a privilege to draw on his enormous learning of German history. David E. Barclay, Eric Dorn Brose, and Geoff Eley read and commented on the manuscript, and their comments undoubtedly improved it. I also thank the two anonymous referees for the Ohio State University Press, who provided excellent suggestions for the final version. I also thank George Basalla, Lawrence Duggan, Willard

Fletcher, and David Shearer, colleagues at the University of Delaware, whose concern for this book make the department of history at Delaware a pleasure to work in. Both as scholars and as parents, Elizabeth Bergen Brophy and James D. Brophy have helped over many years with sound advice and sustained encouragement. Finally, my greatest thanks goes to my wife, Susan M. McKenna, whose indefatigable support and counsel bolstered me throughout the ordeal of researching and writing this book. This book is dedicated to her.

CHAPTER ONE

▼

Capital and Political Authority in German History

"The question who *ought* to rule . . . belongs in the realm of philosophical speculation; practical politics has to do with the simple fact that it is power alone that *can* rule."[1] August Ludwig von Rochau's famous pronouncement in 1853 marked a shift in liberal political thought. A radical democrat turned moderate liberal, Rochau sought to awaken the German bourgeoisie to the realities of state power after the failure of the revolution of 1848. The weakness of the constitutional movement in 1848, he argued, had been its reliance on right rather than might, on the irresistibility of moral idealism rather than on the politics of power.

It was irrational, Rochau wrote, to expect power to subject itself to law: "To rule means to exercise power, and only he who possesses power can exercise power."[2] He dismissed as unrealistic the assumption of German idealism that ideas triumph when their time has come. And yet he clung to the belief that the middle classes would eventually triumph. State power, he maintained, was conditioned by the "relationship of social forces," the most important of which were "wealth, intelligence, and education."[3] Of these, wealth would ultimately be decisive. "The aristocratic tie to the land as a force in the state has fallen," he wrote, because "landed property is more and more outweighed by the daily growing mass of movable capital."[4] In Rochau's scheme of *Realpolitik,* then, it was not the moral force of liberal idealism that would clear the path to power but the growth of a new economic order that would compel Germany's rulers to yield to the interests and values of the middle classes.[5]

The "Structural Continuity Thesis"

Rochau's thoughts on social relations in the 1850s describe the beginning of what has now come to be called the "structural continuity thesis."[6] The power

1

of capital to recast society and politics endowed the German business class with undeniable importance. The expansion of commodities, capital, and services in regional and international networks since the 1830s was changing Germany into a modern market economy. The owners of factories, banks, insurance companies, and railways determined the investments, innovations, distribution of resources, and division of labor. Although they were merely 1.2 percent of the population, the industrial and commercial bourgeoisie (bankers, brokers, manufacturers, merchants, company directors, and owners of coal mines and iron foundries) led the industrial revolution.[7] These businessmen[8] were, as Friedrich Engels wrote in 1847, the "most decisive faction of the German bourgeoisie." Prosperity in industry, he wrote, produced in turn greater domestic and overseas trade, more railroads, and an expanded stock market. The business class and its needs, Engels believed, was the motor of social transformation. It "represents the needs of the entire bourgeoisie and all classes dependent on it."[9]

For both Rochau and Engels the new business elite was also the bearer of a new political order. It possessed the economic means to challenge the political dominance of the landed aristocracy and remodel the state to accommodate more fully the interests of commerce and industry and the emerging mass society. Contrary to their expectations, however, a decisive break with the past never came to pass. Unprecedented economic growth converged with the reassertion of Prussian conservative political power, producing a "historic compromise" in this "age of capital."[10] The decade of reaction in Prussia after 1848 frustrated many who had hoped to achieve decisive political reforms.

For many historians the sociopolitical attitudes of businessmen and their continuing links with the Prussian-German state explain how an aristocratic, landholding political elite retained power in Germany until 1918 in spite of the shrinking economic influence of agriculture. They argue that a structural continuity in the political economy of Germany explains the course of German history from 1848 to 1918. In 1848 the capitalist class abandoned liberal ideals, so the argument goes, and sought stability in the reaction of the 1850s; economic concessions neutralized political aspirations. When liberalism revived in the New Era (1858–62) and the Prussian parliament rejected a military reform bill, setting off a constitutional conflict over the legislature's power of the purse (1862–66), the business class again deserted the liberal front. Following the military victory over Austria in 1866, businessmen formed the core of the new National Liberal Party, which made its peace with Bismarck's "Bonapartism," accepting a new amalgam of authoritarian government, national unity, laissez-faire, and finance capitalism. During the depression that followed the crash of 1873, Bismarck scrapped free trade (1878–79) and (so it has been said) "refounded the empire" with tariff laws protecting both iron and rye, thus securing the political alliance of Junkers and industrialists.

In the period after Bismarck, the structural continuity argument continues, the bloc-building, lobbyist politics (*Sammlungspolitik*) of the 1890s reduced the German parliament to a brokerage house of economic interests, which was also parlayed into a defensive front against the rise of the Social Democratic Party, by 1912 the largest political party in Germany. Businessmen, furthermore, advocated *Weltpolitik:* colonies would bring new markets and cheap raw materials; battleships would sustain the growth of the heavy industries; and the lure of foreign glory would paper over domestic political strife ("social imperialism"). The advocacy of territorial annexation by major economic interest groups after 1911 contributed to Germany's aggressive war aims in 1914. The structural legacies of the Wilhelminian empire, so the thesis concludes, weakened the democratic forces supporting the Weimar Republic and thus prepared the way for the rise of the Third Reich, the Second World War, and the Holocaust.[11] In brief, the structural continuity thesis would explain the long discussed and much debated "special path" (*Sonderweg*) taken by German history during the fateful century after 1848, from the failed revolution to the founding of the Bonn republic.

Betrayal, Alliance, Symbiosis

To discuss the validity of this general thesis in its entirety would far exceed the normal limits of a single historical monograph. Instead, this study focuses on the early years, the four vital decades (1830–71) when the structure's foundation was putatively laid. But first it is necessary to consider a number of subsidiary issues (that is, subsidiary to the central problem outlined above) that have been raised by historians and social theorists concerning the events of these years.

To orthodox Marxist historians, the behavior of the German capitalists after 1848 was an act of betrayal (*Verrat*). The German bourgeois failed to carry out the role assigned them by dialectical materialism. They failed to overcome the aristocratic-monarchical order and replace it with a bourgeois republic in a united Germany—the necessary prelude to the final victory of industrial capitalism over feudal agrarianism. That victory would in turn have prepared the way for the inevitable triumph of the proletariat in the climactic class struggle with the bourgeoisie. Even worse, the bourgeoisie came to terms and even cooperated with the old order, unnaturally extending its life into the twentieth century.[12]

In his study of railway construction in Prussia before 1848 Dietrich Eich-holtz shows how the "Prussian way" veered from the path Marx had charted. The "necessary" class antagonism between the nobility and bourgeois capi-talists, he argues, did not develop to the point of clearing away the remnants of feudal society. Using the railroad industry in its early phase (1830–48), he shows how the bourgeoisie established an "unholy alliance" with the Junkers. He calls the bourgeoisie's use of the Prussian absolutistic state to facilitate the construction of railroads the "method of material corruption." The capital-ists, for example, relied on the state for legal decrees to expedite land appro-priation and to overcome the difficulties of accumulating capital, government subsidies, loans, and the subscription of stock. "From the beginning the Prus-sian way was a compromise between the bourgeoisie and the old ruling classes by which both Junker and capitalist profited." [13] Such a relationship between capital and feudalism encouraged "antirevolutionary tendencies . . . among the Prussian bourgeoisie . . . whose pitiful behavior can be characterized by cowardice, betrayal of the mass movement to the old ruling powers, and mis-erable servility." [14] Karl Obermann, Ernst Engelberg, and Roland Zeise echoed Eichholtz's position.[15]

Most scholars have dismissed the bourgeoisie's "historical mission" and its betrayal as teleological and unhistorical.[16] In the 1960s a new generation of historians sought to use social scientific methods to explain the historical roots of the Nazi dictatorship. In so doing they strove to avoid both the Marx-ist blueprint for social development and the historicist-idealist tradition that accepted Bismarck's empire as a uniquely German social formation.[17] Their principal analytical tool was modernization theory, a sociological model that posits democracy as the normative form of government for urbanized, indus-trialized mass societies. England's gradualism, France's revolution, and the in-dustrialized democracy of the United States were held up as examples against which the deficiencies of Germany's political tradition could be examined.[18]

In this context *alliance* became a key term—a codeword—to describe the relationship between capitalists and Prussia's ruling elite during the 1848 revolution and the subsequent reaction that marked for the middle classes the beginning of a servile, antidemocratic tradition. Faced with a two-front battle against democrats in the street and the ruling aristocratic elites, liberal poli-ticians—many of them businessmen—chose to side with the latter, entering into a junior partnership that guaranteed order and stability but sacrificed a political voice. The term alliance, however, is not completely an ex post facto construct. In 1847 the historian Heinrich von Sybel prescribed an "open, thorough, and practical alliance" among capitalists, the intelligentsia, and the state to prevent the rise of "dangerous communistic tendencies" brought about by the "great contrast between capitalists and the unpropertied." [19]

Postwar historians, however, use the term alliance less for a specific event or agreement than as a general description of the political milieu of the 1850s. First used by Heinrich Heffter in 1950,[20] the word reappeared in Friedrich Zunkel's work on Rhenish and Westphalian entrepreneurs between 1834 and 1878. Published in 1962, Zunkel's lapidary prose, wealth of primary sources, and clear, forceful thesis made the book enormously influential, and it still remains the authoritative study on Prussian entrepreneurs. "It was perhaps the brilliance of this work," noted Hartmut Kaelble in 1985, that discouraged "subsequent social-historical works on the political history of the [entrepreneurial] bourgeoisie." [21]

Zunkel sought to explain the origins of the cartel of economic interests that arose between the landed nobility and the high bourgeoisie in the Kaiserreich. He was the first of Germany's postwar historians to employ social historical methods—attention to social origins, occupations of sons, marriage patterns, and social networks—to clarify the political stance of entrepreneurial groups in the Rhineland and Westphalia. He argued that in the 1830s and 1840s a confident, self-conscious entrepreneurial class arose that provided leadership in the revolution of 1848. While noting some uniquely German characteristics in the prerevolutionary era—rapid industrialization, late development of the bourgeois class—Zunkel clearly views the 1848 revolution and its political fallout as a significant watershed in German political life. Fearing both the democratic demands of radical artisans and the threat of extensive damage to property, the Rhenish leadership became increasingly moderate, advocating a constitutional monarchy, limited suffrage, and, eventually, a "break with the revolution." For the sake of order and economic stability, the bourgeoisie gave up its "political emancipation," "retreated" from politics, fortified a "feudal society," and hindered development toward a "humanistic, democratic social order." [22]

In the 1850s and 1860s the development of the bourgeoisie degenerated, Zunkel suggested, into an "alliance of governing classes" in which the entrepreneurial class remained the "second social power." [23] The alliance of the 1850s and 1860s is presented as a dualism: the once political businessmen of the Rhineland were "diverted" to economics by an "authoritarian monarchy," thus accepting the administrative dominance of the state and the political leadership of the feudal nobility.[24] The combination of economic prosperity and the abandonment of bourgeois values led in turn to a "feudalization of the bourgeoisie": the increasing imitation of aristocratic styles of living and bourgeois conformity to a "half-feudal Prussian society." The building of lavish villas, the cultivation of noble contacts, and the desire for aristocratic titles exemplify the feudalized behavior of entrepreneurs.[25] In short, these developments amounted to stagnation; the "bourgeoisie, which at mid-century

dreamed of ruling in the future, no longer possessed the vitality and influence to assert itself against the East-Elbian nobility." [26] For Zunkel the price
of bourgeois integration into the Prussian-German state was dear.

In this perspective the pivotal era of the German *Sonderweg* was 1848–
66, when leaders of the German bourgeoisie swapped their claim to political
leadership for the privilege of making money. In so doing, commercial and
industrial leaders gradually estranged themselves from any kind of emancipatory social-political movement, thus laying the groundwork for a weak democratic tradition in Germany. When the ascension of Prince-Regent Wilhelm
to the Prussian throne in 1858 revived public forums on liberal politics—the
New Era—and brought about the founding of the liberal Progressive Party in
1861, entrepreneurs ceased to identify themselves with the liberal parliamentary movement. Satisfied with the economic concessions granted by the state,
the business class denied the political movement the economic clout it needed
to succeed. Hence, the alliance thesis dovetails with that of a German tendency
toward "revolution from above": the ability of conservative elites throughout
early modern and modern German history to introduce just enough reform
to preempt social and political change from below.[27] In the context of the
1850s, writes Hans-Ulrich Wehler, the "continuation of the 'revolution from
above' after 1849 proceeded with economic-political reforms and concessions
as compensation for political repression and lack of emancipation." [28]

The alliance thesis, so forcefully presented by Zunkel, pervades the major
social histories on entrepreneurs, liberalism, and nineteenth-century political movements. It is to be found, for example, in the works of Jürgen Kocka,
Helmut Böhme, Richard Tilly, Heinrich August Winkler, Hans-Ulrich Wehler,
Wolfgang Mommsen, Wolfgang Klee, Wolfram Siemann, and others.[29]

Böhme, in particular, uses the alliance thesis to place the role of the "do-
mesticated" bourgeoisie in a larger context. His *Deutschlands Weg zur Grossmacht* (1966) sought to show that the struggle between Prussia and Austria
for political hegemony in Central Europe from 1848 to 1866 was primarily
rooted in economics. Such an approach eclipses the importance of Bismarck's
statesmanship in the 1860s. Writing economic history as diplomatic history,
Böhme argued that Prussia's success in frustrating Vienna's attempts to enter
the German Customs Union in 1853 and 1865 was more decisive in its effects
than Prussia's military victory of 1866.[30] Prussia's "marriage" to the western
industrialized states through the Franco-Prussian customs treaty in 1862 prevented the Habsburg monarchy from attaining the economic leverage needed
to realize its large-German (*grossdeutsch*) design, an "empire of seventy millions" that would have stretched from the North Sea to the Adriatic.[31]

Underlying Böhme's argument is the assumption that free trade had a unifying effect on diverse political interests in Prussia. The allure of free trade

produced a "new political coalition" between "traders, bankers, and [light] in-dustrialists and the conservative feudal agrarian leadership of Prussia." With this "community of interests, not only did the liberal-democratic aims of 1848 fail but also the plans of Austria." [32] Free trade, Böhme asserted, was the nec-essary concession that produced a "division of labor." With the noble land-holding classes abstaining "from modern industrial economic processes . . . [balanced by] the far-reaching abstinence of entrepreneurs from the political arena, the old and new elites laid the basis for the special position and the special development of Germany." [33] For Böhme the politically supine Prus-sian bourgeoisie was an essential component to the Prussian state's drive for political hegemony in Central Europe after 1848.

Under close examination the idea of a political alliance among German elites based on free trade does not stand up. A consensus on free trade existed neither in the business community in the 1850s nor between the National Lib-eral and Free Conservative political parties in the 1860s.[34] It is clear that the "concession" of free trade did not pacify businessmen, who had other de-mands. In the 1850s, the same commercial circles, as we shall see in chapters 4 and 5, sharply opposed the government on banking policy and entered into law suits against the government over control of private railroad companies. The use of "alliance" and "new political coalition" glosses over the com-plexity of domestic politics and the numerous difficulties between business and the state in an expanding economy. The idea of a division of labor between Junkers and entrepreneurs overlooks the Silesian landlords who invested in coal mines, iron foundries, and railroad companies, as well as widespread speculation by Junker landlords in industrial securities. The clean division of economic and political spheres is an unconvincing interpretative scheme for the 1850s—particularly for the entrepreneurial outlook, which usually linked political and economic matters.

The chief shortcoming of Böhme's work, then, is the overemphasis on high politics and state political economy, and an undiscerning attention to the politics of doing business in specific sectors, regions, and business circles. On this point Theodore S. Hamerow's important two-volume study is more astute, giving color and definition to the expanding public voices of bourgeois economic and public life. His studies underscore the import of the postrevo-lutionary period for the empire's social and political foundations, but his com-manding overview is concerned more with the breakthrough of laissez-faire industrialism, bourgeois public opinion, and the growing commercial hege-mony of Prussia than with showing specifically how postrevolutionary eco-nomic politics affected the evolving relationship between businessmen and Prussian state officials.[35] Neither Böhme nor Hamerow shows us the politics of the boardroom: how businessmen, representatives of large-scale capitalism, contested state policy to establish the right to make money.[36] Handbooks and synthetic narratives further reflect this shortcoming.[37]

In the 1970s West German neo-Marxist historians Lothar Machtan, Dietrich Milles, and Michael Gugel opposed the notion of alliance, advocating instead the idea of symbiosis. Gugel, for instance, portrayed Prussia in the 1850s and 1860s as a postrevolutionary, acquisitive, consumer-oriented society that consequently developed a liberalism more reform-oriented than emancipatory. The Progressive Party, Gugel asserted, was not interested in recasting the foundations of the Prussian state by franchise extension, a cabinet responsible to parliament, or a more democratic constitution.[38] Rather, the Progressives sought a greater "embourgeoisement of the power structure" by reorganizing the state for greater efficiency.[39] During the 1850s the concepts of civil law, justice, and the constitutional state, once brimming with radical significance, were emptied of their content by middle-class parties.[40]

The bourgeoisie in the 1850s, asserted Gugel, drew a sharper distinction between society and state. They increasingly viewed the state as an institution through which disputed interests could be arbitrated and resolved; it was "an excellent instrument for the advancement of economic and social interests." [41] After the decreed constitution of 1850 secured the socioeconomic foundation of Prussia, a depoliticized "bourgeois-capitalistic" society unfolded. Gugel deflated the importance of the constitutional conflict, in which a liberal opposition attempted to rein in the authoritarian Prussian executive through greater parliamentary control. The conditions for a liberalization of the constitution and the Prussian political system, Gugel argued, never existed.[42]

Machtan and Milles offered their study, *Klassensymbiose von Junkertum und Bourgeoisie* (1980), as a corrective to the left-liberal modernization theory, which "replaced the nostalgia for the holy world of the authoritarian state" with a "nostalgia for the holy world of the modern constitutional state." They argued that by reconciling capitalistic social development with the *telos* of liberal social democracy, West German modernization theory was putting a square peg in a round hole.[43] Central to their critique is the dismissal of the term alliance. The word presupposes a "voluntary subjective act" rather than a "capitalistically determined, historical-concrete unity of ruling classes." [44] They replaced "alliance" with "symbiosis of classes," a term that in their view more accurately reflects the relationship of the capitalist class to the preindustrial order.

The symbiosis refers to a "fundamental consensus" between Junkers, a noble class of capitalist farmers, and the bourgeoisie, a class granted optimal conditions to industrialize by the state.[45] The relationship had little to do with the conscious actions of either group but was "simply decreed to them by the ambivalent development of German capitalism." [46] Mixing organic and mechanical metaphors, Machtan and Milles stated: "Naturally the real-historical functional mechanism of this class symbiosis crystallized only very slowly and, for the time being, unconsciously behind the backs of the productive agents involved." [47] In this respect, politics were merely epiphenomenal actions to protect material interests. Echoing Gugel, the authors argued that the constitutional conflict was nothing more than an effort by the middle classes to legitimate an already established social position and to attain further economic concessions. In what was hardly an emancipatory movement, the oppositional tendencies of the commercial and industrial bourgeoisie could be dismissed as "pragmatic opportunism." [48] This neo-Marxist view assigns no emancipatory role to the business class after 1849. It characterizes the Prussian experience from 1850 to 1870 as a peculiar form of bourgeois dominance, in which the needs of the class were met without overthrowing the state.

These neo-Marxist interpretations redress the misreading of the bourgeoisie as a subordinated, feudalized middle class but offer only half-truths as alternatives. Certainly the ability of both new and old elites to amalgamate their interests in an undemocratic state is the crux of the matter. But whether the postrevolutionary socioeconomic base (which "objectively conditions" the Junker-bourgeois "form of rule" [*Herrschaftsform*]) [49] was organized as effortlessly as Gugel and others suggest is questionable. Their arguments evade the numerous concrete points of conflict between conservative and bourgeois interests during the first industrial revolution. Equally evasive is Milles and Machtan's use of the biological term *symbiosis,* the process by which two separate organisms live together with a mutually beneficial association. It is ironic that these two historians harshly criticize bourgeois historical writing yet show a historicist penchant for the organic metaphor of symbiosis. Such a metaphor conveys a frictionless process. A metaphor of social process must also account for opposition, exclusion, and competition. Symbiosis evokes the "invisible hand" of capitalism silently transforming German society without showing the antagonistic processes inherent in a capitalist economy. There are no agents in Milles and Machtan's story. We are less apt to consider the politics of the 1850s as a cozy symbiotic process if we look beyond abstractions regarding the "ambivalent development of capitalism" toward the people and parties who represented the varied and vying interests of agriculture, trade, transportation, handicrafts, and light and heavy industry.

Material Interests versus Liberal Idealism

Implicit in all three versions of the *Sonderweg* construct is the idealization of pre-1848 liberalism. Eichholtz, Zunkel, Böhme, and Gugel all take the posi-

tion that a clearly defined democratic-liberal idea existed before the revolution and was abandoned during it. The political interpretations of the 1850s
are colored by the assumption that before 1848 the German bourgeoisie espoused a universalist political ideal calling for a free, rational, constitutional
form of government. Afterward the universal humanism gave way to class-
specific interests, inviting opportunism and compromise. These assertions are
based on the assumption that 1848 was a great political watershed.

To be sure, some German liberals abandoned the universalist political role
of the bourgeoisie as a result of 1848. But the political views of Prussia's liberal
cadres were almost always class-specific—before and after 1848.[50] No ideology of natural-law philosophy or democratic principles led urban notables,
merchant-patricians, and economically ascendant businessmen to advocate a
constitution in the 1830s and 1840s.[51] Urban leaders never believed in a political role for the unpropertied classes and never challenged the legitimacy of the
Prussian monarchy. Rather, this social group believed in the need to end arbitrary government and establish a *Rechtsstaat* (rule by law) to protect property,
person, and marketplace. In so doing they presumed to speak for the masses.

Practical issues such as adjusting the tax base, introducing better property
laws, banning entail and hunting rights, promoting customs treaties, debating
the merits of free trade, and abolishing the patrimonial court system occupied
the political agenda of Prussian businessmen in the pre-1848 era. They were
moderate economic liberals who believed that politics should accommodate
the two principal spheres of civil society: commerce and industry. Joseph
Dumont, newspaper owner, railway director, and urban notable, revealed the
character of entrepreneurial politics in 1833 by advocating "sensible freedom—not because of any theory but because lawful freedom alone ensures
the comforts of life, free activity, industriousness, and freedom of occupation." Ideologies he disdained: "exclusive theories from all sides are much
too rigid." [52] Recent research has rendered a more accurate political portrait
of the pre-March Prussian entrepreneur.[53]

This bias among businessmen toward practicality was equally prevalent
during the revolution of 1848. Although idealistic political issues are usually
the main focus of historical accounts of 1848, the material-economic issues
are hard to avoid. The unification of Germany under Prussia was for Prussian liberals as much an economic goal as a political ideal; it corresponded to
David Hansemann's subsequent plan to unify the German states with a federal *Zollverein* (Customs Union) parliament.[54] The protracted debates on voting and constitutions must not be permitted to obscure the significance of the
many economic associations and advocacy groups that blossomed in 1848.
They promoted a wide spectrum of interests and integrated the question of

free trade, national tariffs, and protective legislation for crafts into the central forum in Frankfurt.[55]

The practicality of economic liberals contrasted greatly with the idealistic posture of the lawyers, professors, civil servants, and other representatives of *Bildungsbürgertum* (the professional middle classes). Wilhelm Oechselhäuser, a businessman from Dessau who worked in Silesia, complained in 1848 about the "enormous phrasemaking" of "illusionists" in Frankfurt who argued over the basic rights of Germans. He demanded that the parliament and the people finally concern themselves with sensible things, such as economic questions.[56] Gustav Mevissen, the Cologne entrepreneur, expressed similar sentiments when he wrote in October 1848, "The volubility of the professors is indefatigable, and I very much fear that German unity will perish because of German thoroughness."[57] It is perhaps not surprising that in March 1848 one of Hansemann's first deeds as minister was to supply credit to Rhenish banks and transform the leading Cologne bank, the A. Schaaffhausen'sche Bankverein, into a joint-stock enterprise.

Whether one interprets the pursuit of material interests as opportunistic[58] or as an indication of political maturity,[59] we must nonetheless recognize this rudimentary element in the political outlook of businessmen. It is unhistorical to impugn these liberal-minded businessmen as turncoats and cowards in 1848 when they consistently held plutocratic, commercially based political views. In 1845 Rhenish liberals reformed the electoral procedure for the provincial diet; its three-tiered voting system based on degrees of wealth became the model for that introduced by Prussia in 1849. Men such as Dumont, Hansemann, and Camphausen believed not in equal citizenship but in active and passive voting rights. Criteria for enfranchisement was based on wealth, property, and influence. It is not surprising, then, that Hansemann believed the constitution of 5 December 1848, which granted universal manhood suffrage, went too far, encouraging "destructive democratic and anti-government principles." The subsequent "relief, if not satisfaction," as Rudolf Gneist commented, with which the "propertied classes welcomed the Three Class System" was not betrayal but consistency.[60]

The betrayal and alliance theses lose much of their force if it is assumed that businessmen (before and after 1848) always presumed to work with the monarchy to achieve reform. Hansemann's pamphlet of 1833, *Preussen und Frankreich,* criticized the state of Prussia by praising France's constitution and enlightened legislation. But Hansemann presented his call for a constitution as advice to the Prussian monarchy and not as opposition; he admonished the king to include the wealthy bourgeoisie in the ruling elite in order to ward off a more radical democratic movement. In 1840 he characterized the Prussian monarchy as a "useful and conservative" protection "against the lower more dangerous democratic elements." [61] Similarly, it was Ludolf Camphausen, the railroad entrepreneur from Cologne, who in May 1848 called back the prince-regent from exile in England and never abandoned his hope of unifying Germany under the Prussian monarchy. To pursue the small-German (*kleindeutsch*) program, he convened the Prussian National Assembly on 22 May 1848. It opened four days after the National Assembly in Frankfurt, whose unifying efforts it undercut. To know the limited reform program of these businessmen in the prerevolutionary or *Vormärz* era is to recognize that their political attitudes in the 1850s were a continuum from the 1830s, not a consequence of failure in 1848. For this reason, this study begins in 1830 to underscore the strong strands of continuity in entrepreneurial politics.

In doing so, this study confirms the thesis of Jeffry Diefendorf's distinguished work on Rhenish businessmen's politics between 1789 and 1834.[62] His research on entrepreneurial behavior under French occupation and early Prussian governance reveals the utterly pragmatist political style of Rhenish businessmen, who sought to weave the needs of business institutions and business politics into the fabric of state life. Although Diefendorf's study ends in the 1830s with the onset of industrialization, his argument that "the old, pre-revolutionary political process which had benefited them and had provided them with their political education" deserves emphasis.[63] The following chapters will confirm the validity of this claim, while also showing the continued flexibility of businessmen in adapting to (and exploiting) the new political conditions after 1830.

As the next chapters will show at greater length, the business class in the 1840s and 1850s sought no radical change in Prussia's social and political order. Before and after 1848, it did not seek to expel aristocrats from the seats of power. More accurately, the business elite demanded to be incorporated into the ruling class, "those privileged people who, without exercising actual political functions, influence those who govern . . . because of the economic and financial power they possess." [64] Not only are the rigid class distinctions anachronistic for this period, but the independent role of the Prussian state is also distorted. Marxist theory asserts that the state is the instrument of the ruling class (*Junkerstaat*) and thus dismisses the problem. The alliance thesis, relying more on Max Weber and Western sociology, recognizes the state as a potential third party but evades the problem with the shibboleth of a "feudal absolutistic state"—inferring a mirror conformity of the state to the political needs of the conservative aristocracy. The symbiosis theory considers the state to have been the stage where the interests of Junkers and capitalists met and negotiated their competing claims, assigning to the state the role of mediator, not player.

The government of Minister-President Otto von Manteuffel (1850–58) and the bureaucracy that served it, however, sought to steer a course between the romantic conservative philosophy of the Prussian aristocracy (expressed best by the Gerlach brothers and the political philosophers Karl Ludwig von Haller and Friedrich Julius Stahl) and the demands of the liberal opposition in parliament.[65] Manteuffel's neoabsolutism sought to reassert the primacy of the Prussian state over all particular estates and classes, and this policy pleased neither noble conservatives nor middle-class liberals.[66] Moreover, one cannot assume a monolithic policy or philosophy when referring to the state. Ministers and high-ranking regional bureaucrats, for example, could not agree on basic economic policy, displaying inconsistencies and contradictions that reveal a divided, uncertain government.

In rendering a more accurate construction of the political dialogue between old and new elites, we must assume a multivocal Prussian state in the throes of remaking itself. Eric D. Brose's study on how the Prussian state lurched into the era of industrialization moves beyond conventional paradigms, throwing new light on the fragile consensus-building procedures that operated in the factionalized, multiparty state apparatus. His research underscores the influence of new social forces that eroded the caste mentality of government elites (*Beamtenstaat*), obviating any absolute distinctions between state and society after the 1840s.[67] Equally important is David E. Barclay's political biography of Friedrich Wilhelm IV, in which his interpretation of the Prussian state in the 1850s as a complex amalgam of countervailing forces opens up new conceptual space for future research.[68] Barclay, for example, demolishes the prevalent view that the Camarilla, the king's ultraconservative shadow cabinet, exercised wide-ranging powers in the period 1850–58.[69] He presents instead a more persuasive interpretation of Friedrich Wilhelm, whose intricate balancing of opposing interests enabled a wider range of political, economic, and social forces to exert influence in the reconstitution of the Prussian state after 1848. Grounded in solid archival materials, these studies give tangible meaning and historical specificity to the important but overly abstract term *state building.*

In many ways, it is exactly the absence of a rigorous context of business politics that mars the betrayal, alliance, and symbiosis theses of structural continuity. They place theoretical arguments ahead of empirical evidence. Although the political and economic attitudes of the capitalist class are the linchpin of this historical problem, the nuances and ambiguities within this social group have been surprisingly neglected. Böhme, Eichholtz, Engelberg, Obermann, Gugel, and Machtan and Milles all assume an unproblematic, docile business class. Hamerow admirably foregrounds the criticisms and tensions of economic politics circulating in the public sphere but does not focus on specific spheres of conflict in government-business relations. Zunkel's portrayal, too, is more differentiated and therefore convincing, but his analysis of bourgeois subjugation rests more on a sociological preoccupation with status and prestige in Prussian society than on an empirical analysis of how the postrevolutionary socioeconomic settlement was actually produced. We are given little idea how businessmen and other middle-class social groups interacted with the governmental bureaucracy at any level, whether local, regional, or ministerial. The question of how three elite groups—businessmen, state officials, and the nobility—confronted one another on such major questions as banking, customs and tariffs, transportation policy, joint-stock banks, and government supervision in this pivotal decade remains unanswered.

In the one case where work has been done on businessmen's behavior, the results fail to confirm the conventional picture. Hartmut Kaelble's study of Berlin entrepreneurs during the period of early industrialization (1830–70) sets aside overarching theories and investigates the social and political actions of businessmen in Berlin. Arguing from solid empirical research, Kaelble stated: "At least in the case of Berlin and its leading entrepreneurs the thesis cannot be confirmed that businessmen after 1848 . . . paid for their social ascendancy and economic decision-making freedom with political conformity." [70] He shows that the 1850s were actually a time when businessmen began to challenge the authority of the state bureaucracy and demanded a greater voice in the decision-making process. Using such associations as the chamber of commerce and the Berlin Trade Corporation (Die Berliner Korporation der Kaufmannschaft), businessmen saw to it that their interests were duly weighed by the government, which relented on many issues. "The thesis that businessmen retreated from politics after 1848," Kaelble concluded, "is at least not valid for Berlin." [71] He noted, however, that Berlin's business class did not challenge the basic autonomy of the bureaucracy. Businessmen contented themselves with winning small business-related gains in the government through quiet advisory channels and did not seek the larger gains of direct political power. Although Kaelble was careful to present his findings as unrepresentative of other entrepreneurial groups,[72] his study suggests that further research could produce a better conception of entrepreneurial politics than the simplistic formulas of betrayal, alliance, and symbiosis.

Bürgertum and the Business Class

Perhaps the most salient feature of modern research on nineteenth-century Germany was its neglecting to explore agency in social spheres other than the conservative establishment. Because paradigms centered on conservative elites pulling wires to direct the movements of a "supine bourgeoisie and a pusillanimous liberalism,"[73] historians' research emphasized the antidemocratic, feudalistic, preindustrial elements. In 1980, however, Geoff Eley and David Blackbourn launched a new research agenda with the publication of essays that challenged the theoretical and comparative premises upon which the *Sonderweg,* or special path, thesis rests.[74]

Eley sets himself the task of illuminating the conceptual flaws in modernization theory and its application to the *Sonderweg* thesis. He especially questions modernization theory's assumption that the benchmark of a successful industrialized country is the presence of middle-class liberalism. The distinction between industrialism and liberalism, he argues, must be better sharpened: the former is a socioeconomic category, the latter a specific ideology. Conflating the two obfuscates the essential differences and further allows the German middle class, whose members were not "good liberals," to be judged as a failure. Overall Eley charges German historical literature with terminological slippage with the terms bourgeoisie-liberalism-democracy: "The conceptual elision of 'liberal' into 'bourgeois' is further compounded by the still riskier equation of 'liberalism' and 'democracy.' "[75] If the terms can be pried apart, he argues, one could begin to recognize a German bourgeoisie, mature and assertive, which found liberalism ill-suited to its political aims.[76] The tendency of the structural continuity thesis to fuse these terms indivisibly, Eley states, further enforces the inclination to measure events with "straightforward polarity"—either liberal victory or aristocratic authoritarianism.[77] "The interests of the bourgeoisie may be pursued and secured by other than liberal means," which leads Eley to place greater emphasis on the German bourgeoisie's economic and juridical successes than on parliamentary liberalism. By stressing the ability of *Bürgertum* (middle-class groups) to develop and profit from industrial capitalism as well as to shape a law code that enabled bourgeois civil society to blossom in imperial Germany, Eley dismisses the "deficiencies" of *Bürgertum.* "Germany did, after all, experience a successful bourgeois revolution in the nineteenth century."[78]

Although Eley's strictures gloss over valid elements of the *Sonderweg* thesis, his critical inquiry is salutary and welcome.[79] Certainly his discussion about what groups actually implemented radical social revolutions in Western Europe and whether liberalism must be the prescribed ideology of the capitalist bourgeoisie was a clarion call to undertake more rigorous comparative history. More important, his pleas to jettison the hardened either-or formulations in judging bourgeois "success" after 1848 and to recognize the many middle-class social groups who became the principal beneficiaries of the reconstituted postrevolutionary Prussian-German state is a theoretical breakthrough. Eley's essay exhorts historians to locate sites and processes of bourgeois agency in state and society.

Blackbourn, too, questions the efficacy of the *Sonderweg* methodology, which examines a social class on the basis of what it ought to be; the German title of his essay, "How it actually did not happen" ("Wie es eigentlich nicht gewesen"), expresses the ironic dig. Blackbourn proposes to examine what is there and keenly observes the cultural influence of the bourgeoisie. At issue for Blackbourn is whether the bourgeoisie had the power and means to stamp German society with bourgeois values. Scrutinizing civil law, public space, and public institutions (zoos, operas, parks, museums, etc.), Blackbourn sees in the more diffuse experience of civil society a smugly optimistic bourgeoisie, proud of its accomplishments. Against the "broader pattern of material, institutional, legal, and intellectual changes," Blackbourn speaks of a "silent revolution." [80] By employing an argument of cultural hegemony, he does not deny the strong aristocratic presence and antiliberal tendencies in German society. But Blackbourn asserts that Germany's antiliberal tendencies, when integrated into the greater framework of European social history, are comparable with other national traditions. Germany, he claims, merely "provided the heightened version of the norm." [81]

Blackbourn's intent to modify perceptions of Germany's "peculiarities" is convincing, and his recognition of multiple identities in bourgeois life and his desire to examine civil society through a prism other than Berlin's court, government, and parliament is noteworthy. In recognizing that the bourgeois revolution may be closer to a gradual, fluid process of opportunities than the event-oriented "failure of 1848," both Blackbourn and Eley have cast new light on the study of bourgeois culture.[82]

German historians have readily taken up the challenge of Blackbourn and Eley to rethink the middle-class role in German history. Numerous collections of essays reexamining the socioeconomic and political world of the nineteenth-century German bourgeoisie have emerged in the last ten years, and numerous other articles and monographs address this subject.[83] Although it is too early to surmise a consensus, it seems that an incremental revision of some *Sonderweg* assumptions is underway.

Hartmut Kaelble and Wolfram Fischer have shown, for example, the relative uselessness of the *Sonderweg* idea when comparing processes of industrialization and social structures to other countries. Kaelble argued in 1983 that, in terms of per capita economic growth, occupational dislocation, growth in the secondary and tertiary sectors, structural economic changes (farming to industry, craft to mechanization), and such demographic factors as urbanization, the putative influence of "rapid industrialization" on Germany's *Sonder-*

weg does not hold up.[84] Wolfram Fischer has added other socioeconomic statistical data to this thesis. In view of the pervasiveness of "deference society" and the general influence of nobility in the bureaucracies, armies, and economies of England, France, Russia, and Spain, the inability of the German bourgeoisie to become the sole ruling class is no exception.[85] Comparisons between French and German entrepreneurs also belie the commonly held assumption that German industrialists were both better trained academically and more authoritarian.[86] The corollary between the *Herr-im-Hause* attitude of German business and the authoritarian state must be rethought. Certainly the careful social historical research of Dolores Augustine-Perez and Dirk Schumann convincingly dismisses the idea that either "feudalization" or "aristocraticization" has little, if any, explanatory power for German businessmen.[87] New research using comparison and social-historical specificity will prune back many of the traits indulgently ascribed to "German character."

Such revisions affect the period of this study. The convenient use of the bourgeois "retreat" from politics after 1848, for example, has been rejected. In his synthesis of German history from 1800 to 1866, Thomas Nipperdey labeled the history of the liberal retreat a "legend": "it is inexact, essentially false—indeed nothing more than moralizing literary criticism." [88] Beate-Carola Padtberg's study of Rhenish liberalism during the reactionary period of 1850–58 also sets aside the notion of "political apathy." In examining the chamber of commerce, the municipal council, and the Cologne newspaper *Die Kölnische Zeitung,* she effectively shows how a broad oppositional political movement (combining both bourgeois and aristocratic classes) grew out of the "rational and flexible" tactics of the city's economic elite to assert its materialist demands during the economic boom.[89] Two recent German textbooks by Wolfram Siemann and Reinhard Rürup also strive to balance the repressive features with the "modern constitutional and democratic elements" [90] of the Prussian state and a politically active bourgeoisie.[91]

Yet paradigms die hard. The staying power of the alliance thesis is evinced in Hans-Ulrich Wehler's new study of German history from 1849 to 1914, which still characterizes the 1850s as an "unpolitical Eldorado" for businessmen.[92] And Rudolf Boch's study of businessmen who first introduced accelerated industrial expansion into the Rhineland equally adheres to 1848 as the great caesura in nineteenth-century business politics. Although Boch documents the robust political agitation of businessmen in the 1840s, he nonetheless posits that Rhenish business elites after 1848 "ceased to exist as a politically competent class." [93] In view of the contentious negotiations between business and government in the second half of the nineteenth century, this claim, and its concomitant assumption that the state acted as an unproblematical facilitator of business needs, is hardly accurate.

A recent study of early railroad building in Prussia and the United States in the 1830s and 1840s by the historian Colleen A. Dunlavy is also germane to this discussion.[94] Dunlavy answered the call for rigorous comparative history whose broader perspective modifies claims about industrialization and political change formulated in national frameworks. Her innovative analysis of the United States and Prussia, for example, offers the paradox that the centralized authoritarian Prussian state (modeled as a "unitary-bureaucratic" state) intervened less in both construction and regulation than the federal U.S. government (a "federal-legislative state"), whose strong promotional and supervisory roles belied its liberal, laissez-faire reputation. Her crisp comparisons illuminate how contrasting political structures determined the different styles of technology and business practices of railroad companies and, conversely, how such large economic institutions affected the political world. But in examining differing styles of railroad technology, the degrees of state intervention and abstention, and the long-term roles of lobbies, legislatures and state ministries, Dunlavy's questions are intended more for reshaping the fields of business history and history of technology than for advancing the political history of German businessmen. Her interpretation of the Prussian state elides the many factions in the court and bureaucracy, province and capital, that resisted unified policy and that, in critical ways, dilute the strength of the unitary-bureaucratic construct. Moreover, the statement that economic liberalism better characterized Prussian policies than it did U.S. policy distorts the intentions of Prussian neoabsolutism and glosses over the state's paternalistic interventionist actions which businessmen sharply criticized in the *Vormärz* period.[95]

The problem of the business class and its operational strategies with the government still remains an underexplored topic. Certainly the recent debates, discussed above, call for reassessing the formulation "alliance," the code word of government-business relations, which essentially precludes bourgeois agency. It is too constrained a term to explore the curious admixture of conflict and cooperation that characterized the rapprochement between business circles and the government after 1848. Although such historians as James Sheehan, Otto Pflanze, and Martin Kitchen have recognized the fundamental flaw in interpreting government-business relations as an alliance, there is no study of businessmen in Prussia after 1848 to draw a more accurate, detailed picture.[96] In 1972 Kaelble wrote, "The rules that allowed non-civil servants to participate in political decisions remains largely unresearched." [97] And Dieter Langewiesche could still report in 1988, "It has so far not yet been clarified to what degree representatives of the commercial and industrial bourgeoisie in the 1850s used their economic position to advocate their political interests to the state bureaucracy." [98]

Railroad Entrepreneurs and the Prussian-German State

What is most needed at this juncture in the debate concerning the German bourgeoisie is new primary research. In view of this, I present here a study of the business class in its relationship to the Prussian-German state during the period from 1830, the onset of industrialization and railroad construction, to the political reorganization of Germany that followed the wars of 1866 and 1870. In order to stake out more credible ground between the polar hypotheses of the putative alliance and the so-called bourgeois hegemony, I examine the relationship between Prussian entrepreneurs and their government in the critical area of railway construction and ownership during the period in which this industry was the leading sector of German industrialization.

The decades upon which this study is focused were also the critical years of the "take off" in which German industrialization reached the stage of "sustained growth." Although today the universal validity of the model developed on this theme by W. W. Rostow is, correctly, rejected, it still has significance for Germany. As Rainer Fremdling's quantitative studies on the railroad industry have shown, there is no reason to doubt his assumption that the leading sector of this acceleration in Germany was railroad construction (seconded by the enlargement and modernization of the armed forces in the 1860s).[99] For that reason I have concentrated my researches on the railroad industry in searching for the actual, in contrast to the assumed, relationships between entrepreneurs eager to promote the interests of private enterprise and a conservative, authoritarian state accustomed for nearly two centuries to directing the country's economic growth. What was true of the railway magnates and financiers was also true of entrepreneurs engaged in other enterprises during the "take off" years, for the development of the joint-stock form of business enterprise multiplied the flow of investment capital and involved businessmen in many kinds of enterprises. The railroad business was a sphere of great importance for bankers, manufacturers, merchants, and industrialists; but it was also important for the landed estates in the eastern provinces, the state ministries of war, trade, and finance, and any town or region that sought access to national and international markets. "The location of railway lines," wrote Frank Tipton, "was always a political decision and always retained its power to create and destroy."[100] For government-business relations, the railroad industry was a touchstone of economic and political conflict.

Before 1848 railroads were the domain of private entrepreneurs. After the revolution the Prussian government sought to buy out private railways and dominate the railroad business with a state-run system, threatening the existence of the twenty-seven private railroad companies operating in Prussia. Government takeovers and aggressive regulation of the remaining private lines produced an adversarial relationship between the government and the directors, financiers, and investors of private railways. The relationship was further exacerbated by Trade Minister August von der Heydt, who used every lever of the state's legal and financial powers to give the state the upper hand in railroad ownership. Heydt's aggressive tactics jeopardized one of Europe's largest investment sectors and antagonized Prussia's leading entrepreneurs.[101]

Owing to close state supervision of railroads, we can monitor the changing relationship of government agencies to the business world with greater accuracy and depth. Previously unexploited sources give new insights on specific areas of conflict between the two groups, enabling us to portray the businessmen's ambivalence to state presence in the economy as well as to accent their influence on government policy. The behavior of railroad businessmen informs us how capitalists modified the terms of dialogue in preexisting political institutions to attain a *juste milieu* for capitalist enterprises in the late 1850s. To understand this evolving settlement, the two sides of government-business relations must be equally weighted: the side of conflict, to affect and change policy; and the side of cooperation, which allowed capitalists to avail themselves of the financial and legal benefits of the state. Friedrich Dahlmann's remark that the Prussian state possessed the "magic spear which heals as well as wounds" also characterizes the equivocal, ambivalent attitude of businessmen toward state bureaucracy in the period of early industrialization.[102]

The integration of the Prussian business class into Germany's political order after 1848 was a complex process of conflict and cooperation that cannot be neatly described as an alliance or a capitulation to a preindustrial order. The business class exerted pressure at certain points in the government, bureaucracy, and economy in the effort to shape policy in accord with their interest. The amalgamation of new and old elites cannot merely be explained as the "defense of inherited ruling positions by preindustrial elites against the onslaught of new forces." [103] The resistance, antagonism, and protest from the business class in economic affairs played a key role in creating a new political establishment after 1848. In structural terms, the series of compromises, successes, and failures that the business class encountered in establishing its terms of dialogue with Prussia's conservative order speaks more of a search for mutual accommodation than of victory or defeat, conquest or capitulation, alliance or symbiosis.

The railroad industry is, to be sure, just one facet of a larger business world. I believe, however, that collectively railroad businessmen represented Prussia's capitalist class better than their counterparts in other sectors of the economy. The men who founded and directed railway companies were affiliated with a great number of other businesses and professions. Such founders and directors of the Rhenish Railway as Gustav Mevissen, Ludolf Camphausen, David Hansemann, Friedrich Wilhelm König, and Joseph Dumont either owned or had extensive investments in coal mines, iron foundries, newspapers, insurance companies, banks, and wool, linen, and cotton mills. Friedrich Lewald, H. Henock, and Karl Milde, Silesian railroad entrepreneurs, were involved in newspapers, banking, and textiles. Heinrich von Wittgenstein, president of the Cologne-Minden Railway, was active in steamships and insurance companies and served as a district governor in the Prussian government. H. F. L. Augustin, director of the Berlin-Potsdam-Magdeburg Railway, was a former judge for a Prussian superior court. Friedrich Engels, father of the famous socialist, owned and ran cotton mills but sat on the board of the Berg-Mark Railway. The banker and silk entrepreneur Hermann von Beckerath also directed the Cologne-Crefeld line. The heterogeneity of their activities makes it difficult to cluster these entrepreneurs into interest groups, such as it is often done in the case of landowners and heavy industrialists. How these businessmen interacted with the government as a social and political force of the bourgeoisie is the primary concern of this study.

Hence this examination of the business class veers away from questions normally asked about businessmen. It does not, for example, seek to enhance the studies of Fritz Redlich and Toni Pierenkemper, who examined the social profiles and business conditions in Germany in order to define successful entrepreneurship and the nature of the entrepreneur.[104] Nor is it a contribution to the macroeconomic studies on the impact of railroads on capitalism, economic growth, and the development of the first industrial revolution.[105] It also does not directly address the developed debate on the role of the state in promoting economic growth.[106] Rather, this study seeks to bridge the gap between German economic and political history, the former ignoring the political components of Germany's economy, the latter paying too little attention to the microeconomic details that shaped political outlooks.

CHAPTER TWO

▼

Private or State Owned?
The Railroad Question, 1830–1848

The opening of both new railways . . . produced a sensation felt by every-
one. . . . We notice how our entire existence has been thrown forward on
a new path and accelerated in new directions—how new conditions, joys,
and fears await us, and how the Unknown practices its dreadful excite-
ment, at once tempting and terrifying. . . . The railroads are . . . a provi-
dential event, giving humanity new momentum and changing the color
and shape of life. A new chapter in world history begins, and our generation can be proud to have witnessed it. What changes must now enter
our outlook and imagination! Even the elementary notions of time and
space have become unstable. Railroads have killed space, and only time
remains for us. If we only had enough money to properly kill the latter![1]

The Rhenish émigré poet Heinrich Heine wrote this paean to railroads
upon observing the opening of two Parisian lines in May 1843. How
starkly it reveals both the fascination and tribulation that gripped the minds of
those who first saw steam railways! Heine appreciated not only the "world-
historical" significance of what he saw but also the power of money to van-
quish space and propel civilization. In marveling at the achievement of accumulated capital seemingly to alter fundamental laws of nature, Heine paid
tribute, if only indirectly, to those who conceived and financed railroads.

But the initial reception of railroads in Germany in the 1830s was less
prophetic, less certain. Early proponents of railroad transportation, such as
Friedrich List and Friedrich Harkort, failed to persuade rulers and statesmen
to allocate the necessary millions to build the new iron roads.[2] In Prussia,
fiscal conservatism, technological skepticism, and political fears among high-
ranking government officials initially blocked state participation in railroad
building. Financial advisers believed the colossal amount of capital demanded
by railroads would overwhelm the budget of the Prussian state; technical experts deemed the innovation of steam-propelled transportation on iron rails
fraught with mechanical problems and thus a money loser; and political elites

saw the financial burdens spilling over into a constitutional crisis if the state attempted to build its own railroads. Constrained by these principal considerations, the Prussian ministers balked at integrating railroads into state economic policy. The job of planning, financing, and building Prussia's first railroads fell by default to the initiative and capital of entrepreneurs.

The position of businessmen on whether railroads should be built by the state or the private sector evolved over the period from 1830 to 1848. As we shall see, there were a number of cultural, economic, and political factors that shaped the outlook of the business class, but the differing positions were guided, not surprisingly, by pragmatism and profit. In the late 1820s and early 1830s, many Prussian businessmen were reluctant to build railroads as private business enterprises, largely because of the likelihood of financial loss but also because of mercantilistic and idealistic conceptions of the state's role in the political economy. But in the late 1830s and 1840s businessmen, in the face of unexpected profits, accepted the position of leadership—provided that the Prussian state offer supplemental financial and legal support to the new industry. The first comprehensive Prussian Railroad Law in 1838, however, failed to provide guidelines for firm state support, provoking criticism from business circles. When new legislation in 1842 finally anchored the state's commitment to private railroad development in the form of dividend guarantees, loans, and stock investment, thereby contributing to a boom expansion period (1842–46), businessmen embraced this brand of private ownership. Yet enthusiasm for state ownership appeared again in the crash of 1846–49, encouraging state officials to draft plans for a state railroad system in 1848. As a general rule in the *Vormärz* period, entrepreneurial support for state ownership was inversely proportional to the prospect of profit.

It is nonetheless ironic that the Prussian bureaucracy, which for decades demonstrated know-how and foresight in promoting economic reform, failed to initiate railroads, perhaps the most significant economic innovation of the nineteenth century. Since the time of Frederick the Great, state officials had spurned the typical Prussian merchant as too parochial to recognize the organizational and technological innovations needed for economic progress. Yet the organizational and financial abilities that businessmen demonstrated to build railroads and expand its allied industries of coal and iron augured a new era of entrepreneurial endeavor. The rise of the railroad marked the emergence of a new assertive, risk-taking business elite willing to accept the challenge of undertaking large capitalist enterprises.[3]

Railroads became icons of the new civil society of capital and industry. Coal, iron, steel, and the new steam-driven textile mills also played an important role in the rise of industrial society. But locomotives, railroad bridges, and railroad stations, more than coal mines and iron works, became cultural symbols: they were dramatic visual expressions of modernity, progress, and technological power—heralds of a new society. Ludolf Camphausen, a grain merchant in Cologne, captured the centrality of railroads to entrepreneurial optimism when he announced in 1833 that Europe had entered a new epoch in its history, an age of trade and prosperity. "It is not politics or religion that will occupy the central position of this age," he wrote, but rather "the striving of all peoples for material welfare." And the "most effective lever of promoting material welfare . . . [is] namely: the railroads." [4]

The Private Era, 1825–1840

Prussian business circles were among the earliest on the Continent to perceive the utility of railroads and build them. In the same year that George Stephenson opened his Darlington-Stockton railway line (1825), and long before the first steam-driven German railway (the Bavarian Nürnberg-Fürth line, 1835), Friedrich Harkort published an essay that outlined the commercial importance of railroad construction, proclaiming it to be a "national obligation." "The railroads," he wrote, "will bring forth many revolutions in the commercial world. When one connects Elberfeld, Cologne, and Duisberg with Bremen, Holland's transit dues are no more. The Rhenish West-Indian Company could consider Elberfeld a harbor once a ton can be transported to Bremen's dockside within two days for 2 silver groschen. . . . Rhenish-Westphalian commerce would prosper with such a connection to the sea." [5] In 1828 Harkort founded the first German joint-stock railway company, building a 7.3-kilometer narrow-gauge, horse-drawn railway from the Himmelfürst coal mine at Überruhr to Kupferdreh and Nierenhof.[6] Between 1825 and 1835 he indefatigably promoted railroads. As builder, publicist, and member of several Westphalian diets, Harkort was one of Europe's first advocates of railroads.[7]

Larger projects followed Harkort's pioneering start. Old manufacturing and commercial centers in the Rhineland and the Ruhr demonstrated their ability to produce enough share capital to start railway projects. Businessmen sought to break the hold of English exports on both finished and raw materials by making Ruhr coal accessible to neighboring valleys, where English coal undersold German coal by half. In its annual report of 1834, the Elberfeld chamber of commerce complained that English metal buttons undersold locally made buttons in spite of import duties and local manufacturers' advantage with raw materials. Connecting coal seams and forges and factories with inexpensive transportation would provide the stimulus to break the English hold on continental trade. Railroads, the chamber asserted, would lower the cost of Ruhr coal, allowing Prussian producers to reclaim German markets.[8] Numerous committees sprang up in the 1830s in Elberfeld, Cologne, Düsseldorf, and Witten that promoted and eventually built important railways: the Düsseldorf-Elberfeld, the Berg-Mark, and the Cologne-Minden railways.[9] Among the first entrepreneurs of railroad construction was August von der Heydt, a merchant banker from Elberfeld, whose early activity prefigured his subsequent role in railway development as Prussian trade minister after 1848.

On the left bank of the Rhine, Ludolf Camphausen, a wealthy entrepreneur active in Cologne, advocated in 1833 the construction of an "iron Rhine" from Cologne to Antwerp. For centuries Rhenish manufactures had suffered from the control of the mouth of the Rhine by the Dutch, whose tolls added to the cost of reaching the North Sea.[10] The creation of the Kingdom of Belgium in 1830, however, offered Prussian Rhineland an opportunity to evade the Dutch monopoly on Rhine transport. Reacting to Camphausen's plan, David Hansemann proposed an alternate route for the Cologne-Belgium line, a longer path that would serve the wool merchant's home city of Aachen and other Rhenish cities. In 1834–35 Camphausen and Hansemann founded rival companies to build the Rhineland-Belgium line, but they eventually merged in 1837 to become the Rhenish Railway.[11] By the early 1840s private businessmen had formed companies to meet the three essential transportation needs in Rhineland and Westphalia: access to Belgium, a route to the Weser and the Hanseatic city of Bremen, and connections between the industrial valleys of Westphalia (Ruhr, Sieg, and Wupper) to link coal and ore producers with foundries and harbors.

Rhenish businessmen clearly set the pace in early railroad development. By 1845 over half of the country's railroad investment was located in this one province.[12] But bankers and merchants in the eastern provinces also constructed and operated lines by the early 1840s: Magdeburg-Leipzig (1837), Berlin-Anhalt (1839), Berlin-Stettin (1840), Berlin-Potsdam (1837), Berlin-Frankfurt (1841), and the Upper Silesian Railway (1841).[13] By 1842 private initiative had built 587 kilometers of railway, resembling the pattern of early construction in England, France, and the United States.[14] These railways were built without direct state involvement, although the state helped indirectly by providing franchise charters, army engineers, and the legal privilege of eminent domain.

These businessmen exhibited independence and a willingness to take risks —definitive qualities of entrepreneurship—but they were not proponents of classic laissez-faire economics. Although Adam Smith's doctrines had taken hold in influential bureaucratic and university circles in Prussia,[15] businessmen opted for private construction of railroads more out of necessity than ideological preference. Such notable businessmen as Friedrich Harkort, Ludolf Camphausen, and David Hansemann looked to the state for financial and technical leadership to build railroads but were repeatedly refused. Harkort built Westphalia's first railway in 1828, but one year earlier he had petitioned for the state to build Westphalia's railways.[16] In 1831, as deputy of the West-phalian provincial diet, he again proposed that the state build a Weser-Lippe railroad, but the plan was officially rejected in July 1832.[17] In the 1833 essay "The Railroad Between Minden and Cologne," Harkort reluctantly advocated private initiative, "because one cannot wait for the state." [18]

Ludolf Camphausen headed the private Rhenish Railway Company, but he too exhorted the government to finance Germany's principal railway routes. In 1833 he warned: "A joint-stock company as exclusive owner would con-stitute a new force in the state and often conflict with the views of the gov-ernment." [19] He likened railroads to highways and canals and saw danger in private ownership of what he felt ought to be, either solely or partly, state property. Camphausen presumed both financial and technical state support for the Rhenish Railway, and he expressed bitter disappointment when his re-quest for state subsidies was rejected.[20]

Hansemann, the organizer of both the Rhenish and the Cologne-Minden railways, also urged the state to monopolize railroads. At the fourth Rhenish Diet in 1833 Hansemann stated that "an enterprise so important and so per-vasive in all material interests should not be left to private speculation . . . it is in the best general interest of the land, when all roads, canals, and railroads belong to the state." [21] The worth of a railroad, he wrote, should be mea-sured not by profit (or loss) but rather by the common good. In a subsequent essay in 1837, Hansemann argued that the state should bear the cost of the institution that would bring general prosperity to the nation.[22] A similar argu-ment came from E. Bülow-Cummerow, a Junker agrarian-capitalist, who did not trust private entrepreneurial interests in the west to develop agricultural markets in the east. Such an important economic and military instrument as railroads, he argued in an 1843 essay on Prussian politics, should not be left to "private speculation." [23] Unlike contemporary laissez-faire publicists such as John Prince Smith,[24] commercial leaders in both the western and eastern provinces perceived the state, in its ideal form, not as an impediment to de-velopment but, rather, as an institution to promote economic change.

Businessmen, however, were disappointed. Harkort lamented in 1835 that ten years had passed and little had been done to encourage railroads.[25] Camp-hausen, criticizing the lack of an assertive economic policy, quipped in the same year, "Such is the order of things in our beloved Germany. It assembles a handsome library of books in German on locomotives, railroads, and canals, but we have neither locomotives, nor railroads, nor canals." [26]

The assumption among business elites that the state should finance, if not own, railroads did not run counter to their financial interests. In this early phase of railroad construction, few believed that private circles could amass the capital needed to build. More important, few believed that railroads would reap dividends worthy of long-term private investment. Behind arguments of the "common good," then, lurked the fear of debt, the belief that just as canals and streets had traditionally emptied state coffers, so would railroads.[27] In 1837 Hansemann assumed that railroads would never earn good profits because the advantage of low tariffs for commerce far outweighed the revenues to be earned from rail transport. Although "the mightiest lever of welfare and German power," railroads would never be a moneymaker.[28] But when railroads demonstrated their ability to make money as well as reduce shipping rates in the 1840s and 1850s, the cry for state ownership rapidly disappeared among businessmen.[29] Profit margins more than economic doctrine affected the positions of Prussian businessmen on railroad ownership.

And yet philosophical-historical considerations did support the idea that the state should take up money-losing enterprises for the common good, intellectual convictions that influenced businessmen as well as scholars. Their minds were nurtured as much by G. W. F. Hegel and the Comte de St. Simon as by the laissez-faire economists Adam Smith and David Ricardo. Since the 1770s German Idealism had depicted the state as the moving force in world history, and utopian socialist St. Simon saw in the growth of science, technology, and factory production a pattern for the future reorganization of society and government.[30] In 1841, when Cologne businessmen (among them Gustav Mevissen, Ludolf Camphausen, Gustav Mallinckrodt, and Dagobert Oppenheim) financed the *Rheinische Zeitung,* they chose as editor the young Hegelian Karl Marx, not a free trader.[31] Early German capitalists saw the state as the key to progress, the lever of national welfare.

More concretely, the Prussian government had heeded the needs of the business community for decades, with both laws and direct involvement. Notwithstanding some glaring and significant clashes with business interests, the state enjoyed the reputation of possessing one of the most progressive economic policies in the German Confederation.[32] Changes introduced by a circle of high-ranking officials in the years 1807–13, the Reform Era, enabled modern capitalism to take root in Prussia. Embracing certain elements of economic liberalism, reform bureaucrats Freiherr vom Stein and Prince Karl August Hardenberg abolished serfdom, guild restrictions on production, and restrictions on occupation and relocation. Tariffs were abolished between provinces but—departing from Smithian economics—set at moderate levels for imports to encourage domestic industry.[33] These reforms allowed capitalists to create open domestic markets, hire (and fire) wage laborers in accordance with business cycles, and rely on migration to urban and rural regions for temporary, nontraditional labor. Although the Stein-Hardenberg reforms failed to achieve many of their chief social and political aims, these laws had practical force for the infant railroad industry.[34] The thousands of navvies that dug and built Prussia's first railroad beds and tunnels in the 1830s and 1840s prefigured the future industrial concentration of Germany's workforce.[35]

In the Rhineland, the Prussian government further enhanced its relationship with the business class by keeping the Napoleonic law code in effect after it acquired the province in 1815.[36] The legal continuity eased the transition from French to Prussian rule and sent a strong signal to Rhenish businessmen, whose prosperity depended on the 1807 *Code de Commerce,* that Prussia recognized the advanced economic state of its new provinces.[37] The French law codes ensured equality before the law and, unlike the Prussian Edict on Municipal Government of 1808 (*Städteordnung*), made no distinction between town and rural residents, provisions which better suited the widespread putting-out system of the Rhenish textile industry. The French jury system also pleased Rhenish merchants; only property owners could be jurors, ensuring "that the law would deal severely with those who committed crimes against property." [38] The Prussian government, furthermore, retained the French commercial courts, which settled commercial disputes more quickly than civil due process. Prussia also kept intact the semiofficial status of the Rhineland's chambers of commerce, through which businessmen shaped local affairs and enjoyed *Staatsunmittelbarkeit*—direct contact to Berlin ministries.[39] This apparent spirit of cooperation encouraged businessmen to advocate state ownership of railroads.

The most far reaching achievement of Prussian economic policy before 1848 was the creation of the Customs Union in 1834.[40] This union of eighteen German states removed many economic barriers posed by particularism and was the essential precondition for Germany's economic takeoff. To improve trade communication the Prussian government radically overhauled its highway and postal system, increasing its highway mileage threefold between 1817 and 1835 and fourfold by 1842.[41] Consequently, the state's interest in improving trade, infrastructure, and economic competitiveness made it a likely candidate for railroad ownership.

More important, perhaps, the long history of direct state intervention in the economy led businessmen to believe that the state would absorb losses to promote railroads. Since the late eighteenth century, it had built model factories, imported new technology through state-sponsored industrial espionage, and offered economic incentives for private investment in steam engines and power looms. The state's commercial investment bank, the Seehandlung, owned and operated an array of enterprises: coal mines, silk factories, textile mills, chemical works, and zinc, iron, and steel mills. It owned fleets of merchant and steam ships and operated tugs in the Elbe, Havel, and Spree rivers.[42] The state founded the Berlin Technical Institute (today the *Technische Hochschule* of Berlin) in 1821 to train civil servants as engineers and machinists. Prussia's first locomotive was manufactured by the royal foundry in 1816, though it was decidedly not a model for entrepreneurs. The steam locomotive was pulled by horses around a track in the factory courtyard, and when it was transferred to Silesia to work in the coal mines the wheels did not fit the track gauge.[43]

With these early economic reforms, reform-minded officials hoped to unleash the creative and productive energy of individuals. Inspired by Kantian views of individual freedom and the economic philosophy of Adam Smith (Hegel made his mark on the next generation of bureaucrats), these state servants of the Reform Era sought to change the fabric of society. Yet, though these laws were cloaked in the spirit of laissez-faire individualism, the cut was distinctively Prussian. Unlike Adam Smith, who envisioned in the *Wealth of Nations* government reduced to minimal functions, Prussian officials introduced these reforms to restore their badly indebted state to solvency and to nurture a new civic spirit capable of generating a popular resistance to French domination. Mercantilism, the economic doctrine of the Frederician state, had become outmoded. The liberal reform faction in the bureaucracy sought to engender greater private wealth that would yield higher tax revenues. The progressive elements of Prussia's economic policy did not serve the laissez-faire program of dismantling government.[44]

In short, the principle of the invisible hand was embraced neither by state bureaucrats nor by businessmen in Prussia. In the early phase of capitalism, both accepted the state's role in guiding, encouraging, and promoting economic prosperity. Harkort, Hansemann, Camphausen, and others cautioned the Prussian government to learn from the squalor and misery created by England's laissez-faire excesses. They exhorted the government to enforce child labor laws, prevent overconcentration of industry to avoid urban misery, and build technical schools to train the unemployed.[45] For most Prussian businessmen, the state was a self-evident component of their economic, social, and political outlook. Businessmen had benefited from state intervention in the past and expected it in the future. And government officials hoped that if commerce and industry were promoted, greater wealth could revive the Prussian state—and the noble and bureaucratic classes that served it. Why, then, did the state not build the railways?

The issue of state railways first arose in the late 1820s. Peter Beuth and Karl Schinckel, two prominent civil servants, toured British industrial regions in 1826, reported on English railways, and subsequently dispatched a state mining engineer and a geologist to study railroad construction.[46] These reports impressed Finance Minister Friedrich von Motz and Foreign Minister

Christian von Bernstoff, who in 1828 proposed a state railroad to connect the Weser and Lippe rivers. But their interest in railroads was grounded mostly in a short-term political aim: to apply political pressure on Hanover and Hesse-Cassel. These states, along with Saxony and the free cities of Bremen and Frankfurt, had formed the Middle German Commercial Union in 1828, a customs league that threatened Prussia's plans for the Zollverein.[47] Connecting the Rhine and Weser would open up a new toll-free trade link between southern and northern Germany that would exclude Hanover and Hesse-Cassel.[48] The line, moreover, would loosen the Dutch garotte on Rhenish shipping.[49] But the king rejected the railroad plan, insisting that the road between the two rivers (connecting the cities Minden and Lippstadt) was adequate.[50] And the idea faded altogether when both political problems found solutions: the Kingdom of Belgium ended the Dutch trade monopoly in 1830, and Hesse-Cassel finally joined the Prussian union in 1831.[51]

The Prussian government's refusal in the 1830s to participate in railroad building stemmed partially from the initial lack of foresight by the king and from the weight of the factions in the bureaucracy and court that opposed railroads. In the early 1830s King Friedrich Wilhelm III took little interest in railroads and was resistant to arguments promoting them. When he announced "that he did not see that it made a great deal of difference whether one arrived in Potsdam a few hours sooner or later," [52] the king clearly failed to grasp the ramifications of railroads. Like the king of Hannover, who expressed his dislike of cobblers and tailors traveling as fast as he did, Friedrich Wilhelm objected to riding with commoners.[53] He probably concurred with other nobles that the mobility offered by railroads would erode the moral fiber of society.[54] He refused to use the Berlin-Potsdam line that connected his two residences for the first few months of its operation, and throughout the 1830s he set a resistant, obstinate tone at court against the "ephemeral fashion" of railroads. Nonetheless, one cannot view the king as an absolute opponent of railroads.[55] In the three years before his death in 1840, he acknowledged the military utility of railroads, thus deferring to his generals, who constituted an important bureaucratic faction backing railroads. In recognition of the military's need for railroads, Friedrich Wilhelm bequeathed one million thalers on his deathbed to a railroad line connecting the western and eastern provinces.[56] Although this sum alone could not finance the railway, which would demand tens of millions of thalers, the legacy represented 1/20 of Prussia's money supply and was therefore not insignificant.

Friedrich Wilhelm's disposition toward railroads was all the more strengthened by the negative views of leading officials who together composed a formidable bureaucratic faction against state involvement in railroads:

Postmaster General Karl Ferdinand Friedrich von Nagler; Peter Beuth, the celebrated promoter of Prussian industry in the finance ministry; and Christian von Rother, the president of the Seehandlung, the director of the Royal Bank, and the chief of the finance ministry's trade department. The king called upon these officials in 1835 to outline a railroad policy. Three charters had already been granted by this date,[57] but these concessions provided scant information in answer to investors' questions regarding the government's attitude toward railroad building. Would it build its own network and remove railroads as an equity on the stock market? Or would it provide incentive to private investors with interest guarantees and favorable loans? The competition for a fourth charter between Magdeburg and Leipzig in 1835, compounded by official and unofficial requests for a policy, compelled the bureaucracy to consider general rules for ownership and administration.[58]

Rother's 1835 report damned state participation in railroads. He doubted whether railroads were a necessity for the European continent; the present demands of transportation, he wrote, were met by the highways and canals.[59] The construction costs, he believed, were also prohibitive. Because continental railroad companies had yet to pay satisfactory dividends, there was no evidence that railroads could pay for themselves. And if profits were earned, he added, they would diminish the revenues from the toll roads and postal roads to which the state was committed.[60] He also feared that capital, which should be invested in industry and state paper, would instead be attracted to railroads.[61] Thus, Rother concluded that the state had no business either building or subsidizing railroads. But private railroad companies, he acknowledged, presented serious problems with both stock swindles and a transportation monopoly that could harm the state. Consequently, he recommended—true to the Prussian bureaucratic spirit—that the government supervise construction and administration of private railroads and reserve the right to final ownership.[62]

Nagler and Beuth supported Rother's position. Focusing on the specific issue of railroads and the postal system, Nagler saw railroads only as a threat to government profits and to the state's sovereign control over conveying post. As a minister who had worked tirelessly to make the Prussian postal system the best in Germany through superior roads and coaches (the latter doubled as a profitable transportation system), Nagler was disinclined to see his success wiped away by a technological innovation.[63] Beuth, on the other hand, believed that industrialization had not yet reached a level advanced enough to support the financing of railroads. Augmenting the oppositional front of these ministries was the Mining Corp, which feared that the promotion of railroads would escalate coal production uncontrollably, keeping the state from responsibly managing the coal industry.[64] The opinions of Rother's faction were accepted by the king, who granted the Magdeburg charter in February 1836 with no subsidies or interest guarantees from the state.[65] These two basic conditions of the 1836 charter became the nucleus of the general Railroad Law of 1838.

The resistance of these three influential ministers to railway development remained throughout the 1840s. In 1837 Rother resigned from his position in the finance ministry because his opposition to railroads brought him into direct conflict with the crown prince, but he was later forced in 1842 by Friedrich Wilhelm IV to manage railroad finance as the head of the Seehandlung—an act by the new king that "amounted to a cruel revenge." [66] Nagler remained a staunch critic of railroads, while Beuth only grudgingly acquiesced in the government's policy. Rudolf Delbrück, a junior official in the finance ministry during the 1830s, remarked in his memoirs that Beuth, once a pioneer of reform, was "too advanced in years and too set in his ways to blaze new trails. This fact was most noticeably—and most sadly—evident with his position on railroads . . . [which] belonged to his administrative sphere but hardly existed for him. He delegated the preliminary work to his subordinates, limited himself to sarcastic remarks during meetings, and merely supplied the signature to finished memoranda." [67] Ironically, locomotives after 1848 bore his name as a tribute to his "promotion" of railroads.

There were, to be sure, proponents of a state railroad system in the Prussian state. The junior ranks of the bureaucracy were filled with railroad enthusiasts who were not scarred by the debt-ridden years of Napoleonic era and were more receptive to the promises of the railway age. More crucially, the war ministry, shifting from its initial opposition to railroads, which was grounded in fear of a quick, indefensible French invasion, came to appreciate the benefits of rapid troop transport. In 1836, during the debate on the Railroad Law, leading members of the war department advocated a state system, which would ensure the military's full exploitation of this new mode of transportation.[68]

But when it came time for the king to arrive at a decision in 1837–38, the economic realities of state life, as presented by Beuth, Rother, and Nagler, overrode the military preference for state lines.[69] Prussia had already tripled the mileage of its roads between 1816 and 1831, from 3,866 to 10,360 kilometers, at a cost of 42 million thalers, giving it one of the best road systems in Europe.[70] For a poor state like Prussia, this was a large infrastructural investment, especially with Rother's efforts to reduce the crushing state debt, standing at 250 million thalers after the Napoleonic era.[71] A commitment to railroads, Rother believed, would burden the state with greater loans and negate the government's twenty-year attempt to stabilize its finances.[72] Echoing Rother, a state council report of 1838 announced: "It is impermissible to jeopardize the fortunate condition of an orderly government budget so that the state, by borrowing money or by depleting necessary reserve funds, can play entrepreneur." [73] Railroads did not fit into the economic outlook of officials who, having witnessed near bankruptcy in 1806–7, resolutely adhered to fiscal conservatism.

But the most compelling reason why state officials shied away from railroad building was political. At issue was the question of the Prussian constitution. In 1810 and 1815 the king promised his subjects a constitution guaranteeing national representation, a major goal for the reform bureaucrats, who saw a constitution as the first step toward transforming the Prussian subject into a citizen.[74] The constitution, however, never materialized. "Fears of a Jacobin revolt in 1818, pressures from Metternich in Vienna, the resistance of conservative ministers and representatives of the East Prussian Junkers, and the conservatism of the monarch," writes Jeffry Diefendorf, "all combined to thwart plans for a constitution." [75] To avoid political change the king never convened the United Diet, the central representative body of estates that would most certainly have exhorted him to fulfill his promise.[76]

But this diet also had an important economic function: it cosigned state loans greater than twenty million thalers. The king considered this law, passed in 1820 to rein in the expenditures of an expanding bureaucracy, an "innocuous concession," because he planned to rule without loans.[77] And, indeed, he never called a diet during his reign, 1797–1840. Hardenberg, the king's leading minister, on the other hand, saw this 1820 law as the third promise for a constitution and as a mechanism to accelerate the building of a national assembly.[78] He was right. With the industrial age imminent in Germany, this law effectively curbed royal and bureaucratic prerogatives, for it linked the state's finances to the constitutional question.[79] Because the cost of railroad construction was too high to avoid the cosignatory, the railroad question was at once political and economic. This fact did not escape entrepreneurs such as Harkort, Camphausen, and Hansemann, all advocates of a constitutional monarchy. Their pamphlets in the 1830s pleading for state railroads bristled with this political subtext. They believed the urgency of building railroads in conjunction with the 1820 debt law would bring the constitutional question to a head.[80]

Unwilling to face the political consequences of raising the credit to build railroads, the Prussian government introduced a general Railroad Law in 1838 that handed the task of finance and construction over to the private sphere. The law's concise forty-nine paragraphs included provisions for upkeep, taxation, charters, stock subscription, police supervision, safety standards, postal transport, military use, eminent domain and compensation, passenger and freight prices, profits (announcement, limitation, and use thereof), and the exclusion of competing lines for thirty years.[81] The law's most salient features were the state's right to supervise administration and the company's need to receive state authorization for any changes, such as branch lines or new stock issues. An appointed state commissioner would act as liaison between the government and company, and he was to be notified of all stockholder and board meetings.[82] The state, furthermore, reserved the right to take over a company after thirty years and set specific conditions for indemnifying stockholders.[83] The law exempted railway companies from commerce and stamp taxes but nonetheless imposed a special levy (as compensation for diminished toll revenues on highways) that would enable the government to purchase stock. Given the political and economic constraints of the state, the law was tailored more to its needs than the needs of railroad builders. The law relegated a task that the state could not carry out to the private sphere but nonetheless reserved the state's right to supervise the industry and eventually own it.

Historians have praised the law for its remarkable prescience of future needs and disputes,[84] but contemporaries were not as sanguine. Karl August Varnhagen von Ense, the writer and perceptive observer of Prussian politics, entered in his diary on 13 April 1838 that the government "even makes a soured face to railroads." [85] Less casual in locution, the Aachen and Cologne chambers of commerce presented stinging critiques of the law, objecting particularly to paragraph 48, which retroactively applied the law to the company charter already granted to the Rhenish Railway for the Aachen-Cologne line.[86] (The railway company, in fact, never recognized the validity of this particular clause.) The restrictive and potentially expensive clauses of the law, such as the company's unlimited liability for persons and goods traveling on the railway and a 10 percent ceiling on profits, led stockholders of the Rhenish Railway to believe that directors had duped them by deliberately founding the company before promulgation of the law.[87]

Such complaints prompted a special meeting of stockholders with Ernst von Bodelschwingh, the provincial governor of the Rhineland, who freely admitted the deficiencies of the law.[88] Officials of the Rhenish Railway, Ludolf Camphausen and David Hansemann among them, promised the stockholders to petition the government to amend the law. For this reason Camphausen immediately published "Toward a Contribution to the Railroad Law," an essay that urged the government to amend the legal vagueness of the law and to recognize the public good to be derived from private railroads. He criticized the spirit of the law, which set the obligations of a railway to the state but not the reverse.[89] He believed the lack of state support retarded railroad development, while the many restrictions and obligations imposed on companies cut into slim profits. Camphausen concluded that the law would drive investors and entrepreneurs away from Prussia.[90]

Hansemann, too, attacked government railway policy with three pamphlets. In 1837 he had already attempted to influence the writing of the law with his "The Railroads and Their Stockholders in Their Relationship to the State." This pamphlet strove to influence the government, which in January of that year had begun to draft the Railroad Law. It ostensibly advocated state ownership, but its title revealed the true aim: to strike a balance between state supervision and the rights of stockholders. To create this equipoise, guarantees of entrepreneurial freedom had to be secured so that speedy construction, efficient management, safe investment, and the needs of the "common good" could all be met.[91] He wrote that the government's alleged plan to design a law that reserved the right to enact future restrictions, interfere in company decisions, and impose its conditions retroactively on already chartered companies resulted in a shaky legal basis for private railroad ownership. He endorsed state supervision, which he believed was proper to avoid the abuses found in the American system, but objected to the absolute power conferred on the ministers by the law. Joint-stock companies were corruptible, he noted, but overweening government control was equally destructive for investment and efficient administration.[92] Instead he advocated commissions in which representatives from government, commerce, and industry would issue, renew, and revoke charters after reviewing companies' performance.[93]

In 1838 Hansemann attempted a second time to influence the final draft of the law. Centering on the relation of the postal system to private companies, the essay "Prussia's Most Important Railroad Question" criticized the power accorded the postmaster general to determine independently the reparation fee for each railroad company. It pleaded for firm laws that would apply the same criteria to each company in fixing compensation and thus avoid arbitrary action by ministers. In this essay Hansemann's belief in private railroad ownership was more pronounced; the argument rested on the premise of private companies and their unassailable right to seek reasonable profit while providing a public service.

In 1841 Hansemann's *A Critique of the Prussian Railroad Law of 3 November 1838* went further and lambasted the one-sided discussion that created a law that, he claimed, failed to provide clearly delineated legal protections upon which private investors could depend. He criticized the fact that all branches of government were consulted, abiding by the collegial system of Prussia's bureaucracy, yet entrepreneurs were not invited to contribute. "Thus a law came into being," he wrote, "that gives stockholders the impression that the state has received the legal means to ruin companies, an opinion that is especially evident in the Rhineland, where one is accustomed to expect legal protection more from laws and less from what the government feels is fair." [94] Hansemann's commitment to constitutionalism emerged in his attack on legislation designed under bureaucratic absolutism: "This condition is to be named lawless, when the legal conditions are so made that the profits of an enterprise depend on state officials' sense of fairness. However beautiful and honorable the state government finds this trust in its own fairness, it honors itself more and appears worthier when the state establishes lawful justice fairly, as opposed to making lawlessness a law and then consoling itself with the belief that there is trust in its fairness." [95] For Hansemann the "unmeasured paternalism and control" which the law reserved for the state, combined with the "unheard of responsibilities" that it imposed on private companies, amounted to flawed legislation inappropriate for a rising commercial and industrial state.[96] He reminded the government that the cost of building public railroads was beyond the state's capacity. Having failed to provide for the common good, the government was wrong to lay unnecessary burdens and restrictions on private companies.[97] The political message was unmistakable: Prussia's business class, its bourgeoisie, merited a greater say in governmental affairs because it could now provide the economic power the state lacked.[98]

The complaints of Camphausen, Hansemann, and the chambers of commerce surfaced in the Rhenish diet, whose 1841 proceedings petitioned the state for a revision of the law.[99] These criticisms seemed to have had some effect. The state council, for example, amended a paragraph in the cabinet's original draft of the 1838 law that allowed the postmaster general to impose compensation fees on individual companies as he saw fit. Echoing Hansemann's critique, the revised version planned fixed terms (to be set at a future date) for compensation. Moreover, two paragraphs heavily criticized by Camphausen and Hansemann—the lease of a company's railways to another company and the 10 percent maximum on company profits—were never enforced. Finally, future discussions on railroad policy included railroad entrepreneurs.

The Mixed System, 1840–1847

In 1838–39 the common stock of the Rhenish Railway fell twenty points below par, forcing its directors to sell reserves of stock to raise money and thereby increasing the amount of devalued paper in circulation and further depressing its price. This downward movement in value, which conformed to a general trend, encouraged the belief among businessmen that the Railroad Law had failed to give private companies enough government backing.[100] Threatened with liquidation, the Rhenish Railway appealed to the government to buy 4,000 shares at market value for one million thalers. The government refused despite Hansemann's threat to sell the 4,000 shares to the Belgian government, which he did secretly in October 1839.[101]

The belief of Prussian businessmen that the direct effect of the Railroad

Law was a bear market is important. They feared that they would lose investors to Bavarian and Saxon railroads, which paid better dividends, and reasoned that the state was obliged to aid the fledgling railways. The lack of commitment embodied in the 1838 law, they believed, harmed the business, and
they complained about the government's inconsistent messages to investors.[102]
Stock returns over the next four years, 1839–42, strengthened this view. Of
the six Prussian railway companies offering dividends, five paid rates either
the same as or lower than those of previous years.[103] Relative to the European
and American railroad market, this performance fell short of investors' expectations—and early railroad owners maneuvered boldly with block shares
to prevent further devaluation. Although the 1840s are generally regarded as
a prosperous period for railroad stocks and bonds, company ledgers reveal a
precarious time. In hindsight, we see the beginning of irreversible industrial
growth, the groundswell of Prussian economic superiority.[104] Businessmen in
the 1840s, however, did not exhibit the confidence often associated with early
capitalism.

In principle the 1838 law consigned all finance and construction of railroads to private hands. Yet the old habit of state promotion of industries
deemed important for its military or fiscal benefit reasserted itself. In 1839, the
Seehandlung, the government's commercial bank, granted the Berlin-Anhalt
Railway a 500,000 thaler loan and purchased shares amounting to one million thalers.[105] Similarly, the government aided the Berlin-Stettin Railway by
purchasing 500,000 thalers worth of company bonds, while promising the
Pomeranian diet to uphold its claim to the railway company to guarantee a
4 percent dividend.[106] Rother, who authorized these transactions, reluctantly
acquiesced in the state's altered policy of aiding certain important lines.

These actions were but overtures to what was to come after Friedrich
Wilhelm IV came to the throne in 1840. Compared to his father's caution
in mediating between rival parties in economic policy, the new king's open-
minded optimism toward railroads set a new tone in matters of economic reform.[107] The Hohenzoller, like his Bavarian cousin Ludwig, had a passion for
railroads and strongly believed in the state's obligation to promote them.[108] As
crown prince he had fought the conservative opinions of his father's ministers in the 1830s, and it was his quarrel with Rother over the Railroad Law
of 1838 that prompted the minister to resign from the finance ministry's trade
department. The new king, with the backing of military advisers, was intent
on building railroads in the eastern lands, especially a railway between Berlin
and Königsberg.[109]

The public discussion on railroads was renewed in 1841 when the king
called upon the provincial diets to select representatives for United Committees of the Estates of the Prussian Provincial Diets (*Vereinigten ständischen*

Ausschüsse der preussischen Provinziallandtage) to meet in Berlin in October 1842. This committee was the first public expression of his commitment to reinstate "Germanic" corporate assemblies, an extension of the provincial diets intended to restore something of the feudal *Ständestaat* that absolutism had destroyed. The king decided when the standing committee would convene and what issues it would address. Its function was to be purely advisory.[110]

But the king also saw the committee as a shrewd way to finance loans without granting a constitution. "A Central Diet [*Reichstände*] can be avoided," the king wrote his brother Prince Carl, "by contracting loans through a body composed of 32 deputies and 32 state councilors." [111] The Committee, he wrote to *Oberpräsident* Theodor von Schön, would raise "the possibility . . . of enjoying all the advantages of a general diet without having to fear the consequences [*Erschütterungen*] that the sudden introduction of the latter might bring." [112]

For bourgeois liberals, though, a joint committee of provincial deputies revived hopes for a constitution.[113] In connection with other reforms, such as less stringent press censorship,[114] the committee appeared as the cautious first step toward fulfilling the promise of a constitution. The enthusiastic reaction of the press and its reform-minded audience, in fact, corresponded to the fears of Metternich, the tsar, and the king's ministers, most of whom implored him not to proceed with the idea.[115]

To throttle political discussion during the committee's sessions, the king's ministers (Bodelschwingh and Eichhorn) drew up a narrow agenda of three questions to be presented to the deputies and furthermore created a protocol that prohibited debate and petition. The result was an agenda in which Hansemann "recognized neither a political nor a practical thought." [116] The three questions posed to the committee that assembled in October and November 1842 were whether the salt tax should be lowered to help the working classes; whether private rivers should be opened for public navigation; and whether the government should establish a Railroad Fund to promote private companies' construction of a national network connecting all provinces.

With the last question, the government proposed to help build five basic lines, whose construction was estimated to cost fifty-five million thalers: a Rhein-Weser line; a railway through Thuringia to the west; a railway from the Oder River to the Russian border; a line from Frankfurt on-the-Oder to Breslau and continuing to upper Silesia; and a line to connect Posen and Silesia. The government guaranteed a 3.5 percent dividend for the stock of private companies but cautioned (to avoid charges of increasing the debt) that it would not spend more than two million thalers.[117]

The first two issues facing the committee were not controversial (the former was a foregone conclusion, the latter technical and trivial), but the question of a national railroad network was not as tame as the government had hoped. First, it raised the age-old Prussian question of whether the government should encourage state unity or preserve the particular political traditions of its provinces. Railroads amounted to economic and infrastructural unity, which liberals hoped would develop a common political consciousness and, ultimately, "unified political representation of all Prussian people." [118] Second, the 1820 debt law, as we have already seen, required that state-financed railroads be approved by the estates in a United Diet, thus raising the question of whether the fund could legally be approved. "There can be no doubt as to the illegality of this kind of support," Ludolf Camphausen wrote his brother Otto. "The question is whether the government will decide to reveal the actual state of our finances." [119] The political dimension of railroad building could not be ignored.

The king's plan to use the committee as a rubber stamp for his economic and political designs was only partially successful. Although the assembled body did not have the right to initiate discussion, engage in debate, or even thank the king in a formal address, unpleasant questions arose. Friedrich Joseph Brust, a merchant from the Rhenish town of Boppard, declared that the committee was not empowered to approve financial operations of the state and asked for exact information on state assets and incomes before discussing financial matters. Moreover, if the state was interested in promoting railroads, he announced, it was obligated to convene a United Diet.[120] August von der Heydt, a deputy representing the Westphalian diet, also broke with protocol, stating that because of the "great improbability of a high dividend from the designated railway lines, it appears wiser if the state took over construction." [121] This comment received the clear support of the majority, suggesting either a belief in state-supported economic enterprises or a political ploy to force the king to convene the United Diet.

Heydt pressed the issue of state railroads so vigorously that Bodelschwingh, the presiding representative of the king's cabinet, forbade any further discussion on state railways. The state, he announced, did not plan to build railroads, and the committee was convened only to consider the state's role in guaranteeing dividends for private construction. When committee members continued to question the legal validity of approving dividend guarantees, Bodelschwingh threatened to retract this question from the agenda and have the king renounce any kind of state support for railroads.[122] Faced with this threat, the committee approved the original request with only fourteen dissenting votes.[123]

Yet the committee unexpectedly exhibited initiative. Led by Heydt, the members of the committee compelled Bodelschwingh to take an additional vote on a tortuously formulated hypothetical question: "Whether the assembly wishes to declare in the protocol that it believes the best means for carrying out the projected railroad lines is at state cost and would have voted for this option had the government not expressly stated its decision not to build railroads in the near future at state expense." [124] This motion was defeated 50 to 47, a narrow but surprising loss for Heydt's popular position. Heydt ascribed the defeat to the peculiar hypothetical nature of the question, but the divided vote also showed the lingering willingness of politically inexperienced liberals to accommodate the wishes of the government.[125] Once it was clear that the government had no intention of building state railroads, many abandoned the position of principled opposition.

Heydt's unflinching support for state-owned railroads in the 1840s merits explanation. His viewpoint, which remained unaltered for the next thirty years, significantly affected German political economy, for he served as Prussia's trade minister from 1848 to 1862. Although we have no primary documentation by Heydt on the origins of his position, his advocacy of state rails most likely grew out of his early trying experiences in launching private railroad projects.[126] In the years 1836–42, Heydt led Elberfeld in attempting to build three railroad lines that would connect the commercial and financial center of the Wupper valley with branch lines to the coal seams of the Ruhr (Elberfeld-Witten line) and Berg regions (Elberfeld-Duesseldorf line), as well as with a trunk line connecting the Rhine and Weser rivers (the Rhine-Weser line). Heydt could hardly claim unqualified success; two of the three projected companies never came to life.[127] Finding investors for the Rhine-Weser line (260 kilometers long) was especially difficult, provoking Heydt in 1838 and 1839 to appeal to the state for a two-million thaler subscription. When the government refused, the company was compelled to stop its preliminary work and dissolve itself, producing in turn considerable regional distrust of future railroad schemes.[128]

Following the coronation of Friedrich Wilhelm IV, whose enthusiasm for railroads produced a new optimism for construction, Hansemann's company received the right to build a Rhine-Weser line in 1841. The Cologne-Minden Railroad, however, planned a route that bypassed Elberfeld, arousing indignation and fury among the city's commercial elites. Heydt was a leading member of the Berg-Mark Railroad Committee that protested to the king both the route and the study, which fixed a prohibitively high cost to include Elberfeld. Challenging the plans of the private Cologne-Minden Railroad, this committee proposed a "Rhenish-Westphalian line," built solely from state funds. This proposal fell on deaf ears in Berlin, but the committee's efforts were not in vain. The government agreed to fund an independent survey to assess the accuracy of Hansemann's cost projections. More important, the ardent wishes of Elberfeld businessmen to be linked to the railroad network were eventually realized in March 1844 with the chartering of a line between Elberfeld and Dortmund, which became the Berg-Mark Railroad.[129] For this railroad Heydt acted as both financial officer and chairman of the board.[130]

Heydt's early engagement with railroads is instructive for two principal reasons. First, it reveals how interwoven political and economic issues were for the business class. Heydt's honorary public offices as a judge for the region's commercial court (1831; president 1840), a city councillor (1833), and a member of the district diet (1834) had always been connected with business and his status as the oldest son of a commercial patrician family. But business and politics were made indivisible by the convergence of Heydt's financially based desire, as a banker and an entrepreneur, to bring rail lines to Elberfeld with his political duties in the seventh Rhenish provincial diet in 1841 and in the standing committee of 1842. Second, Heydt's assertive, almost defiant, support for state railroads in the United Committee in 1842 is most likely explained by his frustrating experience in attempting to control Elberfeld's railroad future. The struggles among rival commercial centers to influence, if not dominate, railroad politics compounded by the difficulty of raising sufficient capital on the private market seems to have left an indelible mark on his thinking. Although most other Prussian commercial elites changed their stance after 1842 and championed private ownership, Heydt tirelessly strove for state ownership. Heydt would champion other economic liberal causes in his tenure as a state minister (joint-stock principle, privatization of coal industry), but he tenaciously advanced state ownership in the heyday of private railroads.

The vote that approved the Railroad Fund in 1842 produced a discrete government account set up in 1843 to promote the construction of the five proposed railways. The government transferred a one-time sum of six million thalers to the Railroad Fund. Additional two million-thaler annual installments replenished it. The government further announced its decision to invest in one-seventh of the capital stock of the five proposed lines and guarantee the remaining six-sevenths of share capital with a 3.5 percent dividend. The interest on the government's stock flowed not to the treasury but to the Railroad Fund, whose assets were to be used to acquire more shares.[131]

The Railroad Fund established the mixed system of railroad building in Prussia. The far-reaching supervisory powers that the government granted itself in the Railroad Law of 1838 were now balanced by financial subsidies and dividend guarantees to private railways. The mixture of private enterprise and state support roughly corresponded to the earlier suggestions of Camphausen, Hansemann, and others.[132] The state support for these five trunk lines signaled a new government commitment to the industry, which entrepreneurs believed would benefit all Prussian railroads. Indeed, railway companies not among the privileged five did receive state help. In 1843 the Rhenish Railway was granted a loan of 1.25 million thalers, and the Berg-Mark Railway received a million thaler loan in 1844.

Under the mixed system, railroad securities experienced a boom between 1842 and 1846, exceeding state paper and all other enterprises in dividends.[133] The boom underscored a new position of strength for railroad businessmen, who could profit from their own enterprises but still have the assurance of government commitment. The arrangement also put to rest the question of whether the state should monopolize ownership. "Since so many private railroads were in operation, in construction, or in the planning stage," wrote Hansemann's biographer, "it could now only be a question of a mixed system of private and state railways, and the experience in Belgium and Baden showed that the state built much more expensively than private companies." [134] Above all, the mixed system worked. Between 1842 and 1848, sixteen private railroads were chartered in Prussia, capitalized at 84,232,500 thalers.[135] By dint of Prussia's surge in railroad construction, Germany's railway mileage doubled that of France.[136]

The mixed system reflected a spirit of cooperation, but this change does not entirely describe government-business relations in the 1840s. Stock market laws introduced in April and May 1844 prohibited trading foreign stocks, buying on margin, and, above all, subscribing railroad stock without permission from the finance ministry.[137] The laws attempted to curb the mania for railroad securities that gripped Prussian society after 1842—drawing in even artisans and the lower echelons of the bureaucracy, many of whom lost substantial savings on reckless, inexperienced trading. The radically increased volume in securities multiplied the number of illegal stock-jobbers, thus weakening the regulatory power of the state. The railroad boom also threatened temporarily the viability of both state bonds and the mortgage bonds of provincial land banks.[138] The latter were the foundation of Junker economic life; since the late eighteenth century these bonds had generated the funds that financed the transition of noble estates from a local subsistence economy to an agrarian market capitalism. Strengthening bureaucratic controls on buying stock while curtailing the number of railroad securities to be traded in Prussia reflected the suspicious attitude of both state officials and landed nobles toward the new joint-stock operations. The action of conservative elites against the new money class demonstrated their fear of industrial capitalism and the ambivalence of state economic policy, which simultaneously hindered and helped business.

The government law intended to crack down on questionable ventures and brokers, but it also contributed to the first modern stock market panic. Investors halted further payments on stocks, banks withdrew their investments from Berlin, and the impossibility of future stock issues threatened the solvency of many existing companies. Contemporaries referred to a *Geldkrisis:*

a shortage of liquid capital because of the government's conservative policies on money supply and commercial loans, compounded by its refusal to allow joint-stock banks to operate in Prussia.[139] This shortage of investment capital was now heightened by a lack of confidence in the stock market. The panic of 1844, a direct reaction to the new law, depressed the value of railroad stocks by 20 percent.[140]

The panic became the overture to a short-term depression (1846–49) triggered by crop failures between 1844 and 1847. The potato blight of 1845 and bad harvests in 1846 raised the average price of basic foods 50 percent and doubled the price of potatoes and rye. It produced a misery that had not been seen since the famine of 1816–17 and the economic privation suffered under the Continental System.[141] In conjunction with bad harvests, the lack of confidence in investment and the drop in production contributed to the social unrest caused by the unemployment, hunger, and social distress of Germany's laboring classes in the years before 1848.

In spite of the harsh laws against high finance, clear entrepreneurial opposition to government is not evident. At the same time as these hostile laws, the government and business circles developed a dialogue that was less paternalistic than in past times. The government recognized its failure to consult those directly affected by the 1838 Railroad Law. In February 1843 the finance ministry issued a rescript, asking its provincial officials (Landräte, Regierungspräsidenten, and Oberpräsidenten) to consult property owners and railroad companies on how to revise the Railroad Law.[142] The report to the Brandenburg Oberpräsident that summarized the results of local officials' inquiries showed a broad enthusiastic response from railroad companies and property owners. The Berlin-Potsdam, Berlin-Anhalt, and Berlin-Frankfurt railways presented a list of complaints, "endorsing more or less Hansemann's *Critique of the Railroad Law,* and the Berlin-Anhalt referred to it directly." [143] Prussia's bureaucracy began to consult businessmen.

By granting a charter in 1846 to the Association of Prussian Railroad Administrations, the government recognized the competency of businessmen to administrate railroad affairs and to propose sensible reforms. Ten railway companies attended the association's meeting in November 1846, convened primarily to draft a unified, thoroughgoing revision of the 1838 Railroad Law. The twenty-five substantial revisions proposed by the committee were published for circulation a year later by a Friedrich Kühlwetter, a Düsseldorf-Elberfeld Railway director, and two directors of the Rhenish railway, Mevissen and Quadflieg.[144] Revolution interrupted this process of modifying the law. The association also presented the state with a list of its supervisory abuses.[145] In addition, it began to formulate regulations for unifying both timetables and operational procedure. By 1848 the association—now expanded to other German states—coordinated all railways to one time standard (*Berliner Normalzeit*).[146]

The government further acknowledged the rising importance of commerce and industry in state policy with the creation of a Trade Department in 1844, which was a subsidiary office of the finance ministry, and the Royal Bank in 1846, a semipublic central bank of issue. Both changes were roundly denounced as insufficient reforms: business factions in the provincial diets had demanded a trade ministry and felt slighted with a mere department and, similarly, the Royal Bank fell far short of relieving the problems of money supply and commercial credit that had plagued businessmen in the last two decades.[147] Although the Trade Department was not an autonomous ministry, the office did ensure greater participation of the business class in economic policy. Responding to the Berlin Trade Corporation in 1844, the president of the Trade Department wrote: "No laws that touch on trade and commerce will be passed, no changes in tariff policy will be adopted, no export and shipping laws with other countries will be settled without the Trade Department, which will in all such occasions consult the ranks of businessmen to apprehend their experiences and views and get to know their wishes."[148] These half-measures pleased few, but the creation of the Trade Department nonetheless showed that bureaucratic absolutism was grudgingly retooling state machinery for entrepreneurial needs.

The higher status and recognition that the state accorded the business class by the mid-1840s was further exhibited in 1846 when the government appealed to chambers of commerce for advice on whether abolishing the 1844 laws would alleviate the business depression. The response was lively but hardly showed a united front of businessmen against government economic policy. Whereas some chambers endorsed maintaining the laws (Danzig, Hagen, Krefeld, Koblenz, Elberfeld) because they were not the cause of the economic distress, others (Cologne, Aachen, Stettin, Königsberg, Magdeburg, Halle, Erfurt) strongly endorsed their abolition. For Friedrich Engels the lack of common aims among business groups and their failure to mount an effective political front indicated political immaturity.[149] Indeed, only Aachen's chamber of commerce pointed to the unfulfilled promise of a constitution to explain the crisis of 1844.[150] But the division more likely points to a belief among businessmen that the Prussian state still advocated economic progress and, more important, showed signs of integrating commercial and industrial interests into state policy. Initiating a dialogue to adjust unfair laws suggested the state's willingness to weigh business interests. And to avoid greater devaluation of the securities market in the 1840s, the government did not levy the tax on railroad companies stipulated in the 1838 law—a rare instance of a government passing up already approved revenues.

It is clear that the position of state bureaucrats toward businessmen's groups (chambers of commerce, corporations, lobbies, diets, etc.) had evolved by the mid-1840s. The Prussian state bureaucracy's longstanding claim of governing effectively in all areas of public life had worn thin among entrepreneurs. It was evident in numerous areas of economic life that the state lacked expertise, and, significantly, the state tacitly acknowledged this. In matters of taxation, tariffs, trade relations, transportation, and industrial development, the state bureaucracy did not always follow its traditional procedure of autonomously formulating policies and instead availed itself of business groups' views for drafting legislation. In matters of banking, credit, and commercial law, such business groups as the Berlin Trade Corporation ceased to be merely councilors but rather became technical experts in drafting policy. Kaelble's research on Berlin businessmen shows that in the 1840s state bureaucrats yielded ground to allow bankers, merchants, and businessmen into the "decision-making sphere" in matters of commercial and credit laws.[151] Although possessing no formal right to participate in policy decision making, business elites were expanding their participation in governmental affairs with meetings and written recommendations.[152]

For certain business elites, then, a qualitative equality existed between themselves and bureaucrats. Hansemann wrote in 1839, "I speak and write freely about the deficiencies of the bureaucracy to people in high places — very high places — and none can fault me and must hear me whether they like it or not." [153] In his memoirs, Rudolf Delbrück, an official in the ministry of finance, acknowledged the respect that such businessmen as Hansemann commanded in questions of commercial and industrial policy. In one instance, Delbrück recalled feeling "ashamed" when a position paper on tariffs in 1846 by "outstanding" Rhenish businessmen was brusquely dismissed by the finance minister; the shame stemmed from the misguided arrogance of a minister not heeding the views of men who were self-evident authorities on the question of differential tariffs.[154] Although examples of haughty bureaucratic behavior toward the business class persisted, it is because of such civil servants as Delbrück who respected the views of businessmen that critical negotiation, not outright opposition, remained for many businessmen the best means of changing bureaucratic policy. The probability of bourgeois entrepreneurs finding like-minded middle-class bureaucrats was great. "Bourgeois membership," writes Eric D. Brose, "in the ministries, institutes, agencies, corps, and services which made up the state stood, variously, between 46–100 percent." [155]

The blurred line between business and government interests can also be seen in how chambers of commerce reacted to the legislation against unfettered stock speculation. Although the law of 1844 was patently hostile to the railroad industry, some business circles agreed with the government. The Berlin Trade Corporation, for example, stated in 1846 that diverting the flow of capital away from railroads would help settle the crisis,[156] thus endorsing the state's attempt to rein in the corporation's business partners in Cologne, Breslau, and Aachen. This endorsement is a reminder of the care one must take not to exaggerate the distance that stood between the business class and the bureaucratic-noble elements of the Prussian establishment.

The division between the public and private spheres is further blurred by an examination of the careers of businessmen and bureaucrats before 1848. Many state officials worked for railroads as engineers, geologists, legal advisers, and directors. The Rhenish Railway directors Ammon, Open, and Hauchecorne were all civil servants on leave, as were the engineers Pickel (Rhenish Railway), Neuhaus (Berlin-Stettin Railway), Hermann (Berg-Mark Railway), Hartwich (Stargard-Posen and Rhenish railways), and Henz (Rhenish Railway).[157] Friedrich Wilhelm von Reden, an official in the foreign service in the 1840s, also worked as "special director" of the Berlin-Stettin Railway. Friedrich Kühlwetter, a civil servant who later became a minister and a provincial governor, was a director of the Düsseldorf-Elberfeld Railway in the 1840s. Hans Viktor von Unruh, the director of the Magdeburg-Leipzig line and later a revolutionary leader, began his career as a state engineer. The lieutenant colonels Podewils and von Kräwel were directors on the Berlin-Hamburg and Berlin-Frankfurt railways respectively.[158] The Puttkammers, a family of Junker civil servants, invested heavily in the Berlin-Potsdam line. Robert von Puttkamer used his influence as a company director in October 1845 to persuade Provincial Governor von Meding to secure a state loan for the railway.[159]

Ernst von Bodelschwingh, the Rhenish provincial governor in the 1830s, complained in 1838 that a Rhenish government councilor and other officials defended the interests of joint-stock companies all too eagerly, owing to their investments in them.[160] Conflicts of interest grew so great in the bureaucracy and the officer corps that the king issued a secret decree in 1844 barring further direct involvement with railroad finance.[161] In short, business and government circles overlapped. Businessmen drew on both technical experience and political connections when employing state bureaucrats. Conversely, many officials welcomed new economic sectors that offered good salaries to professionals frustrated by the lack of advancement in civil service in the 1840s.[162] Railroad directors were also successful in attracting influential nobles to the business. The Hohenzoller Prince Carl, Fürst Radziwill, and Graf zu Dohna were just some of Prussia's high-ranking nobles who sat on "honorary" railroad committees in return for railway shares.[163] The porous divisions separating government and business perhaps encouraged businessmen to work within the bureaucratic system and not categorically oppose it. The above discussion reveals the empirical weaknesses of characterizing the Prussian state as predominantly dominated by the interests of nobles (*Junkerstaat*), or by a government whose officials retained a caste-like loyalty (*Beamtenstand*) which superseded interests of class. Historians should jettison both explanations of the Prussian state and instead recognize the growing interpenetration of state and society in the 1840s that forced the Prussian state to reconstitute its ruling establishment during the first industrial revolution.

The closely knit web of relations that existed among businessmen, bureaucrats, and nobles, however, did not preclude businessmen's criticism of governmental politics. Not only did businessmen express their annoyance at the state's dilatory tempo in responding to the needs of modern finance and industry, but they also objected to the arrogance of the Prussian state in delaying further the promulgation of a constitution. The publication of Friedrich Wilhelm III's testament in 1840, which directly referred to a "central assembly of the estates," renewed the constitutional movement,[164] and such entrepreneurs as David Hansemann, Gustav Mevissen, Hermann von Beckerath, and Ludolf Camphausen—all railroad directors—were among the principal spokesmen of Rhenish liberalism.[165] These men strove to transform Prussia into a constitutional monarchy founded on the rule of law.[166] Writing for an American newspaper in 1852, Friedrich Engels wrote that by 1840 the bourgeoisie of Prussia had "arrived at a stage where it found the development of its most important interests checked by the political constitution . . . [and] assumed the lead of the middle-class movement of Germany." [167]

The conflict between business and absolutistic government came to a head in 1847, when Friedrich Wilhelm issued a patent on 3 February calling for a United Diet. This was hardly the king's wish—state finance necessitated it. Among the more pressing financial projects was the so-called Eastern Railway. Although the king's primary goal in creating the Railroad Fund was to build a line between Berlin and Königsberg, the province of Prussia still had no railroad. The link between the eastern provinces and the capital was economically important for Junkers and militarily necessary for the Prussian army, but it offered little attraction for private investors.[168] When the lack of transportation prevented available grain stocks from relieving starvation in the eastern provinces, the pressure to build mounted. Despite the lack of interested entrepreneurs, the king gave orders to begin preliminary work in October 1845.[169] The Eastern Railway's construction, however, demanded thirty-three million thalers. After several conferences with the cabinet in 1846–47, the king decided to build it at state cost.[170]

The United Diet consolidated representatives from the eight provincial diets into a central body that, if Friedrich Wilhelm III's ordinance of 1815 and 1820 had been followed, would have assembled annually and had the power to approve legislation, taxes, and loans.[171] But Friedrich Wilhelm IV's patent of February 1847 to assemble the diet did not follow this prescription. It made no mention of the constitutional promise of 1815. Under the patent the king alone could summon the body, which was composed so that the noble estate predominated. Although the patent recognized the United Diet's power to approve new taxes and loans, the diet had no power to initiate legislation. In the event of conflict, the king could dismiss the chamber and return to the Standing Committee and provincial diets.[172] In response to the king's pronouncement that no piece of paper be permitted to come between himself and his people, Rhenish liberals drew up a statement of eight points that distinguished their conception of the United Diet from the patent.[173]

Heinrich Simon, a lawyer from Breslau, best expressed liberals' disappointment with the king's patent in an essay, "To Accept or to Refuse?" in which he exhorted the chosen deputies to boycott the United Diet. Liberals did not boycott but instead used the diet as an "organ of opposition against the constitutional conceptions of the king." [174] The range of political issues debated at the United Diet was broad,[175] but the most demonstrative oppositional action taken by liberals was their refusal to grant credit to build the Eastern Railway. "If the deputies could not meet regularly and could not control finances," August von der Heydt declared on the floor of the diet, then they must "take the uncomfortable, highly embarrassing, but necessary step of denying assent to all loans." [176] More succinctly, Hansemann stated: "In matters of money, friendliness ends." [177] Put in the humiliating position of stopping all work on the Eastern Railway, the government parried with the statement: "The government refuses to develop the United Diet further into a constitutional parliament." [178] With the Diet dismissed, the hopes for legal constitutional reforms in Prussia dimmed. Political frustration compounded by unemployment, bad harvests, food riots, and, most important, news of revolution in Paris brought revolution to Berlin in March 1848.[179]

The United Diet offers, indeed, a dramatic closing to the *Vormärz* period in government-business relations, a climactic end in which a formally constituted political body that included Prussia's leading business elites rejected the crown's political manipulations to forestall constitutionalism. But it would be wrong to place too much emphasis on this event as an encapsulation of how government-business relations developed in the 1840s. Although the Diet's proceedings emphatically stressed entrepreneurs' oppositional stance to the state, relations between businessmen and government officials in the 1840s were not one-dimensionally negative. An examination of the efforts of private railroad companies to assert their interests reveals the noteworthy point that business relations to the state had improved by the mid-1840s. The creation of the mixed system for railways, greater consultation with chambers of commerce over economic legislation, increased influence of railroad directors on railway policy, and the select penetration of leading business elites into the bureaucratic decision-making process tokened a process of accommodation, albeit flawed, and not irremediable alienation from the state.

The relationship of business elites to the state was multisided, and business politics must be weighed equally with formal parliamentary politics to achieve a composite assessment. Although political rhetoric highlighted the differences between state and society in 1848, doubly underscored by social distress and governmental paralysis, the perspective of business politics suggests that the Revolution of 1848 does not represent a complete breakdown in government-business relations. In many areas of economic activity, relations were on the mend. Such railroad entrepreneurs as Camphausen, Beckerath, Hansemann, Mevissen, Diergardt, Lewald, and others clashed with government bureaucrats when advocating a constitution that would move Prussia beyond bureaucratic absolutism toward a representative government that could better respond to the needs of public society. But these aspirations should not overshadow the more diffuse political advances in economic policy, whose cumulative impact made business elites generally shift closer to the state rather than away from it. When looking at business politics and business practices of entrepreneurs during the 1850s, one sees important strains of continuity with the *Vormärz* period. The practice of criticizing the state while simultaneously working with it, so evident in the 1840s, would likewise characterize the political-economic behavior of the business class in the postrevolutionary period.

The Railroad Question in 1848

The tumultuous days of March in Berlin witnessed slain demonstrators, the erection of barricades, and a brief period of anarchy. In response to the mobilization of popular forces, the king appointed Ludolf Camphausen and David Hansemann as ministers to demonstrate the crown's receptivity to change. Although the "liberal cabinet" of Minister-President Camphausen was largely cosmetic (key cabinet posts remained in the hands of conservative nobles), the two businessmen nonetheless sought to reform economic policy. They transformed the private A. Schaaffhausen'sche Bankverein into the first joint-stock bank in Prussia, keeping afloat commercial investments affecting over 200,000 workers. In April 1848 the two ministers also created the ministry of trade, commerce, and public works, thus elevating the status of commerce and industry in state affairs. Furthermore, this ministry drafted reforms for municipal, county, and provincial governments in the eastern provinces, and it submitted bills to tax both landed estates and the annual income of nobles.[180]

By emergency decree the ministry also resumed work on the Eastern Railway, primarily to remove radicalized unemployed workers from Berlin.[181]

The Camphausen-Hansemann ministry lasted until June 1848, but Hansemann stayed on until September as finance minister in the Auerswald Cabinet that replaced it. During this time Hansemann, in cooperation with Trade Minister Karl Milde, a Silesian merchant and investor in railroads, turned his attention to the railroad question. In August Hansemann devised a plan for the government to purchase all existing private railways, monopolize the industry, and further develop Germany's railroad network under the aegis of the state.

After 1846 railroad companies suffered considerably from the depressed business cycle. By 1848, their future was bleak. "With the current critical state of all financial conditions," wrote Hansemann in a memorandum, "the dissolution and bankruptcy of numerous domestic railway enterprises is to be feared." [182] Three railway companies, he noted, had halted construction; many had defaulted on interest payments; and most paid little or no dividend money on common stock. Many investors who had bought shares on margin ceased to pay their quarterly installments.

Hansemann believed that the business depression compounded by revolution jeopardized the ability of the railroad industry to develop under the joint-stock principle. The 109 million thalers invested in railroads—"a considerable portion of the national wealth"—was threatened (65). The loss of this capital would not only affect railway companies and their investors, who came from all social classes, but also laborers "who work and produce for the railroads, namely, [those working in] iron and coal works, machine factories, passenger car and freight car factories, brickworks, and the many smaller trades employed by them" (67). The military dimension—"national defense"—was also to be considered (77). Hansemann further noted the local distress. Regional governments, whose administrative spheres were economically dependent on railroad construction, had petitioned the state to fund building to avoid further economic hardship. Perceiving railroads as the foundation of Prussia's industrial economy, Hansemann sought to avert a collapse at all cost: "There is no doubt that the government must forcefully intervene" (65).

Aiding individual railways, Hansemann believed, was not enough to avert this crisis; selective aid would only raise charges of favoritism. Rather, he proposed "that the state complete the construction of unfinished railways, take over the direction and administration of railways, and gradually unite all railways into an organic whole in the interest of the common good." He concluded, "In other words, the railroads must gradually become the property of the state" (67). Under the laws of 1838 and 1842 the state could acquire private railways over a period of fifty to seventy-two years, depending on how much the Railroad Fund had collected and the extent of government financial involvement. Hansemann's scheme, however, envisioned immediate acquisition at an extremely good price. For the price of fifty million thalers, all existing railroads plus the Eastern Railway, valued together at 140 million thalers, could come under state control (75). The state would raise thirty million through government bonds, ten million from treasury notes drawn on the collateral of state domains, and ten million from "railroad notes [*Eisenbahn-scheine*]," which would circulate on the stock market (82, 86).

The memorandum is not explicit on whether fifty million would buy out all stockholders or just a portion of them. The figure suggests that Hansemann initially strove to make the state the majority stockholder in each company, enabling the state to effect a complete takeover when money was available. On the other hand, Hansemann might have entertained the notion of immediate state acquisition in the catastrophic market of 1848.[183] In either case quick action was needed. The scheme turned on the desperate mood of the financial world. Hansemann cautioned that the state should neither expropriate property nor use the stock market to expedite the takeovers. The former would violate property laws, the latter would result in price gouging (73). Instead the government should negotiate with company directors, who were left with the choice between accepting the state's terms or facing imminent bankruptcy. Because the government would convert all common stock into 4 percent state paper, stockholders would welcome the state action and pay no heed to directors' advice to hold out (74–75). The state, he added, could balance its losses by streamlining overhead costs, enabling it to operate more efficiently than could private companies (82, 85).

For a businessmen who for two decades had nothing but contempt for the inefficiency of state officials in commercial enterprises, Hansemann's claim that administrative costs would be cut with state bureaucrats was, to say the least, remarkable. The evolution of his vacillating position toward the state is largely connected with the business trends of the railroad industry.[184] In the early and mid-1830s, when private financing of railroads seemed unlikely, Hansemann advocated state ownership. After 1837, and after the successful and profitable stock subscriptions of several large German railroads, Hansemann shifted his stance from complete state ownership to supplemental support of private enterprise. When railroads made money in the 1840s, Hansemann praised private directors, who were accountable to their stockholders; civil servants, he claimed, could never match their efficiency.[185] Yet when the business cycle radically turned downward in 1846 and made worse by revolution, Hansemann again shifted his view.[186]

Hansemann's memorandum in 1848 exhibited the characteristics of the practical businessman, for it sought to cut a deal beneficial to all involved parties: the state, the stockholders, and, above all, railroad entrepreneurs.

(Whether the customer was genuinely considered is doubtful.) Hansemann's plan enabled the business class to avert a total financial disaster. By cutting their losses and receiving remuneration from the state, entrepreneurs could shift their investments to new areas. Business cycles shaped the political attitudes of this important representative of the business class.

Hansemann's scheme was never put into action in original form. Drafted in August, the plan died when the Auerswald-Hansemann cabinet was replaced in September 1848 by the conservative (and economically more cautious) cabinet of Graf von Pfuel. On 1 November the king appointed Graf von Brandenburg as minister-president and Otto von Manteuffel as minister of agriculture. Manteuffel, a staunch advocate of bureaucratic absolutism, was viewed as the guardian of the government's reactionary faction and succeeded Brandenburg as minister-president in December 1850.

On 8 December 1848, the king appointed the Elberfeld merchant-banker August von der Heydt as trade minister. The appointment came just weeks after the National Assembly had been moved from Berlin to Brandenburg and just days after the king promulgated a constitution by decree. This shrewd move introduced a government of mixed powers whose legislature was elected by universal suffrage.[187] Although the constitution was put into effect by decree—thus marking yet another crucial "revolution from above"—it put Prussia on the map of representative governments. Although many liberals spurned the constitution as another example of Prussian autocracy, the news immediately stabilized financial markets.[188] The bourse rebounded, reflecting the acceptance among business elites that order, no matter what its cost, was better than the anarchy of the "crazy year." "As much as one scorns Brandenburg and Manteuffel and criticizes their infamous politics," wrote the Rhenish textile manufacturer Wilhelm König, "a bad government is better than no government." [189]

CHAPTER THREE

▼

The Search for Mutual Accommodation, 1848–1857

"This parvenu form of wealth, this most colossal creation of modern industry, this peculiar economic mongrel, whose feet are rooted in the earth but whose head rests on the stock market, gives aristocratic land ownership a mighty rival and the middle class an army of new troops."[1] In this statement of 1862, Karl Marx tried with the help of mixed and stretched metaphors to describe the importance of railroads for the ascendant business class in Europe. Yet railroads after 1848 were no longer the exclusive domain of private capitalists. Unlike the two decades preceding the revolution of 1848, when entrepreneurs enjoyed uncontested leadership in railroad ownership, during the 1850s they vied with the state for control of the business. In 1848 the Prussian government neither owned nor administered a single kilometer of rail. By 1860 the state owned 1,494 kilometers of rail and administered an additional 1,270 kilometers of private rail, controlling 49 percent of Prussia's entire rail network of 5,674 kilometers.[2] Competing with the business class to control policy and profit in the railroad industry, the state changed the entrepreneurial dynamics of railroad building.

The tension that developed between railroad businessmen and the government arose from the economic importance of railroads. Massive capitalization and profits reveal the preeminent role of railroads in the industrial revolution. Railroad investment in Germany between 1850 and 1873 represented one-quarter of all investment.[3] In 1849 the 107 million thalers invested in Prussia's nineteen private railroad companies netted profits of 9,271,084 thalers; in 1856, 273.25 million thalers netted profits of 24,083,604 thalers; and by 1866, 499.5 million thalers produced 65,789,856 thalers in net profit.[4] The magnitude of such figures emerges more clearly when we know that the average cost of starting up a coal mine—no small business venture—was around one million thalers in the 1850s and that the Prussian state debt in 1850 stood at 156 million thalers.[5]

The socioeconomic importance of railroads was, however, even greater. Besides employing tens of thousands in construction, maintenance, and administration, they also created a new heavy machinery industry—mostly factories for locomotives, passenger cars, and freight cars. In 1842, the Borsig machine works had produced eight locomotives; by 1858, the company had made one thousand. Iron production soared with the growing need for rails and machinery. Coal consumption rose 183 percent between 1850 and 1860 in Prussia, owing largely to the growing demand for railway fuel and material.[6] Whereas in 1844 80 locomotives and 666 freight cars carried 2.5 tons of freight, in 1856 more than 742 locomotives and 14,648 freight cars carried 170,518,617 tons.[7] Prussia's developing railway network produced new social realities: stagnation or prosperity for villages, towns, and whole provinces depended on access to railway connections. For good reason economists refer to railroads as the "leading sector" in Germany's first industrial revolution and call the long-term upward business cycle from 1840 to 1873 the "railway-Kondratieff." [8] As the undisputed key to national wealth in the "age of capital," railroads provide an opportunity to study the political dynamic between government and business interests.

During 1848–66 the relations between government and private enterprise passed through two business cycles of approximately nine years each. Both cycles were demarcated by depressions, in 1846–49, 1857–59, and 1866–67, the first and third of which were complicated by significant political events (revolution and war, respectively). Each cycle can be subdivided into similar stages—a period of weakness and recovery in which entrepreneurs were dependent upon the state (1848–52 and 1857–62) and a period of renewed strength in which they were inclined to assert their independence from it (1853–57 and 1862–66). The progress of these cycles is particularly evident in the railroad industry. This chapter studies the first nine-year cycle (1848–57); chapter 7 will examine the second (1857–66).

1848–1852: Recovery and Direct State Intervention

August von der Heydt's acceptance of the trade minister post in the Brandenburg-Manteuffel government at the end of 1848 surprised many contemporaries. He had been a vocal advocate of the constitutional movement in the Westphalian diet of the 1830s, the Standing Committee in 1842, and the United Diet in 1847. Because his past political career ran counter to Manteuffel's agenda, his acceptance earned him much scorn. But Heydt's "liberalism" needs to be examined more closely; it stood closer to conservatism than many of his contemporaries believed. Although the young Heydt advocated progressive reforms such as the annual assembly of provincial diets, the right of petition, civic equality for Jews, and a constitution for Prussia, these reforms could be reconciled with a "thoroughly conservative mindset, which was the case in the house of von der Heydt." [9]

The foundation of this conservative mindset was the family's Calvinism and its profound respect for monarchy. Heydt's father (also named August) was a particularly stringent Calvinist whose two other sons, Carl and Daniel, led a large number of Elberfeld coreligionists to secede from the state church when it proposed a new liturgy in 1847. These "Wuppertal separatists," notes historian Jonathan Sperber, "would be politically the most extreme conservatives and Prussian royal loyalists in the entire Rhineland during the 1848 Revolution." [10] Certainly August von der Heydt was affected by the conservatism of his family's Protestant sect, just as he was by the family's ties to the Hohenzollern family. Heydt, in fact, developed personal ties to the crown prince, highlighted by Friedrich Wilhelm's two visits to Heydt's house in 1842 as monarch. Accordingly, the king appointed him in 1845 to head a commission to reform laws on currency transactions in the Customs Union. Hence, when Heydt embarked on a phase of loyal opposition in the period 1842–47, espousing moderate reform, it aroused little suspicion in Berlin.[11] Before the revolution Heydt publicly admonished the government that it should alter its positions on the Rhenish penal code and on biennial convenings of provincial diets, but his fealty to the monarch was above reproach. His opposition consisted of anchoring Prussian monarchy in constitutional legality.

The king, however, felt betrayed by Heydt's persistent support for a constitution and his opposition to the king's religion patent at the United Diet in 1847 (which sought to place Jews in a separate estate), but this contretemps was resolved by a long missive from Heydt that defended his actions as behavior consummate with his allegiance to the king.[12] Heydt clearly drew the line between reform and revolution, having no sympathy whatsoever for democracy or republicanism. In 1848 he refused to run for the constituent assemblies in Frankfurt and Berlin, stating that he could not reconcile these political bodies with his belief in legal continuity.[13] And certainly the course of the revolution in the Rhineland deepened his dislike of popular democratic politics and its excesses. He was a cofounder of Elberfeld's Constitutional Club, which sought to check the radical politics arising in the Rhineland.[14] Elberfeld democrats publicly ridiculed him with a charivari (*Katzenmusik*) in August 1848,[15] and his brother Daniel was taken hostage and extorted for money by an angry mob in Elberfeld in May 1849. In sum, having passed muster with his relationship to king and state, Heydt's experience in municipal and regional government in addition to his skills in banking and commerce made him a thoroughly qualified choice to succeed David Hansemann as trade minister.

"This moderate, elegant, adroit banker possessed a background that made him unassailable for nobles and government officials." [16]

For a private banker, one whose banking establishment (Heydt-Kersten & Sons, est. 1754) was among the Rhineland's leading lenders of credit to merchants and manufacturers, Heydt's advocacy for state railroads appears odd. Although Heydt made large profits from railroads as a director and as a banker in the 1840s and 1850s, he nonetheless viewed state participation as indispensable.[17] As noted in the last chapter, the Rhine-Weser and Elberfeld-Witten projects of the Elberfeld commercial community collapsed in the 1830s because of the shortage of capital. These early impressions perhaps molded Heydt's view that the state, in enterprises of unprecedented capitalization, was the essential instrument for economic improvement.

In contrast to his fellow Rhenish bankers and entrepreneurs, Heydt believed, furthermore, that the state possessed the right to direct the economy for its own purposes and should therefore never relinquish the controls of strong state paternalism. As minister, he proposed a more ambitious bureaucratic apparatus to regulate economic activity. Equating modernization with bureaucratization, Heydt's statism advocated the expansion of the regulatory and promotional roles of the state—an economic corollary of the state's increased political control.[18] In this regard his philosophy as a bureaucrat scarcely resembled the older Prussian mercantilist tradition, which was more modest in dimension, and largely differed with the Prussian Reform-Era philosophy, which sought to efface the state's presence in the private market. Rather, Heydt's views were part of a broader historical trend in the 1850s, when the Austrian, French, and Belgian states took a more a interventionist role in the economy. Promoting the state ownership of railroads, Heydt believed, served the dual purpose of encouraging economic growth in the private sector (for example, the newly liberalized coal industry) while integrating industrial development with the commercial, fiscal, and military interests of the state.

And yet portraying Heydt either as a progressive practitioner of Bonapartistic statism or as a forerunner of modern-day state interventionism is only half the story. Equally important in explaining Heydt's zeal for state railroads was his love of power. As this book will amply show, he was an extremely talented administrator who, in turn, was entrepreneurial in accumulating greater spheres of jurisdiction and influence. In his career as a public servant he antagonized not only the business world but also other ministries. He was consistently at loggerheads with the finance ministry, whose ministers Karl von Bodelschwingh (1850–58) and Robert von Patow (1858–62) advocated budgetary accountability and minimal state paternalism in a private market economy.[19] Heydt, on the other hand, as the ambitious head of a new ministry, interpreted his duties broadly, bending laws and encroaching upon state revenues as benefited his ministry. To be sure, Heydt's calls in the 1840s to check arbitrary government actions with constitutional legality were not always consistent with his actions as a minister. Biographical accounts of Heydt overestimate his regard for parliamentary control over government action. Succinctly described, Heydt was the consummate empire builder. And because bringing railroads (the most capitalized sector in the Prussian economy) under the aegis of the trade ministry became his pet project, it is difficult to separate his own personal ambition from his railroad policies.

Heydt, then, enthusiastically adopted Hansemann's plan of a state railway system, albeit in modified form. Toward this end he attempted to negotiate a government takeover of the Rhenish Railway in the winter of 1849. Heydt believed the company was in desperate financial straits and that stockholders would welcome converting their shares into state bonds. Reluctantly, company directors acceded to the proposal and asked for 4 percent interest on the conversion from company common stock to state bonds. Heydt offered lower, believing the company had no choice but to accept. The directors held out for a better offer, and when the stock market slowly recovered over the course of 1849, they called off the deal. Once financial markets visibly improved, the directors and major stockholders decided to keep the company private.[20] By 1849–50 it was clear that the quick killing envisioned by Hansemann was no longer possible.

In the years 1849–53, plagued by low freight revenues, high construction costs, and obligations to pay dividends, private railroads struggled to stay out of debt. In this unstable period the government played a major role in aiding railways with financial problems, including six in the western provinces of Westphalia and the Rhineland. Railroad companies started in the 1840s in these two industrially advanced provinces now had their solvency threatened by the catastrophic business years of 1846–49. In three instances, the railroads were uncompleted lines that declared bankruptcy during 1848. Two of these were Rhenish lines, the Aachen-Düsseldorfer and the Ruhrort-Crefeld-Kreis Gladbacher railways, with which the state agreed in 1849 to finish construction, administer business upon completion, and guarantee dividends, gaining in return an option to purchase the company shares at par whenever it wished.[21] The Cöln-Minden-Thüringer railway in Westphalia, however, was completely bought out in 1849; the state indemnified stockholders, dissolved the private corporation, and renamed the railway the Westphälische Staatseisenbahn.[22]

Owing to similar financial difficulties and an inability to pay dividends, the Berg-Mark railway, the important Ruhr line that connected Elberfeld, Hagen, and Dortmund, agreed to come under state administration in 1850.[23] The state already owned 25 percent of Berg-Mark's stock, and because the railway connected with the state-run Aachen-Düsseldorfer line, it became a logical choice as administrator.[24] In 1853 the state would add both the Prinz Wilhelm and Cöln-Crefeld railways to this Ruhr-Rhine network, making the state a major railroad administrator in the western provinces next to the large private networks of the Cologne-Minden and the Rhenish railways.

In addition, the trade ministry agreed to guarantee 3.5 percent dividends on stock issued by other companies desperately in need of capital. The stock guarantees to such large, established companies as the Rhenish, the Cologne-Minden, the Stargard-Posen, and the Upper Silesian railways enabled them to pay salaries punctually and continue the construction of branch lines.[25] The government believed that this government support benefited all railroad companies, for it propped up assets on the sagging securities market and restored general confidence in future railroad investment. The state guarantees, in short, helped companies stave off further disaster until the mutually reinforcing relationship between iron production, coal mining, commercial manufacturing, and railroad transportation brought business back to prerevolutionary levels.

Although neighboring railways in the Rhineland complained that state-administered lines and state-subsidized dividends in the area would hurt their stock quotes, investors more generally believed that the state action of either honoring partial value of the company paper or offering subsidies was the best deal to salvage these ill-timed ventures.[26] By stepping in and aiding these fledgling start-ups, the trade ministry was fulfilling its expected role of augmenting private enterprise with state support. Only the state could afford to resuscitate lines that were not economically viable in the short term. These actions by the trade ministry were in line with the expectations of the business class when the ministry was created in 1848.

And yet the early relationship between businessmen and the trade ministry was not without problems, chiefly because of more far-reaching plans for state ownership being hatched within the government. Heydt developed a long-term plan to achieve a state rail system through gradual purchase of private railway stock and through the construction of new state lines.

The key to a state railroad system was public moneys. The new constitution of December 1848 had created a legislature whose Chamber of Deputies possessed the power to approve loans and budgets. Thus the Prussian government's decreed constitution solved the prerevolutionary dilemma of raising loans large enough to build railroads. With the National Assembly in Frankfurt dissolved and the Erfurt parliament not yet convened, the Prussian Chamber of Deputies debated in December 1849 a thirty-three million thaler loan to build the Eastern Railway as well as to complete two unfinished lines in the regions of Saarbrücken and Westphalia.[27] As noted earlier, liberals in the United Diet had rejected a government request for a loan to build the Eastern Railway.[28] With a constitutional government in place, the Chamber of Deputies now backed the Eastern Railway with little hesitation. The ministry viewed the other two lines as commercially and militarily important and argued for their completion as a national task. The Prussian parliament approved the loan package on 20 December 1849.[29]

A significant stipulation accompanied the bill's passage. The Chamber of Deputies' Railroad Committee announced that the government must "use every possible means" to transfer all Prussian rail into the hands of the state.[30] The Chamber, repeating arguments advanced in the Standing Committee in 1842 and in the United Diet of 1847, gave its full approval for the government to pursue a policy of state ownership and supplant the "mixed system" of the 1840s that presumed the leadership of the private economy. Although advocacy of railroad nationalization was intermittently popular among elected officials in the decades after 1848, the commission's report of 1849 was the Chamber's most pronounced statement of support for state railroads between the years 1849 and 1866. The Chamber's enthusiasm for state ownership reveals the pessimism among public circles and businessmen over the problems of private ownership.

And yet when Trade Minister Heydt launched an aggressive supervision of the industry, railroad businessmen criticized and resisted the ministry's claim to shape policy in the industry. In 1849–50 Heydt compelled Prussian railways to schedule night mail trains. Because the ministry issued the order during a time of heavy financial losses, many companies protested bitterly. We shall see in chapter 4 that this issue became a significant confrontation between private railroad companies and the trade ministry. The government levied fines and threats of suspension for those who refused to comply, and Heydt filed lawsuits against three railways that persisted in their refusals. The government occupied the Bonn-Cologne railway, replacing its privately employed administrators with state officials for a month until the company relented.[31]

Private companies also resisted Heydt's orders to aid Police President Karl von Hinckeldey and Minister of Interior Ferdinand von Westphalen in discharging employees involved in the 1848 revolution. The government's order that company presidents draw up lists of politically questionable workers was met with a poor response, prompting Heydt to turn the task over to the Royal Railroad Commissions, the government administration supervising railroad affairs. Considerably less informed about company employees and their histories, the commissioners' inquiry into railroad personnel and their politics produced meager results. In several instances, railroad companies refused to discharge workers believed to be politically undesirable and reinstated workers fired on orders of the government.[32] In 1852 stockholders of the Düsseldorf-Elberfeld Railway ignored the governmental wishes during the reactionary period and elected a director who had played a prominent role in 1848, prompting Heydt to nullify the election.[33] Although companies eventually acceded to certain government wishes, their capitulation was grudging and carried out only as a result of repeated threats and monetary fines by the ministry. During the years of acute political reaction, 1851–54, private railroad companies, headed predominately by moderate liberals, did not cooperate with attempts of the Prussian state to purge business and bureaucracy of democrats.[34] The general reluctance to comply with the government's new political direction provoked Heydt to carry out a protracted effort in the king's cabinet from 1853 to 1857 to classify private railway officials as "indirect state servants" for purposes of security.[35]

The most salient example of government-business friction in the early 1850s was the controversial government takeover of the Lower Silesian–Mark Railway in 1850–52. Against the wishes of both directors and stockholders, Heydt replaced the private administration of the Lower Silesian Railway with state officials in 1850. Because the company was one of the largest and oldest railways in Prussia, the incident raised the question of whether the trade ministry wished to work with railroad companies or subsume them. Whereas government takeovers in previous cases had been viewed largely as benevolent—mostly because they rescued unfinished railroad projects depleted of capital—contemporaries deemed this takeover as an unnecessary, hostile intrusion into the affairs of private business. The government justified the takeover with a technical stipulation in a state loan to the company which allowed the state to manage the company if it failed to turn a profit in three years. The company complained that it was grossly unfair to expect a profit in 1847 or 1848 and attributed the losses of 1849 largely to the expense of running Heydt's night trains.[36]

Heydt's action was undoubtedly part of his nationalization scheme. The profitable Silesian line between Berlin and Frankfurt a.O. became the center for a large network of state-owned railways built in the eastern provinces over the next decade. In 1852 Heydt dissolved the company as a private business and incorporated it into the Prussian state railway system. The company contested both Heydt's final appropriation of the company by executive fiat and the stockholders' vote he later manipulated to approve the state takeover.[37] The first two civil court appeals backed the company's claim; the third (in Berlin) ruled in favor of the state. The trade minister had won his case and in the process revealed his intent to use the legal, political, and economic leverage of the state to weaken the power of private management and assume control of Prussia's railway system. The incident sat well neither with entrepreneurs, whose projects seemed at the mercy of an arbitrary minister, nor with investors, who were denied a lucrative option on the securities market.

By the end of 1852, the government owned 912 kilometers of rail and administrated an additional 332 kilometers of private rail. The 2,113 kilometers of independently operated, private rail overshadowed the state-owned system (63 versus 37 percent), but it was, by all calculations, a formidable start.[38] The trade ministry had made good use of this recovery period after the Revolution of 1848 to establish the state as a railroad power.

1853-1857: A Mixed Legacy

The years 1853-57, the most prosperous of the decade, were a period of unparalleled expansion in manufacturing, mining, and overseas trade. The railroad industry also prospered, yet because Heydt's ministry consolidated its power over railroads, railroad entrepreneurs described their success in qualified terms. The ministry not only increased the mileage of state railroads through more takeovers, but it also exercised greater indirect control over private companies through its supervision of company charters, stock issues, bonds, and the use of foreign capital. Although the mileage of private rail still exceeded that of the state, the trade ministry's restrictive supervision and expansionist designs put railroad directors in a defensive position.

The trade ministry put new revenues to work to accelerate its nationalization plan. In May 1853 the Chamber of Deputies enforced the railroad tax, a provision of the 1838 law that had never been implemented because of economic crises of the mid-forties. The levy was progressive and drained off profits exceeding 5 percent from private railroad companies that had borrowed from the state.[39] These so-called extra-dividends flowed into a fund controlled by the trade ministry designated exclusively for railroad nationalization through gradual stock purchase. Thus the profits of private railroads would fund their own eventual demise. This was indeed bitter fruit for such efficient, profitable companies as the Cologne-Minden and Upper Silesian railways, which together over the course of the 1850s contributed over four and a quarter million thalers in extra-dividends.[40] As we shall see in Chapter 6, the passing of this tax produced lengthy debate in the Chamber where Georg and Karl von Vincke and their faction of old liberals protested the intrusion of the state. In the king's cabinet, Finance Minister Karl von Bodelschwingh strongly objected to Heydt's control over the fund independent from the state treasury. In spite of parliamentary and ministerial opposition, Heydt secured by means of the railroad tax additional revenue for quicker acquisitions. The purchased railways, Heydt stated, would "ensure the state a property of immeasurable worth." [41]

State regulation of transportation reached new heights in the mid-1850s, encroaching on private administration of railroad companies in a number of ways. In 1857 the government introduced renewal funds for private companies, an additional sinking fund to supplement the already mandatory reserve funds. The latter was a stipulation of the 1838 railroad law that required companies to set aside a portion of annual profits (from .5 to 1 percent of total capitalization) for renovation. Although the additional fund added more security to company assets, it also restricted private railways from offering higher dividends in order to maintain a competitive profile on the stock market. The fairness of the trade ministry's ordinance appeared especially questionable when it was not enforced on all state-owned railways.[42] The exemption of some state railways from the sinking fund clearly put private railways at a disadvantage.

The trade ministry intensified its supervision of private management in several different ways that companies interpreted more as interference than regulation. Heydt transformed the once perfunctory requirement of having all annual dividends approved by the government into a rigorous ordeal, often denying petitions from companies to issue higher dividends.[43] In addition, he insisted that railroad companies publish their profits monthly and punished those directors who refused with heavy fines.[44] Further, company directors needed permission from the trade ministry to issue bonds or a new series of common stock, the negotiations for which were long, arduous, and not always successful.[45] Even worse for railroad directors was dependence on the trade ministry to guarantee company bonds and preferred stock, a power that Heydt used to his advantage.

Moreover, the trade ministry favored the state lines by denying new charters to private companies. To cite but one example, the extension of the Rhenish lines southward to complete the north-south axis in western Germany was delayed at least five years, in part because of military considerations (Cologne and Coblenz were fortress towns), but also because Heydt hoped to win the concession for the state system and deny it to the Cologne-Minden and the Rhenish railways.[46] Overall, during the period 1849–62, the government allowed only two new railroad companies to be founded, rejecting dozens of petitions to build or extend lines.[47] The shortage of funds and the difficulty in placing shares on the market were Heydt's standard excuses, but this answer was not consistently credible during 1850–57, a period when ninety-four joint-stock companies (coal mines and iron works making up fifty-nine of these) placed shares amounting to over 107,985,699 million thalers with little difficulty.[48] It was not the stock market but rather state aims that frustrated both domestic and foreign businessmen in their effort to construct and administrate private railways.[49]

Although the Prussian state's interest in owning and administering its own network of rails in all provinces put private railroad interests at a disadvantage, in some cases it helped railroad investors sell unprofitable lines. In the years 1849–55, for example, the state attempted to take over the Münster-Hamm railway, a small line in Westphalia. The Münster-Hamm was a private line of less than thirty kilometers that was sandwiched between a Prussian state line on one end and the Hannoverian state railway on the other. Because this stretch logically figured in with the governments' planned network of state lines, the directors and stockholders approached the government with an offer and drove a hard bargain. The negotiations began in May 1849 and were finally ended in 1855; the terms of sale to the state consistently changed to keep pace with the improving stock market and to fetch a higher price. In 1849 the company approached the state ministry offering the sale of its stock at 70 percent; in 1850, the terms were raised to 86 percent and an additional dividend guarantee of 3.5 percent; and by December 1853, the company agreed to sell the railway for state paper yielding 4 percent.[50] The tenacity and persistence of the company nettled state officials, who broke off negotiations three times before finally accepting the deal in 1855. Because the average dividend rate stood at 2.6 percent between 1849 and 1853, investors received a generous settlement. Unlike the Lower Silesian–Mark takeover, this private company was not opposed to state ownership or government takeovers; the stockholders were merely opposed to an unprofitable transaction and knew that they had the upper hand in negotiation.

Overall, businessmen raised little general objection to state involvement in railroads in the early 1850s, for they assumed that the state would serve business needs. This expectation was partially fulfilled. By 1858, for example, the state administrated over 46.7 million thalers of Rhenish private railways, whose average dividend return was 1.37 percent. Privately administered railroads in the Rhineland, on the other hand, capitalized at over 81.1 million thalers (chiefly the Cöln-Minden and Rhenish railways) received an average 5 percent dividend.[51] Over the course of the 1850s the state had become the caretaker of indispensable but unprofitable private railways. This curious mixture of private capital and state management in Germany's leading industrial sector is a feature that has not been satisfactorily integrated into the discussions on the role of the state in industrialization.

Objection to state involvement arose in particular instances when businessmen believed that government policy served only the state. Businessmen believed the state was unnecessarily aggrandizing its administrative influence when the state-managed Berg-Mark Railway absorbed the Düsseldorf-Elberfeld company or retarded the expansion of such profitable lines as the Rhenish and Cologne-Minden railways because of conflict of interest. Similarly, the Stargard-Posen railroad shrugged off the state's attempt to enlarge its role in the railway. The company was contractually obliged to accept state administration in 1851 following three consecutive subventions to the company from the government to guarantee a 3.5 percent dividend.[52] But the company shareholders, in spite of government pressure to vote for a government take-over, voted against complete state control in 1855. The trade ministry's offer to substitute 4 percent state paper for the company's common stock was rejected in the expectation that the railway could fare better as a private enterprise.[53]

In the mid-1850s business circles increasingly criticized railroad take-overs by Heydt's ministry, producing a new level of concern for state involve-ment in business. Against the staunch opposition of stockholders and direc-tors, Heydt took over the highly profitable Upper Silesian Railway in 1856. The railroad company had resisted and criticized state regulation through-out the 1850s, especially concerning the question of freight rates for coal.[54] In 1855 the company protested the ordinance which allowed the provincial railroad commission to change unilaterally rates on third-class carriages and challenged the jurisdiction of a provincial state commission to meddle in pri-vate business.[55] Relations between the railway and the government were made worse when the directors involved themselves in politics and openly backed the opposition party. "In the fall election for the Chamber of Deputies," wrote a government official, "the most influential executives of the Upper Silesian railway—among them director Kuh—made appearances which aroused gen-eral outrage among government loyalists." [56] The political behavior of the di-rectors annoyed the governor of the province considerably; it was "politically objectionable," he wrote to the trade minister, that a company employing over a thousand workers should be directed by such people.[57] Shortly thereafter Heydt exploited his ministerial power to bring the railroad under state control.

In the railroad industry charters were needed to incorporate as a joint-stock company, lay new lines, and issue new series of stock. When, in Novem-ber 1855, the railroad directory submitted its request for a charter to build a branch line into the coal fields of Tarnowitz and the surrounding coal seams of upper Silesia, Heydt refused. The company considered the procedure of a charter pro forma, for the railway had been promised the right to connect its trunk line with this valley: logic dictated that only this railway should have this charter. Heydt, however, withheld the charter and threw the company into a crisis; investors assumed this branch line, with its long-awaited profits, was a part of the Upper Silesian's network.

Knowing that these branch lines were vital to the company's future, Heydt then offered the charter to the company on the condition that the state take over the railroad's administration. The tactic aroused much resentment from the company directors, who initially rejected it in strong language. They charged the government railroad commission with intrigue and dishonesty, accusations that provoked the commissioners to threaten the directory with suspension.[58] The company directors were all the more appalled when the railroad commission insisted—under orders from Heydt—that the board of directors present the option to the assembly of stockholders not as a demand from the state but, rather, as a request from the company. The Prussian government's attempt to cover up its initiation of the deal and not to appear as the aggressive party was, however, quickly leaked to the press.[59]

The charter became Heydt's wedge to separate the board of directors from its stockholders. Heydt knew that the company directors could not justify any principled legalistic fight against the state over private administration to their stockholders if it meant inferior dividends. In this instance, defying the government's move on the basis of business principles ran counter to the company's prosperity and profits, giving little or no room for the private management to fight. Resembling nothing less than economic blackmail, the "offer" had its intended effect—the directors capitulated.[60] At the annual company meeting in August 1856 the Upper Silesian railroad directors presented their stockholders with the option of either remaining a completely private company with no charter (and lower dividends) or becoming a state-administered railway that would build the branch line and thereby ensure the future health of dividends. As a Breslau newspaper wrote, "The action of the government, in principle, is certainly not to be defended in all respects, but the transfer of the administration to the state is only a matter of time." [61]

The takeover needed a two-thirds majority, and it passed narrowly by 20 votes. More stockholders voted against the measure than those that voted for it, but the latter held more shares. The state, which owned stock in the line and which normally refrained from participating in votes, cast its 54 votes for the takeover.[62] Through clear abuse of governmental powers, the Upper Silesian Railway fell into the hands of the government. Heydt received heavy criticism both in the Prussian parliament (the *Landtag*) and in the press, but the new arrangement came into effect nonetheless on January 1, 1857.[63]

Months later, the government took over the administration of the Wilhelmsbahn (Cosel-Oderberg), another large Silesian railway. Owing to overexpansion and a depressed money market, the privately owned Wilhelmsbahn —Germany's most profitable line in 1855—went bankrupt in 1857.[64] During the early 1850s the railroad undertook plans to extend two branch lines (Nicolai-Idahütte, Ratibor-Leobschütz) and build a new one (Leobschütz-Neiss) which would not only connect its lines to more Silesian coalfields but also unite with the Upper Silesian Railway in Idahütte.[65] The construction of these lines was approved by the government, but the initial construction costs were grossly underestimated, making it necessary for the company to seek an additional 5 million thalers in 1856 to cover costs. The company decided to raise half the sum by doubling the stock and to raise the other half with a 5 percent bond. In January 1857 Heydt's ministry granted permission to the company directors to follow this course of action.[66] This financial maneuver was a risky undertaking; the bourse was already depressed and could not easily handle the volume of these issues. Moreover, new northern Austrian lines were completed which robbed the Wilhelmsbahn of its freight traffic to Galicia, Russia, and Austrian provinces.[67] In March the directors publicized the precarious state of the company's finances. Investors were told to expect heavily slashed dividends, a move that sent the stock into a downward tailspin on the market. By April of the same year, the company could not pay creditors.

Showing signs of severe insolvency, the directors submitted a proposal to the general assembly of stockholders for a state takeover. The assembly, which was controlled by an elite consortium of Berlin financiers (Bleichröder, Wolff, and Hirschfeld), voted overwhelmingly for state control, believing the government would compensate investors fairly in this fiasco. The state's below-par indemnification of stockholders, however, was nowhere near to matching the prices that investors had paid for the stock in the 1850s, which had soared to quotes above 200. Stockholders lost fortunes. Many embittered investors spoke of collusion between Berlin banks and government and, more specifically, of ministerial criminality.[68]

During the bankruptcy proceedings, the business community blamed company directors, but, significantly, the state railroad commission received equal, if not greater, condemnation. Investors and financiers were shocked that the commission, which supervised board meetings and ledgers, could allow the business to issue a 16 percent dividend to stockholders in 1855, yet watch it collapse months later. The ability of the state to supervise the industry properly was gravely questioned. The state's assertion that it preempted private greed and overzealous ambition with a disinterested, above-party expertise was roundly criticized.[69] The prestige of Heydt and his ministry was further compromised when, to finance the state takeover of the Wilhelmsbahn with a 1.5 million thaler bond, he raided the Silesian miners' welfare association to back a 5 percent bond.[70] The miners' association (*Oberschlesische Bergbauhülfskasse*), which was created by Friedrich the Great, became a detail of special concern for one journalist who criticized Heydt in July 1862 for misusing the fund and "experimenting with it to death." (Heydt prosecuted for libel; the reporter's acquittal in 1862 was a cause célèbre for the Progressive Party.[71]) In a similarly coercive move, Heydt forced Silesian coalmine owners to subscribe to the same 1.5 million thaler bond. Those who did not participate were threatened with higher state surcharges. He specifically browbeat the region's major coal magnates (Herzog von Ratibor, Herzog von Wiese, Kaufmann Dorno, and Furst von Pless) with a surtax of 2 groschen per ton if they did not accede to his wishes. The legality of such a surtax was highly dubious, but "the ultimatum," as the Breslau railroad commissioners wrote to Heydt, "seems to have had a decisive effect."[72] The takeovers consolidated the state system in the east, which, combined with the Eastern, the Stargard-Posen, and the Lower Silesian railways, had grown into an extensive network.

These issues of nationalization and increased government control of private industry exemplified government-business confrontations of this era. The conflicts often centered on the personality of Heydt, who was alternately viewed as a bold, assertive proponent of state planning, or as an autocrat who, to paraphrase Rudolf von Delbrück, often confused the interests of the trade ministry with the common good.[73] Few would question the competency of Heydt, whose technical, administrative, and financial skills were widely respected. But there was certainly a conflict of interest at work in his role as minister whose ostensibly impartial status as arbitrator in commercial affairs clashed with his other role as director of state railroads. In another example of a conflict of interest, Heydt, who also oversaw the construction of public works, had no compunction in extracting large contributions from all Prussian joint-stock companies for the building of the Berlin cathedral, an action that businessmen interpreted as unethical solicitation.[74] As Hans Viktor von Unruh wrote, his "tendency toward arbitrary action and deficiency of solid principles" led railroad directors to believe that "the paralysis of private management appeared to be exactly the intention of the minister, who alone wanted to rule." [75]

Economic issues took on a political edge. As already seen, the entrepreneurial circles that built and financed the Upper and Lower Silesian railways backed the opposition party in 1855, contributing to the election of a liberal wholesale merchant, Theodor Molinari, to the Landtag. The esteemed status of Molinari as president of Breslau's chamber of commerce rankled state officials, for he lent great credibility to the opposition party.[76] Other chambers of commerce also adopted an overtly political attitude in lengthy introductory commentaries to their annual reports, criticizing the unwarranted intervention of government into private business and emphasizing the need to end Prussia's patronizing tutelage in economic and civic affairs.[77] The reports of Prussia's chambers of commerce grew so critical in the 1850s that the trade ministry issued a circular in 1857 ordering them to confine their reports to statistical materials—and to leave out complaints and political editorials.[78] The many local committees in the eastern provinces that mushroomed after 1857 to promote the building of railroad lines soon became political bases for the "Young" Lithuanian Faction (*Fraktion Junglitauen*), the nucleus of the future Progressive Party formed in 1861.[79] Oppositional stances in elections, outspoken petitions and reports, and railroad committees transformed into political caucuses demonstrated how intertwined economics and politics became in the 1850s.[80]

The Prussian state's control of money supply—finance politics—also brought railroad circles into conflict with the government. Rhenish entrepreneurs, frustrated by the ministry's tight loan policy, founded commercial banks outside Prussia to fund large-scale enterprises like railroad construction. Similarly, in 1856, a number of prominent railroad men and bankers established commandite banks in Prussia, a maneuver that circumvented the need for a government charter. This act—the subject of chapter 5—greatly annoyed Manteuffel's cabinet, which interpreted it as defiance of government control. The *Diskonto Gesellschaft* and the *Berliner Handelsgesellschaft* were founded by a new breed of entrepreneurs opposed to state tutelage and desirous of greater autonomy in business affairs.

After 1848 the efforts of the Prussian state to participate directly in the railroad business led to the creation of several railroad associations whose purpose was to organize and collectively represent the interests of private companies. The creation of the *Norddeutscher Eisenbahn-Verband* (1848/52), the *Verband mitteldeutscher Eisenbahnen* (1852), the *Rheinisch-Thüringischer Eisenbahn-Verband* (1853), the *Ostfriesich-Thüringischer Eisenbahn-Verband* (1856), and the *Westdeutscher Eisenbahn-Verband* (1857) enabled private railways of different states to coordinate timetables, fares, and freight rates independent of government treaties. These associations introduced the innovations of a general bookkeeping office, luggage transfer, and commonly owned freight trains. They also played a major organizational role in the mobilization of the Prussian army in the Rhineland in 1859.[81]

The associations strengthened the liberal argument that private commerce could handle the larger, overarching problems of the new industrial age without state intervention. Their pragmatic achievements contradicted Prussian government assertions that only the state could coordinate and manage an efficient, interlocking rail network. It was not coincidental that these Verbände arose in exactly the same period that Heydt's ministry asserted its increasingly larger claims to organize the industry. Their creation was largely a defensive response, and Heydt's uncooperative behavior toward these private administrations confirmed their success. Called upon by the king to justify a number of prohibitory decrees against the North German Railroad Association, Heydt admitted in June 1857 that the "prevalent" services of this *Verband* "weakened the influence of the Prussian government." [82] In spite of Heydt's arbitrary actions to control the growth of private railroad organization, the associations nonetheless throve and showed German governments that private companies could indeed serve public needs.

▼

In spite of numerous problems in government-business relations, the Prussian state did have something positive to offer. The Prussian legal system, for instance, often supported the interests of the business class. Central to the needs of businessmen was civil law, the juridical sphere that presumed "civil society was shaped by contractual relationships freely formed by equal partners." [83] The octroyed constitution of 1850 upheld this tenet—first set down in the Prussian law code of the late eighteenth century—and thus provided commercial circles with what Max Weber called "the calculability and reliability in the functioning of the legal order and the administrative system [that] is vital to rational capitalism." [84] Furthermore, the continued use of commercial courts after 1848 greatly aided the resolution of financial disputes, and the civil courts handled eminent domain disputes fairly.[85] Finally, by its role in drafting of a new Commercial Code for the German Confederation (1857 to 1861), the trade ministry promoted German capitalism.

The ministry of justice, furthermore, restrained the Prussian army on issues important to business interests.[86] The minutes of the state cabinet record its resistance to the war ministry's desire to impose arbitrary ordinances on railway companies, fearing drawn out and unsuccessful court cases.[87] On three occasions in the mid-1850s, the war ministry was forced to compromise with railway companies on the question of payment for military fortifications. Likewise, private railways abolished reduced fares for military personnel. Although the ministry had enforced such exactions on companies earlier, the litigious attitude of businessmen in the 1850s produced more cautious governmental behavior. The protocols of private railroad companies reveal the businessman's confidence in both the independence of the judiciary and its ability to reach fair decisions.[88] Yet the courts could not always check the far-ranging independence of government ministries, whose ordinances often fell outside the purview of the legal system. For this reason, many merchants and entrepreneurs joined liberals in the New Era to demand that ministers be held accountable to the courts under the judicial code.[89]

Positive aspects can also be seen in the relations between the government bureaucracy and private railroads, at least on the lower bureaucratic levels. Although the trade minister desired a tightly coordinated bureaucracy of clearly delineated hierarchies controlled from above, this was not always the case.[90] The mediators between the Berlin ministry and businessmen were the local Royal Railroad Commissioners, who created a dialogue that permitted businessmen to dissent and negotiate. Often recruited from private companies, railroad commissioners possessed the technical expertise and practical experience to form opinions independently of both the trade ministry and the railway companies. Although local officials enforced the ministry's unpopular decisions, they were frequently sympathetic to the needs of private business. Commissioners in Cologne, Breslau, Münster, and Berlin often questioned the pragmatism (and legality) of Heydt's orders and provided a conduit for businessmen to communicate their viewpoints to the higher echelons of government.[91] In this respect, the dialogue between businessmen and the trade minister was, if not always harmonious, open and fluid.

Entrepreneurs were thus ensured a voice in matters pertaining to their railroads. On such issues as freight rates, line construction, administrative procedures, taxes, personnel, and government bond guarantees, company directors were able to present their views to the government. Railroad directors had excellent access to railroad commissioners, deputy prefects (*Landräte*), district governors, and provincial governors, allowing a company to enlist the support of other bureaucrats when commissioners or the trade minister were uncooperative. Rhenish and Westphalian companies made full use of their district governor, Eduard Moeller, who was receptive to commercial needs, and they successfully played him off against the more conservative provincial governor, Hans Hugo von Kleist-Retzow.[92] In the Saxon province of Prussia, businessmen played a similar game with Provincial Governor Witzleben and the trade minister.[93]

Many railway directors also infiltrated bureaucratic and court circles. Although overwhelmingly bourgeois in social origin, some had earned the honorary titles of commercial councilor (*Kommerzienrat*) and privy commercial councilor (*Geheimer Kommerzienrat*), a status that allowed them to attend court, where connections and influence were found.

The *Eisenbahn-Zeitung*'s lists of Prussian railroad directors attending the annual conference of the *Verein deutscher Eisenbahnverwaltungen* in 1850, 1857, and 1860 provide clues to the social composition of Prussian railroad directorships in the 1850s. Of the 68 directors who attended in 1850, 60 were of middle-class origin, with three bearing honorary titles; the remaining eight were aristocrats, with two bearing honorary titles in addition to their noble patent. In 1857, 29 of Prussia's 32 attending directors were bourgeois, and 15 of these carried honorary titles; of the remaining three, one was a noble with the honor of Regierungsrat, while the other two were military officers. Finally, in 1860, 39 bourgeois and four noble Prussian directors attended; 28 of the 39 bourgeois directors had honorary titles, as did two of the four nobles. Although the percentage of bourgeois directors remained constant from 1850 to 1860 (88 versus 91 percent), those who had closer contact with the bureaucracy and the court by dint of their cachet rose (5 versus 66 percent).[94] In short, bourgeois businessmen apparently gained access to the Prussian establishment and used its networks to their advantage. There is little evidence, however, to correlate honorary titles and political docility. In the many disputes between the government and railroad companies, most of the directors of the larger railroads bore honorary titles.[95] Access to court did not stop them from criticizing and resisting orders from the trade ministry and other government agencies. The increase of honorary titles among businessmen points more to an entrepreneurial pragmatism, the exploitation of influential affiliations, rather than to obsequious "feudalization." [96]

Access to higher echelons of the government bureaucracy presupposed a certain social status. Government officials perceived these businessmen as members of the commercial estate (*Handelsstand*), which had the right to petition and negotiate with the government. Prussian ministers followed the growth of rail networks in neighboring countries—especially France—and respected the practical achievements of Prussia's entrepreneurial class. Railroad entrepreneurs also saw themselves as an urban elite, leaders in the country's commercial affairs. These patricians, bankers, and entrepreneurs wanted a greater voice in the bureaucracy's decision-making process. Nurtured by a long tradition of state promotion of economic enterprise, businessmen expected close contact with the Prussian state—and the influence that accompanied it.

This attitude toward the state was not necessarily inconsistent with businessmen's ties to liberalism. These businessmen had grown up in the milieu of notables' politics, the prerevolutionary tradition of elites assuming leadership in urban civic affairs. Although they opposed the aristocratic belief in the privilege of birth and rank, business elites nonetheless believed that men of wealth and property deserved a greater weight and representation in the affairs of government than those with little or no means. As noted earlier, such railroad entrepreneurs as David Hansemann, Ludolf Camphausen, and Gustav Mevissen all participated in designing the three-class voting system, first used in the Rhenish local government law of 1845.[97] This suffrage system, which distributed voting power according to income, suggests why the business class was made up of moderate liberals in 1848. The system was intended to assign wealthy businessmen and landed aristocrats equal political power. Their advocacy of such a system in the 1850s demonstrates the businessmen's consistency; their aim was not to undo completely the underpinnings of status society but to attain greater recognition within it for the new monied class. Understanding railroad entrepreneurs not only as market-oriented businessmen but also as notables with presumed privileges and honors is not unimportant. Recognizing the residual persistence of status relationships and the slow, uneven movement toward a class society in mid-century Prussia helps explain the negotiating behavior of business elites.[98]

In spite of shared elitist attitudes, it would be extravagant to characterize this interaction as "symbiotic." [99] Local government officials often imposed controversial ordinances on railway companies. As the agents responsible for overseeing all public stockholder meetings, attending board of director meetings, and inspecting company books, local commissioners embodied the government's suspicion of private association and private commercial enterprise. What resulted was not a mutually beneficial friendship but, rather, a hard-fought process of negotiation. Mutual respect existed, but both sides recognized the fundamentally adversarial relationship between the trade ministry and the business world, whose interests and aims were often diametrically opposed. Hardly symbiotic, relations between businessmen and the state are better described as tenuous, fluctuating, and variable. The business class displayed its willingness to use semipublic institutions such as the chambers of commerce to achieve reforms. But when these internal channels of representation ceased to deliver results, businessmen turned to public criticism and the Chamber of Deputies. It is the combination of using the new power of the public sphere (the public opinion of Landtag and press) while continuing to negotiate directly with the state that characterized the ambivalent political practices of the business class. It welcomed the new constitutional advances but in no way wished to surrender the older privileges of the *Handelsstand* acquired during the era of absolutism.

▼

In July 1859, Anton von Polski, an aggrieved railroad investor, approached August von der Heydt while dining in his Bad Kissingen hotel (Bavaria) and publicly slandered the state minister in a menacing manner. Von Polski hurled a packet of worthless stocks at Heydt, insulting him loudly with an impressive string of expletives.[100] The act of slander brought von Polski immediate arrest and eventual prosecution for public defamation of character. The man had lost 40,000 thalers in the Wilhelmsbahn crisis of 1857. He believed that the Prussian government had illegally colluded with Berlin banks to drive down Wilhelmsbahn stock to enable the state to take over the railway's administration. His verbal abuse of the minister was the culminating act of a long fruitless campaign in 1858–59 to petition the trade ministry, the parliament, and the king for just recompense.[101] "The blood of investors, widows, and orphans," he wrote King Friedrich Wilhelm IV, "stains the state moneys that purchased the railroad."[102]

The image of a wronged investor publicly sullying a Prussian trade minister's good name is striking. Rarely did the actions of high railroad finance and government economic policy cause public scandals, and such financial dailies as the *Berlin Börsen-Zeitung* were quick to report "l'affaire Heydt" with tinges of schadenfreude. But as exceptional as von Polski's response was, it does point to important changes in Prussia's economy in the 1850s, a period when the Prussian government significantly altered its prerevolutionary relationship with the leading sector in big business. In the years 1848–57 it became a prominent competitor in the railroad business, realigning its connections with the business class. In this period the Prussian state not only regulated private railways with a new severity in regard to finance, taxes, personnel, and day-to-day procedure but also constructed five state-owned railways and, in addition, administrated twelve out of the twenty-six private railways in Prussia. Of the 301,264,000 thalers capitalized in Prussian private railroads in 1858, over one-third (105,343,000) stood under state administration.[103]

Prussia's economy in the 1850s underwent great changes and clearly affected the politics of businessmen. While there is some validity in pointing to 1848/49 as a significant mark on the political economy of the Prussian-German state, one must not exaggerate the revolution's impact on businessmen's dealings with government officials. The creation of the constitution, bicameral legislature, and the trade ministry were indeed important milestones. Yet this "turning point" did not achieve a fixed settlement in government-business relations, and it does little to explain to explain how the Prussian state and the business class came to terms with one another over the politics of making money. As the railroad industry demonstrates, there was much to be resolved on the question of state power and private profit.

The changes in the original terms of the mixed system produced in turn a mixed legacy in the years after the recovery, 1853–57. Although railroad entrepreneurs showed a willingness to do business with the state and accept the Prussian government's role as owner and administrator of railroads, they were also quick to contest state actions believed to be unfair and injurious to businessmen. Spurred by an unprecedented boom in economic growth, the business class articulated positions independent from the government. Conflicts between the trade ministry and business interests reinforced the identity of the business class as a new interest group.[104] Mixing equal doses of conflict and cooperation, businessmen were resolute in insisting on an economic and political framework that would accommodate business as well as government.

The relationship between the business class and government elites is explained not in discrete events (such as 1848 and 1866) but rather as a fluid, opportunistic, politically ambivalent process. The most marked feature of government-business relations is not clear oppositional identities but, rather, the shifting, unfixed postures of both government and business. During the 1850s the Prussian government vacillated between two positions: whether to continue a two-hundred year tradition of directing and intervening in economic life or to allow businessmen the freedom to pursue profit as they pleased—and tax them accordingly.[105] While relinquishing its "direction principle" in coal mining in favor of a laissez-faire policy, the state intervened and asserted control over the railroad industry. The trade minister repeatedly attempted to weaken private railways, but he failed to break their power. He vacillated and steered a course that simultaneously hindered and promoted private railways. The inconsistency was caused partly by the lack of state funds to pursue a more radical policy of takeovers and by the exigencies of time, which demanded that Prussia keep pace in railroad construction to maintain its preeminent role in the Zollverein. As we shall see in chapter 6, Heydt was forced to capitulate to public and parliamentary resistance in 1859 and accept the supremacy of private railways.

The numerous spheres of conflict that arose between business and government in the 1850s suggest that explanations assuming an unproblematic alliance between business and government fail to recognize the economic and political complexities in reconciling an expanding capitalist economy with Prussia's conservative political establishment. Instead, the 1850s are better characterized as a decade-long search for mutual accommodation between business and government, a search for an equipoise between private entrepreneurial profit and state power. The search for this balance was an ongoing, case-by-case process and one that was never adequately completed in the reactionary period, 1850–58. The following three chapters amplify this theme.

In 1857–59 significant changes in Prussia's political economy would alter the course of government-business relations, making this brief period an economic and political watershed. The depression of 1857–59 clipped the wings of industrial and financial circles that strove simultaneously for expansion in industry and greater independence from state economic policy. After 1857, curtailed production and scarcity of investment capital reinforced an older pattern of large-scale enterprises looking to the state for aid and favorable legislation to promote long-term development. The depression, however, was accompanied by important political changes in central Europe, among them the moderate-liberal cabinet of Wilhlem I in the "New Era," the brief period of political thaw (November 1858–March 1862) between the decade of reactionary politics and the Constitutional Conflict. After November 1858, the new Prussian trade minister's economic policy eased strained relations between businessmen and government officials. This economic and political rapprochement between the business class and the Prussian state (the theme of chapter 7) would have a long-term impact on the course of liberalism, capitalism, and state building in Prussia-Germany.

CHAPTER FOUR

▼

The Conflict over Night Trains

In the spring of 1849, Minister of Trade, Commerce, and Public Works August von der Heydt issued an ordinance requiring Prussian railroad companies to schedule night trains to expedite the country's mail. The directive from Berlin came as a harsh blow to private railroad companies. With day and evening trains running at significant losses, the order to introduce night trains, whose unprofitability was foreseen, came as a complete surprise. The revolution had brought trade and industry to a near standstill, and the railroads were the first to suffer from the overstocked warehouses, silent factories, and severely depressed financial markets. There was little freight to transport and even less confidence in investment. Stock quotes in 1848 fell to new lows and improved only slightly in the first half of 1849.[1] Railroad companies drastically cut back on personnel and schedules to stave off total ruin. Three railroad companies went bankrupt and numerous others defaulted on dividends and loans.

Decreed in the name of general welfare, the government order was perceived by business circles as an act of unnecessary intervention and a new example of bureaucratic paternalism, a trait that entrepreneurs had long deplored. The order overlooked the industry's poor financial condition, and the government failed to consult the company directors. It was doubly crushing that the order had emanated from the trade ministry—a creation of the revolution, a so-called concession to the middle classes.

The problem was significant for government-business relations. Issued four months into Heydt's career as a state minister, the order established a tone for ministerial relations with capitalists investing in the expanding Prussian infrastructure. Combined with Heydt's attempt to exploit below-par stock prices and buy out private lines, the policy of introducing night trains against the wishes of railroad companies alerted stockholders, financiers, and railroad directors at an early date that Prussian state interests did not always coincide with the needs of private capital. The standoff over night trains illuminates a frame of mind in the business community toward the government, an attitude that does not correspond to the assumption of a cooperative alliance between the business class and the Prussian government. Rather, the relationship is better characterized as defensive and, at times, oppositional. The incident suggests that in the harshest years of the reactionary era, 1851–54, when the state sought to impose its political order through purges and decrees, directors of private railroad companies did not passively accept government dictates limiting their business freedoms.[2]

The protest from private railroad companies was considerable, both in magnitude and form. Eleven companies representing 95 percent of all Prussian private rail—60 percent of the country's total rail lines—protested in one form or another to the government, ranging from written remonstrations to lawsuits to refusals to comply with government orders.[3] The controversy lasted from 1849 to 1852 but its legal decisions stretched into 1855 and its political tone resonated into the New Era.

▼

In April 1849 Heydt ordered the Lower Silesian–Mark Railroad to run night trains between Breslau and Berlin. Although protesting the command with strong words, the company directors submitted but asked for funds to defray the cost. A subsequent stockholders' meeting amended the directors' decision and voted to pull the trains by horse rather than by locomotive, a measure partly to cut costs, partly to defy the government. Heydt threatened all directors with fines if they did not comply, and night trains pulled by locomotives began to run in May. The losses that year for the railway amounted to 350,000 thalers; 80 percent of that deficit, 280,000 thalers, stemmed from the cost of the night trains.[4]

Over the next three years similar demands were made on a number of Prussian railways. The Bonn-Cologne, Cologne-Minden, Prince Wilhelm, Rhenish, Berlin-Stettin, and Berlin-Hamburg railways all introduced night trains against their wishes. Every company protested. The order to introduce a night train on the Berlin-Hamburg Railway was especially questionable, because the line traversed the territories of Prussia, Mecklenburg-Schwerin, and Lauenburg and terminated in Hamburg. A branch line extended to Lübeck. An international treaty signed in November 1841 by five states—Denmark represented Lauenburg—had enabled the company to lay rail. The treaty stipulated that the railway company was to treat all governments equally; Prussia would act as the supervisor but could only expedite orders on which all parties agreed.[5] Hamburg and Mecklenburg-Schwerin were major shareholders in the railroad and possessed an additional veto right.

Both the governments and the stockholders opposed the idea of night trains, but Heydt persisted. He maintained that the company had to follow Prussian law, because the company was registered in Prussia and its directors met in Berlin. When in April 1852 the board of directors refused to schedule night trains, Heydt threatened directors with one-hundred thaler fines for every night without a train. The fines totaled three thousand thalers before Heydt threatened the directors with a takeover and notified the now nationalized Lower Silesian–Mark Railway to prepare for the absorption of the Berlin-Hamburg administration.[6] The company capitulated before the deadline of 15 April but sought redress in the Prussian courts and through diplomatic channels. In the following years, the company lost an average of 130,000 thalers annually, which amounted to 1.5 percent loss in dividend earnings.[7]

It is of particular interest to follow the actions of railways in the Rhineland, for the evidence available on these lines provides us with a closer view of business attitudes toward the state in the immediate years after 1848. Like the Silesian and Berlin Railways, companies in the Rhineland and the Ruhr also protested. The first affected was the Rhenish Railway. It, too, was ordered in May 1849 to start night trains to Paris via Antwerp. In contrast to the Silesian and Berlin lines, however, the trade ministry initially underwrote the costs of the company's night trains until January 1850.[8] Thereafter the minister expected the company to absorb the losses, which promptly halted night service.

A director of the Rhenish Railway, Dr. Gerhard Compes, a lawyer by trade, drew up a brief outlining the company's objections. His summary at the board meeting emphasized the ministry's tacit recognition of the act's illegality by initially paying for full costs without objection. After seven months of subsidies, the revocation of financial assistance for night trains constituted an inconsistent and arbitrary action. Moreover, he noted, the government had no right to change company statutes or alter timetables, for the company statutes, drafted in the early 1830s, predated the Railroad Law of 1838. Technically, then, the company did not need to seek approval for timetables as other Prussian lines did. Fundamentally agreeing with his position, the board requested that Compes, assisted by two other lawyers, review more closely the rights of the company and draw up a legal recommendation.[9] With this recommendation, the board could then decide what course of action was most appropriate.

Gustav Mevissen, the president of the company, dissented and opened a discussion that proposed a more cautious, diplomatic approach. He noted that the Royal Railroad Commission wished to reach a settlement regarding the transport of royal mail wagons. An agreement had already been reached with the Cologne-Minden, the Rhenish Railway's important counterpart on the right bank of the Rhine. Because the commission was anxious to coordinate schedules in the western provinces, Mevissen implied that the issue was not one that could be ultimately won. Thus the problem regarding long-term strategies with the government loomed as more important. If the company decisively rejected the government demands, even if it had the legal right to do so, it had to be that much more careful in opposing Minister Heydt when he himself had legal recourse.

In this instance Mevissen believed that Heydt still had a legal leg to stand on, if only a slim one. The Railroad Law (paragraph 36, clause 3) gave the government the right to have their post coaches transported at no charge.[10] Because the stipulation of night trains was not so disadvantageous, the company should look on it as an onerous concession whose long-range advantage outweighed the immediate burden. By accepting the present demand from the government, Mevissen reasoned, the company might be able to sign a separate contract more agreeable to the specific needs of the company. Through tactful compliance the company could effect a better settlement with the government's railroad commission, perhaps even demonstrating that night trains were not needed for speedier mail service to Belgium. Persuaded by this argument, the board agreed to submit to the demand of night trains but to pursue the necessary steps for a legal defense.[11] The company's acceptance of the government's order for night trains was couched in terms of general cooperation with minor technical disagreements, a tactic that delayed a final governmental decision. Meanwhile, a team of lawyers worked out the legal position that upheld the government's obligation to compensate the company for night trains.[12]

The delaying tactic worked until 13 November 1850, when the trade ministry ordered the resumption of night trains as of 1 January 1851 without compensation. Punitive threats accompanied the directive; the ministry demanded that the Railroad Commission fine each director one hundred thalers for failure to obey the order.[13] The company's directors, strengthened by the unanimous assertion of seven lawyers that compensation was necessary, defied the order, drafted a letter of rejection to Heydt, and waited for the trade ministry to bring suit against the company.[14] From January to March the directors, in cooperation with their technical and administrative directors, refused to run night trains. In April Heydt threatened the company with sterner measures. Faced with a possible government takeover of the company's administrative posts, the directors temporarily capitulated and reintroduced the night trains while preparing for the lawsuit. A victory in court, the protocol reassuringly noted, would reimburse the company's losses.[15]

News of the lawsuit prompted other Prussian railways to take action. Heinrich von Wittgenstein, former district governor and president of the Cologne-Minden Railway, wrote the directors of the Rhenish Railway and expressed his company's disapproval of Heydt's imperious behavior. He, too, had protested against the "dictated changes" in the train schedule, "partly because they [the changes] are unfeasible, partly because they oppose the company's interests." [16] Wittgenstein stressed that they were not alone. Many of the neighboring railways, he believed, would reject the demands as decisively as the Rhenish Railway. "Like us," he wrote, they were "equally worried that the interests of railroad companies were endangered to a great degree, if the overbearing behavior of Berlin toward railways regarding mail connections was not vigorously opposed." Wittgenstein invited the directors to attend a conference of all private railway companies within the jurisdiction of the Rhineland-Westphalian Railroad Commission in order to adopt a common response to the "increasing encroachment of the trade ministry." [17]

On 23 April 1851 directors of the Rhenish, Cologne-Minden, Prince William, Bonn-Cologne, Münster-Hamm, and Düsseldorf-Elberfeld railways met to form a united front protesting the schedule changes dictated by Heydt. The written protest disputed the government's interpretation of paragraph 36 of the Railroad Law that allegedly empowered the state to introduce night trains against the will of the railroad companies. In addition, the meeting brought about the collective decision to disobey Heydt's order to run night trains for the summer schedule.[18] The meeting's resolutions were the first acts of disobedience against the new trade ministry. The conference further revealed railroad directors' willingness to organize in defense of private business interests. A corporate spirit of mutual cooperation began to evolve.

The protest to Heydt, drawn up by the directors of the Bonn-Cologne and the Cologne-Minden Railways, addressed the problem of coordinating railroad schedules with postal administration. According to paragraph 36 of the Railroad Law, the two operations should be adjusted "so far as the nature of the business permits it." Relations had soured, the directors inferred, because the ministry failed to apprehend the "nature" of railroad companies and what was "permissible" as a business practice.[19] Railways operated under the joint-stock principle, which obliged directors to fix prices so that capital investment yielded a dividend for their investors. The essential factor for a joint-stock company was efficient management. Its directors, entrusted with stockholders' money, were obligated to promote profit.[20] Imposed regulations that drastically minimized profits could inflict irrevocable harm to the "nature" of railroads. The falling value of railroad stocks was inversely proportional to the rising scarcity of investors inclined to offer funds under such conditions.[21] Not only were expansion and prosperity put in doubt, but the order also threatened the viability of the entire industry. The diminution of already poor dividends would imperil investment, the lifeblood of a capital-starved industry.

In this instance, the economic philosophy of these railroad directors was clearly one of laissez-faire liberalism. The market decided the necessities of life. The interests of the public and joint-stock companies, argued the directors, go hand in hand: "Like manufacturers and merchants, companies must satisfy the customer. A train that is needed and meets a demand will be occupied and pay for itself. Its installment would not be objected to. It is another question, however, when a train is installed to transport merely a mail bag, especially when a rider and horse could punctually expedite the matter without much cost and difficulty." [22]

The companies did not oppose promoting the general good, which was invariably Heydt's defense; they merely measured it by the yardstick of market conditions. If the government insisted on nightly mail trains, it must subsidize them until the service became profitable; it could not expect the investors to do so. This "immoderately extended use" of the government's right to influence timetables robbed directors of their managerial role, for a government agency was assuming responsibility for the financial interests of company stockholders.[23] More crucially, the letter expressed a sharp distrust of the way the trade ministry interpreted the law and questioned the ministry's actual intentions. The minister's implementation of the law contradicted, the directors believed, the "obvious intention of the law to define reciprocal privileges." The unreasonable demands amounted to "an interpretation that subjects one party to the arbitrary will of the other." [24]

But why was the spirit of the law broken so blatantly by the trade ministry when the finance ministry and railroad companies had cooperated with one another for years? The entrepreneurs believed the answer lay in Heydt's desire to nationalize railways and in his intent to use night trains to drive down dividends in order to purchase railways at a radically cheaper price. The Railroad Law allowed the government the right to appropriate railways, provided the company was fully remunerated. The criterion of full remuneration was to pay the company twenty-five times the average of yearly dividends paid out in the last five years. By driving down dividends to unacceptable levels and thereby maintaining the bear-market trend that had begun with the financial crisis of 1846 and continued through 1849–50, the government could purchase companies at unrealistically low prices. The implication of Heydt's aims was guardedly formulated but nonetheless accusatory:

When, now, it lay in the legal power of the state to enforce orders against the wishes of private companies—orders that did not absolutely fulfill the needs of general welfare—which lowered the income or dividends to a preferred minimum, so also would the buying prices of railroads be lowered. In other words, the state could become the judge in its own affairs and possess the means to render illusory—under the appearance of legality—the noble intention of the law and thus dispossess a private party, which in good faith had given its trust to the government.[25]

The accusation was not based on mere speculation. By introducing night trains on the Lower Silesian–Mark Railway, Heydt had indirectly caused immense losses, which in turn allowed the government in 1849 to take over the administration of the railroad. The petition charged the government with unfair trading and mocked its self-image as an impartial arbiter of the public welfare. A "judge in its own affairs," the ministry interpreted the commercial code to favor its own financial interests.[26] But Heydt continued on his course. In directives to several railway companies in the Rhineland he ordered new night trains for the summer schedule and rejected the Rhenish Railway's request for either compensation or suspension of its night trains to Belgium.[27]

In June 1852 he took even harsher steps against the Bonn-Cologne Railway, a local railroad line of forty-three kilometers with little significance in the Prussian rail network for either freight, passengers, or mail. This small railroad company refused to obey the new order for night trains without a subsidy, maintaining that the government, in imposing such dictates on private companies, was overextending its authority.[28] In response Heydt authorized Hans Hugo von Kleist-Retzow, the newly installed provincial governor of the Rhineland province, to give the company a deadline of five days to comply. When the deadline was not met, the government fined the company directors one hundred thalers each per day and, more important, drew up a protocol that transferred control over the company's administrative duties to the Royal Railroad Commission.[29] Heydt insisted that the company pay for the costs incurred by the government's assumption of administrative duties and, furthermore, proposed to create a new government agency solely to administer the railway if the company "persisted in its oppositional behavior." Of course, Heydt noted, the "obstinate company directors" would have no role in this new administration.[30]

The Bonn-Cologne directors held out for over a month, which both surprised and worried the government. Three weeks after the administrative takeover, Heydt, concerned by the directors' persistence, authorized the Railroad Commission to offer the return of administrative powers to the company. The commission stipulated that the company must run the prescribed night trains, but it could contest the order in court. Otherwise, the government would have to proceed with the costly step of installing a permanent state administration.[31]

Although this proposal was rejected, a deputation of Bonn-Cologne directors met with Heydt a week later to negotiate an out-of-court compromise and achieved a modicum of success. Directors Stahl and Mühlens argued that the company had not refused to run night trains per se, but merely refused to run them without compensation. Heydt proposed that the directors resume control of the company, operate the night train as ordered, and lodge a protest against the executive order with the proper authorities.[32] As recorded in the company protocol, he added "that as far as he was concerned, the company should receive special consideration if the cost of night trains significantly injured its financial interests."[33] The next day the directors officially accepted the terms of settlement, though still noting that they did not recognize the legality of the government order.[34]

The settlement was advantageous for both sides. Heydt and his ministry were spared the burden of finding administrators to run the railway efficiently. The month-long occupation had produced a number of problems for the government. Among them was the failure of the Railroad Commission to integrate night trains into an acceptable work schedule for locomotive drivers and machinists; it instituted eighteen-hour work days in four-day rotations with a half day off—a clear safety hazard.[35] In turn, the company directors were given honorable terms of defeat. Although they were bound to run night trains, Heydt recognized their right to seek redress and conceded that the railroad's situation constituted a potential exception to the law. They had neither won nor lost but could interpret their actions as a spirited defense of company interests at the next stockholders' meeting. Heydt had shown courtesy when asking the company to return, and there was still a chance—as shown by the case of the Rhenish Railway—that a lawsuit could bring the compensation they thought the railway deserved.

The reconciliation between ministry and company, however, was short lived. Three weeks later, Heydt refused to retract the fines imposed on the directors, citing their "unjustified obstinacy."[36]

▼

That the small Bonn-Cologne Railway had the courage to defy the trade minister was owed to the victories of larger lines over the government in the courts. In April 1852 the Rhenish Railway won its decision against the trade ministry. The lower court found no merit in the ministry's claim that the law permitted the government to assume certain supervisory duties.[37] The ministry appealed the decision, of course, but the first round was a clear victory for private business.[38] The Berlin-Hamburg Railway also won its first decision in 1853. The two cases sent a powerful signal to the business community that its interests could be defended against the government.

Throughout the dispute the government characterized the companies' opposition as a stubborn defense of Manchester liberalism, a fear of innovation, or a pure willfulness to disobey the trade ministry.[39] Heydt criticized the companies as blind to the bigger picture of national economy and thus deserving of harsh treatment.[40] Whether this indictment of the private railroad system was warranted is questionable. Rhenish railway companies recognized the need for a Berlin-Cologne night train and never opposed it, demonstrating a pragmatism that Heydt did not want to acknowledge. Passengers traveling from Paris or London had been obliged to stay the night in Cologne because of the lack of a night train to Berlin. Although the same companies opposed certain night trains exclusively for mail purposes, the directors responded to this need. Acting under the auspices of the North German Railroad Association, the directors of all railroads involved in expediting the Cologne-Berlin express met in 1852–53 and worked out the particulars.[41] The success of the night express had hinged on the willingness of the Hanoverian and Brunswick governments to grant persons and baggage direct transit through their lands without changing or unloading. The state railway administrators of the two territories agreed to participate, and in 1853 an agreement was worked out.

The Prussian government, however, annulled the schedule contract, told the Brunswick and Hanoverian governments that the three governments must inaugurate a night train, and that the private companies must not influence the decision.[42] The Prussian ministry subsequently altered the original treaty in several ways, which the directors believed outweighed the advantages of the night train. Even the Railroad Commission, Heydt's own instrument, admitted that certain provisions of the treaty (regarding the order for the Berlin-Anhalt Railway to run a fourth night train) were entirely useless.[43] It was not the resistance of private companies but the insistent claim of the Prussian government to determine policy in northern Germany that added fuel to the continuing conflict. In this situation, as in others, Heydt worked to check the innovations of private railroad associations.[44] Even though the Cologne-Berlin night train appeared to be unprofitable, private companies demonstrated a willingness to look beyond their own ledgers and consider greater interests. Heydt's intervention in this case appeared to be motivated more by political principle than by administrative need.

Heydt's fiats often appeared to be simply assertions of ministerial power, but he always justified them with the need to serve the general good. Evoking the needs of the postal system in 1853, Heydt ordered the Magdeburg-Leipzig line to run another night train. After a year and 70,000 thalers in company losses, however, night service was eventually canceled, because the postal authorities stated they were never interested in the train and it was a burden to them as well as the company.[45] Not without irony, the *Berliner Börsen-Zeitung* noted in March 1859 that the trade ministry canceled a night train on the state-owned Upper Silesian Railway because of financial losses.[46] Clearly Heydt's interest in regulation was not always exercised for the welfare of the post or better schedules for freight and passengers. The examples of the Berlin-Cologne night train and the Magdeburg-Leipzig mail train suggest that there

was a reasonable side to the companies' requests and that efficiency and pragmatism did not always motivate the ministry's actions.

Over the long run, though, the railroad companies' opposition to night
trains diminished, for the directors' principal objection—hindrance to efficient management—lost its sting after night trains showed signs of profitability by the end of 1852. The frequency of night freight shipments steadily
increased, mostly because of the coal industry, and night trains became a
component of the competitive edge to draw customers. In fact, the trade ministry offered the Rhenish Railway in May 1853 the right to suspend their
night trains from Cologne to Belgium; the Aachen-Düsseldorf-Ruhrorter line,
a state-administered railway, the Railroad Commission explained, could assume its routes. The company, however, refused the offer. Using the same
principle but reversing their previous position, the Rhenish Railway directors
sent a letter to Heydt, stating they had never recognized the ministry's right
to influence their timetables and they intended to retain their night trains,
"merely to promote competition with the Aachen-Düsseldorf trains." [47] Similarly, the Berlin-Hamburg Railway, although actively involved in a suit against
the Prussian government over night trains, admitted in its 1853 report to stockholders, "One large railway line after another has introduced night trains and
it cannot be denied that the public, especially the businessman, have decisively demanded them—our railway cannot be left behind." [48] Thus the legal
issue over the government's right to impose night trains on private railroad
companies quickly became a moot point. Competition for freight contracts
had forced the issue—in Heydt's favor.

It was in this changed climate that the ministerial litigation against the
railway companies swung in favor of the governmental position in the second and third appeals. In September 1855 the government finally won its right
to refuse compensation.[49] The court case with the Berlin-Hamburg Railway
never actually addressed the original complaint of the stockholders and the
foreign governments: the legality of imposing night trains on a private company. The Berlin court stated it had no jurisdiction to decide such a matter;
the company could merely sue for compensation. The court proceeding, then,
changed in significant ways. The question over the legal right of the Prussian
government to order night trains fell into the background; the civil suit merely
centered on whether such an order should be accompanied by compensation. Consequently, the railroad company's role shifted from the accused to
the accuser, the former always holding an advantage.[50] Similarly, the Rhenish
Railway case was decided not on the letter of the law but on a broader interpretation by a judge who believed trains to be the instrument of the general
welfare. In so doing, commented one railroad director, the judge went beyond
the law code into the sphere of national economy, something that he knew

nothing about.[51] The most damaging evidence against the companies' cases, however, was that by 1855 they had voluntarily accepted night trains in the face of higher revenues and competition.

The Berlin-Hamburg line attempted to play its last card in the Federal Diet in Frankfurt. The Diet discussed the matter until 1858, but no decision was reached—a small yet telling example of how the Diet in its last years failed to meet the practical needs of German economic life.[52] The Rhenish Railway stoically accepted the decision, letting it pass in its board and stockholder meetings with little comment.

It would be wrong to dismiss the night train dispute as an ephemeral affair that ended in defeat for Prussian businessmen. On the contrary, the issue remained a central question for stockholders, financiers, and railroad directors from 1849 to 1852; railroad companies held their ground, defied government orders, and won in court. It was only after railroads started to schedule night trains voluntarily that the courts accepted the government position.

As early as 1849 it was clear that the Prussian government was not entirely wedded to private railroad interests and that companies had to resist government control. The Rhenish Railway's protocols are especially revealing, for the company directors weighed their two basic options of either hard-line legal confrontation or appeasement. On the one hand, some directors evinced confidence in the Prussian tradition of lawful rule and believed their claim could be upheld legally. Yet even more revealing is the position of Mevissen, the company president, whose estimate of Minister von der Heydt and his bureaucracy was shrewd. He advised the company not to exercise its legal prerogatives for fear of the minister's long-term wrath and suggested the greater advantages of maintaining a dialogue with the trade ministry. He recognized that success in litigation would be a Pyrrhic victory if it antagonized this powerful minister. Although the Rhenish Railway opted for open confrontation on this occasion, we will see that this same company joined others in adopting the more pragmatic modus operandi of responding flexibly to problems with state railroad policy and negotiating a reasonable settlement out of court and the public eye. The night train dispute confirms that the business agenda was not set by the government and that cooperation between business elites and government officials could not be taken for granted. In the harshest years of Manteuffel's reactionary era, railroad entrepreneurs advocated free enterprise against state interference, showing their alacrity to use the courts to check the government's arbitrary action.

The matter was not forgotten. It became an integral part of businessmen's grievances during the elections of 1858 and in the New Era. The night trains dispute served to display the continuity of disagreements between business and government since 1848 and strengthened the argument of commercial newspapers that businessmen had to elect deputies willing to defend business interests.[53] The issue was furthermore used to attack Heydt personally in 1858, when it was rumored that he would not survive the New Era. The week-long rumor of Heydt's imminent dismissal in November 1858 occasioned many philippics against the minister (presumably to reinforce the prince regent's decision), and the night train dispute was incorporated into the arguments that Heydt was never a friend of Prussian business.[54] This controversy spilled over into the political sphere, where businessmen frustrated by Prussia's business policy influenced the political agendas and platforms of liberal parties.

When we place this incident in the greater context of the aggressive government takeovers of railroads from 1849 to 1857, the introduction of an unpopular railroad tax in 1853, the controversial second reserve fund in 1857, a restrictive bank policy throughout the 1850s, the parliamentary opposition to state railways from 1855 to 1859, and the continuing policy of paternalism over joint-stock companies, we see that this issue was not an isolated phenomenon. Rather, it was an early indicator of a decade-long trend. The thousands of thalers in fines, the government takeovers of administrations, the collective action of private businesses against the government, and, of course, the protracted court cases evidence strained government-business relations in Prussia in the early 1850s.

CHAPTER FIVE

▼

Banking and the Business Class

The emergence of commercial investment banks after the Revolution of 1848 was an institutional breakthrough for modern capitalism and one of the central factors in the accelerated development of the industrial revolution in Germany between 1848 and 1871. The accumulation and mobilization of capital in concentrated and accessible forms was indispensable for undertaking such large-scale projects as railroads, coal mines, and iron works. Long-term promotional loans that enabled entrepreneurs to start up new businesses became an evident necessity in the growth of modern business. As one bank director noted, "Capital, more than water, steam, or electricity, put the machines into motion." [1] In view of the unprecedented magnitude of capital needed to build railroads, the railroad industry's need for joint-stock commercial banking was crucial.

Given the immeasurable importance of commercial investment banks for industrialization, the establishment of such banks as the Bank für Handel und Industrie in Darmstadt (hereafter the Darmstädter Bank), the Disconto Gesellschaft, and the Berliner Handelsgesellschaft in the 1850s represented a milestone for the political and socioeconomic aspirations of Prussia's business class. Economically, investment banks were the catalyst for what we now know as the "industrial take-off," the attainment of sustained, irreversible economic growth in Germany after 1851. Politically, these institutions were the expression of an assertive middle class, enabling businessmen to practice trade free of government wishes and restrictions. The liberal aspiration for freedom of association and self-administration in commercial and civic affairs was partially realized by the creation of joint-stock commercial banks.

Although German banks have never suffered from a lack of historians, rarely are they studied in a political context. Alfred Krüger, Karl Erich Born, Wilhelm Treue, W. O. Henderson, Richard Tilly, Fritz Seidenzahl, Hans Jaeger, Hubert Kiesewetter, Hans Pohl, and Manfred Pohl have all written extensively about the development of German banking in the 1850s, but most gloss over the political aspects of the story, primarily because they are interested in questions of continuity in the national economy or the role of the state in industrialization.[2] Surveys of German economic and political history reflect this deficit.[3] Karl Obermann and Helmut Böhme are two exceptions to the trend; both splice together economic and political events for a more integrated argument. Obermann first attempted to ascribe some political meaning to the bank foundings of the 1850s. In orthodox Marxist fashion he argued that the bank openings were the result of the alliance between the bourgeoisie and the crown-aristocracy following the estrangement of the middle classes from the proletariat after 1848.[4] The new joint-stock banks of the 1850s, Obermann argued, formed an essential part of the bourgeoisie's "compensation" for "recognizing the political power of the king and aristocracy." By assuming, though not demonstrating, that the Prussian state supported the joint-stock principle to promote the bourgeoisie's economic needs, Obermann interpreted joint-stock banks as the crucial link between the failed revolution of 1848 and the "revolution from above." [5]

Böhme, too, ascribed the development of the banks to an alliance between the bourgeoisie and Junkers, thus viewing the bank foundings as an outgrowth of the reactionary period.[6] He sketched how proposed bank reforms in 1848, which intended to serve a more liberal society, emerged in 1849–50 as a banking policy that served the interests of reactionary government. Böhme's narrative portrayed David Hansemann as the lone champion of progressive economic reforms. Hansemann's attempt as a government official to charter credit associations for lower middle-class artisans (and thus continue the liberalizing process of the revolution) threatened the monied interests of both the rural and urban elite: "What Hansemann strove for, wealthy businessmen, bankers, and large landholders wanted to hinder." [7] Thus Böhme argued that because both private bankers and government officials stood to lose economic and political influence with banks independent of state interests and old money, Hansemann became politically isolated. This led to his dismissal as finance minister in 1848 and his resignation as chief director of the Prussian bank in 1851.[8]

Although Böhme's account of Hansemann's political struggles with the Prussian government over the course of 1848–51 is instructive, it conveys the mistaken impression that Prussia's leading businessmen uniformly sided with the Prussian state. Hansemann, however, was neither politically isolated from entrepreneurial elites nor the sole critic of Prussian economic policy. Böhme's thesis, although seemingly well documented, is less than convincing. In 1851 Gustav Mevissen, a director of the Schaaffhausen'sche and later of the Darmstädter Bank, assisted Hansemann in working out the statutes of his credit bank, the Disconto Gesellschaft, and later asked Hansemann to be president of his Darmstädter Bank.[9] Mevissen and Abraham Oppenheim, two key Rhenish entrepreneurs who were railroad directors as well as bankers, were also being sued by the trade ministry during this period for their unwillingness to comply with ministerial orders to schedule night trains (see chap. 4). Further, they and other private railroad directors were inclined to disregard government directives to discharge workers connected with the Revolution of 1848, exhibiting a reluctance to cooperate with reactionary policies (see chap. 3). In sum, the argument for an alliance between businessmen and authoritarian government in the postrevolutionary era is flawed and needs modification, for it does not recognize the many frictions between Prussian entrepreneurs and the state.

The bourgeoisie should be recognized as an additional force in Prussian politics; their political ambivalence in the 1850s both defied and accommodated the conservative Prussian government. Having practiced business before 1848 in a bureaucratic-absolutist state that accepted principles of free trade, entrepreneurs of the 1850s learned to use the Prussian bureaucracy and simultaneously practice free enterprise in piecemeal fashion to achieve their interests. Consistent neither as unfailing parliamentarians nor as obedient subjects of the crown, Prussian businessmen were nonetheless resolutely unwavering in attaining bourgeois social and economic needs. And, more important, the ambivalent position of the entrepreneurial class toward authoritarian government expressed a strategy of successful negotiation, not defeatism or compliancy. The banking sector is just one area where the business class adopted a position independent of the crown, one which was tantamount to defiance.

To underscore the element of friction and defiance between the state and the bourgeoisie in Prussia's banking history, this chapter focuses on an episode that has hitherto failed to be integrated into the secondary literature: a decree (*Octroy*) drafted and signed by the king and the cabinet on 12 July 1856 to ban commandite banks.[10] This decree is the most concrete evidence we have documenting the failed attempt of the Prussian state to control the political and economic power of the business class. The principal businessmen involved in this episode were connected to the railroad industry.

That historians have neglected the decree is somewhat understandable— it was never promulgated. Otto von Manteuffel, the minister-president, opposed the bill on political grounds and worked persistently to block publication of the signed law. Although originally outvoted in the cabinet, Manteuffel quickly undermined the majority position by obtaining a postponement of the law's promulgation. In late August, Manteuffel convinced the king and cabinet to bury the law permanently and averted what he believed to be a serious misadventure. Yet the successful maneuvers of Manteuffel do not diminish the decree's significance. Though never put into action, it reveals a crisis within the Prussian government in the summer months of 1856 regarding commercial banking, the control of capital, and the political power that might be derived

from high finance. And it dispels the idea that commandite banks were accepted, if not welcomed, by the Prussian government.[11] For these reasons this
incident deserves analysis, because it illustrates concretely how businessmen
confronted government restrictions and how officials reacted to their circumvention.

The decree was the cabinet's reaction to the bold move of David Hansemann and Gustav Mevissen, two railroad entrepreneurs who established
capital-share investment banks using the commandite principle. Commandite
companies were a substitute for joint-stock banks, which the government refused to charter. Inactive or "silent" partners in a commandite contractual
relationship were protected with limited liability, while active partners—company directors—were burdened with unlimited liability. Commandite companies also did not possess the legal character of a juridical person; property, for
example, could not be bought in the company's name. But not having the legal
status of a juridical person brought one great advantage: a commandite company was not a legal corporation and therefore did not require a charter, the
mechanism by which the government controlled commercial development. In
fact, because Prussian businessmen had used commandite companies infre-
quently and on a small scale, only two paragraphs in the Rhenish and General law codes addressed the status of such companies.[12] The establishment
and practice of joint-stock companies, in contrast, were carefully prescribed
in laws passed in 1838 and 1843.[13]

Hansemann set the precedent in January 1856 by reorganizing his credit
association, the Disconto Gesellschaft, into a commandite bank. A consortium, organized by Gustav Mevissen, followed in July by founding the Berliner Handelsgesellschaft. In the same month, commandite banks were opened
in Breslau, Königsberg, and Magdeburg, as well as in Coburg and Hamburg.[14]
The decree expressed the reaction of an angry government regarding these
banks which, totaling over forty million thalers in nominal capital,[15] had no
charters from the state yet had been established in full accordance with the
law. The lack of a charter requirement meant freedom from government pro-
scription and supervision. Promotional investment banking, heralding a new
era in the movement of capital, had arrived in Prussia against the will of the
government.

Prussian businessmen resorted to the commandite principle as the last
step in a long confrontation with the Prussian government over banking privileges. Banking freedom (*Bankfreiheit*) had been a point of contention between
entrepreneurs and government officials since the 1820s.[16] The government's
tight control on the money supply and its continued refusal to set up more af-
filiates of the Royal Bank produced a sizable store of ill will among business
circles.[17] In spite of its professed aims to liberalize the economy after 1806–

13, the Prussian state, with an eye toward its own financial problems, failed to meet the needs of businessmen in leading sectors of the economy in the following decades.[18] Owing to public and internal pressures, some concessions were granted, however slight. In 1846 the Royal Bank of Prussia was transformed into a semipublic central bank of issue; ten million thalers of share capital were added to its reserves, and in 1847 it was renamed the Prussian Bank. An advisory board of shareholders exercised some degree of input, but the state still retained dominant control.[19] The multiple requests for bank reform at the United Diet in 1847 confirmed the continued dissatisfaction of the business class.[20]

During the revolution, the "liberal" cabinet of Camphausen and Hansemann transformed the A. Schaaffhausen'sche Bankverein into the first joint-stock bank in Prussia in August 1848. In March 1848 the imminent collapse of the private bank, whose investments in the Rhineland and Westphalia affected over 170 factories and 40,000 workers, had compelled the government to accept the reform as preferable to further radicalization of the Rhineland. Yet the bank's low share-capital base (5,187,000 thalers) and its restriction on note issue did not appease Rhenish businessmen. And once the crisis of 1848 abated, the government canceled any plans for further joint-stock charters. The A. Schaaffhausen'sche bank owed its joint-stock status not to a progressive policy shift of the Prussian state but, rather, to the emergency conditions of 1848.[21]

After 1848 the problem became more acute, for it was clear that the twenty-one million thalers of the Prussian Bank, the central bank of issue, were grossly inadequate for the growing economy of Prussia. In 1848 the Camphausen-Hansemann ministry introduced normative statutes (which had been codified in 1846 but never enforced) for banks of issue to issue notes as well as engage in Lombard and discount. Banks in Berlin, Cologne, Magdeburg, Stettin, and Breslau were accorded the privilege, but this did not quell criticism. The maximum on note issue, set at one million thalers per province and at eight million thalers for the entire country, made the reform more cosmetic than meaningful. Moreover, the restrictions on discounting bills and receiving deposits by these banks limited their usefulness; critics claimed it deterred rather than promoted the growth of banks of issue.[22] This de jure "reform" of banks, however, did aid the government in staving off criticism from the Landtag and chambers of commerce and help the Prussian state maintain its mercantilist policy on money supply and private banking.[23] Thus, from businessmen's perspective, Prussian banks at the beginning of the boom business cycle of 1851–57 were woefully undercapitalized.[24]

The refusal to charter joint-stock banks was the most prominent cause of the bourgeois discontent with the Prussian government. Businessmen felt greatly disadvantaged, for the joint-stock bank, with its capacity to amass and lend capital, was the motor of business expansion. Although government officials dwelled on the problem of note issue, the businessman's primary concern was credit. Unlike the traditional banks that handled mostly state paper and safe investments in established enterprises, these new banks actively sought to start up businesses and promote underdeveloped branches of commerce and industry. The banks' principal attraction was floating long-term loans to new companies, but they also gave clients lines of credit, advanced raw materials for production, accepted future consignments of manufactures as collateral, and recognized promissory notes, securities, mortgages, and bonds as legal tender. The Société Général du Crédit Mobilier, the institution set up under the auspices of Napoleon III in 1852, set the standard in promotional banking with its capacity for massive loans, its know-how in the business world, its speculative willingness to start up new companies, and its unprecedented stock dividends. With its capital base of sixty million francs, the Crédit Mobilier was a dramatic breakthrough in commercial finance.[25]

The example spread quickly to Germany. The first such joint-stock bank to be established on German soil was the Darmstädter Bank für Handel und Industrie, founded by Cologne merchant-bankers Abraham Oppenheim, Wilhelm Ludwig Deichman, Viktor Wendelstadt, and Gustav Mevissen.[26] Oppenheim was a charter shareholder in the Crédit Mobilier and was in fact related by marriage to one of its principal owners, Benôit-Fould. With this connection, Oppenheim secured the backing of the Crédit Mobilier to invest in a German counterpart. Because of the hostile behavior of both the Prussian government and the traditional banking houses of Frankfurt, Oppenheim turned to the Grand Duchy of Hesse-Darmstadt, whose government granted him a charter on the provision that the bank raise the capital to complete the Hessian railroad line from Mainz to Aschaffenburg.[27] The bank opened for business in April 1853. After an initial rough start (due mostly to the difficulty of placing its shares at a satisfactory quote on German exchanges), the bank soon established itself as a leading industrial investor in Germany. In 1856 it raised 1.6 million gulden for the establishment of joint-stock companies; by 1870, it participated in no fewer than thirty-four major railroad transactions between 1853 and 1870.[28] By 1856, sixteen such credit institutions existed in Austria and the German states.

The Prussian government's response to the Darmstädter Bank's opening indicated its general position on large-scale joint-stock banking in and outside Prussia for the coming years. Calling the new bank a form of "French propaganda" and its founders "agents" of the French, by whom Cologne was "most endangered," King Friedrich Wilhelm IV warned his cabinet, "This institution is intended to transfer to Germany the credit swindles that have raged in Paris to exploit the entire Rhineland, and [it] . . . will have an undeniably disadvantageous political influence." [29] In consequence, the cabinet drafted a diplomatic note to the Hessian government expressing its utmost disapproval, assured the king that the bank's plans (as stated in its statutes) to open branches in Prussia would be stopped, and authorized Heydt to prohibit any transaction between the Darmstädter and the Schaaffhausen'sche bank, whose directors included Mevissen and Oppenheim.[30]

Undaunted by their government's dislike of joint-stock credit banks, Prussian businessmen and merchant bankers invested in prominent joint-stock banks at Leipzig, Dessau, Luxembourg, Karlsruhe, and Vienna—as well as in other smaller institutions ringing the borders of Prussia. In turn, these banks did not shy from investing in Prussian enterprises. The Darmstädter Bank, for example, advanced millions of florins to the Rhenish Railway to complete the construction of its Rhine lines.[31] Because the official money supply (21 million thalers) was patently inadequate, these banks provided the welcome stop-gap measure of feeding the Prussian economy with currency. In return they used Prussian enterprises for investment and speculation. The Prussian government responded to this with a law in 1855 that forbade the use of foreign notes under ten thalers. The law did not produce the desired effect, prompting Heydt and Bodelschwingh, the trade and finance ministers, to publish an article in the *Staatsanzeiger,* the Berlin journal of record, exhorting commercial circles to cease using foreign money substitutes. Reflecting in retrospect on this effort, Rudolf Delbrück, a member of Heydt's ministry, wrote, "Voluntary help from the commercial estate [*Handelsstand*] regarding foreign notes was not to be counted on, for its most influential members themselves were founders and directors of these foreign banks." [32] (Delbrück failed to note, however, that he and other top officials had also invested in Darmstädter bonds.)[33] Consequently, another law was introduced in 1857 that extended the ban to all foreign currency.[34]

By 1856, joint-stock credit institutions had been erected in all corners of the Continent. Their influence extended from "the plains of Castile to the valley of the Danube, from London to Constantinople and from Moscow to Trieste." [35] Even the ultra-conservative Habsburg government consented to the Credit-Anstalt in 1855. The trend toward joint-stock banks seemed irreversible, and Prussian businessmen believed that their government would eventually capitulate and recognize such institutions as indispensable to industrialization and economic growth.

In February 1856 two prestigious consortiums petitioned the government to permit the chartering of joint-stock credit institutions. The simultaneity of the petitions was not coincidental; they were part of a larger European struggle between the upstart Crédit Mobilier and the Rothschilds vying for supremacy in the years 1852–56. Waged first in Madrid and Vienna, the battle then shifted to Berlin.[36] Mevissen, Oppenheim, Mendelssohn, and the Crédit Mobilier headed the first project, the "Prussian Credit Institute for the Promotion of Agriculture, Trade, and Industry," and proposed a base capital of thirty million thalers with the expectation of raising it to fifty million. The Rothschild House, P. L. Ravené, and Gerson Bleichröder backed the second project, the "Prussian Society for the Advancement of Commercial and Agricultural Industry," and requested twenty-four million thalers as an initial capital base with the option to expand to eighty million.

Submitted within four days of one another, these two proposals—because of the magnitude of the propositions, the prestige of their proponents, and the public attention they received—stirred the government to reconsider its stance on joint-stock commercial banking in Prussia. The petitions noted that the country was in danger of falling behind France and Austria in the tempo of industrialization but stressed that investments in agriculture in the eastern provinces were the banks' first concern. To underscore the latter point, prominent aristocrats not only signed the petitions but also agreed to sit on the board of directors. The Erbprinz zu Bentheim was featured in the Rothschild petition, while the Herzog von Ratibor, Graf von Redern, Graf von Arnim-Boitzenberg, Graf von Solms-Baruth, Graf von Keyserling, and the Fürst von Hohenlohe-Öhringen lent their names to the Mevissen proposal.[37]

A two-month ministerial debate ensued on whether the charters should be granted. The debate divided the cabinet into camps supporting and opposing the enterprises. The argument for approval came chiefly from Heydt and Marcus Niebuhr, an adviser in the king's Privy Council. Their memoranda argued that rigid opposition to promotional banking was no longer a viable option. Blanket condemnation of joint-stock banking, Heydt maintained, had not enabled the government to control commercial and industrial investment. Moreover, this policy was out of step with rapid expansion in recent years. Fully aware that the government's railroad funds were already overextended for the coming years and that the Prussian Bank and the Seehandlung did not possess the capacity to service the existing enterprises in Prussia, Heydt reluctantly recognized the desirability of more joint-stock banks. Although in public the trade minister held firm to the government's restrictive position, he began around 1855 to question the policy in government memoranda. He stated that the government should return to the philosophy embodied in the bank reform of 1846, which worked toward a compromise between private banking and state control. After 1848, Heydt noted, the government had become "frightened in following the newly embarked course." [38]

Niebuhr advanced a stronger argument by asserting that the government "no longer has a free choice with this charter." Prussia's restrictions on domestic banks had encouraged joint-stock banks in neighboring Dessau, Brunswick, Rostow, Weimar, Gera, Thuringia, and Darmstadt (two), and now a rejection of a credit company would produce "more than one on our borders. This would be far worse than allowing one within the country, because a border crédit mobilier would draw all its business from Prussia and simultaneously be free of all government control." [39] In pleading for a joint-stock investment bank, neither Niebuhr nor Heydt sought to abandon the state's philosophy on controlling finance and the use of capital. (Niebuhr, an early protégé of Ludwig von Gerlach, was part of the ultra-conservative *Kreuzzeitung* circle.[40]) Instead, they argued that new conditions required a change in tactics to meet this end. Introducing joint-stock banking to Berlin would diminish the business of foreign border banks and allow the state to exercise greater control over financial affairs. Heydt conceded that these banks would influence Prussian business whether or not they had their seats in Prussia; hence the state should garner what control it could.

Actually the proposals came at an opportune time to dovetail with other planned changes by the government. In May 1856 Heydt and Bodelschwingh increased the note issue of the Prussian Bank more than threefold, from twenty-one to seventy-one million thalers, in an effort to reassert the state's control over the economy and permit the government to ban all foreign currency. Allowing a major credit institution to operate in Berlin would enhance the plan, for it would use government notes and stand under the trade ministry's supervision. He proposed that rewording the statutes in more restrictive terms to prohibit activities outside of Prussia and limiting the type of enterprises funded in the country would preempt the major dangers. With such arguments, it was clear that Heydt and Niebuhr did not ground their advocacy of the charters in the liberal doctrines of self-administration and economic freedom. Firm advocates of a bureaucratically controlled economy, the two government officials saw the charter as a way for the state to guarantee "a long-lasting and influential intervention." [41]

The tactic, however, did not sit well with the minister of the interior, the minister of agriculture, and the directors of the Prussian Bank, who together formed a bulwark against the new charters. Heydt had perhaps anticipated their opposition, for he appealed to the king for his consent without a cabinet vote. All three parties protested this action, stating that these charters touched on their spheres of administration and therefore required a cabinet vote.[42] In consequence, they submitted written rejections. The Prussian Bank directors disclaimed any need for new credit banks. The enormous economic growth in the last five years hardly bespoke of lethargy or the danger of being outstripped by France and Austria, the report stated. On the contrary, the bank directors warned Heydt of too much activity and drew a parallel between the current speculative fever and the financial panic of 1844. Moreover, they saw no guarantee that the bank's capital would flow to agriculture instead of commerce and industry. Not least, they objected to the Prussian Bank's potential loss of status as the primary instrument for shaping the domestic financial market and controlling the interest rates.[43]

Minister of Agriculture Karl von Manteuffel also argued that a private institution would eclipse the power of the state bank and thus limit the freedom of the government to make decisions. For the state to be beholden to such an institution for loans would be regrettable.[44] Yet Manteuffel undercut his own position with the admission that, if the government was predisposed to permit such banks, he favored chartering not one but both banks. In this way the "government can avoid the accusation that it chose one company over another without sufficient justification." [45] This fear of adverse public reaction suggests the extent to which potential public pressure affected even the most arch-conservative members of Otto von Manteuffel's government.

The forceful rejection of the charter came from Ferdinand von Westphalen, the minister of the interior, whose criticisms were clustered around the two interconnected themes of economics and politics. The economic objections centered mostly on the minister's belief that the proposed institutions' primary aim was to pursue stock speculation. As evidence he cited the intention of the Rothschild consortium to reserve eighteen of the twenty-four million thalers in stock for the bank's ownership, including eight million for Rothschild alone. A liability of such large dimensions, he argued, would strengthen an already overly strong hand and invite rash and risky speculations.[46] The sole interest in quick profits was apparent in the stocks of crédit mobiliers, whose volatility could only be attributed to deliberate manipulation.[47] And, he continued, credit institutes in Berlin would be no different. "Among the founders of the Prussian Credit Institute are people whose connection with the Darmstädter Bank is notorious; and among the promoters of the other company are founders of the crédit mobilier in Vienna. The businesses of both institutions and their stockholders have until now merely been active in unsolid enterprises and stock-jobbing." [48] He dismissed as farcical the petitioners' assertion that the banks would make a "solid contribution" to the economy.

The minister's political objections addressed the potential power that would accrue to the credit institutions and the corresponding loss of power to the state and the Junker class. Initially Westphalen criticized joint-stock banks as injurious to the moral well-being (*Sittlichkeit*) of the lower classes and to the benevolent, nonpartisan status of the state, but the actual reason for rejecting such banks lay in their deleterious effect on the Junker class. He remonstrated that the recent new stocks were devaluing state paper, above all the mortgage bonds (*Pfandbriefe*) issued by the Kurmark, Neumark, and

Pommeranian *Landschaften,* the land banks (first established by Frederick the Great after the Silesian wars) that had become the financial bulwark of the Prussian landed nobility.[49] Whereas these bonds held bravely at par through the financial panic of 1846 and the revolution, their market value fell 2 to 3 percent in the bull market of the 1850s. Speculation, he maintained, explained the low quotes; there were too many new industrial and commercial securities promising lucrative, short-term profits that overshadowed the older, more stable equities. The slackened growth of the provincial mortgage bonds in the 1850s was cause for alarm.[50] The sluggish trend endangered the viability of a newly established agricultural institution in Posen and, overall, might force landowners to resort to normal mortgages as a substitute. "The worth of these bond mortgages," he reminded Heydt, "is that they cannot be called in and make ownership of land a stable, conservative element." [51] More directly, Westphalen stated, "The credit of the larger landowners . . . rests in the credits of these agricultural institutions and in the worth of the bonds they issue." [52] Westphalen feared an expanded stock exchange that would drain capital out of land banks. To invite promotional banking to Berlin was tantamount to shutting off investment in agriculture.

In his first written opinion, Westphalen suggested not an outright rejection but two major revisions. First, the two proposed institutions were to be amalgamated and the base capital reduced from thirty to ten or twelve million thalers. Second, the securities should be issued not as common stock with fluctuating dividends but, rather, with a fixed dividend, much like a bond or a preferred stock.[53] The offer of a compromise might have been nothing more than a tactic, for the two consortiums would not have accepted such conditions. Two days later, however, Westphalen retracted the proposal in a brief final *Votum* and flatly opposed approval of both charters.[54] Nonetheless, the reluctant spirit of compromise displayed by both Westphalen and Manteuffel merits interest: even the most conservative members of Friedrich Wilhelm's government were resigned to some form of modernization, as long as the state possessed preeminent control. On this dictum the whole cabinet could agree.

Of central importance was the position of the king, who was initially inclined to support the projects in some form. On 11 March he wrote Heydt, "I have decided to demand either the merger of both companies or to confirm one of the two." [55] Confident of approval, Heydt had already opened negotiations for a merger of the two credit institutions.[56] But the king, troubled by the various arguments mounted by the conservative side, wavered and finally decided to support the ministerial vote on 26 March 1856 that ended in defeat for any kind of reform. The cabinet's recommendation to the king to reject both charters summed up the arguments of Karl von Manteuffel, Westphalen, and the Prussian Bank, and the king accepted and authorized the rejection of both charter petitions. The report drew attention to the danger of neutralizing the aims of the Prussian Bank, of unwarranted stock speculation, and of threatening the stability of railroads and agriculture. Lamprecht, the Prussian Bank director, stressed the possibility of an impending money crisis on the international market and the need for Prussia to act prudently.[57] The attempt of the merchant class to modify Prussia's banking system with the cooperation of the government had failed.

The refusal to charter joint-stock banks proposed by the two most prestigious banking circles in Germany sent a powerful signal to the Prussian business class, and it was this decision that most likely convinced financiers of the need to employ the commandite principle. Trade Minister Heydt drew this connection in a memorandum to the Privy Council, stating that "for reasons of an objectionable nature, many big Berlin bankers have prepared an enterprise [Berliner Handelsgesellschaft] that has not yet been made public in which the rejected joint-stock crédit mobilier will be established as a commandite company." [58] The connection was also evident in the identity of the founders of the Berliner Handelsgesellschaft. Most had been backers of the two joint-stock proposals.[59] In March 1853, Mevissen, who helped organize the consortium, wrote: "We are patronized by Berlin in one letter after the other in a manner of which I do not at all approve. The gentlemen in Berlin, who are entirely ignorant of finances, want to give us special directions, draw balances, etc. If that continues for long, I will seriously consider the idea of transforming the [A. Schaaffhausen'sche] Bankverein into a commandite company and double its capital." [60] Mevissen, then, had long toyed with the option of a commandite company as a counterstroke to government obstinacy and saw the need for the commandite principle after the government's reaffirmation of its refusal to charter joint-stock banks.

In 1856 the commandite principle, hitherto applied to small firms involving one entrepreneur (unlimited liability) and a few dozen notables (limited liability), was now used to found large companies with a wide ownership. By using the legal status of a trading company, which, because unincorporated, fell outside legal restrictions imposed on joint-stock companies, directors of a commandite company could acquire investment capital from "inactive partners" not unlike the directors of a joint-stock company. In effect, such a company was no longer a genuine commandite association but, rather, a commandite joint-stock company (*Kommanditgesellschaft auf Aktien*): a distinction that enabled financiers to mobilize capital and split it up in shares, while simultaneously avoiding government supervision.

The loophole was worked out by degrees. David Hansemann first employed the strategy in 1851 soon after resigning the directorship of the Prussian Bank. While still director he petitioned the government in 1849 for a charter to start the Berlin Credit-Gesellschaft, a credit bank designed to aid craftsmen and shopkeepers in Berlin during business slumps. In 1848 the Belgian government had responded to the scarcity of money by creating the Union du Crédit in Brussels, and Hansemann proposed a similar institution in the Prussian capital. After a delay of eleven months the government refused Hansemann's request. The refusal angered Hansemann greatly and was one of several incidents that prompted his resignation from office.[61] Once a private businessman, he pursued the idea further and realized that the law allowed him to operate a credit bank if the statutes were established along the lines of a trading company (*Handelsgesellschaft*), a form of association that did not require a government license.[62] In October 1851 the Disconto Gesellschaft began business. The government treated Hansemann's maneuver with disdain; the Prussian Bank refused to discount any bills of the Disconto Gesellschaft or otherwise recognize it as a financial institution.[63]

The credit company's initial reserves of approximately 500,000 thalers did not threaten the government's bank policy, and, moreover, its statutes forbade speculation with securities or promotional investment. Hansemann's idea in January 1856, however, was to reorganize his credit company into a share-capital commandite company and to issue stock in two series totaling ten million thalers—an elasticized application of the limited partnerships. Having had a charter rejected as a high-ranking government official and having subsequently experienced mixed relations with the trade ministry, Hansemann did not apply for a charter to issue public shares. His willingness to accept the risk of unlimited liability was motivated by the need to bypass the petitioning process.[64] Within days the stock was privately subscribed and Prussia's largest private bank (in respect to capital) was launched.[65] The bank's success in attracting investment capital ensured its long-term viability and became the precedent for widespread use of the commandite principle.[66] The bank, however, only became a lodestar for other bankers in the spring of 1856 after the government turned down the two bids to bring joint-stock banking to Prussia.

Forewarned by Hansemann of the statute changes,[67] Heydt did not attempt to forestall it. Most likely he tolerated it because he had to—there was little the trade ministry could do legally to block it. Tacitly, the government granted Hansemann a privilege, earned perhaps through a conservative and sensible banking practice in its first five years.[68] Heydt should have been more concerned about the second statute change in November 1856, when the Disconto Gesellschaft partners empowered its directors to speculate with its reserves on the stock market and promote new businesses. But again the minister and cabinet did not react. By its failure to check the changes inaugurated by the Disconto Gesellschaft and by its continued rejection of joint-stock charters, the government opened the way for investors to follow Hansemann's lead. "The Hansemann'sche Disconto Gesellschaft," wrote Heydt, "has, as is well known, opened up the escalation of large joint-stock commandite companies . . . this has had the necessary consequence that every enterprise which shies from a government license for joint-stock status appears as a commandite company." [69]

Reacting to rumors of imminent commandite bank openings, the king asked the cabinet to convene and discuss the advisability of outlawing commandite banks. The cabinet met on 1 July. Unable to reach a unanimous decision, the report to the king contained a majority vote and a dissenting opinion. The majority decision, led by Heydt, Westphalen, and Bodelschwingh, supported the idea of imposing a regulation on the crypto joint-stock banks. These ministers recognized "justifiable objections," namely, doubts about the constitutionality of the decree, and consequently recommended immediate action—a provisional decree, allowing the Landtag's subsequent approval. The founding of a few large-scale commandite banks compelled the state to establish new regulations. The decree must distinguish between normal, small-scale commandite companies, deemed to be a healthy component of the economy, and the newer stock-issuing commandite companies, whose emergence was clearly a circumvention of the commercial code. Hence the report recommended that the decree restrict the number of silent partners to 100, ban transferable shares (thus canceling their attraction for the bourse), and institute bureaucratic controls to supervise all new commandite companies.[70]

Otto and Karl von Manteuffel mounted the dissenting opinion. These ministers did not believe that "an emergency situation was at hand" justifying "a deep invasion" into the rights of business enterprises." [71] Without denying the negative aspects of these banks, the Manteuffels maintained that such "outgrowths cannot at all be avoided, if one does not want to destroy simultaneously the healthy development" of business in Prussia.[72] Such "aggressive intervention" (*gewaltsame Eingreifen*) against commandite companies would prevent undesirable companies but would also hinder the establishment of "solid and useful enterprises." [73] The cure, they argued, was not to be found in government intervention but in the market; speculators would soon learn not to invest in unsound enterprises. Finally, the two ministers claimed that such an ordinance did not justify departing from the normal legislative process.[74]

Outnumbered in the cabinet, Otto von Manteuffel sought to assert his will by telegraphing additional appeals to the king's councilors. Writing from the Hague on 8 July, Manteuffel sent a long telegram to Privy Councilor Illaire, an influential adviser attending the king during his cure in Marienbad. He announced that two new commandite companies had been founded, but their moderate reception by the market confirmed his opinion that the Berlin public was "coming to its senses by itself." In view of the imminent decree, Manteuffel questioned whether these companies should receive the same privileged status as Hansemann's company or whether Hansemann should be denied the privilege as well. The legal questions were unclear and he believed that the problem would best be solved by leaving it alone. Heydt, Manteuffel wrote, "favors decisive intervention, but I see neither a legal nor a political reason why the government alone should take on itself the odium of adopting an aggressive measure instead of sharing it with the Landtag." [75] The argument failed to convince the king and the decree on commandite companies was drafted and signed on 12 July.

On the following day Manteuffel sent another telegram to Illaire exhorting the king to delay publication of the decree. He argued that the legality of the measure was "at the very least dubious." The constitution's article 63 granted the crown the power to rule by decree only in times of emergency. It was difficult to argue that an emergency existed. The decree, he wrote, "is impractical and therefore impolitic." A law severely restricting commandite companies, he reiterated, had to be reached in agreement with the Landtag, which would most likely approve the measure. Arbitrary intervention with a decree, on the other hand, would only alienate those parties in support of the government's position, for the means were too questionable. The larger public would disapprove of the decree, argued Manteuffel, because it appeared to favor the "Capitals-Aristocratie"; moreover, the public would recognize that to restrict competition would increase interest rates. Only the established commandite companies would approve.[76]

Manteuffel's opposition to the decree was grounded more in his government's fragile relationship with the House of Deputies than in a principled regard for the constitution, which he saw fit to alter on numerous other occasions. Banking policy had been an issue in the lower house during the 1850s and one that aroused strong opposition. Friedrich Harkort, citing the "insufficiency of the Prussian [state's] credit organization," called in February 1851 for a twenty-one member commission to examine the government's competency to meet the country's growing banking needs.[77] Although the government contested the right of the lower chamber to occasion a formal inquiry as an unjustifiable expression of mistrust, the commission and three subcommittees were nonetheless formed in April 1851. The committee's massive report to parliament a year later raised several problems. It criticized the government's reluctance to issue small loans to artisans; the restricted money supply, especially the eight-million thaler ceiling on notes issued by the provincial banks of issue, which impeded growth and encouraged the inordinate import of foreign currency; and, finally, the government's unwillingness to lift the restrictions on joint-stock banks in Prussia. In particular, the commission faulted the government's rejection of Hansemann's credit bank. The commission recognized the government's right to oversee general banking practices and to prohibit the circulation of foreign currency but concluded that the credit needs of an entire land could not be met by one state bank. Prussia's banking system, it concluded, must be reformed. In subsequent debate on the report during May 1852, the Landtag rejected both the commission's draft for a bill and its own reworked bill. Harkort submitted a new bill in February 1856, which underwent intense debate but was dropped in April.[78] In spite of the liberals' failure to bring about a new law, it was generally recognized that Prussia needed reform.[79] To have promulgated the decree three months after the government had narrowly defeated a reform bill would have been politically unwise. The government's economic policy and its reputation as the Zollverein's leader would have suffered, as would Manteuffel's attempt to steer a course between the Camarilla's reactionary neoabsolutism and the democratic parliamentarism of 1848.[80]

The minister-president's second telegram warning the Privy Council to take heed of the parliament and public opinion had its intended effect: the king began to doubt. Unable to make the final decision, he ordered on 14 July that the decree's publication be delayed until further counsel with the minister-president and his cabinet.[81] Between sojourns in the Hague and his estate in Lausitz, Manteuffel returned to Berlin and submitted another recommendation (18 July) that the decree be abandoned. Two additional commandite companies in Berlin were now in business, he noted, and the decree's efficacy was all the more diminished. The cabinet had met to discuss the issue, he reported, but only two ministers were in town, Minister of Interior Westphalen and Minister of War Waldersee. Both thought it wiser to delay the final decision until their colleagues returned.[82]

Westphalen, however, recognized Manteuffel's delaying tactic and saw an opportunity to thwart it. When the minister-president left Berlin three days later, Westphalen submitted a memorandum directly to the king. With diffuse moral arguments he implored the king to publish the decree. The minister asserted that the new commandite companies were speculating in grain, driving up prices already elevated by the forecast of a bad harvest. Their price gouging endangered the welfare of the poor, the "less well-off classes of the population," and especially "the minimally paid civil servants." The stock-jobbing of these companies furthermore harmed the general welfare by attracting capital for quick profits and not for useful investment. "They are nothing more than a means of circumventing the existing restrictive laws on joint-stock companies, and therefore I must believe that the enactment of the ordinance is fully justified." [83]

Heydt, too, attempted to counterbalance Manteuffel's efforts by sending one of his top aides in the trade ministry, Rudolf Delbrück, to Marienbad to persuade the king of the decree's necessity. "The matter," wrote Delbrück in his memoirs, "did not belong to my jurisdiction, rather to Herr Hoene's, but my minister believed that I, because favorably received by the king, would be able to exert some influence on the decision." Although the king had in principle no objection to the decree, "for he despised anything resembling stock swindles," Delbrück noted, Friedrich Wilhelm hesitated to oppose his minister-president. After three days Delbrück left the spa with the postponement of the decree's proclamation still in effect.[84] The king wished that the decree, technically a law since 12 July, be reviewed again by the cabinet before its promulgation.

By the time the cabinet congregated on 19 August to submit an opinion to the king, the situation had changed enough to force a shift toward Manteuffel's position. Five commandite companies had been established in Prussia (two in Berlin, three others in Breslau, Magdeburg, and Königsberg), thus rendering the decree, in practical terms, useless. The original intention had been to prevent companies that had been denied corporate status from establishing themselves in some other form. Although the decree would prevent future companies from reorganizing as commandite banks, the damage already incurred by the recent company start-ups had greatly reduced the efficacy of the decree. The opinion concluded that it was not worthwhile to depart from the normal legislative process, for the "aim has been thwarted." [85]

The cabinet opinion, however, took particular notice of the persisting division of opinion: collegial unanimity did not exist. All ministers save the two Manteuffels recognized the legitimacy and legality of the king's decree and refused to concede to the minority opinion that it was "neither political nor constitutional." And yet the cabinet recommended that the decree be abandoned for purely pragmatic reasons. To avoid further discussion on constitutional and legal questions, the majority agreed to forgo a second vote and acquiesced in the minority position. In return the minority surrendered the right to elaborate its position in writing.[86] The waiver was a magnanimous gesture that swept the legal and political issues under the carpet, emphasizing instead the decision's practical side. Having received his wish to drop the decree, Manteuffel avoided rubbing salt in the wounds of royal prerogative and ministerial authority.

Manteuffel's victory translated into a silent, grudging consent to commandite banks and companies. With the decree formally buried, the government took no action, issued no statement. The lack of reaction did not go unnoticed. Mevissen, for example, both publicly and privately pointed up the government's hypocrisy in rejecting the petitions of the credit institutions yet allowing the Berliner Handelsgesellschaft to form as a commandite bank with no difficulty whatsoever. The *Bremer Handelsblatt* echoed this complaint.[87]

To the public the government presented a fitful, contradictory policy that was logically indefensible. Behind the scenes, however, the government's effort to be consistent in its banking policy was frustrated by quick-acting businessmen, a potentially troublesome Landtag, and Manteuffel's delaying tactic.

The incident of the abandoned decree is important chiefly because it documents a vital stage in the decline of the government's power to control and direct the Prussian economy. During the same decade that witnessed the Prussian government's abandonment of the direction principle in the coal and iron industry, it grudgingly relinquished to private enterprise its authority to channel and restrict the availability of credit for industrial expansion. The Prussian government opposed the establishment of commandite banks in Prussia and resented entrepreneurs who evaded their control over banking and finance. Clearly the relationship between the government and business class was not one of "alliance."

Later, the Darmstädter Bank, Disconto Gesellschaft, and Berliner Handelsgesellschaft became financial pillars for the Prussian-German state. But they were founded in a circumventive, rebellious operation, launched in the face of governmental opposition. The economic recession of 1857 drastically curtailed the program of promotional underwriting that these banks envisioned; it forced them to retreat for a while from the large-scale, company promotion that the government had feared.[88] After 1859 these banks participated in the "Prussian Consortium," which found it profitable to float government bond issues that financed the wars of German unification. Their later relationship to the government is not descriptive of the time of their origin.

These frictions in business-government relations during the 1850s raise questions about the validity of attempts to explain the ruling establishment in Prussia during 1848–66 as an unholy alliance or unhealthy symbiosis between capital and authoritarian government. In such vital areas as banking the relationship was hardly conflict free. Clearly the politics of the Prussian business class were more complex than has been generally assumed. The story of the suppressed decree of 1856 shows that the progress of industrial capitalism in this critical decade was not the result of cooperation between officials and entrepreneurs. The archives reveal the contrary. The business community had to oppose and outmaneuver the government in order to further its vital interests.

The crisis over commandite banks, furthermore, should not be consigned merely to economic or banking history. The alacrity with which the king and the cabinet resorted to a decree shows that bank openings had political overtones. The decree poses the question why the king and his cabinet felt such urgency to bypass the Landtag on a commercial matter. Royal commands were provided for in the 1850 constitution (the "Notenverodnungsrecht" in article 63) but only for emergency situations—and the opening of commandite banks hardly constituted a state emergency. The move to unconstitutional executive action underscores the perceived threat of the business class's operations and the growing frustration of the government in its effort to harness the influence of this group. The incident demonstrates that the government did not always grant economic concessions to ensure the quiescence of the business class. More crucially, this instance contradicts the binary paradigm of economic concession versus political reform.[89] The Prussian government perceived this particular economic reform as a political issue. Friedrich Wilhelm and the ministers Westphalen, Karl von Manteuffel, and Heydt objected to bank reform on grounds that were partially political. The king attributed the demand for credit banks to an insidious French influence; the ministers Westphalen and K. von Manteuffel believed bourgeois self-administration in banking would expand capitalism and destabilize the traditional social order; and Heydt rejected the change because it threatened his capacity to determine how industrial growth should serve state interests.[90] The government documents bearing on this issue show no clear separation between economic and political spheres.[91]

Minister-President Otto von Manteuffel also viewed the problem in political terms, albeit differently from his cabinet members. Manteuffel, usually characterized as the architect of reactionary state policies, emerged as the unlikely defender of bourgeois interests. His support is largely attributed to the role the Prussian parliament played in Manteuffel's policies in the 1850s, a role that has not yet been fully appreciated.[92] His defense of commandite banks was part of a greater strategy for maintaining his brand of bureaucratic absolutism, which needed the constitution and a body of elected deputies as an essential counterbalance to check the patriarchal conservatism of the Junker class—most visibly embodied in the Camarilla. For this reason he chose to tolerate commandite banks rather than unduly injure his status in parliament by forbidding them. Although this decision was unpopular with his cabinet, Manteuffel recognized that a royal decree on banking practice would greatly harm his relations with the lower house by revealing too starkly its impotence under the constitution. Manteuffel's political strategy had, however, a double-edged quality; to neutralize the ultraconservative right as well as the democratic left, his government was required to concede undesirable measures to the moderate liberals of the center. The influence of public opinion and the presence of the Landtag—albeit indirect—had grown more powerful. Manteuffel's repeated references to the decree's unconstitutionality and the adverse impact it would have on public opinion and in parliament reveal the silent pressure of business interests on his policy. For this reason, his protestations that the decree was a "deep invasion into the rights of businessmen" rang true.

No longer could the crown impose its will without considering how the business class would react. In other words, the *Rechtsstaat* and the parliament possessed some genuine worth.[93] That parliamentary commission reports, chamber of commerce protests, and newspaper articles could affect government policy reveals an erosion in the state's autocratic power over the economy.

In this respect the question of agency is of central importance. The party exhibiting instrumentality, demonstrating action, and exerting power was the middle class and not Prussian state officials. The business class introduced modern banking to Prussia in spite of and not through the government. The increased accessibility to capital in northern Germany resulted from a shrewd evasion of government controls by businessmen who wrested rather than received reforms from the government. That reform was hard-earned and achieved in spite of official resistance enhanced the bourgeois belief in the inevitability of political progress.

Although the transformation of governing authority from bureaucratic control to a negotiated consensus between government and a broader range of elite groups was a gradual process over the course of the 1850s, the decree of 1856 presents a concrete instance in which to view the change.[94] This example of assertive middle-class evasion of state control gathers greater significance when placed in the larger context of Prussian political culture in the 1850s. Providing new reference points to examine how the bourgeois class interacted with an authoritarian government in the 1850s (and vice versa) will enable us to reconstruct and understand a political style that was neither democratic nor defeatist. If the construct of German exceptionalism is to have any application to the 1850s, it should presuppose an active, assertive bourgeois class willing to resist the government and successfully affect the decision-making process. Deficiencies and omissions of the bourgeoisie do not explain the middle-class disregard for parliamentarism, but rather the success such groups as the business class had in the 1850s in attaining material and social goals that weakened the need for democratic procedures. The July decree was one of the last attempts of the Prussian crown to assert its will arbitrarily in the marketplace. Its repression provides a sharp illustration of the latent power in the capital and commercial networks of the business class. It allows us to understand how the business class accrued more influence in the Prussian ministries and why the business class became particularly successful in arranging its terms with the Prussian state on a more favorable basis.

CHAPTER SIX

▼

The Railroad Fund, 1842–1859

In 1842 the Prussian government established the Railroad Fund, a special account to aid private investment in railroad construction. This fund was the financial basis of Prussia's mixed system of railroad building: private businesses assumed ownership and administration of railways, while the government, in keeping with its tradition of state paternalism, fostered the infant industry with favorable legislation and financial assistance. After 1848, however, the role of the Railroad Fund changed under Trade Minister Heydt's administration. Heydt used the fund to bridge Prussia's transition from a privately owned railway network to a state-run system. The ministry's vision of a speedy transition to state ownership, however, was not shared by all, and opposition from other governmental ministries, parliamentary factions, and the liberal press contributed to the dissolution of the Railroad Fund in 1859, thus ending Heydt's bid for state ownership.

Uniting the financial power of the fund with other government monies, the trade ministry became the largest, most important investor in Prussia, building over 2,960 kilometers of railway by 1860. The fund reached sixteen of Prussia's twenty-three railway companies, underwrote 33,907,003 thalers in direct loans, and indirectly generated 140,590,000 thalers in share capital through interest guarantees. Private railways received 5.3 million thalers in direct construction funds and a further 2.4 million in dividend subsidies; 19.8 million were given to state construction and 2.5 million for dividends. Thus, the trade ministry's activities represented one-quarter of Prussia's entire railroad market. Hence, while recent historiography has taken great pains to redress earlier overstated claims about the state's role in industrialization, the importance of state involvement in the railroad boom of the 1850s should, at the same time, not be underestimated.[1]

The debate over the Railroad Fund sheds light on a transitional period in Prussian history, when governing circles were uncertain as to what role the state should adopt in the new capitalist economy. The execution of a coherent economic policy from the executive branch of government was hindered by the lack of harmony between Finance Minister Bodelschwingh and Heydt, the ministers jointly responsible for governing the state's economic activities. Although this division was in part a personality conflict, the clashing attitudes of the finance and trade ministers embodied broader differences. They advocated two predominant economic policies of the 1850s.

Finance Minister Karl von Bodelschwingh advocated a minimal role for state paternalism in the private market economy that the government had promoted since 1806. By introducing liberal economic principles (abolition of serfdom, freedom of occupation and movement, free sale of noble estates, self-administration of cities) during the Reform Era, the Prussian state had taken a pathbreaking step in Central Europe in unleashing the energy and industry of individual initiative.[2] This viewpoint found ideological buttresses in Immanuel Kant and Adam Smith, whose philosophies of individual freedom supported the tenets of economic liberalism. Bodelschwingh stood for continuing this policy and applying it to railroad building: private capital should assume leadership and the fund should nurture the growth of private railroads. Staunchly conservative, Bodelschwingh advocated not a laissez-faire economy but an economy that subordinated state involvement to private activity. His outlook was further shaped by a prevailing value of Prussia's prerevolutionary bureaucratic caste that, since the near bankruptcy of the Prussian state in 1806, looked upon all large state expenditure as an anathema—unless absolutely necessary. The state's willingness to allow private business to initiate economic modernization and avoid state expense accounts for the relative compatibility between liberal businessmen and Prussian state officials in the early nineteenth century.[3]

Heydt, on the other hand, strongly believed in state control of the economy and had no compunctions about expanding the bureaucratic apparatus of the trade ministry to meet this end. As we have already seen, Heydt exercised strong state paternalism in the railroad industry and with other joint-stock enterprises and broadly interpreted the powers of his ministry to reconcile economic activity with the interests of the state. Although willing to concede that the coal industry would best serve Prussian state interest as part of the private sector (reinvigorated and expanded through private capital), Heydt averred that the state with its own system could profit from railroads while promoting the needs of commerce and industry. Thus, the fitful ambivalence that characterized Prussia's economic policy in the 1850s can be traced largely to the shifting balance of power between Bodelschwingh and Heydt.

Heydt's policy with the fund, however, had one chief problem: funding. By 1856, the Prussian government had invested over 65 million thalers in railroads, over one-quarter of Prussia's state debt. The railroads' prominent role in swelling the state debt from 150 million thalers in 1850 to 250 million in 1856 drew the attention of the press and, eventually, both houses of the Landtag. Pressure from the parliament and the liberal press, which together produced a public discussion on state finance, constrained Heydt's railroad policy and was partially responsible for dissolving Heydt's fund in 1859. Prussia's legislature (the Landtag) exercised a political influence that, if still weak, could nonetheless at times check and modify the policies of the king's cabinet.

▼

The original aims of the Railroad Fund were modest. The immediate goal in 1842 was to promote the construction of rudimentary east-west and north-south corridors that would unite Berlin with its provinces. The finance ministry (under the auspices of Christian von Rother and Ernst von Bodelschwingh) laid aside the one-time subsidy of six million thalers for direct investment of the railway companies' start-up capital. It also created a running account to cover the payment of dividend subsidies (between 3 and 3.5 percent) that the government offered the fledgling railway companies to attract investors. The account received annual replenishment from the finance ministry (500,000 thalers), the state salt monopoly (an unfixed sum), and the interest off the fund's investments. Equally important, this expense account had a limit: the law of 1842 stated that the Railroad Fund's running account could not exceed an annual expenditure of two million thalers.

The fund stayed within these restrictions until Heydt's trade ministry took over its administration from the finance ministry in 1848. Heydt's first task was to remedy the fund's chief shortcoming: the failure to attract entrepreneurs to build the Eastern Railway between Berlin and Königsberg. He used the newly constituted lower house to approve a loan that would enable the state to build the Eastern Railway itself. The loan would also be used to complete two other lines, the Westphalian Railway, which would connect the western provinces with the rest of Prussia, and the Saarbrückener Railway, which would integrate Prussia into the commercial corridor between England, France, Belgium, Switzerland, and Austria. The total building costs for these three lines was thirty-three million thalers. Heydt submitted a bill for a loan of twenty-one million thalers to the lower house in December 1849, with the promise that the fund would cover twelve million thalers of the building costs as well as underwrite subsidies on the preferred stock for the Westphalian and Saarbrücker lines. Both houses passed the bill and supported Heydt's long-term aim to purchase all railways in Prussia.[4]

The Landtag's compliance with Heydt's loans and dividend subsidies in 1849–50 was criticized by the liberal press. Newspapers questioned the houses' approval of the thirty-three million thaler loan in 1849 without instituting control mechanisms to check how the money was actually used: "Because we are not in the position to prevent any unlawful use, we will never recognize the legal validity of the houses' vote."[5] Why, asked the editors of the *National-Zeitung* and the *Ostsee-Zeitung,* allot the loan in one lump sum instead of annual increments to maintain supervision of the finances? The *Kölnische-Zeitung* expressed their dissatisfaction in even blunter terms: "You so-called constitutionalists, are you so afflicted with blindness as not to see . . . that the counter-revolution stands in our midst fully organized and builds a finely linked chain throughout all of Germany, and you put in the hands of these counter-revolutionaries the only thing they are lacking—money"?[6] The rhetoric of such editorials smacked of the bitterness of liberal setbacks in 1848, but their mistrust of how the Prussian government would use the money was not far off the mark. One clear misuse of the Railroad Fund can be cited. When the threat of war loomed in the Lower Danube and the Crimea in November 1852, and the Prussian government prepared for the possibility of mobilization for war, the king's privy councilor Marcus Niebuhr drew up a mobilization loan for twenty-six million thalers, whose collateral was to be drawn from the unused funds of the 1849 railroad loan.[7] The truism of liberal journalists that "the financial administration [of a government] goes hand in hand with the political system" indeed had validity.[8]

Early criticism of state railroads also stemmed from the laissez-faire belief that the less intervention and expenditure by the state, the better. Echoing the doctrines of Jean Baptiste Say, Adam Smith, Christian von Schlözer, Wilhelm von Humboldt, and David Ricardo, such free-trade organs as the *National-Zeitung* criticized the burden of dividend guarantees on the taxpayer. The newspaper complained, for example, that the Prussian taxpayer would pay over one million thalers in 1850 for state railroad subsidies.[9] The *Vossische Zeitung,* observing the parliamentary debate on dividend subsidies for two Rhenish railways, questioned whether the unnecessary expenditure was also destroying competition and creating unfair business practice.[10] This criticism spilled over into the upper house's debate on whether to extend government support to the Aachen-Düsseldorfer and the Cologne-Crefelder railways. The motion passed with a slim majority of six votes (69 to 63).[11]

The terms of payment on the 1849 loan taxed the fund's resources considerably. Within one year of its management, Heydt had technically exhausted the fund's supply for the next six years. Amortizing the principal on twelve million thalers, covering the interest on twenty-one million thalers, and meeting the subsidy obligations on other lines fully absorbed the fund's assets until 1856.[12] Heydt, however, sought to change the restrictions of the fund's spending limits and radically aggrandize its capacity as railway owner.

The best evidence of Heydt's changed policy was his proposed loan of thirty-four million thalers in 1852.[13] The fund's financial outlook had changed enough, Heydt believed, to plan bolder investment for the mid-fifties. By 1852 the fund's running account had risen to 1,513,000 thalers and would stand at 1,800,000 after 1855.[14] According to Heydt's calculations, railroads that once burdened the fund with heavy subsidies (the Stargard-Posen and the Lower Silesian–Mark railways) now demanded only 200,000 thalers, in contrast to the 1,137,000 thalers required in 1849–51.[15] In conjunction with the fund's rising income, the relatively low dividend subsidies plus administration costs (70,000) left 1,530,000 thalers free. With this 1.5 million thalers, Heydt proposed on 16 June 1852 to float a loan that would build seven lines at the cost of twenty-eight million thalers: in the west, lines between the Sieg and Ruhr valleys, Rheine and Osnabrück, Münster and Rheine, Saarbrücken and Trier, and the Rhine bridge at Cologne; in the east, lines between Breslau and Posen, and Bromberg and Thorne.[16] The fund's running account would act as the sinking fund to pay for the loan's interest and principal. This annual cost Heydt figured as 700,000 thalers, thus leaving over half of the running account for the original use of meeting subsidy payments.[17] The loan, he insisted to the finance minister, was "not a matter of preference, but rather a political and financial necessity." The state could not rely on private speculation to build its railroads when competitive neighbors threatened to outstrip Prussia.[18] Two months later (23 August), Heydt asked for another 6,161,495 thalers for the further construction of the Eastern Railway (Creuz-Frankurt/Oder via Landsberg and Cüstrin), bringing the loan's sum to thirty-four million thalers.

The loan proposal shows the trade ministry's new view of the Railway Fund. Heydt had ceased to see it as a discrete pool of money limited to two million thalers designated for subsidizing private railroads. Rather, he perceived the account as venture capital, a sum of money to be exploited to its greatest value by his ministry. The fund, he believed, should be put to work as collateral for large building loans and thus give the state the leading role in railroad construction. With clever management, Heydt noted to Bodelschwingh, the loan could be followed by an even greater loan that would allow the state to build ten other important lines.[19]

Heydt's vision shifted the fund's function from state promotion of private railways to state ownership of Prussia's newest lines. In a memorandum to the finance minister, Heydt clearly stated his preference for state-owned railways. In reference to the seven railway lines in question, he admitted that the railways could indeed be built by private enterprises with state subsidies. But, he noted, "insofar as it is a choice between a dividend subsidy or state construction, I am decisively for the latter, because experience has not shown us that joint-stock companies build railways more inexpensively than the state, and under state administration railways are much more useful for the direct interests of the state and the public." [20] Heydt further advocated state ownership for revenues: "After the state has taken over the administration of the Stargard-Posen, bought the Lower Silesian–Mark, and nears completion of the Eastern Railway, there can be no question that filling in the gaps in the provinces in which the state itself owns railways is not only in the interest of more efficient travel but also more profitable for the entire eastern state rail network." [21]

Although Heydt stressed efficient, profitable lines in the eastern provinces, his overall selection of proposed lines suggests a keener interest in establishing an equally large network in the west. Eleven of the seventeen projects proposed by Heydt in 1852 were in the Rhineland and Westphalia.[22] Most connected with the older private lines of the Berg-Mark, Cologne-Minden, and Rhenish railways. The proposal of state construction and ownership for such lines as the Sieg-Ruhr, Dortmund-Soest, Münster-Rheine, and Deutz-Frankfurt indicated that Heydt wished to deny the older, private railways their logical points of expansion and growth. By establishing an integrated state network in the western provinces by the end of the decade, Heydt would have concentrated blocks of state railways in the most strategic provinces, thus making nationalization of all railways in Prussia a greater likelihood.

This strategy added up to a policy shift. Starting with the 1849 loan of twenty-one million thalers, Heydt sought to transform the Railroad Fund into an open-ended source for government loans to construct a state railway system. Under Heydt the fund ceased to promote only private railroad interests and, in fact, worked against private interests. The state network was intended to compete with private companies, deny them room for growth, and eventually take them over. The loan signified a radical break with Prussia's mixed system.

Finance Minister Karl von Bodelschwingh opposed Heydt's use of the Railway Fund and from 1852 on acted as the principal brake on state spending in railroads. As supervisor of the general treasury and the state budget, Bodelschwingh believed it was incumbent upon him to oversee the fund's uses and challenge its independent status. He used his leverage as chief of finances to fight a policy he strongly opposed. The ministers' conflict over the use of state revenues became a highly personal, decade-long feud that occasioned long cabinet disputes and a mutual unwillingness to compromise on this issue. The two ministers would lock horns over the Railroad Fund in 1851, 1852, 1855, 1856, and 1857–58. The patent incompatibility of the two ministers leads one to ask why the king did not dismiss one of them to effect a more consistent economic policy. A divisive cabinet is perhaps what the king sought. Friedrich Wilhelm IV, Bismarck noted in his memoirs, cultivated an antagonistic triangle between Minister-President Manteuffel, Heydt, and Bodelschwingh to help maintain a balance between royal and ministerial power.[23]

Bodelschwingh's reply to Heydt's 1852 loan proposal argued against the loan and the idea of a state railway system. Earlier Bodelschwingh had opposed Heydt's argument for state construction of two of the lines included in the loan proposal.[24] In February, furthermore, he had participated in a protracted battle of principle to oppose the government's takeover of the Lower Silesian–Mark Railway.[25] In justifying the twenty-million thaler purchase of the railway to the legislature, the cabinet had stated that this was an isolated case and did not mark the beginning of a state system.[26] The jump from proposals for individual lines to railway systems that encompassed entire provinces, however, alerted the finance minister to a new attitude: "If not explicitly stated, it must be factually recognized that this is the first time the proposal of state construction has arisen." [27] Bodelschwingh recognized Heydt's intent and criticized both its budgetary oversights and its assumptions about the Railroad Fund.

Bodelschwingh dismissed the plan on both fiscal and philosophical grounds. He declared that the numbers Heydt presented to show that the fund had the money to finance the loan were misleading. Heydt's proposal, furthermore, disregarded continuing obligations for the 1849 loan and considerably underestimated the reserve needed for dividend guarantees. When these obligations were added to the costs of the new loan, Bodelschwingh estimated that the fund exceeded its legal limit by nearly two million thalers.[28]

Bodelschwingh attributed Heydt's attempt to hide the Railway Fund's financial obligations to the trade minister's basic view of the fund. The trade ministry, he wrote to Heydt, claimed there was an essential difference between the fund and the general treasury. According to this viewpoint, the fund's budget, however fraudulently balanced, was free from the scrutiny of the finance ministry's bookkeeping principles. This claim to independence was wrong. Whether a loan was contracted by the fund or by government agencies, Bodelschwingh argued, the loan still represented an increase in state debt: "The revenues that make up the Railroad Fund flow from the same source and are subject to the same changes and conditions as other state revenues." Ultimately, then, the proposed loan touched on the administrative sphere of the finance ministry, whose primary duty was to safeguard the fiscal health of the state.[29]

Moreover, the state could never replace private enterprise as Prussia's railroad financier. Not only did the state not possess the capital to undertake such immense investments and meet the demands of every region, but the contingencies of state finance also militated against tying up large sums for six years at a time. The development of a political crisis "would necessarily postpone execution of the whole plan." [30] Echoing his earlier stance on the state takeover of the Lower Silesian–Mark Railway, Bodelschwingh concluded that this loan had no proper place in the budget.

The crux of Bodelschwingh's critique, however, lay not in the accuracy of numbers or the realities of state debt but rather in the basic policy of railroad construction in Prussia. The proposed loan radically deviated from the original purpose of the Railway Fund, which was designed to aid, not supplant, private investment. State support, he reminded Heydt, was intended only for exceptional cases and could only be implemented through dividend guarantees. The fund, Bodelschwingh wrote, was intended to awaken and stimulate investment and should never intervene in such a way as to paralyze it. "Fundamentally, railway construction can and must be left to private enterprise." [31]

The function of the fund's annual account as a supplementary stimulant for private investment explained its low ceiling of two million thalers. Bodelschwingh lectured Heydt on the philosophy that underpinned the fund's design: "Private speculation forms the wide foundation upon which the Railroad Fund can build. The Fund's administration and application presumes that this base should not be weakened, shaken, or removed. Thus the state should intervene only where general interest justifies it and when the particular conditions of the enterprise demand it." [32] The central problem with Heydt's plan was that "development of private speculation was excluded from the start." Bodelschwingh questioned whether the state could assume "the entire responsibility for the punctual completion of the railway network. Once departed on this course, the state will not be able to leave it." [33] The danger of Heydt's loan was dual: it undermined the investing power of the private market and presupposed a state role in finance that it could never fulfill.

Bodelschwingh further inveighed against the centralization of finance that encouraged people to look to the state and not to local initiative. He pointed to the unfortunate pattern of investment in contemporary Prussia, a time when "a surfeit of disposable capital is thrown into state paper and railroad securities, while local interests have become accustomed to expect everything from the state." [34] Earlier Bodelschwingh had rebuked Heydt for allowing two railway companies to hoodwink the state into subsidizing the Rhine bridge's construction. It was a task, he opined, that the companies and the city government of Cologne could have easily accomplished themselves. Similarly, Bodelschwingh asked why the state should intervene and build the Sieg-Ruhr line without first tapping local capital that would directly benefit from the railway.[35]

Local enterprises, Bodelschwingh asserted, could attract this capital themselves if they were called upon or forced to do so. Such newspapers as the *National Zeitung* agreed with Bodelschwingh: "In recent times the receptivity toward new railroad projects has been ambitious. . . . in most cases private investment is fully sufficient and would assert itself even stronger if it was not hindered by so many legislative obstacles." [36] Heydt, however, claimed to see no relationship between state expenditure and diminished local investment. In a memorandum to Manteuffel, he pointed to the great number of petitions requesting charters to start new railways as evidence of private initiative, yet defended the need for state lines with the assertion that his specific lines did not attract private investment.[37] This defense, however, shows a disingenuous argument. All of Heydt's lines in his 1852 proposals had private bidders save two.[38] It also contradicted his earlier argument with Bodelschwingh that the state was the preferred, not the necessary, builder.[39] Indeed, Heydt failed to note to Manteuffel that although many new companies actively sought charters, few received them. In the 1850s, the trade ministry granted only two charters to establish new railway companies.[40] By denying new companies the initiative to build, Heydt created a need for state construction.

Bodelschwingh's opposition defeated Heydt's proposal. Heydt succeeded in bringing the issue to cabinet meetings (3 and 6 November 1852) by convincing Manteuffel to put it on the agenda.[41] The king, Minister of Interior von Westphalen, and Minister of War von Bonin reacted favorably to Heydt's idea, but the finance minister's strong resistance was enough to stop it.[42] Although Heydt's position on state ownership of railways actually carried a majority in the cabinet, the king and minister-president were reluctant to act against the finance minister's wishes in budgetary matters. Heydt later protested to Manteuffel about the unreasonableness of the finance minister's opposition,[43] but Bodelschwingh persevered. In a final memorandum to Manteuffel, Bodelschwingh demonstrated that the fund lacked the assets to float a thirty-four million thaler loan.[44] Heydt's bid to transform the fund into a protonationalization program failed.

Nevertheless, Heydt's energy in keeping the state a leading promoter in railways did not diminish. The failed 1852 loan made clear, to be sure, that Heydt would have to tolerate and work with Prussia's private railways and thus continue the mixed system. Heydt, however, did not abandon his hope of using the fund to float large loans. The trade ministry's administrative report for 1852–54 explicitly included this option.[45] Nor did it stop Heydt from finding other ways to generate new sources of capital to enlarge the fund's sphere of influence. The Railroad Tax is one example.

In 1853 Heydt submitted a bill to the Landtag to activate the Railroad Tax (*Eisenbahnabgabe*), a provision of the 1838 Railroad Law that empowered the government to tax the net profits of railways. The law freed railway companies from the normal commercial tax (*Gewerbesteuer*) but included a possible levy on net profits as just recompense for the losses to the state from lower highway tolls and diminished mail-coach revenue. The law stipulated that the tax revenues be used to replace monies lent to railway companies and thereafter to purchase their stocks.[46]

The Railroad Tax, however, had never been levied. The fragile first years of railway construction and the money crisis of the 1840s dissuaded the government from ever imposing it. But with the financial crisis over and with many companies earning good profits, 1853 appeared to Heydt a propitious time to introduce the tax.[47] For Heydt, the crucial aspect of the tax was that it did not flow to the general treasury but, rather, to a stock-acquisition program, now administered by the Railroad Fund. "The tax," Ludwig von Gerlach stated two years later in the lower house, "is actually no tax at all: it is the price tag for a monopoly." [48] For this reason Heydt emphasized that the tax revenues be called "extra-dividends" to emphasize their status as an accelerator of state railway ownership.[49]

The Railroad Tax of 1853 became a prominent public issue. In the Landtag the debate for its legislation stretched from February to April and extended the legislative period past the Whitsuntide recess. Eleven versions of the bill were debated in the lower house; the discussion in the upper house was equally long.[50] Ludwig Kühne, an old-liberal in the lower house, introduced an amendment that would have siphoned the tax into general treasury funds.[51] The lower house voted down Kühne's amendment but narrowly approved the tax. The upper house also approved the tax but not without questioning the future debts of the state, the putative advantage of shareholders with state involvement, and whether the state could match the progress of private railways.[52] The Landtag thus continued to support Heydt's aim of state ownership, albeit with more restraint and qualification than in 1849.

The debate on the bill's passage centered on the legality of taxing the railway companies progressively and the rates at which they should be taxed. A petition from five railway companies to the lower house protesting the tax's progressivity found support among many deputies, resulting in a long, "rather strong" debate.[53] The petition asked that one fixed tax percentage be agreed upon for all profits and that legal procedures be instituted to ensure the government's proper execution of stock acquisition.[54] The first point revealed the railway directors' self-interest in not paying new "socialistic" taxes; the second manifested a distrust of Heydt. The request for stock-purchase controls was a response to a motion by Marcus Niebuhr, who was also the financial adviser in the king's privy council. He proposed to strike the passage in the original law that required the government to reinvest stock in the same proportion in the company that it taxed. Redacting this provision gave the trade ministry greater freedom in shaping its stock portfolio and prevented delay in "acquiring all railroad equities." [55] The houses passed Niebuhr's amendment and, of the eleven versions, passed the one that least modified the executive branch's bill. The lower house succeeded in removing the highest tax rate from the law (30 percent from net profits exceeding 70 percent) and, contrary to Heydt's wishes, the legislature's final version recommended that the general treasury supervise the stock-acquisition program.[56]

While the Landtag quibbled mostly over the tax's form, newspapers questioned its substantive legality. The *Spenersche Zeitung* attacked the injustice of taxing stockholders twice, once with the stamp tax upon purchase (*Stempelsteuer*) and then again on annual net profits. It also called progressive taxation a "dangerous thing," a product of "socialistic, national economic theories," and a "central doctrine of Proudhon." [57] The *National-Zeitung* argued that the tax was a dead letter of the 1838 law. To revive the law's original intention—that the state should be the sole owner of railways—ran counter to the principles of railroad economy. We should not blame the legislators in 1838 who could not have known better, wrote the editors, but rather the politics of 1853:

> Where the finance minister is at a loss to find a need to justify a new tax, the trade minister enters and declares, "I must buy the railways." And where the trade minister is at a loss to find the means to undertake such an immense undertaking, the finance minister enters and declares, "I must find an equivalent of a commercial tax for the railroads and thus introduce a long-promised tax." Out of this conundrum of reasons arises a law that robs from stockholders a portion of their legal profits and purchases their property with this money. That is nothing more than the gradual expropriation of stockholders without compensation.[58]

The tax's intent to divest the private market of railroads provoked the newspaper to liken the tax to the work of "naked communism" and to the French socialist utopians of the day, "Cabet and the Icarians." Taxing property at all was linked to radical socialism: "What one calls here ground rent, Proudhon regards as theft." [59] This hyperbole that denounced progressive taxation and sanctified private property illustrates well the extreme dogma of free traders in the 1850s.

On 24 April 1853 the Landtag approved the Railroad Tax, which the king signed into law on 30 May.[60] The law fixed progressive tax rates for these so-called extra-dividends, since they had never been set in the original law. Accordingly, net profits of 4 percent or less of the company's nominal capitalization yielded 2.5 percent of that profit to the government; 5 percent, 5; 6 percent, 10; and 7 or more percent profit, 20 percent.[61] By today's standards, the tax's progressivity was not harsh: 100 thalers profit from 10,000 yielded 2.5 thalers to the state leaving the company with 97.5 thalers; 800 thalers net profit yielded 65 thalers to the state leaving 735 thalers.[62] Large, prosperous railways thus paid taxes ranging from 63,750 thalers, as did the Berlin-Anhalt Railway in 1857, to 129,333 thalers, which the Cologne-Minden Railway paid in 1856.[63] In 1859 the *Berliner Börsen-Zeitung* cited 150,000 thalers as an annual representative figure for large railways.[64] In spite of the tax's relative mildness, investor's dividends for Cologne-Minden Railway common stock diminished by 1 percent, the Upper Silesian by 2 percent, and the Magdeburg-Leipziger by 4.5 percent in the mid-fifties.[65] Heydt admitted that skimming this premium off investors' returns was a "considerable burden" for profitable lines.[66] If Rainer Fremdling's average of railroad stock dividends in the 1850s of 5.8 percent is correct, investors most likely agreed.[67] Certainly railroad directors found the tax steep.[68] By 1857, for example, the state collected a profit of 600,000 thalers from the Cologne-Minden and the Upper Silesian railways through the new tax and stock dividends. Heydt reported that this sum represented an 87.3 and 28.2 percent return, respectively, on the government's investment—a lucrative deal.[69] With such prospects in mind, he reported to the lower house in 1855 that the more profitable lines would fall into the state's hands within fifteen to twenty years.[70]

The tax gave new significance to the fund's assets, for it meant the creation of a sizable stock portfolio. Heretofore, the government only possessed stock from its 1842 investments, which by 1859—the year of the fund's dissolution—earned 1,452,328 thalers in dividends.[71] The extra-dividends, however, accumulated approximately four million thalers by 1859, giving the Railway Fund a total of five and a half million thalers in dividend earnings for further stock purchases.[72] For railroad finance, this sum was not especially formidable. Yet by 1866 these earnings would have increased to fifteen million thalers, thus approaching the dimension Heydt desired for the fund's stock-acquisition program. If the fund had not been dissolved in 1859, the tax would have achieved its purpose: private companies would have gradually financed their own demise.[73]

▼

The Guarantee Fund, created in 1854, is another example of Heydt's attempts to expand the power of the Railroad Fund. With the fund's running account fully committed, Heydt turned to the new possibilities created by the extra-dividends. Using the extra-dividends of the Cologne-Minden and the Upper Silesian railways, Heydt created a sinking fund to enable these private railways to raise share-capital to build lines that were originally part of his rejected building schemes in 1852: the Oberhausen-Arnheim, the Sieg-Ruhr line, the Breslau-Posen-Glogau line, the Deutz-Giessen-Frankfurt a.M., and the Rhine bridge at Cologne.[74] In addition to acting as collateral for stock issue, the Guarantee Fund also functioned as the subsidy fund that backed minimum dividend rates on the stock.

By agreeing to the terms of Heydt's Guarantee Fund, the Cologne-Minden Railway received the charters to build the bridge and three lines in the Rhineland and Westphalia. The company agreed to channel to the Guarantee Fund an annual sum of 50,000 thalers from its net profits, including a portion of its own stock dividends from 1854. In addition, the company contributed the one-time sum of 100,000 thalers, while the city of Cologne and the Rhenish Railway—two clear beneficiaries of the bridge—donated a combined sum of 500,000 thalers. This money was collected in one interest-bearing account, a money pool that enabled the company to issue new series of stock worth over thirty million thalers. The government administered this account, assuring investors their dividends and guaranteeing the Cologne-Minden Railway that the government could always raise a minimum of 300,000 thalers for such needs. It further promised to suspend its reinvestment of Cologne-Minden stock and channel its dividends into building the bridge (the state owned one-seventh of the company's original common stock purchased in 1842). The account, according to the contract, would last until the lines were constructed and the capital for the bridge was amortized. The account could be dismantled after five successive years of profits fully covered the annual interest payments.[75] The same conditions were applied to the Upper Silesian Railway for the building of the Breslau-Posen-Glogau line, which in turn supported 12,250,000 thalers in stock issue.[76]

The Guarantee Fund typified Heydt's administrative and financial talents. Even before the Landtag had approved the Railroad Tax, Heydt had devised a shrewd scheme to put those tax revenues to immediate action under his auspices. Hardly a minor account, the Guarantee Fund summoned to life fifty-one million thalers of railroad securities over the course of the 1850s.[77]

Heydt's resolve to use private companies so readily, and not to persevere with a state program, bespoke a change in attitude, yet his strategy with the assets belied the spirit of cooperation. He secured from the Cologne-Minden Railway, for example, the right to purchase the Oberhausen-Arnheim branch line at any time. In 1857–58 Heydt also sought to revise the contractual agreement with the railway companies to aid state ownership. He proposed to dissolve the independent status of the Guarantee Fund and transfer its assets—mostly in the form of company stock—to the state treasury, while keeping the subsidy pledge intact. The "increasing demands of the general treasury" justified the move, Heydt wrote to the governor of the Rhenish province. The same memorandum, however, revealed that Heydt also planned to use its assets to acquire greater blocks of stock: "The additional purchase of Cologne-Minden stock for the Guarantee Fund . . . would accelerate the means of transferring the property of the railway over to the state." [78] In addition to an increased stock portfolio, Heydt wrote to Bodelschwingh, the transfer would also give the Railroad Fund's new revenues between 550,000 and 900,000 thalers.[79]

The Upper Silesian Railway's management, which had just been replaced by the government in a controversial takeover in 1857, agreed to this proposal. As Heydt predicted, the Cologne-Minden directors rejected it.[80]

▼

The Legacy Fund (*Legatenfonds*) also demonstrates the lengths to which Heydt went to find money for the Railroad Fund's projects. Although the use of this fund spanned three decades, its story in connection with the Railroad Tax and Guarantee Fund underscores Heydt's resolve to accumulate capital for his railroad projects. The fund derived from the private estate of Friedrich Wilhelm III. In 1840, he bequeathed one million thalers on his deathbed to a special account to finance the building of a railway from Halle to Cassel to the western provinces.[81] Although initially hostile to railroads, the Hohenzoller had finally recognized the military importance of a railroad connecting Berlin, Halle, and the western provinces via Cassel. The hilly terrain around Cassel and the lack of investors prevented the construction of a direct Halle-Cassel line. Consequently, in the mid-forties, the fund's executor, Baron von Alvensleben, in cooperation with the state ministry, had invested the money in two railways: 810,000 thalers in the Thuringian Railway, a line that approached Cassel through a circuitous southern route (Halle, Merseburg, Leipzig, Erfurt, Gotha); and 190,000 thalers in the Cologne-Minden-Thuringian Railway, whose rails extended from Hamm to the eastern border of Westphalia in Paderborn. This last line, burdened with outstanding debts and not yet turning a profit, was bought by the state in 1849 and renamed the Westphalian Railway. It immediately saddled the Railroad Fund with its losses.

Because the terms of the Legacy Fund never explicitly stated the destination of its investment dividends from the Thuringian Railway, Heydt claimed them for the Railroad Fund. In 1850 the trade minister squeezed 31,310 thalers of back interest payments from the very reluctant, financially troubled directors of the Thuringian Railway.[82] The money went directly to the Westphalian Railway. After 1852, the Legacy Fund's administration was transferred from the finance ministry to the trade ministry, thus allowing Heydt greater flexibility in supervising the properties of the Railroad Fund. The dividends from 1852 (39,200 thalers), for example, were invested in Aachen-Düsseldorfer bonds, a railway administered and subsidized by the state.[83] By 1857, the trade ministry had channeled over 215,000 thalers of Legacy Fund earnings into stock acquisitions.[84]

Several parties contested the Legacy Fund's jurisdiction and use. In December 1849 the directors of the Thuringian Railway lodged a protest with the Hohenzollern house—the king and his three brothers, Princes Wilhelm, Carl, and Albrecht. The directors claimed that the entire fund should be invested in their railway. The Hohenzollern princes rejected this demand (21 January 1850), but they complicated matters by upholding the company's ancillary claim that the interest from the 810,000 thalers of Thuringian stock should be reinvested in the railway.[85]

Heydt disregarded the Hohenzollern decision and continued to use the interest as he saw fit. When prevailed upon to defend his recalcitrance to the king in March 1853, Heydt maintained that the Legacy Fund should hold to its "original intention" and finance the quickest route from Halle to the western provinces. For this reason, he wrote, the Railroad Fund was entitled to the interest from the Legacy Fund. The best route, he believed, was one north of Cassel that could connect with the Westphalian Railway. Such a line would give greater economic importance to the state railway and cancel the Thuringian Railway's future claims for remuneration. Satisfied with Heydt's arguments, the king issued a decree (4 April 1853) denying the company's claim to the interest. The railway consequently paid 40,000 thalers to the state treasury, with which the Railroad Fund acquired securities.[86]

Heydt's victory over the Legacy Fund's management was short-lived. Two years later (June 1856), the Hohenzollern princes submitted a long protest to King Friedrich Wilhelm IV about the use of the fund. They demanded that the comptroller of the Hohenzollern entailed estate (*Fideikommis*) manage the account and its income. The king asked his ministers to review the matter. Because the question was a financial and legal matter, the key opinions were those of Finance Minister Bodelschwingh and Justice Minister Ludwig Simons, and both rejected the princes' claim. Caught between his cabinet and his family, the king turned to the crown's lawyer, whose recommendation favored the princes. On 25 March 1857 the king, after a long delay, decreed in favor of his brothers: the interest earned from the 810,000 thalers was to be supervised by the family comptroller. The cabinet, not accustomed to the king's independence, petitioned Friedrich Wilhelm to repeal the decision two months later, but the king refused. On 14 July 1857, the funds were transferred.[87]

Heydt, however, was not ready to acquiesce in this royal decision. After Prince-Regent Wilhelm assumed governing responsibilities from Friedrich Wilhelm in 1858, Heydt resubmitted his claim to the money. Simons backed the trade minister in another written opinion (*Votum*), but Robert von Patow, who had replaced Bodelshwingh as finance minister in the New Era cabinet, decided he had nothing against the standing agreement. The staunchest opposition came from Ludwig von Massow, minister of Hohenzollern house affairs, who told Heydt that it was futile to seek a cabinet vote. Although the cabinet did not deliberate on the issue, the prince-regent nonetheless agreed in November to review the matter. As he was one of the original parties in the

royal protest, Wilhelm's opinion was not surprising: he supported the standing decision. A second edict (11 November 1859) defeated Heydt's plan.[88]

With characteristic tenacity, Heydt persisted. He had earmarked this
money to help fund preliminary work on a line between Halle and Cassel via
Nordhausen, which offered a drastic shortcut over other options. He hoped,
furthermore, this line would be state-owned.[89] In January 1860 he presented
an obscure interpretation to the king: the royal rescript, he said, had established the "material settlement," but it could not be considered a "final, legal
settlement." Moreover, Heydt conferred with Patow about negotiating a cash
settlement with the princes' comptroller. If the Hohenzollerns were set on
controlling the interest, he wrote, they should be prepared to pay a fixed sum
to the state treasury as a kind of tax.[90] This proposal fell on deaf ears, as did
Heydt's idea of funding a state line. The new executor of the fund, von Uhden
(Alvensleben died in 1858), told Heydt that a state rail built with Legacy Fund
money "could not be allowed," for Friedrich Wilhelm III had only envisioned
a private enterprise.[91]

Heydt haggled with the royal house until the end of his tenure as trade
minister (March 1862), at which time no decision had been reached. Eventually, in 1863, a private railway (Magdeburg-Leipzig) received the concession
to build the line and, with Heydt gone, the Hohenzollern house minister suggested that the finance ministry take over the administration of the stock and
interest. Ironically, Bodelschwingh, who returned as finance minister in September 1862, had to refuse. The test of constitutional principle between the
parliament and the crown over the army bill had produced a budgetless government, and the treasury did not have the authority to effect the transfer
of funds.[92]

The dispute over the control of the Legacy Fund was not, comparatively,
a major financial issue. Nonetheless, Heydt's struggle with the Prussian royal
house sheds light on his determination throughout the 1850s to find capital
wherever possible to maintain the state's role as promoter and owner of railroads. Not content with the fund's limits, Heydt elasticized its legal, budgetary parameters through the creation of discrete accounts within the fund. The
Railroad Tax, the Guarantee Fund, and the Legacy Fund all served the function of accelerating the fund's acquisition of private railroads.

▼

It was clear by 1854 that Heydt needed supplementary income to maintain
the state's bid for leadership. By 1853, the Railroad Fund's debts exceeded the
legal limit of its expenditure. Rather than trim back state railway construction,
Heydt disregarded the law limiting the Railroad Fund's annual expenditure to

two million thalers. In the four years from 1853 through 1856, Bodelschwingh, in one of a series of critical memoranda, estimated that the fund's budgetary limit was exceeded by the cumulative sum of 1,366,000 thalers.[93] This figure did not include other debts that Heydt should have stated in his budget. The 952,950 thalers earned by the Lower Silesian–Mark Railway between 1853 and 1857, for example, were never included in the formal budget, although they made up part of the fund.[94]

Heydt further violated budgetary agreements by failing to transfer all profits of state-administered and state-owned railways to the general treasury. Although the 1849 loan allowed him to use profits (temporarily) from the three lines it funded (the Eastern, Westphalian, and Saarbrückener railways), Heydt also used profits from others. In 1856 he authorized the sale of one million thalers of Berg-Mark Railway stock and appropriated the money for the fund's payment schedule in 1857. Similarly, the finance ministry challenged the legality of the trade ministry's use of state railroad profits to cover the additional construction costs of the Münster-Rheine-Osnabrück line, which had swelled to 1,226,755 thalers.[95] A 45,000 thaler discrepancy in Eastern Railway profits that failed to reach the treasury also aroused the attention of the finance ministry.[96] During the mid-1850s, Heydt's budget was easily double the permissible limit.[97] The finance ministry's concern over such sums was understandable: it was in dire need of budget-balancing revenues. Whereas the state budget ballooned over one hundred million marks between 1848 and 1856, the tax yield rose 10.5 million thalers in the corresponding time span to net fifty-seven million thalers.[98] Heydt, however, had his own ambitions and thus his own debts.

Heydt's problem with debt perhaps explains his attempt in 1854 to stretch the fund's spending power with unorthodox financial maneuvers. In an attempt to liquefy assets to attain the greatest amount of capital to cover burgeoning railroad construction costs, Heydt made inquiries in March 1854 with the Frankfurt bankers M. Bethmann and M. A. Rothschild and the Amsterdam banker W. Bischoffsheim regarding a *Depôtgeschäft*, a personally tailored stock-based loan. He wished to sell one of these banks two million thalers of railroad securities at a quote above the market price, which he would repurchase by the end of the year for an agreed upon premium. All three banks declined the offer.[99] The negotiations failed because Heydt wanted until the end of the year to repurchase the stocks (eight months), whereas these banks only allowed three to six months for such deposits. Heydt also wanted to discount the securities at a quote of 107.5, which (although under the market price) these bankers found too high for the sum of money in question. The other crucial question for the Frankfurt bankers was the exchange rate between gulden and thalers; curiously, Heydt refused to cite a specific rate.

The trade ministry's usual banks of business, the Prussian Bank and the

Seehandlung, were not asked, and Heydt requested from the private bankers complete confidentiality. Clearly, Heydt was undertaking a risky and unconventional deal without the knowledge of other ministers. Bodelschwingh would most likely never have approved the undertaking, owing to both the uncertainty in financial markets caused by the Crimean War and the unconventional nature of Heydt's wheeling and dealing.

To the finance ministry's principal accusation of exceeding the budget by over a million thalers, Heydt answered with silence. Previous rebukes had shown that Heydt was not shy in justifying his position vigorously—when defensible. Most likely Heydt knew that Bodelschwingh was right, but he also knew that neither the lower nor the upper house had yet exerted any strict controls on his administration and that he had greater support in the cabinet than did Bodelschwingh.[100] His decision to ignore the law limiting the size and function of the Railroad Fund for four straight years is telling of his willingness to overlook any legal control impeding what he believed to be the best interests of the trade ministry. How serious was such an action? By the standards of his peers in the cabinet (who saw the constitution on which they took oaths as an elastic entity), Heydt's disregard of the law was probably not perceived as criminal or worthy of dismissal. Yet deputies and liberal journalists, in view of wanton neglect of budgetary constraints, acquired an increasingly critical view.

After 1855, the question of the Railway Fund became bound up with the larger issue of parliamentary control of the budget. The conflation of the two issues was partly by design. Bodelschwingh, frustrated with his lack of power to control Heydt, encouraged a more critical posture on the budget from the lower house. In January 1855, he engineered enough votes on the right to put two critical liberals on the budget committee: Robert von Patow, the former trade minister of 1848, and Ludwig Kühne, the tax specialist.[101] In the same month, Bodelschwingh also proposed to Heydt to dissolve the fund and transfer its assets to the finance ministry—in vain. That the finance minister resorted to parliamentary stratagems to influence cabinet policy suggests his relative isolation in the cabinet and inability to rouse his colleagues to act. (It further shows the growing role of parliament in Prussian policy making, even for conservative ministers such as Bodelschwingh.) He had long been concerned with the trade ministry's railroad debts and its liberal spirit with dividend subsidies, a financial obligation that he believed was crushing the state.[102] The finance minister pointed up the Eastern Railway's confused budgets, late payments, and inefficient administration but received no support to rein in Heydt. Heydt did not deny that the general treasury paid the fund's overdrafts annually but avoided substantive debate by interpreting the finance ministry's memoranda as an affront to his person and authority.[103] Heydt seemed to brush aside Bodelschwingh's persistent criticisms easily, taking months to reply, which perhaps explains why Bodelschwingh appealed to parliamentary factions.

Bodelschwingh's move had its desired effect. In April 1855 the budget committee of the lower house presented revisions to a government bill regarding an additional loan to complete the Eastern Railway and construct the Münster-Rheine-Emshafen line. The trade ministry asked for 4,309,000 thalers. Heydt promised the budget committee that the Railroad Fund's means were "fully sufficient" to meet the payments on a new loan, which, against the backdrop of the fund's deficits since 1853, was a bald-faced lie.[104] The committee recommended that the sum be reduced to 3,976,000. Although a minor monetary reduction, the intervention itself was significant. The committee changed the route of the Münster-Emshafen line favored by the ministry, shaving off a Prussian mile (7.4 km) to cut costs, and made other minor revisions with the Eastern Railway. It rejected Heydt's plan to amortize the debt at an unfixed rate, insisting instead that the loan should be repaid in 1 percent installments like all other railroad loans.[105] It further advised that "if the government's proposal is accepted, then the ongoing state construction and subsidization of railroads must be postponed entirely for a number of years." [106] The committee recognized that the fiscal limits of the fund were saturated and announced the lower house's unwillingness to approve future loans.

This new regulatory role galled Heydt. "I mind very much," Heydt wrote the king two days later, "that the houses have intervened for the first time in questions of bookkeeping." It was indeed questionable whether the Landtag had the jurisdiction to concern itself with cabinet decisions, "but with a railway over fifty miles long [370 km] one could hardly contest the right. Where that right begins and where it ends is difficult to determine." [107] Unwillingly Heydt conceded that confusion existed between the executive and legislative branches regarding the control over government spending.

In the same session of the lower house, Ludwig Kühne, modifying his 1853 proposal, submitted an additional motion to suspend temporarily the fund's stock-acquisition program (funded by the Railroad Tax) and channel its profits into paying this new debt.[108] Kühne, a gifted speaker who knew the value of wit and anecdote, offered compelling reasons to abandon the plan for a state monopoly of railways. Why, he asked, should the government undertake the financially impossible task of purchasing all of Prussia's railways — priced at 180 million thalers — when other pressing debts were at hand and when private railways continued to reduce rates and expand Prussia's lines? To adhere reverently to the letter of the 1838 law, he argued, was foolish. Kühne reminded the lower house that he had chaired the state commission in 1838 that had written the Railroad Law. He was well aware of the law's premises but noted that in 1838 there was only one mile of steam-driven railway on the European continent. Subsequent experience showed that state intervention was unnecessary.[109] The lower house rejected Kühne's amendment but accepted the committee's proposals to alter the terms of the loan.[110]

Thus, in spite of the overwhelming victory of government parties in the election of 1855 (which installed the so-called *Landratskammer*),[111] liberals kept the budget question alive as a political issue. Since 1849, industrial and commercial interests had objected to the disproportionate tax burden placed on the Rhine and Westphalian provinces, the continued tax exemptions of the landed nobility in the east, and the increasing size of the budget. According to Patow in 1857, it was the liberals alone who consistently motioned for greater control of taxes and the budget.[112] After 1855, however, the liberals found unexpected support on this issue from conservatives.

Ludwig von Gerlach, the clarion of the right, called upon the Landtag to unite the Prussian virtue of thrift with the constitutional regime in a forceful speech in the lower house on 22 February 1856.[113] He introduced a new finance doctrine designed to curb the government's appetite for centralization and bureaucratization by refusing all new proposals for taxes. The move, he wrote to his brother Leopold, "was the only *practical* way to make the houses an instrument of the estates." [114] Exercising budgetary control was one element in Gerlach's larger political strategy, which planned that conservatives should not let the constitution perish through inactivity and rejection but, rather, through constant use and practical application transform it into a conservative tool.[115] Meeting with Gerlach days afterward (27 February), Bodelschwingh supported the new tactic. Only the king's civil cabinet or the houses, he told Gerlach, could begin to monitor the budget and dissolve the trade ministry.[116]

By February 1856 the array of Heydt's critics and opponents had reached formidable proportions. They included liberals and conservatives in both houses of the Landtag who were concerned about the condition of the Prussian budget, the financial manipulations of the minister of trade, and his continued efforts to nationalize the Prussian railway system. But they were not alone in their concerns. The Prussian cabinet was itself divided in its support of Heydt's activities; the collegial system worked poorly when confronted by a man of his temperament. Bodelschwingh would even have dissolved the ministry of trade in order to be rid of him and his schemes. But Heydt had one advantage; his opponents were too varied in social station, economic views, and political purposes to unite against him.

Gerlach's initial tactic was to oppose the extension of a tax surcharge presented in the government's 1856 budget. In May 1854 the houses had approved a 25 percent surcharge on the income and meal and slaughter taxes and extended it to the fiscal year of 1855. In spite of Gerlach's threat, this extension was eventually passed,[117] but both the upper and lower houses warned the executive not to consider the surcharge again. The lower advised a thorough reform of state finance to streamline expenditure. The upper, more concretely, announced that only revenues already approved by law would be accepted in the next budget; all new forms of revenue would have to be approved separately by special legislation. The resolutions of both houses pressured the cabinet to come to a definite settlement on finances. If the cabinet was to avoid a greater conflict with parliament, it had to secure state revenues already approved and, furthermore, maximize their profitability.[118]

The new conservative position posed greater problems in the legislative session of 1856/57, for the government sought new revenues of 4,080,000 thalers for an army reform, which proposed to extend military service from 2.5 to 3 years. In addition, the revenues would raise the salaries of civil servants.[119] The debate on the budget went on for months and marked the "highpoint and turning point of the [reactionary] era." [120] The protracted debate caused Ludwig Gerlach to speculate on cabinet changes and bemoan the "power and popularity the leftists — Auerswald, Patow, etc. — possess with their edifying principles of government and the chance they have to take the helm." [121] The "edifying principles" Gerlach feared were the left's attempt to transform the budget debate into a constitutional reform providing for a more precise definition of the lower house's role in the budget. A similar campaign had failed by a narrow margin in 1850/51. It was the same issue that eventually turned the army reform of Wilhelm I into a constitutional crisis in 1862.[122]

Both houses rejected the raise in government officials' salaries. There was little objection to reforming the army, but the question of who and what to tax was problematic. Fiercely protecting its own material interests, the upper house advised raising the levy that pressed against the poor the most: the salt tax. The second house, however, proposed using the Railroad Tax to finance the army reform. The latter's motion was worked out by its finance committee, a twenty-one member body controlled by liberals but chaired by Ludwig von Gerlach. For the liberal faction, Kühne stated: "If the house recognizes the necessity of three-year service and salary raises, then I do not doubt that the trade minister and the government will be willing to suspend the stock acquisition and apply the tax to more urgent needs." [123] Clearly Kühne strove to use the Railroad Tax as a bargaining chip to negotiate control over the budget between the executives and the legislature. "The commission," reported a member who supported the government, "has declared war." [124]

The plenum debate on modifying the Railroad Tax to alleviate the budget deficit focused on whether such a move was legal. Some argued that suspension of the stock-acquisition program would transform it into a commercial tax, because the revenues would flow to the state treasury like any other levy, but the 1838 law forbade commercial tax on railways. Others proclaimed their freedom from stockholders and commercial companies and their right to change the tax. The debate ended in stalemate. The lower house watered down the amendment by introducing a new motion that proposed to suspend the stock-acquisition program temporarily—until finances were put in order. This proposition was voted down by the committee itself and also defeated in the plenum, 168 to 130. The upper house, however, approved the bill, 62 to 17. The proposal's mixed support allowed the cabinet to disregard it, but the debate nonetheless registered changing views on the fund's status.[125] Thus, when Bodelschwingh renewed his complaints to Heydt in April 1857, he told the trade minister that he should not count on next year's funds for railroads. The debate on taxes in the Landtag and its calls for reductions could "not ensure with full certainty that the fund will remain in its present form." [126]

Parliamentary criticism of government spending, administrative inefficiency, and new taxes prompted Bodelschwingh in the summer of 1857 to draft a memorial that exhorted the king to reform state finances. Bodelschwingh's report, which received the influential backing of Privy Councilor Marcus Niebuhr, prompted the king to appoint an advisory committee to consider such a reform. This "State-Council Commission" was composed of eight men drawn from the privy council and parliament. Among them were Ludwig von Gerlach, the new critic of state budgets, and Kühne, the longtime opponent of state railways. The king asked the council to address three specific questions with regard to the railroad industry: whether enlargement of the state's railroad network was politically advisable; whether Prussia's state and private railroads could maintain interest payments; and whether the advantages of further railroad acquisition outweighed the burden of additional railroad bonds. In addition, the commission should address organizational improvements in the postal and mining administrations, both of which belonged to Heydt's sphere of administration.[127] The initial report and proposed agenda placed the blame for the state's financial problems at Heydt's door. "When one reads Bodelschwingh's very interesting and thorough finance report," wrote General Leopold von Gerlach, close adviser to the king, "it is clear that Heydt's actions are very destructive." [128]

The king's call for an advisory council produced a written protest from the cabinet, stating that the move undermined its authority. "Certainly it does not harm you," Friedrich Wilhelm replied, "when I want to listen to other men over an important matter." In a sharper tone the king reminded his ministers, "This concerns something that stands higher than the authority of the cabinet: my responsibility as the king of this land." [129] The king's independent course of action underscores the historic concern for state debt that weighed on the Hohenzoller, the disregard for correct governmental procedure that characterized his whole reign, and the degree to which the parliament and public discussion had influenced the court. But it further confirmed the king's strategy of encouraging actions that weakened the governing strength of the cabinet. For this reason, Bismarck noted, the king enjoyed seeing the houses reject the government's tax bill.[130]

Before the commission convened to discuss the printed agenda, Heydt offered his resignation to the king on 8 September 1857.[131] The creation of the commission and its formal agenda insulted Heydt; he believed the king no longer trusted him.[132] Heydt probably tendered his resignation to force the king to choose between the commission and himself. As was so often the case with ministerial resignations, the king rebuffed it, telling Heydt that he had "indefinitely postponed" the convening of the commission. This was a political victory for Heydt but nonetheless a qualified one. The incident revealed the uncertainty of the king and his advisers over Heydt's railroad policies. Because the commission was suspended, not dissolved, it could be reconvened at any time and thus be used as a mechanism to rein in Heydt's activities.

While the court reassessed the desirability of state railways, the liberal press also questioned the putative advantages of state ownership. The growing burden of railways on the government budget was a frequent complaint. "The Prussian debt has nearly doubled since 1848," wrote one critic of the debt in 1856, "and it is mainly because of the cost of the state railways." [133] Equally newsworthy was the government's claim that the state could offer cheaper prices and freight rates than private railways. The *National-Zeitung* reminded its readers that Heydt was responsible for making the Westphalian Railway cost prohibitive for the working class by abolishing the fourth class.[134] The newspaper also asked why the state raised the coal tariffs on the Upper Silesian Railway and the Wilhelmsbahn after taking them over. Earlier the trade ministry had imposed the "one penny tariff" on private railways but now did not adhere to its own rule. Long editorials strove to demonstrate that, although Prussia's state system could offer fair rates, it could not offer better rates.[135] Practice showed that only the most efficient state railways (i.e., former private railways such as the Upper and Lower Silesian railways) matched the low costs and cheap rates of private railways. But even in these cases, it was questionable whether state railways were cheaper or more advantageous; such performance was based on borrowed money, whose interest burdened the taxpayer.[136] Equally important, free-trade publicists exposed the fallacy of state railroad "profits." Indeed, state commissioners boasted millions of thalers in gross profits, but, when tallying the costs of construction, administration, and finance charges, they never ceased to use red ink.[137]

The development of public criticism against state railway management grew with the bankruptcy of the Wilhelmsbahn railroad in 1857. As already seen in Chapter 3, the business community blamed company directors, but the state railroad commission also received condemnation. The state's regulatory role and its overall inability to supervise the industry were severely criticized. Such grievances left the minister and his quest for a state monopoly open to further criticisms.

Not surprisingly, the question of the Railroad Tax was once again raised in the Landtag in 1858. The issue of legality, which had preoccupied the houses a year earlier, was pushed aside to discuss the primary question of state ownership of railroads. The lower house's new budget committee voted 14 to 13 to suspend the stock-acquisition program. The plenum voted the measure down, but the upper house again approved the suspension. The bill also included a warning to the cabinet that the upper house opposed the raising of the maximum two million thaler limit on the Railroad Fund.[138] The budget committees of both upper and lower houses submitted stronger recommendations to the cabinet than they had in the previous session. Although this bill, too, was unsuccessful, a sea change was evident. As one newspaper remarked in March 1858, "We believe it is safe to say that, when similar conditions arise, that is, when the government demands new revenues, the result will be different." [139]

Following the two legislative sessions that debated the Railroad Fund so thoroughly, the cabinet met in April 1858 to review its position, and on 1 May summarized its deliberation to the king. The cabinet noted the waning interest in the state ownership of railways, though it believed the Landtag's proposal to suspend further state ownership was only a temporary measure until the financial situation improved. In recounting the Landtag's position, the cabinet stated that the two houses could not justify expending funds on a project deemed dispensable when money was lacking to settle pressing, urgent needs of the state. Because tariffs were low and industry and commerce prospering, the Landtag reasoned, there was no great need for further state ownership. Hence, "whether it is desirable for the state to take over all railways and, with it, their attending problems is still very dubious." [140] The last two legislative sessions had questioned the logic and rationale behind state ownership. The conjunction of a prosperous economy with the rising popularity of laissez-faire capitalism among Landtag members prompted the cabinet to reconsider its position on railroad acquisition and ownership.

Heydt dodged this central issue and defended the acquisition program as a legal obligation: it must be pursued out of fairness to railways, which benefited from the stability provided by state stock holdings, and to the stockholder, who was guaranteed stocks over par. Only the directors opposed state ownership, Heydt claimed, for it was in their personal interest to keep the lucrative business for themselves. Further, if the stock-acquisition program was suspended, the Railroad Tax would act as a commercial tax, and the state would be obliged to compensate all stockholders for the tax revenues. Exhibiting a new sensitivity to legal commitments, Heydt maintained that a commercial tax was unjustified, if not illegal.[141]

Ministers Simons and Bodelschwingh dissented from this opinion. The state, they claimed, had the right to change laws, and specific passages in the 1838 law (paragraphs 6, 39, and 49) gave the government the right to alter the law to suit the times. Stockholders were aware that conditions can change and, therefore, such narrow legal objections ought to be overruled.

Bodelschwingh offered a fuller critique of state ownership. Competition kept down rates more than a state monopoly ever could. Full state ownership, furthermore, would only make sense if profits exceeded the costs of interest and amortization payments — "how seldom is this the case." Moreover, Bodelschwingh argued, the process of acquiring railroads in this manner was bad business. The state had artificially propped up stock prices since 1842, and when it came time to acquire the remaining railways (and indemnify stockholders) the government would pay extremely inflated prices. It was also unwise for the state to be the sole owner of railways; if destroyed in war, they would have to be replaced entirely at state expense. Bodelschwingh also noted that most had neglected to factor the increased number of civil-servant salaries into the price that would accompany state ownership. And although others were sanguine about the "improved" budget of 1858, the state would still run a deficit of over eleven million thalers.[142]

Bodelschwingh's opinion was the sole vote against sustaining the acquisition program.[143] Although Simons backed Bodelschwingh on the legal right of the state to change the law, he sided with Heydt's philosophy of a state monopoly. The remaining members of the cabinet believed the advantages of state railroads were greater. Their theses were derived from earlier statements and tended to stray from concrete argumentation. The military importance of railroads remained incontestable. Although freight rates were low, they could still be lower. Prussia should also not deny itself the advantage of this lucrative source of income, especially when bordering states enjoyed this privilege: "How hopeful Prussia's future appears, if the present system is consistently and uninterruptedly carried out. For Prussia will end up in possession of its railways much earlier than its neighbors." Finally, the majority opinion noted that it was chimerical to accept the Landtag's suggestion for a temporary measure — such remedies always remain permanent.[144]

Bodelschwingh's written opinion against the Railroad Fund was his last as finance minister. In October 1858 the New Era cabinet took over, and Robert von Patow assumed control of the finance ministry. As a former minister in the liberal cabinet of 1848, an opposition leader against Manteuffel in the lower house, a critical voice on the budget committee in 1856/57, and a confirmed free-trade advocate, Patow opposed Heydt's policy with even more verve than his predecessor.[145] The views he shared with Rhenish liberals in the lower house and with Kühne on allocating the Railroad Tax to the general treasury ensured private railroad interests a voice in the cabinet.[146]

Heydt, undaunted by either the new appointment or the near-dissolution of the fund, continued to maneuver for greater spending power. Seeking immediate control over the new minister, Heydt submitted to Patow a plan to appropriate all railroad profits for the fund in addition to the annual two million thalers. Aggrandizing the fund's revenues, he claimed, was legal. His tactical move turned on the pivotal phrase in the 1838 law that stated the fund must "not be allowed to exceed" two million thalers. Whereas in the past the phrase had always been interpreted as the ceiling for the fund's activities, Heydt now proposed that the phrase referred only to the finance ministry's contribution, not the fund's budget. The conventional reading set a fixed, concrete limit on the Railway Fund; Heydt's interpretation left room for additional spending power. Patow's response was complete rejection. The fund's aims, he wrote to Heydt, no longer fitted financial conditions: "It seems to be the right time to dissolve the Fund . . . the Railroad Fund is no longer reconcilable within the principles of an ordered budget."[147] Patow rejected Heydt's claim that the king allowed him to manage the fund alone and announced his intention to wrest railroad profits from Heydt's accounts for the treasury.[148] The New Era cabinet thus continued the struggle over the fund between the trade and finance ministries. The debate, however, had one marked difference: Patow, unlike Bodelschwingh, had more support than Heydt in the New Era cabinet.

The continuing tendency of the government toward budget deficits magnified the Landtag's scrutiny of the fund. Recognizing the houses' reluctance to approve new taxes and the government's need to reapportion revenues already approved in the annual budget, Heydt agreed to surrender the extra-dividends of one railway—the Upper Silesian—to the general treasury in February 1859.[149] The piecemeal reform was not enough, however. In March, the lower house reviewed the government's railroad budget, discussed the principles of state involvement in railroads, and debated the dissolution of the fund.[150] Kühne, Leonor Reichenheim, and Karl Milde, all liberals, led the attack against the government role in railroad ownership. Again Kühne proposed his amendment to disband the stock-acquisition program. The "stultifying state omnipotence" with its "overweening bureaucratic influence," the *Berliner Börsen-Zeitung* reported, was the liberals' salient reason for abolishing the stock-acquisition program.[151] Lorenz Stein, a national economist, and Karl Overweg, a Westphalian protectionist with iron interests, defended the state, and Heydt fended off Kühne by declaring to the house that the cabinet was unanimously behind its preservation.[152] Indeed, commented the news-

paper, as long as there was no outstanding need in the budget to justify sus-
pending the fund, the cabinet had the freedom to ignore both public opinion,
which for a long time opposed state railways, and the houses' proposals to
suspend it. But when the need arose to raise money from either a tax or from
the fund, the newspaper predicted, the fund would go.[153]

The occasion for its dissolution arose two months later in May 1859. In
response to the war between Austria and the coalition of France and Sardinia,
Prussia prepared for mobilization and armed mediation. Money was needed
and, not surprisingly, the first source Finance Minister Patow turned to was
the Railroad Tax. On 5 May 1859, Patow, with patriotic flourishes, asked the
lower house to change the Railroad Tax of 1853, dissolve the Railroad Fund,
and channel its revenues into paying for mobilization.[154] Significantly, the bill
was not presented as a temporary expedient but as a permanent statute. Both
houses overwhelmingly approved the bill, which was enacted into law.

▼

The imperatives of foreign policy thus settled the fate of the Railroad Fund.
The exigencies of the 1859 mobilization, however, should not deflect our attention from the longer history behind the fund's dissolution and the debate
over its utility.[155] By March 1859, opposition to the fund had developed so
strongly that, even without the Prussian mobilization, the fund would eventually have perished. The growing belief that the "natural laws" of capitalism
were a far better regulator of prosperity than state intervention enabled both
journalists and liberal politicians to criticize the logic of state railways. Since
1855 the Railroad Tax and the special status of the fund had become a central
issue for liberals in the effort of parliament to enforce parliamentary budget rights. The liberal election victory of 1858 combined with the ministerial
appointment of Patow, the laissez-faire advocate, enabled the protracted agitation for private railways to attain its goal.

Parliamentary procedure in Prussia had some worth for business interests. The attack on the proposal for a state railway monopoly by the liberal
press and the opposition to it in both houses did eventually affect government
policy. Parliament, press, and cabinet combined to form one integrated discussion that forced resistant ministers to acquiesce.[156]

The policy reversal was an important victory for economic liberals. Saving Germany's largest capitalist market from state ownership augured a new
era of free-trade legislation and economic prosperity. Other legislation was
to follow in 1861 and 1862: the property tax on landed estates, the creation
of the commercial law book, the final abolition of the direction principle in

coal mining, and the commercial treaty with France in 1862. Such legislation addressed the new, growing needs of Prussia's business class and indicated that the Prussian establishment was undergoing change. Old and new elites searched for suitable terms on which to accommodate one another in the new society. But, as we have seen with the failed bid for a state monopoly in railroads, the process of reconciling the interests of a conservative government and the emerging elite of commerce and industry was anything but quick and easy. The Railroad Fund is one indication that the balance struck between old and new forces in the 1860s was a series of actions constituting a political process with a longer history.

CHAPTER SEVEN

▼

The Juste Milieu, *1857–1870*

The dissolution of the Railroad Fund in 1859 was not an isolated event but, rather, one element of larger policy modifications in the New Era. Saving Germany's largest capitalist market from state ownership augured a new era of free-trade legislation and economic prosperity. Other legislation followed that addressed the needs of Prussia's business class and indicated that the Prussian establishment was undergoing tangible change. Old and new elites searched for suitable terms to accommodate one another. The period 1858–66 is, in fact, a critical era in the sociopolitical formation of the entrepreneurial bourgeoisie. The business politics of large-scale industries played a key role in reconstituting the Prussian state, affecting both government policy and political liberalism. Although the decisive period of Prussian-German state building is often viewed as the years 1862–66—the years of the constitutional conflict and Bismarck's "revolution from above"—this interpretation, while valid, has little explanatory value for the social group of business elites whose relationship to the state was affected by their economic-political advances in the years of the New Era, 1858–62. These goals, first articulated in the *Vormärz* era and developed in the 1850s, centered on the creation of a *juste milieu* for a maturing capitalist class: a social-political atmosphere in which entrepreneurial elites saw their interests nurtured by the state. Entrepreneurs wanted not only to protect the expanding private sphere of the economy from government interference but also to preserve the state's traditional role in the economy in matters as yet beyond the reach of private capital.

Although the new political milieu after 1858 deserves emphasis explaining why the bourgeois business class came to support Prussian conservatism, this study avoids characterizing the New Era as a turning point or fundamental break in state policy. The New Era must be placed in the context of a complex, evolving relationship between government and business during the period 1830–70. This long-term, unspectacular process fits poorly with dramatic turning points and other narrative designs of political history. In rethinking the importance of the New Era, we should not place the accent on the newness of the New Era reforms; indeed, many of the reforms discussed below were haltingly initiated before and after 1848. Nonetheless, the New Era is significant because it was after 1858 that businessmen felt that the reform path of the last two decades had widened into a central avenue of state concern. The state's responsiveness in clearing obstacles to greater expansion and growth during the New Era brought to fruition the practical, concrete demands businessmen had articulated since the 1830s. There were, of course, many grievances still outstanding, but the incremental advances made by the business class toward assimilation into the Prussian establishment substantially explain why entrepreneurial opposition ebbed in 1862–63. The *juste milieu* of the New Era illuminates one key dimension of the multifaceted explanation regarding the collapse of the liberal parliamentary opposition in 1863–66.

The Depression of 1857–1859

Relations between capitalists and the Prussian government were affected significantly by the onset of a sharp downturn in the business cycle in 1857. For a brief period in the mid-1850s entrepreneurs displayed a willingness to abandon bureaucratic ties. The increase in businessmen's criticism of government actions after 1853 was approximately proportional to the health of the economy. The numerous private joint-stock and commandite banks founded in 1853–56 provided capital-hungry entrepreneurs with a fresh source of long-term financing free of government restrictions (see chap. 5). The door to entrepreneurial autonomy opened by a growing international financial network was soon closed by the depression of 1857–59. These new banking institutions might have ensured entrepreneurial independence from state economic policies in the next decade, but the 1857–59 depression reasserted the older pattern of negotiating with the state for financial and legislative aid.

In 1856 overproduction in both agriculture and manufacturing compounded by financial panic unleashed a chain of bank failures in the United States that spread to Europe by 1857. Prussia's and the Zollverein's newer industrial enterprises were not struck as hard as London's and Hamburg's older commercial networks (especially those in grain exports), but the impact of the business depression was nonetheless considerable.[1] The foreign trade of the Zollverein declined by 300 million marks in 1857–59; wholesale prices and stock quotations fell drastically; and the nominal value of the national wealth shrank by approximately 25 percent.[2] The war between Italy and Austria in 1859, and its ensuing diplomatic complications for all of Europe, prolonged the depression in commerce and production. The Prussian Bank's money supply in 1857–60 provides a reliable indication of the depression's persistent effect on economic growth. In 1857 the money supply stood at 889 million thalers, falling to 820 million in 1858, 815 in 1859, and hitting its low point of 766 in 1860.[3] By 1860 business optimism was evident once again, though raising capital for large-scale projects still remained difficult.[4] In April 1860, Rudolf Schramm could still write to F. W. König, a technical director of the Rhenish Railway, "In these times I believe you [when you write] that you are having difficulty to cover the colossal ongoing costs of construction." [5]

The onset of the first financial crisis of world capitalism enabled the Prussian state to emerge once again as a necessary participant in large-scale business. Under these circumstances Heydt reasserted state leadership in finance. Between November 1856 and February 1857 he lowered the discount rate from 7.5 to 4 percent and advanced loans to companies in need of capital. At the same time he banned the circulation of foreign currency in Prussia, introduced stricter measures to prevent railroad companies from floating loans without government authorization, and forbade the inclusion of future revenues in calculating assets for loan payments.[6] The economic crisis allowed the state to wield greater control over private business.

The 1857 economic crisis narrowed the options for large-scale capitalism. Money and confidence were scarce. Whereas 139 joint-stock companies had been formed in the Zollverein states in the years 1855–57, only 12 were chartered in 1857–59.[7] Business failures greatly curtailed commercial underwriting from joint-stock banks and public investment in the stock market. The depression prevented the joint-stock Darmstädter Bank and the commandite Diskonto Gesellschaft from pursuing their original aim: to supply pools of capital large enough to free German businessmen from restrictive government policies. After 1857 the new commercial banks sought safe investments, practicing conservative finance by taking refuge in state paper and loans. During the depression, the financiers of the new banks became part of the financial establishment of northern Germany known as the Prussian Consortium.

The consortium was a group of leading Prussian financiers, many of them railroad directors, who sporadically aided the Prussian state in raising money for the 1859 mobilization and the subsequent wars of unification. Here one sees evidence of the sea change that had occurred since the mid-1850s. The joint-stock and commandite commercial banks, once considered "French" devices inimical to Prussian state policy, were now included among the members of the financial establishment invited to raise capital for Prussia's bid to establish hegemony over northern Germany. But the consortium's early efficacy in financing bonds is often exaggerated: putting together the loan for mobilization in 1859 was faltering and uncertain. The attempt to float a multimillion thaler loan (which was initially set at ten but whose expansion to fifty million was foreseen) among selected German financiers in May 1859 did not produce a spectacular subscription.[8] The Frankfurt bankers, wrote Ludolf Camphausen, were "swamped in paper and stocks"; the Darmstädter Bank was "impotent and distressed to fill its own obligations"; and the Luxemburg Bank "also appears to have little capital at its disposal."[9] In view of the loan's precarious reception among German banks, Otto Camphausen, president of the Seehandlung, wished that "we could experiment with treasury notes, which would be preferable in the event of peace."[10] In the end, after refusals from London's Baring Bros., the government opted for a public subscription of a twenty-four million thaler loan at 5 percent, whose success surpassed the finance ministry's expectations.[11]

In spite of the depressed stock quotes and the disappearance of investment capital, the railroad industry in general survived the crash of 1857–59 in good condition. Railroad capitalization increased 38.7 percent, swelling from 273.25 million thalers in 1857 to 379 million thalers in 1860, an investment that expanded the Prussian rail network by 23.5 percent.[12] Hence, while the depression's bear market impinged on the plans of established railways to complete trunk lines and delayed the undertaking of new projects, railroad entrepreneurs spoke more of caution than of catastrophe in the depression of 1857–59. And, not surprisingly, railroads also used the depression to their advantage. The Rhenish, Cologne-Minden, and the Upper Silesian railways, for example, used the crash to postpone the construction of unprofitable lines that earlier state charters obliged them to build and, following the political shift in 1858, to extract better financial concessions from the government, such as the right to borrow against bonds and issue stock without the delay of formal state authorization.[13]

But such companies as the Rhenish, Cologne-Minden, Upper Silesian, and Wilhelmsbahn railways remained in a difficult position. All were committed to extending their lines, plans that required millions in future stock issues. For railroad businessmen the most salient feature of the depression was probably the continued dependency on state dividend guarantees. In absolute numbers, the state commitment to backing railroad issues grew by fifty million thalers. In 1860, 99.7 million thalers of the 286.75 million invested in Prussian private railways were guaranteed (34 percent); in 1863, 140.6 of 334.25 million (42 percent); and in 1866, 154.6 of 377.75 million (35 percent).[14] Although the state's actual payment to investors was comparatively small (5,039,329 thalers),[15] railroad entrepreneurs continued to use the mixed system's risk-free offer to investors for expansion in the 1860s, continuing a pattern of government-business relations established in the 1840s.

Placing new issues on the market was perceived by financiers to be hazardous. Abraham Oppenheim aptly summarized the financial market's condition in 1858: "The market still suffers from indigestion with old issues; the country only has enough capital for the completion of railroads already under construction." [16] To attract that capital (both in new issues and bonds) without driving down the value of stock demanded expertise. The attempt by the Wilhelmsbahn to do so failed dramatically, causing scandal, bankruptcy, and quick government intervention in 1857. The protocols of the Rhenish Railway during these years document efforts to effect a good placement, using to its advantage the experience of seasoned financiers, connections to banking circles, a first-rate network of domestic and international intelligence, and access to government officials.[17] Directors also employed the services of the press, which could bolster confidence in railroad stocks. To fight slumping quotes in October 1859, A. Oppenheim instructed Gerson Bleichröder to place an article in the *Berliner Börsen-Zeitung.* It "would simply say that, according to reliable reports, the directors of the Rhenish Railway do not presently consider issuing a new series of common stock; and such an act would not happen unless they could be placed over par." [18] Such tactics denoted the precarious state of high finance; railroads drew on all of their resources to stay afloat. An integral part of this resourcefulness was reaffirming ties to the Prussian state and its dividend guarantees, subventions, and loans.

Business Politics in the New Era

Although the depression reasserted state presence in large-scale capitalist enterprises, the political tenor of government-business relations differed significantly from the Manteuffel-Heydt era. Had there not been a change of government, the effect of the depression would have exacerbated the existing problems regarding the trade ministry's intrusive and imperious behavior and strengthened Heydt's hand in dominating the railroad business. But the prince's new cabinet put government-business relations in a new key, offering a more receptive ear to business. The political shift in Prussia after 1857 helped private enterprise. Upon assuming the governing duties from the ailing King Friedrich Wilhelm IV in 1858, Prince-Regent Wilhelm dismissed the conservative ministers of the king's cabinet, most visibly Otto von Manteuffel and Ferdinand von Westphalen, and inaugurated the so-called New Era. Prince Wilhelm's anti-reactionary views and his promise in 1858 to promote "wise legislation at home" and to support "unifying elements like the customs association" underscored his accommodating attitude toward unification and business needs.[19]

The crown prince's phrases, which pointed to a generous state policy for the upper middle classes, greatly appealed to businessmen whose pragmatic, moderate politics largely strove for progress in alignment with the Hohenzollern crown. In October 1858, Otto Camphausen, who hailed from Rhenish entrepreneurial wealth, wrote to his brother Ludolf in Cologne:

> On Oct. 26, 1858 I attended the swearing in of the country's leader, just as I did on Feb. 6, 1850. In 1850, I attended as a deputy of the lower house and rebellious councilor third class; now I took part as a loyal councilor first class and even a possible ministerial candidate. This time the act had something uncommonly captivating. The prince spoke plainly but with a dignified voice and conveyed to the world the feeling that such an oath was truly not meaningless, that the constitution had finally attained its true confirmation, and that we further stand on firm ground — as if the confusions of 1848 had never disturbed the path of legal development started in 1847.[20]

These words capture well the optimism of moderate liberals for the political era that lay ahead under the reign of Wilhelm. The prince-regent's views on constitutions and legislatures moved steadily to the right after 1858, but for the business community the *juste milieu* of establishing a legal economic framework that promoted capitalists' needs in the New Era remained throughout the 1860s. Although little political headway in constitutional liberalism was achieved in the years 1858–61, the legal and economic advances for the monied bourgeoisie in the New Era were many.

One immediate consequence of the New Era was a deluge of public criticism against Heydt and his economic policies during the 1850s.[21] In 1858 the *Berlin Börsen-Zeitung,* the major financial daily in Prussia, used the less restrictive censorship laws to denounce Prussian economic policy; its editorials urged the Prussian crown to dismiss Trade Minister August von der Heydt and to appoint ministers more responsive to the needs of capitalism.[22] Responding to reports that the prince would ask for resignations from Manteuffel's ministry, the criticism against Heydt sharpened. "We must," stated the newspaper, "unfortunately place in the foreground of our statement that the entire industrial and commercial estate, including those whose interests were directly served by Heydt, greet his resignation from office with genuine joy."[23] Without denying the expansion of the Prussian economy that occurred under Heydt's aegis, the newspaper questioned whether the prosperity should be ascribed to his influence: "We would not let the issue go unquestioned, whether all of this would not have developed to be larger and better without the special effect of Herr von der Heydt and whether his many measures had a harmful effect."[24]

During 1858 Westphalian, Rhenish, and Silesian businessmen bombarded the government with letters and petitions requesting Heydt's dismissal.[25] In the following year, H. F. L. Augustin, a director of the Berlin-Potsdam-

Magdeburg Railway, attacked Heydt in two long essays, charging the minister with gross governmental misconduct.[26] "In short," he concluded, "there is no sphere of business that he does not more or less rule and influence; he has the power to bless or punish any person who pursues a material interest." [27] Leonor Reichenheim, a parliamentary advocate of free trade, followed in 1860 with a pamphlet that denounced Heydt's continued defense of the 1849 commercial code, whose paternalistic laws restricted the free movement of labor (guilds) and the free association of commercial enterprises (joint-stock charters).[28] The Chamber of Deputies joined in to criticize Heydt's protracted role in Manteuffel's cabinet.[29] What surfaced after 1858 in the business world was not a defense of the trade ministry and its accomplishments but, rather, criticism of the heavy hand with which it regulated taxation, money supply, banking practices, coal mining, and the railroad industry. If the 1850s were an unproblematic period for capitalists, for whom Heydt acted as a governmental administrator for their industrial program,[30] then the enthusiasm with which businessmen, economic associations, and financial newspapers greeted the New Era is mystifying. Entrepreneurs, too, sought relief from the reactionary era.

When Heydt survived the purge of conservative ministers and remained as trade minister, business circles and their newspapers complained vociferously.[31] Heydt never recovered a political base in the New Era, finding little support either in the public sphere or among his peers in business and finance. Upon hearing of Heydt's appointment as the leader of the short-lived cabinet from March to September 1862, Otto Camphausen wrote, "Our worst fears have been surpassed by reality—the poor, poor king." [32] As cabinet chief, Heydt was perceived to have drifted so far to the right that such liberal government officials as Rudolf Delbrück, Otto Camphausen, and Friedrich Kühlwetter refused to enter his cabinet.[33] The minister reached the nadir of his political career in the election of May 1862, when his entire cabinet lost in the elections: "Never has a government been so thoroughly defeated." [34] Even his hometown of Elberfeld, which had consistently put him in provincial diets and the chamber of deputies for over twenty years, failed to elect him.[35] "Politics," Heydt wrote in 1863, "has discarded me." [36] The pronouncement was premature. Heydt returned to parliament in 1865 and to Bismarck's cabinet as finance minister in 1866. But it surprised few that Heydt's small faction of arch conservatives in parliament was popularly dubbed the "feudal party" and that his return to government was principally ascribed to his demonstrated talent in circumventing constitutional procedures to generate revenue.[37]

In spite of Heydt's survival, the business class did find relief in the New Era for three leading reasons. First, moderate liberals in the New Era cabinet ended Heydt's ministerial dominance over economic policy. He had little backing from either his colleagues or the Chamber of Deputies and stayed in office only at the king's request. Had Heydt been an English minister, remarked W. O. Henderson, he would have resigned (or have been dismissed) much earlier.[38] Finance Minister Patow, a staunch opponent of Heydt's bureaucratic abuses throughout the 1850s, became the leading voice in the cabinet for shaping economic legislation. Patow's philosophy of curtailing statist intervention in the economy better reflected the wishes of the business class and consequently the railroad business encountered less government interference after 1858.

Second, the return of liberal majorities in the Chamber of Deputies after 1858 produced a new parliamentary attitude toward government-business relations. The banker David Hansemann remarked: "Three years ago no one would have hardly proposed me as an elector, let alone have me as a deputy." [39] After 1858 the legislature moved away from a state-controlled economy toward greater liberalization in a number of key industries. As already seen, the demise of the Railroad Fund in 1859 marked a signal reversal in the legislature's accommodation to state policy. Whereas the chamber in 1853 had supported Heydt's scheme for railroad nationalization, it now advocated less government intervention in the economy's leading sector. The dissolution of the Railroad Fund was the first among several key economic bills that promoted the material welfare of businessmen.

Finally, high-ranking bureaucrats of the trade and finance ministries in the New Era were sympathetic to the needs of large-scale business. Among them were Rudolf Delbrück, M. Phillipsborn, Baron von der Reck, Eduard Moeller, Adolf von Pommer-Esche, Friedrich Kühlwetter, Richard Hoene, and Otto Camphausen. With the assistance of their staffs, they drafted the key legislative bills on economic policy, largely anticipating the expectations of the business class. These men knew and socialized with business elites and were not only in better touch with the practical problems of commerce and industry but were also ready to change how the state regulated and promoted the economy.[40] Since the 1830s, competing interests had eroded the Prussian state bureaucracy's once-uniform identity, replacing it with a more multisided character, whose numerous factions jostled for policy-making influence.[41] It was only during the New Era that the cohort of liberal administrators rose up to bureaucratic levels that allowed them to influence economic policy. As minister-president, Bismarck resented this power. He believed that the majority of the finance ministry's technical advisers controlled the opinions of their ministers (Patow and Bodelschwingh) and sided with the opposition in the constitutional conflict. These men, Bismarck wrote, were capable of passive resistance and saw the political struggle as a "short episode in the liberal development of the government's bureaucratic machinery." [42]

In the period 1858–61 economic changes, long demanded by the business class, became law. The coal industry, for example, attained long-sought legislation in 1860 and 1861. The state had initiated the process of restructuring the coal industry in 1851 with pathbreaking laws that reduced its excise tax on mining by half (from 10 to 5 percent) and replaced its paternalistic supervision of mine operations—the much criticized *Direktionsprinzip*—with one of periodic inspection.[43] But Ruhr, Westphalian, and Silesian coal mine owners still had many complaints; laws still supported guild privileges which restricted the free movement of coal miners between regions and mines; and the continued bureaucratic autonomy of the state's regional regulatory offices (*Bergämter*) remained. Regulators' old habits of intervention and supervision did not entirely cease. During the New Era, business interests criticized Heydt's failure to adhere consistently to the laws of 1851 and, above all, his unwillingness to effect further reform.[44]

After 1858 the government undertook further reforms: in 1860, a law secured freedom of mobility for miners, thus completing the liberalization of the industry; in 1861, the state further reduced excise taxes and abolished the coal mining offices' bureaucratic independence, whose remaining jurisdiction over coal operations was transferred to the general state bureaucracy.[45] Mine owners could now mine coal and ore with their own methods and at their own tempo, hire and fire as they saw fit (thus inaugurating a new era in labor relations), and better coordinate hewing and hauling with transportation and forging. Freed from state tutelage and interference, mining and iron firms pursued unrestrained economic growth with greater vigor and began to consolidate their enterprises into the large concerns that would become a major economic and political force in the Kaiserreich. For the Silesian and Westphalian railway directors involved in the coal industry, the possibilities of vertical integration only fully emerged after 1861.

Another landmark of the New Era's economic settlement was the Commercial Code. Begun in 1857, drafted in 1859–60, and revised throughout 1861, the code was finally published in 1862. The new legal framework for a rising capitalist society received much praise from the business world not only because it demonstrated the state's commitment to promoting economic growth in northern and western Germany but also because the business class was consulted so thoroughly in revising it. Prussia's leading business associations and chambers of commerce assessed the bill, offering copious emendations.[46] At its 1859 annual meeting in Trieste the Association of German Railroad Administrations heard and debated the recommendations of the special commission, whose report was submitted to the German Confederation's diet in Frankfurt.[47] In 1860, Prussia's railway administrations submitted to the Prussian trade ministry their own position paper which critically detailed how the code's "complete lack of expertise" in railroad tariffs and finance "could only harm commercial traffic." The report especially emphasized the disproportionate amount of authority it assigned to state railroad commissioners over private railroad directors.[48] The Prussian government, which played the leading role in drafting the code, incorporated such suggestions. The railroad clause of the code underwent three readings before a settlement could be reached between the interests of state and private railways.[49]

Equally significant for commercial legislation was the Franco-Prussian Trade Treaty, signed at the end of the New Era in March 1862, which erected a framework for greater commercial expansion. Although controversial among businessmen in heavy industries (and those from Austria and the middle German states), the free-trade treaty connected Prussia to the leading western economies and reinforced Prussia's economic leadership in Germany.[50] When Otto Michaelis, the secretary of the Chamber of Deputies' trade committee, sought approval from the legislature for the bill, he argued: "The treaty is a compromise of protectionist interests with free-trade demands; it is the first step to the creation of fairness. For this reason one needs to judge openly and freely, so that the discussion of the fatherland's welfare can cease. . . . the contradictions, the interests, and the principles of the provinces have found their reconciliation in the position of the treaty and its tariffs." [51] The bill passed easily in both houses. Similar treaties followed in 1865 with Belgium, England, and Italy.

These laws and treaties delimited the new space that the state was staking out for industrial and commercial enterprise,[52] but the most impressive legislative signal that the state was making room for bourgeois civil society was the property-tax reform of 1861. This tax law became one of the essential touchstones of parliamentary political conflict in the New Era, and yet, although a well-known fact, it is not a weighted factor in the literature.[53] Since the incorporation of the western provinces into Prussia in 1815, Rhenish and Westphalian businessmen had complained of the unjust tax burden on the western provinces. French occupation had eliminated all tax exemptions in the west, whereas in the east there existed over one hundred varieties of land tax and thirty-three forms of land tax systems—most of them to ensure tax exemption for the nobility.[54] In 1858, 41 percent of Prussian land was exempt from taxation,[55] compelling the Rhineland province to pay almost eight times as much land tax as the province of Prussia.[56]

Ending property-tax exemption (*Grundsteuerfreiheit*) was a reform long advocated by Prussian liberals. The issue resonated among Rhenish liberals in the 1840s, was debated in the National Assembly in 1848, and became one of Hansemann's proposed reforms before the Auerswald-Hansemann cabinet was dismissed in the fall of 1848.[57] Equitable taxation of property was further included in the Prussian constitutions of December 1848 (article 100) and January 1850 (article 101), though it was never enforced.[58] In January 1850 and in November 1852 the government drafted bills to tax landed property in the east, but this attempt was defeated on the lower house floor in March 1853.[59] The property tax continued to be championed by liberal and business circles (Vincke, Kühne, Harkort, Camphausen, and Hansemann, as well as chambers of commerce) throughout the 1850s.

For this reason, a law barring exemptions on landed property was a leading issue in Wilhelm's interviews with candidates for finance minister during the formation of the New Era cabinet and became a central goal of Wilhelm's cabinet.[60] For Otto Camphausen the reform of the property tax was so important that in November 1858 he declined the king's offer of the post of finance minister so that Robert von Patow could take the portfolio. Patow's status as a "non-Rhinelander," Camphausen explained to his brother, could better persuade the upper house to accept the tax reform, and he should therefore—in spite of other shortcomings—fill the post.[61] Camphausen's belief that Patow's rank as noble and *Gutsbesitzer* was essential to passing the law was probably correct, for the bill's passage through the legislature was a rough one.[62] The lower house defeated the first presentation of the bill in March 1859 because it contained too many loopholes for nobles; the second bill was defeated by the upper house in 1860 because it contained too few. In 1861, however, a coalition of the crown, cabinet, and the lower house's finance commission overcame the opposition. The strong endorsement of King Wilhelm, who coveted the revenue the tax would provide for his army reform, overcame the fierce opposition in the upper house led by Graf Arnim-Boitzenberg, who in March and April successfully led two rejections of the property tax bill. Even with the strong pressure applied by the king himself, who used his birthday greeting in 1861 to remind the upper house of its duty to pass the bill, the law only passed by a vote of 110 to 81.[63] The crown's two-pronged parliamentary program, which exhorted the chamber to prevail over the upper house for the property tax while employing the latter to overcome the chamber's opposition to army reform, would remain only partially fulfilled.

The law of 1861 erased exemptions from the property tax in the six eastern provinces and taxed property uniformly and equally throughout Prussia. The real-estate tax more than doubled in fifty-five counties in the east; ninety in the west paid less.[64] One of the oldest liberal grievances had come to an end. The revised tax structure laid the base for a new social contract; the inviolate privileges of nobility, stemming ostensibly from ancient fiefs and royal prerogative, were dealt a severe ideological, political, and economic blow. And because the finance ministry directly appraised the land and supervised the tax's collection, the great estate holders were prevented from watering down the reform through the county and communal governments, which the Prussian nobility had virtually controlled since the Reform Era. Hence the noble class was further brought under the jurisdiction of a centralized, bureaucratic modern state—another tenet of mid-century liberalism.

The property tax reform was, of course, a questionable move for political liberalism. Liberal factions, so focused on using the state to strip Prussian nobles of their birthright, failed to understand that they, by granting the state a new source of steady revenue, were weakening their power of the purse in parliament.[65] By making the annual budget less critical for the administration of the state, they diminished their power to influence state policy after 1861.[66] Once Wilhelm had gained the property tax for his army, he began to repair the divisions between crown and nobility to steer a course away from the liberals—a course, to be sure, more true to his nature. Because four years were required to reappraise all landed property, the tax could not be levied until 1865, at which time, ironically, its revenue helped Bismarck to continue governing without parliament's approval of the state budget (the constitutional conflict).[67]

For many businessmen and political liberals in 1861, the law demonstrated the state's willingness to mediate between an old established elite and a newly emerging one. Otto Camphausen wrote to his brother Ludolf: "We can all be very satisfied with one another about the results of the legislative period. The number of important bills passed into law is quite considerable; above all the property tax reform. . . . Personally both of us can be very satisfied and congratulated for our hard work." [68] The legislative sessions from 1859 to 1861 had produced undramatic but solid, concrete gains for businessmen. The property tax reform, the commercial code, the liberalization of the coal industry, the reaffirmation of private enterprise in railroads—all spoke of major victories for a social group that saw in commerce and industry the foundation of civil society.

Special-Interest Politics

The Camphausens' buoyant mood is perhaps justified by an examination of how enmeshed business interests had become in the Prussian political network. Businessmen, business associations, and lobbies successfully peddled their interests publicly (Landtag), semi-publicly (ministerial channels), and privately (personal contacts). The history of economic lobbying in Prussia certainly did not begin in 1858. Small associations can be traced back to the early nineteenth century,[69] but it was the railroad associations of the 1850s (discussed in chap. 3) that provided other industries with a model for both political lobbying and industrial organization.

Citing the success of the railroad associations in the 1850s, directors joint-stock companies founded the Central Association of Rhenish-West-phalian Joint-Stock Companies in 1858 to lobby more effectively for the modi-fication of commercial law and for the general interests of stockholders.[70] Friedrich Hammacher, one of principal organizers of the association, subse-quently helped to start the Coal Mining Association, whose widespread gen-eral support, he noted, was partially attributable to the "moral force" of the central association.[71] In December 1858 the Trade and Commercial Associa-tion for the Rhineland and Westphalia was founded to provide a better link be-tween businessmen and the press, government, and chambers of commerce.[72] The era of commercial and industrial interest groups had arrived.

The principal task of the Central Association of Rhenish-Westphalian Joint-Stock Companies in 1858 was to protest both a 2 percent tax on the net profit of joint-stock companies in 1857 and the accompanying state supervi-sion of internal business affairs that this tax demanded.[73] In 1861 the Landtag rescinded the tax, and the association disbanded with its chief mission accom-plished.[74] The Coal Mining Association achieved similar success with efforts to stimulate the eastward shipment of Ruhr coal. "The agitation for the re-duction of coal tariffs seems to have had good success," wrote Hammacher in 1858.[75] More impressively, the association not only contributed to the pas-sage of the coal mining laws of 1860/61, but it also attained from the state the provision that all future government ordinances on security and supervision of mines must first receive the approval of the association.[76] In this instance, the special-interest group had become an advisory organ of the government. By 1861 business associations in Prussia numbered more than one hundred, an indicator of their success in affecting the legislative process.[77] Economic associations became an important component of Prussian politics during the New Era.

The protocols of the state cabinet during the New Era reveal that the criticisms and recommendations of chambers of commerce were reviewed at the highest level of government. Businessmen's positions on postal reform, the stamp tax, banking laws, and railroad freight were weighed at the highest level. Even the demand by business circles that a professorial chair for com-mercial law be established at a Prussian university was given serious consider-ation by the cabinet.[78] The Berlin Trade Corporation thanked the government in 1859 for its "liberality" by heeding the association's advice in reforming the insurance industry after ignoring "so many earlier annual reports." [79] When ascribing causes to the abolition of the Customs Union's transshipment tariffs in 1860, the *National-Zeitung* cited the participation of chambers of commerce in the public agitation for change as decisive.[80] The chambers acted once again as both lobbies and advisory organs to the government, roles that Heydt had often denied them in the 1850s.

In 1860 the government acquiesced in the request of chambers of commerce and business associations to convene collectively (Handelstag) to discuss amendments to the Commercial Code and the Customs Union's tariff system. Certainly the presence of David Hansemann and Hermann Beckerath as presidents of the government-authorized Handelstag in 1861–62 was significant. Both had been active critics of the government during the 1850s.[81] "It had taken battles, many battles, before the enterprise [Handelstag] came into being," trumpeted the *National-Zeitung.* "But the promising idea of a convention of the monarchy's entrepreneurial classes has won, and it is the first step toward this common enterprise, which is not merely [a recognition] for those directly participating but also highly advantageous for the advancement of our economic conditions." [82] The Prussian Handelstage of 1859 and 1860 were followed the next year by the Deutscher Handelstag held in Heidelberg, a national forum for commercial and industrial interests that lent further strength to the growing unification movement.[83]

In the 1860s chambers of commerce and other business associations exercised additional influence on bills affecting the economy. When the Landtag deputy Heinrich Kruse, a Rhenish journalist connected with business circles, sought to prevent passage of a bill in 1863 that would grant the state a monopoly on telegraphic communication, he appealed to Mevissen to mobilize chambers against the move. "It would be of assistance, when petitions from chambers of commerce could be *quickly* assembled and presented to the president of the lower house (within eight days) to either oppose the drafts of the government and the commission or, more generally, appeal *for* more moderate legal guarantees to benefit private telegraph companies." [84] This connection between the legislature and an extraparliamentary association of businessmen enabled Kruse to sink the bill.

The legislature's responsive behavior toward specific interests suggests greater public access to policy making. F. Diergardt, the Rhenish entrepreneur who sat in the upper house, complained in 1860 that requests and petitions from his province kept him working "deep into the night." What troubled him was not his toil but the petitioners' belief "that one can execute affairs around here as if we were on the Rhine—that is, discuss the matter over a bottle of wine and settle the issue." [85] Business elites possessed privileged contacts with both parliamentary lawmakers and government policy makers. Gustav Mevissen used his fellow Rhenish businessman Diergardt as his proxy in the legislature. During the parliamentary deliberations on the army bill in 1860, he easily made his views known to key actors, although he was nowhere near Berlin. "I have done as you said," wrote Diergardt to Mevissen, "and gave copies of the political content of your letter to the diligent president of the military commission, Herr von Vincke, as well as to the president of the Chamber of Deputies, Herr von Simson, and discussed the same with Professor Duncker, a member of the house." [86] In matters of business, Mevissen's Berlin contacts also garnered important information for his railroad company from trade ministry officials regarding sensitive procedural matters for procuring charters, loans, and company mergers.[87] The presence of businessmen in Berlin's political circles was certainly not new, but the increased willingness of politicians and government officials to respond to their concerns after 1858 visibly increased. Moreover, businessmen's ability to influence the political process through lobbies, personal contacts, and bureaucratic channels strengthened their inclination not to seek positions in the lower house. Wealthy businessmen sought entry to the ruling classes of the Prussian establishment but not necessarily to the political class of lawmakers.

After 1858, the Prussian state accorded more official respect to business elites than before, signaling a willingness, albeit reluctant, to assimilate them into the establishment. In 1860 Friedrich Diergardt and Ludolf Camphausen were called into the upper house; Mevissen followed in 1865. Diergardt interpreted the honor, which was accompanied by the entailment of his estate, as a "welcome sign that in Prussia closed castes no longer exist." [88] By 1861, over 130 businessmen in the county of Düsseldorf had been given honorific titles (mostly Kommerzienrat) by the court.[89] Although certainly ancillary to the priorities of business politics, the assimilation of commercial elites into political, bureaucratic, and court circles speaks persuasively of an embourgeoisement of the Prussian establishment.

Railroads and Politics

In the New Era the railroad industry also registered positive advances for entrepreneurs. The Rhenish Railway, for example, experienced immediate relief from the new ministries. Throughout 1858 it had sought permission to issue a new five million thaler bond (4.5 percent interest), but Heydt repeatedly denied the company's request. The directors refused to accept the minister's rejections, in which they recognized a "form of paternalism being practiced." [90] Permission was finally granted, however, in December 1858—a month after the political shift to the New Era—without explanation for the reversal, suggesting that Heydt's heavy administrative hand was less tolerated in the new cabinet.[91] In 1860 the government also permitted the Rhenish Railway to absorb the Cologne-Crefeld Railway. The Rhenish Railway had attempted to absorb the smaller company in 1855 and 1857 but was denied because of the restrictive demands of the state, which administered the private railway. In 1859, however, the government dropped the charter's more onerous obligations (among them, building a branch line between Heerat and Neuss) and enabled the Rhenish Railway to acquire this important line connecting the middle and lower Rhine commercial centers. The company advanced toward its long-term goal of establishing an unrivaled network on the left bank of the Rhine.[92]

The company gained the upper hand in its affairs with the government. It repeatedly rebuffed the government's attempts to compel the company to adhere to deadlines to begin construction on two branch lines (Düren-Schleiden and Herbesthal-Eupen), provoking the trade ministry's undersecretary to comment, "The directors of the Rhenish Railway appear to assume it is merely up to them when and if the branchline between Herbesthal and Eupen should be built and, moreover, that it is solely their financial interest that decides the matter." [93] The trade ministry nonetheless cooperated with the company in its project to extend its lines to Nassau and erect a bridge in Coblenz, volunteering to abide by its dividend guarantee in the event of delayed construction and promising to defend the company's cause in the Landtag.[94] The ability of the Upper Silesian and Cologne-Minden railways to modify or repudiate contractual promises to the state also suggested that directors and investors of joint-stock companies found themselves on better footing with the trade ministry.[95] Overall, one sees a gradual shift back to the earlier mixed system, with private business reasserting its leadership but gladly accepting the supplemental support of the state.

The business politics of railroad companies were further aided by the Prussian Landtag, which continued its trend of upholding the principle of private enterprise. In September 1859, following the abolition of the Railroad Fund, the legislature comprehensively reviewed the impact of Heydt's interventionist policies for the growth of Prussia's railroad industry. It questioned the ratio of growth to state investment, noting that while 113 million thalers of state investments produced 1,946 kilometers of rail in 1844–50, 56 million thalers had produced merely 548 kilometers in 1850–57. More crucially it stated that one could consider the entrepreneurial spirit in Prussian railways to be "fully oppressed." In paraphrasing the debate, a Berlin daily wrote, "Nobody wishes to place money in operations whose profitability shrinks when it no longer rests on the natural conditions and objective development of traffic but, rather, on this element of administrative regulation that one has tried in vain to put on a lawful basis numerous times." [96] If Prussia was going to sustain its necessary rate of expansion, it needed to return to a more rigorous basis of legality. With arguments of arbitrary regulation and unhealthy intervention, the legislature fiercely opposed Heydt on his newly proposed freight rates on state railroads and further criticized the state's unprofitable involvement in the Rhein-Nahe Railway, which needed an additional unforeseen six million thaler bond to resume construction.[97]

In 1860 and 1862, Leonor Reichenheim introduced motions to reform the Railroad Law of 1838, proposing the revision of fifteen paragraphs. The reform took aim at the trade minister's overly large scope of power, because his function as impartial supervisor of the financial affairs of private railroads (loans, reserve funds, fixing of dividends, etc.) was incompatible with his other role as administrator of state rails, which competed with private rails. The reform also sought to limit the demands the state could enforce on railroads. Using the night trains incident of the early 1850s and the more recent demand that the Rhenish Railway build the unprofitable Düren-Schleiden line as examples of excessive state inference, Reichenheim called for greater limitation of state authority.[98] Although the proposal initially received the support of all liberal factions and spurred a public debate critical of Heydt's railroad policies, it fell from the agenda.[99]

Reichenheim's oratory was not completely in vain. He sat on the committee for trade and commerce that in 1862 rejected the proposed charter for a state railroad between Kohlfurt and Waldenburg. The committee cited the state's past "unhealthy" railroad policy, especially its unfair pressures against private companies, as the reason for the rejection.[100] A month later the same committee ruled in favor of petitioners who requested full access to the books of the Rhein-Nahe Railway, which had been a perennial loser since the state took over its administration in 1856. The petitioners challenged both the competency of the Railroad Commission and Heydt's right to forbid any inspection of state administration.[101] Heydt's autocratic tendencies during the Reaction were no longer tolerated in the New Era.

A parliamentary commission also reviewed the petition of a Silesian businessman who in 1862 asserted that the government had mismanaged the affairs of the Upper Silesian Railway, whose profits had steadily declined since the government's administrative takeover in 1857, as well as those of the province for not building a line on the right bank of the Oder River.[102] The petition grew out of a movement of company shareholders, who had striven since 1859 to put the company back in private administration.[103] The commission upheld the claim, submitting a stinging indictment of governmental mismanagement. It charged the government with fixing artificially high freight rates, which "a private administration never would have permitted," and attributed the neglect of the province's canals and overall infrastructure to the government's interest in protecting the revenues of the state-owned Lower Silesian–Mark railway.[104]

Although the trade ministry defended its overall record publicly, intraministerial memoranda show that the ministry recognized its own shoddiness. For example, in 1861 Albert Maybach, a ministry official and future minister of railroad affairs, harshly criticized the "deficient operational competency" of the government officials managing the Saarbrücken and Rhein-Nahe railways, which had cost the government millions in dividend subsidies. Portraying them as inefficient, irresponsible, unqualified, dilatory, and technically limited, Maybach recommended transfers for all (save the chief director) and reorganization of the entire office.[105]

By 1862 the business cycle had completely recovered from the downturn in 1857–59, showing signs of strength in both production and trade. Significantly, free trade and the growth of the private railroad system prospered during the years of the constitutional conflict, the parliamentary struggle that began over a military reform bill but became a constitutional issue when Bismarck began to govern without a budget approved by the Chamber of Deputies. Count Heinrich von Itzenplitz replaced Heydt as trade minister in September 1862. Unlike Heydt, the new minister had little interest in retaining the state railway system and supervised economic activity with a lighter hand. During his tenure as district governor in the coal-mining region of Arnsberg in the 1840s, Itzenplitz had acquainted himself with businessmen and come to respect their efficiency and pragmatism. With regard to business politics, Itzenplitz effected a seamless transition between the *juste milieu* of the New Era and the constitutional conflict.

Businessmen were, of course, acutely aware of Bismarck's reactionary reputation and his hard-line defense of royal prerogative, but the key question for many of Prussia's capitalists was whether or not Bismarck's cabinet would roll back the economic policies of the New Era. When Itzenplitz reaffirmed Patow's noninterventionist policies, it appeared that the decade-long struggle to accommodate capital and political authority had borne fruit; the conservative political establishment had recognized the needs of the new elites of commerce and industry and would not touch the reforms. It is nonetheless evident that alongside spheres of cooperation there remained spheres of conflict. Ambivalence, as we have seen, is the operative word for businessmen's relationship to the Prussian state from the *Vormärz* period through the 1870s.

Itzenplitz's alacrity to reduce the role of government in the economy eased the strained relationship between the trade ministry and railroad companies that had developed under Heydt. His inclination to charter new private railroads and authorize the expansion of established companies prompted Bismarck to dub him a "signature machine."[106] In his memoirs Bismarck judged him to be a weak leader who lacked the "necessary energy" to run a complex ministry. Unable to master the technical details of railroad legislation, administration, and regulation, Itzenplitz effectively surrendered ministry policy to such subordinates as Rudolf Delbrück,[107] who favored a private railroad industry. Indeed, the governmental ministries offered fewer obstacles to building and administering lines than ever before, and parliament enthusiastically backed private ownership. The financial world's good will toward private railroads also increased in direct proportion to rising dividends. Public confidence in private enterprise grew; many new lines were proposed and constructed without government support.[108]

In this era, private companies completed the major trunk lines and began the development of branch lines. The year 1862 surpassed 1857 as the most profitable railroad year, with increases in passenger conveyance (1.1 percent), freight transport (14.5 percent), gross income per mile (63,271 thalers versus 61,839 in 1857), and ratio of profit to invested capital (7.27 percent versus 3.76 percent in 1857).[109] After 1862, stock market quotations swelled,[110] drawing even more investors and businessmen (many of them English)[111] into the Prussian railroad world. Private railroad companies were in their heyday.

In piecemeal fashion, the state reduced its direct role in the railroad business. Between 1860 and 1863 the state relinquished administrative control of Cologne-Crefeld, the Aachen-Düsseldorfer, and the Ruhrort-Crefeld-Kreis Gladbach railways, lowering the percentage of private rail under state administration from 41 percent in 1857 to 32 percent in 1866.[112] The trade ministry continued the completion of its earlier projects but granted charters to private firms to build and operate lines within the state rail network in the eastern provinces (the Tilsit-Insterburger and the Ostpreussische Südbahn). These charters announced tacitly the state's capitulation to private railroad construction. Itzenplitz's statement, "I don't care who builds the railroads—as long as they are built," reflected the new pragmatic attitude in the trade ministry.[113] Whereas private rail swelled from 2,960 to 4,280.7 kilometers between 1858 and 1863, the state's portion of the industry rose modestly in the same period from 1,265 to 1,580.6 kilometers.[114] This development, which amounted to a new policy, canceled Heydt's vision of a state network and promoted consolidation of larger railways.

In the years 1858–66 the rising advocacy of private capitalist enterprise dovetailed with the growing issue of national unification. The founding of the *Kongress deutscher Volkswirthe* in 1857 tokened a "growing awareness of economic problems and a widespread desire among liberals to give their search for freedom in Germany a more practical orientation." [115] Railroads were, of course, topics at the economic congresses. Unanimity did not exist on the question of how railroads could best facilitate a single German market and whether private ownership was the best course. Nonetheless, the principles of self-administration, free association, and free competition in business prevailed.[116] Financiers championed private railways, for they were more profitable than state administered lines, as did industrialists, who thought it better to sell their goods to many clients instead of one.[117] Friedrich Hammacher expressed a commonplace sentiment in 1863, when he stated at a meeting of German chambers of commerce that "placing the railroads in the hands of the state governments . . . means nothing other than practicing communism . . . and paralyzing the railroads in the fulfillment of their industrial mission for the common good." [118]

But the advocacy of private railroads among business circles was not completely uncritical. Whereas private companies had earlier charged the government with unfair business practice, chambers of commerce and industrial businesses now criticized private railroads for exploiting their consolidated networks and better organized associations to fix unfair freight rates.[119] Laissez-faire advocates further argued that Prussia's railroad system should be thoroughly overhauled; it was "unnatural" that railroad companies should enjoy monopolistic charters, dividend guarantees, sole use of rails, and other arbitrary practices that produced higher prices.[120] In 1863 Rhenish and Westphalian chambers of commerce and business associations protested extensively against the Rhenish Railway's bid to absorb the Aachen-Düsseldorfer and Ruhrort-Crefeld-Kreis Gladbach railways, fearing the Rhenish Railway's exclusive control of the left bank of the Rhine. Itzenplitz was inclined to permit the merger but yielded to regional protests.[121]

In this instance, the laissez-faire principle of fair competition prevailed. But, although much ink was spilled in the cause of Manchester laissez-faire policies, the practice of businessmen showed little purist devotion to the doctrine. For this reason the editors of the *National-Zeitung,* a decidedly laissez-faire liberal daily, criticized the lack of political independence among business elites, who, when it suited their interests, were all too willing to work within bureaucratic agencies. "For every petition that demands free and independent movement of trade and commerce, there are ten requesting support in one form or another; for every one that is braced with the consciousness of autonomy and its own power, there are ten appealing to dependency on the zealous, good will of the state powers." [122] In this editorial the *National-Zeitung* summed up the fundamental ambivalence that characterized the economic and political stance of the Prussian business class in the 1860s. On the one hand, this increasingly self-confident interest group supported the liberal economic agenda of laissez-faire, which called for ever more freedom from state direction of economic life. On the other hand, it could not bring itself to abandon fully, perhaps prematurely, the benefits and privileges that stemmed from the state's long-established role as the promoter and director of economic growth. There were benefits in both directions, and Prussian businessmen wanted to have it both ways—both the new and the old, the way of the future and the way of the past.

Itzenplitz's policy of relaxing regulation did create room for abuse, illegal profit, and schemes for stock market killings. The most prominent exploiter of the trade ministry's leniency in these years was the "railroad king" Bethel Henry Strousberg, who amassed millions through his "general contract" procedure in the 1860s. His shady business operations, mistreatment of stockholders, and many contacts in the Prussian government occasioned a scathing Reichstag speech by Eduard Lasker, which led to a public scandal and brought about Itzenplitz's resignation in 1873.[123]

Businessmen and Constitutional Politics

The dovetailing of the business cycle's upswing in 1862 with the mounting conflict between parliament and crown posed a potential dilemma for the railroad industry: would the Landtag use its right as cosignatory for all railway-building charters as a political weapon in its confrontation with the crown? Dividend subsidies to railroad investors were part of the budget, so railroad finance could be employed to obstruct government policy. In the early phase of the conflict, however, the chamber budget committee avoided bringing such areas of finance into the debate about a 25 percent increase in taxation to cover the planned expansion in the army. Bills on state aid for railways pitted liberal principle against local self-interest and would serve Bismarck's aim of dividing the opposition.[124] Hence most spheres of railroad policy were left alone, which enabled railroad companies to receive twenty-four major charters involving trunk and branch lines in this period.[125] In the years 1863-66, the government distributed 4,885,662 thalers in subsidies to railroad companies.[126] Some charters came with immediate subventions from the budgetless government: in June 1863 the Landtag approved a 200,000 thaler subvention for Berg-Mark Railway's branch line between Rittershausen and Lennep.[127] In December 1864 the chamber did modify the language of a Rhenish Railway charter to emphasize more fully the chamber's power of coauthorization (which the cabinet accepted) but did not challenge the 4 percent dividend guarantee that accompanied it.[128] Up until 1865 the Landtag's liberal factions avoided linking business politics directly with parliamentary politics. And railroad directors clearly had not objected to receiving charters and moneys for their companies from a budgetless government in conflict with parliament over the power of the purse.

In mid-1865, however, the Landtag's liberal majority did turn to its budgetary power and elements of railroad finance to press the government for concessions. The time for a shift in tactics, wrote Ludolf Camphausen in June 1865, appeared propitious: "By the end [of the legislative session] the relationship has changed. In five months the government has had no foreign-political success; it has made no forward movement, even regressed, and the government must build internal strength through approbative declarations from the lowly regarded deputies, who refuse to do so. The deputies have used this predicament to gleefully reject railroad projects." [129] The factions that made up the liberal opposition to Bismarck's government, however, were initially divided on how to use railroads as a political weapon. In March 1865, when a railroad bill was put before the chamber, the commission reviewing it (headed by Otto Michaelis) recommended postponing the vote until the budget had been legally established. The recommendation was voted down 178 to 108, with members of the Progressive Party defecting. Instead, the chamber passed the alternative motion that the government should sell its railroad stock, which had accumulated in the years of the Railroad Fund, to cover the costs of proposed construction. [130] By rejecting the loan, the chamber retained its stance of principled opposition yet did not undercut the future prosperity of the railroad market. With this maneuver house members upheld constitutional right without injuring economic self-interest.

In 1865 the Landtag rejected the government's bid to tax foreign railroad companies using Prussian rails. [131] It further blocked the government's attempt to sell its Westphalian line to the Berg-Mark Railway in 1865 for fourteen million thalers. But the chamber had been unable to prevent an earlier deal closed between the railroad and the government. In 1863–64, when the government surrendered administrative control of the Aachen-Düsseldorfer and Ruhrort–Crefeld–Kries Gladbacher railways to the Berg-Mark Railway (another private railway administered by the state), it exercised its option to purchase all privately held shares in the two railways. The Berg-Mark Railway bought the options in May 1864 but paid the actual sum (1,247,000 thalers with common stock) much later, in January 1866. [132]

The chamber was also unsuccessful in thwarting the government's sale of its options on shares of the Cologne-Minden Railway in August 1865. By selling its stake in the company, the government stood to gain nearly thirty million thalers with which to finance a possible war against Austria. [133] This incident, in conjunction with the Berg-Mark deal, caused considerable debate in the chamber's liberal factions, raising the question of what the finance and trade ministries would do with the vast portfolio of railroad stock acquired over twenty-five years. [134]

The initiative for the transaction came not from the government but from the railroad company. In December 1862 Gerson Bleichröder, the railway's financial agent in Berlin, prepared a deal that proposed a purchase price of ten million thalers for the government's options on the Cologne-Minden Railway. Bleichröder noted to Bismarck that "the leading idea of the enclosed proposal is to serve the fatherland," but the trade ministry believed that his patriotic efforts undercut the worth of the government's share in the railroad by nearly ten million thalers. [135] The deal was refused.

The matter remained dormant until negotiations were once again resumed in the first half of 1865. Dagobert Oppenheim, a director of the railway, negotiated for the company and packaged a larger deal in May. The new deal offered a ten million thaler indemnity for the surrender of the government options amassed under the Railroad Fund; the government's release from retaining company stock acquired under the Guarantee Fund of 1854, whose liquidation value was reckoned between seven and ten million thalers; and the conversion of the government's remaining financial commitments into common stock, which the state was entitled to sell.[136] The company directors boldly planned a split in the common stock to create the necessary paper for the transaction. The deal enabled the government, if it exercised all elements of the plan, to realize the sum of 28,828,500 thalers.[137] Three weeks later, Oppenheim sewed on coattails, requesting a number of charters for branch lines that would guarantee the company's dominance in Westphalia's emerging coal and iron industrial complex.[138]

The government contested only the company's ten million thaler amortization offer for its options, claiming the figure was much too low. Officials in the finance ministry fixed the sum at 14,903,632 thalers, but the government settled on a compromise of 13 million, which the company accepted.[139] On 18 July 1865, the two parties signed a provisional contract, whose final form was notarized on 10 August. The agreement became binding upon the approval of the company shareholders (28 August) and the crown (13 September).[140] On three occasions in 1865 officials in the finance ministry demonstrated the illegality of signing a deal that involved equities of the Guarantee Fund without the legislature's approval, but these legal considerations were overlooked.[141]

The deal benefited both parties. For the government, the immediate receipt of millions was the driving logic of the deal: the trade minister knowingly accepted a low price in order to obtain the funds for mobilization in the event of war with Austria.[142] The company paid 3 million in hard currency in October and another 2.7 million in January 1866.[143] Without these cash infusions Bismarck could not have pulled the trigger in 1866. In addition to Cologne-Minden's partial cash payment of 5.7 million thalers, the liquidation of other railroad stock in 1866 contributed to the war chest. The sale of Berg-Mark (1 million), Upper-Silesian (500,000), and Cologne-Minden stock (2.2 million) in 1866 helped cover the costs of the Austro-Prussian War.[144]

For the Cologne-Minden railway, the purchase was nothing less than salvation, for the acquisition of the options nullified the government's right to buy out the railroad. According to the contract of the 1842 Railroad Fund, to which the Cologne-Minden was bound, the government retained the right to purchase the company after thirty years; the Guarantee Fund of 1854 also stipulated state ownership of certain lines after fifteen years. Facing imminent absorption into the state rail system in the 1870s, the private company negotiated with the government on several occasions after 1858 to abrogate the state's claim to ownership and did not hesitate to exploit the government's need for money after 1862.[145] Although doubling the common stock produced consternation among shareholders (for fear of value loss), the directors argued at the extraordinary stockholder's meeting convened to vote on this change that dividends after the split would fall from 15 to 9 percent, a drop that represented gain for the 1:2 conversion.[146] The shareholders approved.

The willingness of railroad directors to conduct million-thaler transactions with the government had a direct bearing on the ongoing constitutional crisis, since it suggested the readiness of business interests to allow the government to continue operating illegally (by acquiring funds through extraparliamentary means) as long as such tactics served the economic interests of private business. For Heinrich von Wittgenstein, the president of the Cologne-Minden Railway, as well as the company's directors, the release from eventual state ownership appeared more important than constitutional principles.[147]

The incident is important because it typifies the behavior of Prussia's industrial, financial, and commercial elites. In 1864, following the Prussian-Austrian victory over Denmark, Adolf Hansemann, G. Bleichröder, G. Mevissen, Alexis Meyer, and a long list of notables (headed by Heydt) initiated proceedings with the Prussian government to organize a joint-stock company to build a Baltic-North Sea canal, an enterprise promising great profit.[148] In the same year Alfred Krupp offered the Prussian government a long-term credit for armament deliveries amounting to two million thalers.[149] In August 1865, following the Cologne-Minden sale, the directors of the Rhenish Railway entered into negotiation with the government to purchase the state-owned Luxemburger Railway; they further offered to buy the state-owned Saarbrückener Railway in 1866.[150] In 1863 and in 1866, Cologne financiers approached the government with the offer to convert state coal mines into joint-stock companies.[151] It is clear that the business politics of entrepreneurs did not play a supporting role for the parliamentary opposition. Their eagerness to buy the state's capital assets, receive government subventions, and cooperate with the government in matters of pragmatic business to pursue consolidation and expansion strongly suggests that the politics of business were more paramount than questions of constitutionalism.

It would certainly be wrong to exclude all entrepreneurs from the political struggle in the years 1862–66—a clean, conscious break is not there. Businessmen, according to E. N. Anderson, served widely on election committees and "devoted many hours of service to secure the election of liberals from their districts." [152] Of the 448 electors chosen in Cologne in the 1861

November election, 181 (40 percent) were businessmen, which rose to 222 in 1862.[153] Hartmut Kaelble's study of Berlin *Wahlmänner* in 1862 shows that 89 percent of businessmen voted for the Progressive Party.[154] Of the 231 names that accompanied the printed election program of the Berlin chapter of the Constitutional Party (old liberals) in November 1861 — backed prominently by David Hansemann — 41 identified themselves as businessmen.[155] And, to be sure, some businessmen directly engaged in political activity: Friedrich Hammacher, Hans Viktor von Unruh, and Hermann Beckerath were prominent in the Progressive Party's right-wing faction in the struggle against Bismarck. Most financial and business elites, however, were even more moderate in their views and leaned toward the old liberals, whose political outlook demanded that the constitution and the interests of the *Handelsstand* be recognized but rejected a direct confrontation with the crown.

The rift between moderates and the left-wing Progressives was evident by 1860. The old-liberal stance of loyal opposition had little in common with the principled constitutionalism and confrontational style of such emerging popular leaders as Benedikt Waldeck and Hermann Schulze-Delitzsch. In 1860 Hermann Beckerath publicly criticized Waldeck as a "political nullity," whose name was "connected with revolution, blood, and civil war" and who was one lawyer among too many jurists in parliament. Similarly, Graf Schwerin, a New Era minister, declared to his constituency in 1860 that he would resign as chamber deputy if Schulze-Delitzsch were elected in the same district, announcing his incompatibility with Schulze-Delitzsch's democratic views.[156] The central difference between old liberals and Progressives was the former's willingness to accommodate liberal reforms within the royalist-bureaucratic traditions of the Prussian state. Ludolf Camphausen, writing in 1859, succinctly captured the ambivalent posture of the old liberals, whose deference toward state power precluded genuine parliamentary governance: "In domestic affairs much has happened and we are entitled to expect more, if the deputies succeed in convincing the prince that they are very good, right-minded, and also rather obedient but nonetheless people whose will, even to the crown, has meaning." [157] Old liberals such as Camphausen sought greater political recognition and social esteem for the bourgeoisie but ultimately believed that constitutional development should only be aligned with monarchical prerogative and state interest. Such a view precluded a decisive break with Prussia's brand of mixed-powers government, for it was unwilling to advocate either popular sovereignty or firm, parliamentary procedures that would enable the legislature to check arbitrary actions of the executive.[158]

Regardless of political stripe, few businessmen stood as Landtag candidates during the New Era, and even fewer lent their economic clout to the liberal cause after 1862.[159] Liberal newspapers lamented the lack of experienced businessmen in the Landtag: "Although the people vote in its interest . . . and although the class division in the electoral system apportions the great powers of trade and industry a privileged influence, it is nonetheless evident that few representatives of these elites have entered the lower house." [160] Indeed, D. Hansemann declined the nomination to stand as a candidate in Berlin, but he urged Mevissen (in vain) to do so, noting that "it would be very unjust, if Cologne did not send a businessman or industrialist to the Landtag." [161] Friedrich Diergardt also disapproved of the "passive behavior" of "independent industrialists" who chose to use the new business associations rather than bring their expertise to the Landtag.[162]

During the constitutional crisis, the elites of the business class further refrained from active engagement in oppositional politics. When reporting to his brother about a political gathering of Cologne's liberals and democrats in October 1862, Ludolf Camphausen noted that the "estate of wealthy businessmen was completely missing," adding that their absence "is attributed primarily to indifference; that they also show a new direction is clear in itself." [163] The accuracy of Camphausen's remark is borne out by businessmen's subsequent public displays of solidarity with the government, such as the Rhenish Railway's lavish banquet in November 1862 to celebrate the laying of the cornerstone of its Coblenz bridge. Attended by the queen and high-ranking government officials along with the company's principal investors and the region's economic notables, the banquet's convivial atmosphere was in sharp contrast to the open break between the chamber and crown that began in September.[164] Mevissen's banquet peroration, "Such jointly created enterprises of peace form the tight knit that inextricably ties together nation and monarchy," was not just harmless, ceremonial phrasemaking; it also signaled support for the crown.[165] In 1865, the company's political stance was explicitly articulated when a director issued an advisory that admonished company workers not to vote for Progressive Party candidates "like Classen-Kappelman and Horst, who stand in constant opposition to the government." [166]

The swan song of elite businessmen's political engagement during the constitutional conflict was the petition of 6 January 1863 and its accompanying meeting, which was held in a Cologne hotel and hosted by Joseph Bürgers, Heinrich Claessen, and Dagobert Oppenheim.[167] Drafted by Hermann Beckerath and signed by one hundred Rhenish and Westphalian notables, who reportedly represented over 300 hundred million thalers in capital assets,[168] the petition was strategically submitted to the king on the eve of the new legislative session to "warn, remind, and maintain [to the king] that an understanding with the present chamber is possible." [169] Its text viewed the government's course as illegal: "The basis of a constitutional monarchy is the law, and when the state government does not operate its finances on the basis of a constitutionally confirmed budget, the law is broken." The petition underscored the people's loyalty to the crown, their recognition of the king's power, and the monarch's "wise views" on reforming the army. Although conciliatory in tone, the petition concluded by requesting that the crown consider the "reduction in service time that is generally desired" and the implementation of army reforms within the limitations set by Prussia's "economic conditions and financial capacity." [170] It thus asked the crown to abide by the present norm of a two-year service period and relinquish its demand of enforcing the legally permissible three-year service period, which would require higher taxation and larger appropriations.

The exhortation to the king to seek a compromise with the parliament evoked the voice of muted, moderate opposition. It pointed up the ambivalence of industrial wealth in Prussia, which saw no reason to jeopardize the prosperous reign of Wilhelm, yet yearned for the court and state to recognize the supremacy of law. Typical for the business class, the petition stressed the financial burdens of three-year service rather than the political objection of left-wing Progressives regarding the ramifications of extended military service for a liberal civil society. Although Beckerath, Diergardt, and Abraham and Dagobert Oppenheim signed the petition, doubts about the wisdom of public agitation arose. Camphausen, for example, declined the invitation to sign the petition and refused to attend the conference.[171] Diergardt worried about the petition's reception in court circles and conferred with Mevissen and Heydt about placing a "correct commentary" on the petition in the *Spener'sche Zeitung* to redress any misperceptions about the intentions of the *Handelsstand.*[172] Mevissen, too, criticized the spirit of the petition, which implicitly supported the parliamentary opposition. At the meeting he recognized that Bismarck's ministry had broken constitutional law, but he argued that the parliament's obstructions were also unlawful, being "injurious to the welfare of the state." [173] This argument, which posited that political opposition undermining material prosperity was unjustifiable, was not solely Mevissen's. The annual reports of chambers of commerce in 1862–66 echoed the belief that the economic well-being of Prussia overrode political doctrine.[174]

At the height of the political crisis in July 1863, with the new press restrictions in effect and the breach between Bismarck and the chamber ever wider, Cologne's liberals and democrats fêted Rhenish deputies in public demonstrations of "passive resistance" that included a banquet, a Rhine cruise, and entertainment criticized as "saturnalia of the German bourgeoisie." [175] Yet "none" of the city's business notables "was to be seen, which very much astonished the visiting guests." [176] In September of the same year F. Diergardt acknowledged the de facto dissolution of the old-liberal faction, to which many businessmen belonged. "There is no longer an organized old-liberal party. Of communal action and personal sacrifice there is not a word. This is unfortunate but not to be changed."[177]

The low profile of the business class in the legislature affected the terms of debate during the constitutional conflict, which for businessmen became overly theoretical and impractical, remote from reality. Friedrich Hammacher, who joined the Progressives in 1863, lamented this development. In 1865 he wrote, "I won't complain any more that a large part of the country's businessmen remain apathetic and have abandoned the [political] terrain to doctrinaire democracy."[178] Hermann von Beckerath, who attempted reconciliations with the crown in 1862 and 1863, retired from the party in 1863, frustrated with the party's course of action. Heinrich von Sybel, the historian who represented the commercial center of Crefeld, also remarked that "most of the Progressive Party's activity is averse to practicality and reality."[179]

The rapprochement between Otto von Bismarck and Hans Viktor von Unruh in 1865 also revealed one businessman's search for a way out of the fruitless stalemate. Although Unruh was a founding member of the Progressive Party, his experience as a railroad entrepreneur (Magdeburg-Leipzig Railway) embodied the practical, nationalist sentiments of many businessmen who had prospered during the economic boom of the 1850s but still criticized Prussia's excessive bureaucratic supervision. In 1865 Unruh tried to persuade Bismarck that he, with greater restraint, could have received budgetary approval from the Chamber and that liberals were prepared to work with his government.[180] A year later, Unruh led the moderate faction of the Progressives to form the National Liberal Party and to work with Bismarck by consolidating the economic foundations of the Reich. The old-liberal party, which atrophied in 1862–66 because of its hesitancy to abandon its position of loyal opposition, saw many of its precepts about law, commerce, and civil society resurface in the program of the National Liberals.

▼

Salus publica suprema lex was the motto Mevissen quoted in July 1866 to frame his written arguments for ending the constitutional conflict, repairing the division between crown and legislature, and building the North German Confederation into a vital political and economic entity.[181] Mevissen's political credo, that the public welfare is the supreme law, can be seen as a palimpsest that reveals deeper traces of political ambivalence and economic opportunism. Progressives unconnected with commerce and industry were quick to infer baser motives. As a chamber deputy in 1866, Rudolf Gneist inveighed against the forces of materialism that had ostensibly divided the opposition.

"We know that acquisition rules the world," he stated, and "that . . . a separate governing system has arisen, which on ethically foul-smelling ground has shrewdly combined all the factors to control people through the salability, characterlessness, and the shortsightedness of interests."[182] In 1866 Hermann Baumgarten sarcastically posed the question: "How could these millionaires inconvenience themselves with the predicaments of a nation that did not want to advance loans, approve lucrative charters, and generally live in disadvantageous conditions?"[183] The bitter anger of Gneist and Baumgarten was grounded in their belief that the business class had been lured away from the liberal parliamentary opposition by the commercial policies of the Prussian state during the constitutional conflict, which split the forces of Prussian *Bürgertum* and allowed conservatives to divide and conquer. Many historians have since adopted this position.

Yet it would be wrong to assign the conflict ministry's economic and foreign policies in 1862–66 as primary factors for the economic-political behavior of the business class during the years of German unification. Although 1866 is the decisive year of political conversion of the liberal opposition, it is apparent that Mevissen, Hansemann, Camphausen, Bleichröder, and others of the business class worked with the budgetless government throughout the conflict years. The support the business class lent to Bismarck after 1866 is partially explained by the military victories in 1864 and 1866, but Bismarck's dramatic steps in foreign policy do not explain the prevalent disposition of businessmen to work with the government before 1864.

Before the parliamentary contest of 1862–66, the Prussian government of the New Era demonstrated its flexibility in bending to the needs of industrial capitalism. For businessmen the economic reforms of the New Era largely obviated the need to remake the Prussian state, thus partially decoupling bourgeois capitalism from political liberalism. In the New Era we see how moderate liberalism's emphasis on economic and juridical reforms in civil society became more estranged from the political-constitutional vision of liberalism. Although the sociopolitical formation of the business class is a fluid process stretching back to the eighteenth century, the New Era was a moment in this development at which political affinities between capitalists and liberals were not strengthened but weakened. The conflict and cooperation of the 1850s left a decidedly mixed legacy, but, significantly, a *juste milieu* emerged for commercial and industrial capitalism during the New Era. Its economic settlements reconfigured the terms of dialogue, reconfirming the belief of the business class that the Prussian state and crown, while primarily the instrument of agrarian interests in the east, was nevertheless capable of acting as an honest broker in balancing the needs of the new and old elites. Before the constitutional conflict and Bismarck's "revolution from above," the New Era government had demonstrated to the emerging elite of industry and commerce that the Prussian state still remained flexible in bending to the needs of industrial capitalism. The crucial transition of the monied bourgeoisie from old liberals to National Liberals occurred less with the military victories of 1864–66 than with economic reforms of 1858–62.

CHAPTER EIGHT

▼

Conclusion

I n 1864 Otto Michaelis, an editor of the *National-Zeitung,* labeled the Prussian state a "lazy serf" of railroad entrepreneurs.[1] Michaelis, to be sure, knew hyperbole when he wrote it: between 1848 and 1864 the business class never wielded political dominance over the state. As a political economist, however, he sought to point up the favorable conditions for building railroads in Prussia: a government that had shelved plans for railway nationalization; a trade minister who since 1862 had practiced laissez-faire policies; and a state that used the ample share-capital of the railroad industry to promote Berlin as Germany's leading financial center. The mixed system had successfully nurtured the railroad industry; its further development and greater profits were now left to businessmen.

Historians have focused on this kind of success to reduce the story of business-government relations to the convenient formula of an alliance, which neatly explains the mid-century amalgam of finance capitalism, laissez-faire, and authoritarian government. The evidence adduced in this study, however, suggests that the idea of an alliance serves more as an assumption to fit larger interpretations of German history than as a description of actual relationships in the political economy of mid-century Prussia.

The idea of an alliance rests on the premise of revolution from above, an overarching view of German history that emphasizes the ability of Prussian conservative elites to introduce just enough reform to stave off revolution from below. The importance of the revolution from above in early modern and modern German history is undeniable; it remains the most secure conceptual handrail to guide students through German history. And yet this interpretation only half explains the formative era of German industrialization. Certainly the Prussian state's constitution by decree in 1848 was a revolution from above. It sapped bourgeois revolutionary vigor and refashioned the principle of a mixed-powers government toward conservative ends. But this does not explain how the preindustrial Prussian state harnessed the accelerating force of the new capitalist economy, a central element of its *Staatsraison.*

It does not provide a sufficient explanation of how the bourgeois class that led the industrial revolution established its relationship with the Prussian government after 1848.

The problem is not the term "alliance" but what is meant by it. The assumption that businessmen capitulated to the wishes of conservative elites and swapped political docility for economic concessions distorts both the actions and the sociopolitical outlook of this social group. This oversimplified interpretation fails to convey the complex process by which commercial and industrial elites joined forces with the Prussian establishment. More accurately, the amalgamation of new and old elites in postrevolutionary Prussia constituted an unresolved settlement, a process of accommodation in which opposing interests produced compromises for both sides. To render accurately the political resettlement after 1848, we must recognize entrepreneurial elites as agents of their own interests. Proponents of the structural continuity thesis must modify their conception of the social forces that produced modern Germany's economic foundations.

Conflicts arose between railroad entrepreneurs and government officials. This was hardly surprising. Eager to promote private enterprise and greater financial independence in the 1850s, businessmen were bound to oppose the policies of a state apparatus accustomed to directing the economy for its own purposes. Businessmen registered their resistance to government policy early on, with their refusal to run night trains. The standoff from 1849 to 1853 between Heydt, who made no secret of wanting to own and administrate all railways in Prussia, and numerous railroad companies characterized the defensive posture of railroad directors toward the trade ministry for the rest of the decade. The litigation over night trains rendered a serviceable image for government-business relations in the 1850s: businessmen opposed to government actions using the state to seek a just, legal settlement.

The strained relations with government are further confirmed by the suppressed royal decree of 1856. Government officials perceived the creation of commandite and joint-stock banks as a powerful instrument of a monied bourgeoisie, whose financial clout posed a threat to the political and economic status of the Prussian establishment. The suppressed decree of 1856 marks two important features: the antagonism of the Prussian cabinet toward the business class in the mid-1850s, and the decline of the power of the state to direct and control the economy. The episode revealed that, when prevented from making money, Prussian businessmen did not abide by government wishes. And by undermining and circumventing state policy, Prussian businessmen set their own terms.

The behavior of railroad entrepreneurs in this period reveals a business class capable of both opposition and cooperation with the Prussian state.

When government interests coincided with theirs, businessmen worked with the state. They welcomed state backing in 1842, state intervention during railroad bankruptcies in 1848, and state construction when private investors showed no interest in building the Eastern Railway. This pattern continued through the 1850s. The Rhenish and Cologne-Minden railways, for example, shrewdly negotiated state subsidies and long-term loans to build the Cologne-Deutz bridge, completed in 1858. Prussian businessmen expected and received state support. They tapped state resources when they could and exploited the state's long history of funding private projects of public interest.

Yet entrepreneurs equally demonstrated defiance when material interests were at stake. Although dependent on the trade ministry for loans, charters, and authorizations for stock issue, dividend rates, and timetables, railroad directors refused to comply with orders deemed unfair or injurious to business. In addition to opposing night trains and banking policy, railroad businessmen also protested the terms of the 1853 Railroad Tax, the publication of monthly profits, the state order to build a second reserve fund, the government's refusal to charter new railway companies, and the discharging of employees involved with the Revolution of 1848. Directors incurred thousands of thalers in fines while challenging the encroachments of government. The protocols of the Rhenish Railway (one of the few company papers extant) reveal a decade-long adversarial relationship with the trade ministry. The interests and aims of government officials and railroad entrepreneurs were usually in conflict, not in concert.

It is hardly accurate, then, to speak of a symbiotic alliance, when elites of business and finance were compelled throughout the 1850s to fend off an acquisitive government interested in absorbing the most profitable financial sector in Germany. Heydt not only supervised with a heavy hand but also took over financially strapped companies against their will. (Having taken over seven railway companies within seven years—amounting to tens of millions of thalers of lost share-capital—Heydt might well deserve the epithet of the first "corporate raider.") That the business class was able to ward off total state absorption speaks of its political ability to use bureaucratic channels, the new parliament, and the press to defend its turf.

At issue in the struggle between state and private ownership was the need of the business class to develop means to press its claims. Individually each company defended itself through bureaucratic channels, chambers of commerce, and courts of law. On a corporate level, the creation of five railroad *Verbände* in the 1850s protected private railroads against state dominance; Heydt's hostility toward these associations confirmed their purpose. And on the parliamentary level, various factions—among them free traders—challenged Heydt's use of public funds for state railroad construction. The increasingly vigilant position among liberal deputies (such railroad investors as Robert von Patow, Karl Milde, Friedrich Harkort, and Ludwig Kühne) transformed the issue of the Railroad Fund into a battle of principle over the legislature's budgetary powers. Heydt's illegal bookkeeping and his penchant for constructing state railways on borrowed money exacerbated his relationship with the legislature, which passed the cabinet's bill to dissolve the Railroad Fund. The Chamber of Deputies and House of Lords secured the profits of Prussia's leading sector for private enterprise.

In short, the continued existence of Prussia's private railroad industry was not a concession. The economic-political activity of the business class was not passive or a retreat from politics. Rather, the various dialogues and protracted exchanges that defended and secured private railroad ownership unfolded as a struggle. Railroad entrepreneurs exerted pressure on the government to win particular business-related gains and scored important successes. They showed no hesitation in articulating their material interests, a form of politics that should not be dismissed as secondary to parliamentary activity. Establishing the right to make money is a political process. As Thomas Nipperdey noted: "Economic interests, economic growth, and economic crises became rudimentary political-social facts. The politics of the economy became a central part of politics." [2] Entrepreneurial assertiveness contributed to Prussia's new economic policies in the 1860s, a political shift that had far-reaching consequences for both domestic and foreign politics. The National Liberal party, for example, derives its political origins as much from the modus operandi of the business class in the 1850s as from military victory in 1866.

The assimilation of the entrepreneurial elite should thus be seen as a dual process of two mutually reinforcing factors: a forceful business class that applied pressure on the state to abandon its tradition of paternalism; and the subsequent government response, which reformulated economic policy and gradually retreated from the marketplace over the course of the 1850s. To understand this process, both elements need to be weighted equally. Responding to business interests, the Prussian state acquiesced in key economic questions. It reformulated its economic policy to give the business class greater space to pursue private enterprise. And the business class, by achieving discrete economic reforms through protest, negotiation, and compromise, ultimately lent support to the Prussian state, enabling it to survive in the era of industrial capitalism.

The eventual nationalization of Prussian railroads in 1878/79 merits attention, especially in regard to how it affects this study's argument on government-business relations. By 1865 private railways dominated the Prussian network; their 3,672.75 kilometers outweighed the 1,701.95 kilometers of railway owned and operated by the state.[3] After the reorganization of Germany in 1866, the balance tipped once more in favor of the state, for the Prussian state absorbed the Hessian and Hanoverian state railways. This addition of approximately 1,200 kilometers to the state-owned network gave Bismarck the impetus to propose the nationalization of all railways in 1866–67.

Examining railroad companies in the years 1866–78 reaffirms the assertiveness of business elites in shaping the railroad industry to their needs and not necessarily to those of the state(s). The railroad industry rebuffed plans for nationalization as long as railways wished to remain private, that is, as long as they persisted as a lucrative sector for capital investment. With the help of particularist interests of southern states, profitable private railroads were able to fend off the growing cries for state ownership and a simpler tariff system in 1866–67.[4] An Imperial Railway Office was established in 1873 to streamline the tariff system for private railways but remained ineffective because of what Bismarck called "the railway powers," finance capitalists who refused to accept the interventionist presumptions of a new imperial agency demanding lower and simpler freight rates.[5] In 1876 Bismarck sought again to nationalize the empire's railways and was defeated on two counts: first, by the middle German states and private railroad interests; and second, by his own ministers Otto Camphausen and Heinrich von Aachenbach, who in the space of two years could not agree on a smaller bill that would focus exclusively on Prussia. He accused them of passive resistance to his policies because of their close connection to entrepreneurial circles, which was largely true.[6]

Bismarck and Albert Maybach, the chief of the newly created ministry of railroad affairs, did however succeed in nationalizing railroads with a law in December 1879. Nationalization was part of the broad-scale tax reform that "refounded the Reich" in 1878/79, jettisoning free trade to revive the interventionist state. Tariff protectionism and a nationalized rail system promoted the interests of both heavy industry and agriculture and appeared to bludgeon railway capitalism—financiers and capitalists were apparently denied the right to profit from administrating railways and trading their shares on the bourse. But, although other commercial circles did complain vociferously about the sweeping changes of 1878/79, the view from the railroad industry suggests that the law was mostly welcomed. Hans Viktor von Unruh and Ruhr industrialists opposed the plan, but most railroad entrepreneurs saw it as a fair settlement. Since 1873 railroad stocks had experienced a downward trend, and the late 1870s were particularly hard.[7] Whereas the average interest rate on German railroad stock stood at 7.3 percent in 1871, it slid to 4.7 in 1874 and 4.4 in 1879. Such returns were not much better than state paper.[8] Railroads yielded to other economic sectors as stock market leaders (electrical engineering, chemicals, and machine building), compelling railroad directors to accept generous state compensation for shares that might never rise to previous levels.[9] Thus, unlike earlier attempts in the 1850s and 1860s, a consensus for state ownership existed—most railroads surrendered willingly, seeing it as an opportune time to bail out. Making the best of a persistent commercial slump (and disappointing freight volume), railroad capitalists also benefitted from the swing to state interventionism.[10] Hence the railroad industry, as a sector involved in shipping and international commerce, does not conform neatly to the interpretation that Bismarck, by splitting commercial and heavy industrial interests, could ally iron with rye. The railroad industry was brought into the purview of the interventionist state with the blessings of the major private lines. In this respect, we do not see a great "second founding" in government-business affairs but, rather, a longer continuity of business sectors using the state for their needs. The eventual nationalization of railways was as much a triumph for smart capital as it was for state power.

Overall, then, the revolution-from-above model to explain the political economy of the first industrial revolution clearly has grave limitations. Through the window of the railroad industry, one can mark the growing connections between the state and the business world and the latter's ability to influence policy. Businessmen penetrated ministerial policy-making before 1848, contested state economic policy in the 1850–58 period, and successfully agitated for favorable economic and legal settlements after 1858. Business elites never abandoned their privileged status of direct access to ministries (manifesting the impact of the bureaucratic state on business political culture) yet also used the growing public sphere of the press, lobbies, parliament, and chambers of commerce to press for their needs. After 1858 the government responded to the agitation of railroad companies, lobbies, stock market investors, and the press for business reforms with key economic legislation. The willingness of the trade ministry to prepare bills that pleased the business world marks the many ties, formal and informal, between the bourgeois businessmen and the Prussian state. In fact, business politics after 1840 confounds German historians' general dichotomy of state vs. society and the more specific binary paradigm of bureaucratic-noble state vs. bourgeois civil society. The embourgeoisment of the Prussian establishment is pervasive in sectors pertaining to political economy. In sum, characterizing the state's ability to control the political and economic dimensions of industrialization as a "revolution from above" is empirically inaccurate and conceptually skewed. More satisfactory is viewing postrevolutionary state building as a mutual accommodation of capital and political authority: an evolving settlement negotiated to the full satisfaction of no one party.

In viewing the economic-political goals of railroad entrepreneurs during period 1830–70, we see significant limitations. Businessmen's chief concerns were attaining particular, business-related needs; even economic principles were dispensable. They ostensibly defended the inviolate rights of free trade, the joint-stock principle, the right to association, and the superiority of private over state enterprises. But the driving element behind these principles was the practical necessity of making money. When their material interests so dictated, businessmen abandoned such time-honored doctrines as free trade and private railways, as they did in 1878/79. The abandonment of economic liberalism in 1878/79 was consistent, however, with the political tactics of the business class since 1830, regularly vacillating between state intervention and free trade as an expedient to profit.

The sole principle consistently upheld by businessmen throughout this era was perhaps the belief in law, especially as it affected property relations. Before 1848 the antipathy for arbitrary government among liberal businessmen fueled their espousal for a state ruled by constitutional law (*Rechtsstaat*). But their proposals for a constitutional settlement (before and after 1848) revealed what kind of lawful state they envisioned. It was not such inalienable rights as liberty or universal suffrage (which most businessmen firmly rejected) that made the business class press for a constitution. Rather, they sought laws that distributed taxes equitably, secured property rights, and promoted commercial progress. Rhenish burghers, as we have already seen, devised the three class system of voting in 1845, an electoral procedure that underscored the primacy of wealth and property over equality. The economic brokering that reached new heights in the Reichstag in the 1880s and 1890s was not a "deviation" from German parliamentary tradition. On the contrary, it was the logical outcome of Rhenish-Prussian political practices articulated since French rule on the Rhine.[11]

Because the business class never challenged the political rule of Prussia's conservative elite, it receives poor marks from historians, who assume modern capitalists should prefer democracy to authoritarian forms of government. This assumption, while perhaps noble, is not historically grounded. Although the entrepreneurial class was the engine of a new economic order, it is anachronistic to assume that industrial capitalists were irremediably estranged from the aristocracy and state apparatus of the old political order. We should place the actions and attitudes of businessmen within the context of early industrialization, a time when businessmen tried to accommodate new economic forces to old social structures. Prussia's entrepreneurial elite, too, was acculturated in the estate mentality of status and occupation. As men of property and intellect, the *Handelsstand* aspired to rise above local government and strove to integrate into the ruling elite, not to supplant it. Most important, between 1830 and 1870 the Prussian business class never intended to raze the state, but rather to modify it to better serve the interests of commerce and industry.

This accommodating, reformist attitude of the business class derives partly from its relations to the state in the late eighteenth and early nine-teenth centuries. Prussia's bureaucratic machinery preceded the emergence of an entrepreneurial class, which partially owed its early successes between 1770 and 1820 to government reforms. Businessmen first practiced capitalism under state paternalism and benefitted from loans, subsidies, customs unions, and market-oriented law. In spite of manifest disadvantages, businessmen rec-ognized Prussia's economic achievements and consequently admonished the monarchy after 1830 to reform politically or be overthrown. In the pre-March era (1830–48) they advocated modifying bureaucratic absolutism with consti-tutional checks, a political system that would reform but not undo the army, aristocracy, or even the bureaucracy. Before 1848 businessmen commonly dis-paraged the Prussian government for its arbitrary actions, unwarranted pater-nalism, and its slow execution of policy. Nonetheless the business class en-visioned political and economic reform within the structure of the Prussian state, which it largely perceived as a guarantor of commercial prosperity. It is not surprising—nor a bourgeois "surrender"—that in 1848 such businessmen as Camphausen, Hansemann, and Heydt accepted ministerial positions and worked with the king and his bureaucracy to arbitrate between new and old. Radical democratic upheaval was never an element in their political outlook.

In the 1850s the business class continued on a similar course. It pursued specific material gains and, in so doing, sought to reform state economic policy. (That many idealist participants in the 1848 revolutions subsequently converted to the *Realpolitik* of the 1850s should not prevent us from recog-nizing the political continuity of the business class.) After 1849 businessmen worked with the government but criticized it, too, much as they had be-fore 1848. The lesson of the 1850s, however, was perhaps more significant. Through both conflict and cooperation the business class tested the capacity of the Prussian state to bend to the needs of modern capitalism. With banks, railroads, and coal mines, the Prussian state relented to protests and reformu-lated its economic policy to accommodate the demands of its business class. Sometimes voluntarily (as with coal mines), sometimes grudgingly (as with commandite banks and railroads), the state relinquished certain controls over the economy, acceding greater autonomy to private enterprise. In a slow and unspectacular way the dialogue that the business class had developed with the Prussian state since the 1830s produced profitable results by the late 1850s.

It is striking that Prussia's business class remained content to negotiate with the state for particular gains; wealthy capitalists sought neither direct political power nor resolutely pursued constitutional issues. The trade minis-ter's unchecked authority, for example, was commonly criticized by business circles. But railroad businessmen readily accepted Heydt's dictatorial powers when it meant the swift execution of favorable decisions (a dividend guarantee, a charter, credit). For short-term gains businessmen tolerated ministerial authority whose potential for abuse they knew first hand. Direct negotiation with ministries also undermined the power of parliament. Ministers like Heydt often presented retroactively the financial transactions between railroad companies and the government to the parliament, making the chamber's task of enforcing its budgetary powers more difficult. In brief, businessmen alternated between direct negotiation with the bureaucracy and indirect arbitration through the parliament, press, and courts to attain their desired settlement. This blend of strategies reveals a greater interest in expediency than in adherence to legal spheres of political rule and administration. The fluid, ill-defined spheres of power in the business world of mid-century Prussia suggest much about the commitment of business elites to constitutions and their ambivalent attitude toward the state.

Business cycles played an important role in the dialogue between businessmen and state officials. It would be an exaggeration to link directly the behavior of businessmen to cycles of economic growth, but a rough correlation is present. The constitutional movement of 1830–47, and its accompanying criticism of state paternalism, occurred during an overall period of economic expansion. The decline in production between 1846 and 1849 and the threat to property in 1848 encouraged greater reliance on both state credit and state authority.

Similarly, the boom cycle of 1850/51–57 produced a critical, independent spirit among business elites. The willingness of railroad entrepreneurs to undermine state banking policy and to contest numerous ministerial rescripts spoke of assertive opposition. But the depression of 1857–59 returned government-business relations to their old course. The first financial crisis in world capitalism reasserted the business class's reliance on the state, for it narrowed the options for large-scale capitalism. With money and confidence scarce, railroad entrepreneurs looked to the state for regulatory laws (increased money supply, suspension of usury ordinances), direct assistance (loans, dividend guarantees), and safe investment (state paper, loans to government). With promotional commercial banking made riskier after 1857, Germany's new investment banks turned to state loans as a cautious but profitable undertaking. Once reviled as "agents of the French" by the government in 1853–56, such railroad financiers as Gustav Mevissen, Abraham Oppenheim, and David Hansemann became the chief figures of the Prussian Consortium, the collection of bankers that intermittently financed war loans during the era of unification, 1859–71.

In retrospect the contingency of the 1857 crisis and the accompanying shift in government-business relations was a critical juncture in German history. It decisively influenced relations between high finance and political power. By reestablishing the Prussian state as an economic necessity, it shaped the contours upon which the economic foundation of the future German empire was laid. How this change exactly affected the business class during the Prussian constitutional conflict of 1862–66, which occurred during a pronounced upward swing in economic growth, is difficult to measure. It is, however, hard to dispute the overall effect of the long business cycle of 1850/51–1873, which benefited both the business class and the Junker landholding class (whose grain sales rose on the free market). That the economic interests of these two classes coincided with each other during a crucial period of state building—especially during the constitutional crisis—remains an essential structural peculiarity of modern German history. We could speak, then, of a conjunctural *Sonderweg,* but only in qualified terms.[12] To refer to business cycles without reference to the larger context of Prussian political culture would be a facile, unconvincing approach to the problem.

The effect of the 1857 crisis was consolidated, furthermore, by the political-economic gains of businessmen in the New Era. Their interests were weighed by both the cabinet, which researched and initiated important economic reforms, and the legislature, which cooperated with ministers and passed their bills. Between 1859 and 1862 strong signals of a *juste milieu* between old and new elites appeared. In 1859, at the tail end of the depression, the government plan to buy out all railways was abandoned. In 1861, the Landtag passed a property tax for the landed estates in the eastern provinces, and the government lifted in the same year the final restrictions of the direction principle in coal mining. In 1862 Prussia signed a free trade treaty with France and completed the Commercial Code (begun in 1857), which earned the applause of businessmen.

These changes suggested the willingness of the Prussian establishment to compromise on long-standing grievances (like the disproportionate tax burden borne by the western provinces) and grant legal and practical reforms that allowed businessmen to expand their markets and industrial base. These gains showed the ability of Prussia's New Era cabinet and legislature to arbitrate between business and landed classes, state and private interests. Similarly, such incidents as the suppressed decree of 1856 showed the relative worth of the constitution as a check to royal arbitrary actions.

The developments from 1858 to 1862 supported the contemporary popular belief that material progress would inevitably bring political advances. The appointment of Heinrich von Itzenplitz as trade minister in 1862 capped a series of events that seemed to anchor bourgeois interests in the center of Prussian politics. By the time the constitutional conflict began to escalate to crisis proportions in 1862, business elites had seen that pressure on the government brought results—a favorable economic policy. Business elites had learned over the course of the 1850s that industrial capitalism could flourish within the constraints of the Prussian conservative state.

The case-by-case process through which business and government elites established terms to accommodate capital and conservative political authority played, then, an indisputably important role in the consolidation of Prussian state power after 1848, and it became an essential precondition to unification. If historians are to understand the structural continuities in German history, we must begin to recognize the role played by businessmen in establishing the conditions for that continuity in the postrevolutionary state building period. Placing the political aims and actions of Prussian entrepreneurs in proper context in the period 1830–70 supplements our explanation of how industrial capitalism and authoritarian government uneasily accommodated one another in mid-century Germany.

ABBREVIATIONS

ARbdB	Archiv der Reichsbahndirektion Berlins
BA Potsdam	Bundesarchiv, Abteilungen Potsdam (formerly Deutsches Zentralarchiv, Potsdam)
BBZ	*Berliner Börsen-Zeitung*
BLHA	Brandenburgisches Landeshauptarchiv, Potsdam (formerly Staatsarchiv Potsdam)
EbZ	*Eisenbahn-Zeitung*
GStA Berlin	Geheimes Staatsarchiv preussischer Kulturbesitz, Berlin
GStA Merseburg	Geheimes Staatsarchiv preussischer Kulturbesitz, Abteilung Merseburg (formerly Deutsches Zentralarchiv, Dienststelle Merseburg)
HAStK	Historisches Archiv der Stadt Köln
LHAK	Landeshauptarchiv Koblenz
NZ	*National-Zeitung*
SBHA	*Stenographische Berichte über die Verhandlungen des Landtags: Haus der Abgeordneten*
SBHH	*Stenographische Berichte über die Verhandlungen des Landtags: Herrenhaus*
SEG	Heinrich Schulthess, ed., *Europäischer Geschichtskalender*
SpN	*Berlinische [Spener] Nachrichten*
VBMHGA	*Verwaltungs-Bericht des Ministeriums für Handel, Gewerbe und öffentliche Arbeit*
VZ	*Vossische Zeitung*

Note on Archives and Translation

The research for this study was undertaken between 1988 and 1993, years which witnessed not only the unification of West and East Germany but also the relocation and renaming of state archives. In 1993 the lion's share of the Prussian state archive was moved from the East German archive, Deutsches Zentralarchiv, Dienstelle Merseburg, to its site before the Second World War, the Geheimes Staatsarchiv, Dahlem-Berlin. The Deutsches Zentralarchiv Potsdam was renamed Bundesarchiv Potsdam, just as the Staatsarchiv Potsdam, located in the orangerie at Sanssouci, reverted to its old name, the Brandenburgisches Landeshauptarchiv. In the above abbreviations I note all current and earlier names of archives. I have, however, decided to continue to cite those repositories used in the former Deutsches Zentralarchiv at Merseburg as a separate section of Berlin's Geheimes Staatsarchiv: GStA Merseburg. This usage enables the reader to discern with greater accuracy where the information was found. Moreover, at my last visit to the Geheimes Staatsarchiv in Berlin (July 1996), I found that the Merseburg repositories are still stored separately from the Berlin repositories and, more importantly, the archive still uses the old classification system. And because it is unlikely that the system will change, the interested reader should still be able to find individual documents with the citations used in the notes.

I have translated the offices of *Regierungspräsident* as district governor and *Oberpräsident* as provincial governor. I have mostly used the awkward term deputy prefect for *Landrat,* although the German term is used too. The bicameral legislature of Prussia is referred to as a parliament; the *Haus der Abgeordneten* is designated the lower house or chamber and the *Herrenhaus,* the upper house or chamber. The elected representatives are called deputies.

NOTES

Chapter One

1. August Ludwig von Rochau, *Grundsätze der Realpolitik angewendet auf de Zustände Deutschlands,* ed. Hans-Ulrich Wehler (Frankfurt a.M., 1972), p. 25.

2. Ibid., p. 25.

3. Ibid., pp. 42–43.

4. Ibid., p. 32.

5. For discussions on Rochau's thought, see Leonard Krieger, *The German Idea of Freedom: History of a Political Tradition* (Boston, 1957), pp. 354–57; Andrew Lees, *Revolution and Reflection: Intellectual Change in Germany during the 1850s* (The Hague, 1974), pp. 107–8, 113–15; Rochau, *Realpolitik,* pp. 7–21.

6. I borrow the term "structural continuity thesis" from R. J. Evans, "The Myth of Germany's Missing Revolution," *New Left Review* 149–54 (1985): 68 ff.

7. Hans-Ulrich Wehler, *Deutsche Gesellschaftsgeschichte,* vol. 3, *Von der "Deutschen Doppelrevolution" bis zum Beginn des Ersten Weltkrieges 1849–1914* (Munich, 1995), p. 113; see also Jürgen Kocka, "Zur Schichtung der preussischen Bevölkerung während der industriellen Revolution," in Wilhelm Treue, ed., *Geschichte als Aufgabe: Festschrift für Otto Büsch zu seinem 60. Geburtstag* (Berlin, 1988), pp. 368–69; and Kocka, "Bürgertum und bürgerliche Gesellschaft im 19. Jahrhundert: Europäische Entwicklungen und deutsche Eigenarten," in Kocka, ed., *Bürgertum im 19. Jahrhundert: Deutschland im europäischen Vergleich* (Munich, 1988), 1:12. Also instructive is Wilhelm Stahl, *Der Elitekreislauf in der Unternehmerschaft: Eine empirische Untersuchung für den deutschsprachigen Raum* (Frankfurt a.M., 1973), p. 126. Stahl's figures are slightly higher, because his tabulations refer to the entire nineteenth century.

8. I use the gender-specific term *businessman,* because there were, to my knowledge, no women working at the upper echelons of railroad companies, or in the state bureaucracy. Gender-neutral terms thus do not seem appropriate in this historical discussion. This is not to say that the question of gender in the age of capitalism is unimportant. On the contrary, the widening difference in gender roles created by the capitalist market economy for bourgeois and working classes is an extremely important premise in understanding the full impact of capitalism on social relations. For these classes the separate roles of breadwinning and child rearing, house work and office work, became more pronounced over the course of the nineteenth century, sharply engendering the roles of production and reproduction. See Ute Frevert, *Bürgerinnen und Bürger: Geschlechterverhältnisse im 19. Jahrhundert* (Göttingen, 1988); Ursula Vogel, "Patriarchale Herrschaft, bürgerliches Recht, bürgerliche Utopie: Eigentumsrechte der Frauen in Deutschland und England," in Kocka, ed., *Bürgertum im. 19.*

Jahrhundert, 1:406–38; Ute Gerhard, "Die Rechtsstellung der Frau in der bürgerlichen Gesellschaft des 19. Jahrhunderts: Frankreich und Deutschland im Vergleich," in ibid., 1:439–68; and Ute Frevert, "Bürgerliche Familie und Geschlechterrollen: Modell und Wirklichkeit," in Lutz Niethammer et al., *Bürgerliche Gesellschaft in Deutschland: Historische Einblicke, Fragen, Perspektiven* (Frankfurt a.M., 1990), pp. 90–98. Leonore Davidoff and Catherine Hall's *Family Fortunes: Men and Women of the English Middle Class, 1780–1850* (Chicago, 1987), pp. 272–315, has thrown light on the role of English women and their capital in business.

9. Friedrich Engels quoted by Heinz Wuttmer, "Die Herkunft der industriellen Bourgeoisie Preussens in den vierziger Jahren des 19. Jahrhunderts," in Hans Mottek et al., *Studien zur Geschichte der industriellen Revolution in Deutschland* (Berlin, 1960), p. 145.

10. For the thesis of a historic compromise, see Theodor Schieder, *Staatensystem als Vormacht der Welt 1848–1918* (Frankfurt a.M., 1975), pp. 141 ff; E. J. Hobsbawm's *The Age of Capital, 1848–1875* (New York, 1975) provides a panoramic portrayal of the first industrial revolution.

11. A representative (and by no means comprehensive) selection of monographs advancing the structural continuity thesis are Friedrich Zunkel, *Der rheinisch-westfälische Unternehmer 1834–1879: Ein Beitrag zur Geschichte des deutschen Bürgertums im 19. Jahrhundert* (Cologne, 1962); Helmut Böhme, *Deutschlands Weg zur Grossmacht: Studien zum Verhältnis von Wirtschaft und Staat während der Reichsgründungszeit 1848–1881* (Cologne, 1966); Hans Rosenberg, *Grosse Depression und Bismarckzeit* (Berlin, 1967); Dirk Stegmann, *Die Erben Bismarcks: Parteien und Verbände in der Spätphase des wilhelminischen Deutschlands; Sammlungspolitik 1897–1918* (Cologne, 1970); H.-J. Puhle, *Agrarische Interessenpolitik und preussischer Konservatismus im wilhelminischen Kaiserreich 1893–1914* (Hanover, 1966); Puhle, *Von der Agrarkrise zum Präfaschismus* (Wiesbaden, 1972); Dieter Groh, *Negative Integration und revolutionärer Attentismus* (Frankfurt a.M., 1974); Peter-Christian Witt, *Die Finanzpolitik des deutschen Reiches von 1903 bis 1913* (Lübeck, 1970); Eckhart Kehr, *Schlachtflottenbau und Parteipolitik* (Berlin, 1930); Kehr, *Der Primat der Innenpolitik: Gesammelte Aufsatze zur preussisch-deutschen Socialgeschichte,* ed. by Hans-Ulrich Wehler (Berlin, 1965); Hans Jaeger, *Unternehmer in der deutschen Politik (1890–1918)* (Bonn, 1967); Fritz Fischer, *Griff nach der Weltmacht: Die Kriegszielpolitik des kaiserlichen Deutschland 1914–1918* (Düsseldorf, 1961); Fritz Fischer, *War of Illusions: German Policies from 1911 to 1914* (New York, 1975); Hans-Ulrich Wehler, *Das deutsche Kaiserreich* (Göttingen, 1973); Wehler, *Bismarck und der Imperialismus* (Cologne, 1969); Hartmut Kaelble, *Industrielle Interessenpolitik in der wilhelminischen Gesellschaft: Der Centralverband der deutschen Industriellen* (Berlin, 1970); Michael Stürmer, ed., *Das kaiserliche Deutschland: Politik und Gesellschaft 1870–1914* (Düsseldorf, 1970); and Volker Berghahn, *Germany and the Approach of War in 1914* (London, 1973). Synthetic overviews of this thesis can be found in Martin Kitchen, *The Political Economy of Germany, 1815–1914* (London, 1978); Helmut Böhme, *An Introduction to the Social and Economic History of Germany* (New York, 1978); and Fritz Fischer, *From Kaiserreich to Third Reich: Elements of Continuity in German History, 1871–1945* (Boston,

1986). Robert G. Moeller provides an instructive introduction to this paradigm in "The Kaiserreich Recast? Continuity and Change in Modern German Historiography," *Journal of Social History* 17 (1984): 655–84.

12. For a representative orthodox Marxist survey on the broad sweep of German history, see Joachim Streisand, *Deutsche Geschichte in einem Blick,* 5th ed. (Berlin, 1980), chap. 3. For the standard account on the 1848 revolution, see Karl Obermann, *Deutschland von 1815 bis 1849: Von der Gründung des Deutschen Bundes bis zur burgerlich-demokratischen Revolution* (Berlin, 1961), pp. 217 ff. Karl Marx's own scheme of social organization and his critique of the timid German bourgeoisie can be seen in *The German Ideology* (1845) and *Critique of Hegel's Philosophy of Right* (1844).

13. Dietrich Eichholtz, *Junker und Bourgeoisie vor 1848 in der preussischen Eisenbahngeschichte* (Berlin, 1962), p. 201.

14. Ibid., p. 203.

15. Obermann, "Zur Genesis der bürgerlichen Klasse in Deutschland von der Julirevolution 1830 bis zu Beginn der 40er Jahren des 19. Jahrhunderts," *Jahrbuch der Geschichte* 16 (1977): 33–66; Obermann, "Ludolf Camphausen und die bourgeois Konterrevolution," *Zeitschrift für Geschichtswissenschaft* 18 (1970): 1448–69; Ernst Engelberg, *Deutschland von 1848 bis 1871: Von der Niederlage der bürgerlich-demokratischen Revolution bis zur Reichsgründung* (Berlin, 1962); Roland Zeise, "Die Rolle des Zollvereins in den politischen Konzeptionen der deutschen Bourgeoisie von 1859/66," in Helmut Bleiber et al., eds., *Bourgeoisie und bürgerliche Umwälzung in Deutschland 1789–1871* (Berlin, 1977), pp. 433–56. The historiography of the former GDR toned down the betrayal of 1848 thesis in the 1980s, opting more for a long-term structural shift from 1789 to 1870, but the counterrevolutionary, weak-willed portrait of the bourgeoisie remained intact.

16. West German historiography is not completely free of teleological underpinnings and moralistic indictments of the bourgeoisie. And notions of betrayal can also be found in early West German literature on liberalism. See F. C. Sell, *Die Tragödie des deutschen Liberalismus* (Stuttgart, 1953), p. 226; Wilhelm Mommsen, *Grösse und Versagen des deutschen Bürgertums: Ein Beitrag zur politischen Bewegung des 19. Jahrhunderts, insbesonders zur Revolution 1848/49,* 2d ed. (Munich, 1964).

17. The best treatments on German historicism and its effect on political views are Bernd Faulenbach, *Ideologie des deutschen Weges* (Munich, 1980); and Georg G. Iggers, *The German Conception of History: The National Tradition of Historical Thought from Herder to the Present* (Middletown, Conn., 1968).

18. Thorstein Veblen, *Imperial Germany and the Industrial Revolution* (New York, 1913); Talcott Parsons, "Democracy and Social Structure in Pre-Nazi Germany," in Parsons, ed., *Essays on Sociological Theory* (Glencoe, 1954); Ralf Dahrendorf, *Society and Democracy in Germany* (New York, 1967; German edition 1959); Barrington Moore, Jr., *Social Origins of Dictatorship and Democracy* (London, 1967); Reinhard Bendix, *Work and Authority in Industry* (New York, 1963); Bendix, *Nation Building and Citizenship* (New York, 1964); Alexander Gerschenkron, *Economic Backwardness in Historic Perspective* (Cambridge, Mass., 1962); Hans-Ulrich Wehler, *Modernisierungstheorie und Geschichte* (Göttingen, 1975); Charles Tilly, ed., *The Forma-*

182 · Notes to Chapter One

tion of National States in Western Europe (Princeton, 1975); Raymond Grew, ed., *Crises of Political Development in Europe and the United States* (Princeton, 1978); Jürgen Kocka, "Theory and Social History: Recent Developments in West Germany," *Social Research* 47 (1980): 426–57; Michael Lowy, *The Politics of Combined and Uneven Development* (London, 1981); Thomas Nipperdey, "Probleme der Modernisierung in Deutschland," in *Nachdenken über die deutsche Geschichte: Essays* (Munich, 1990), pp. 52–70. Also important for German modernization theory is the critical theory of Jürgen Habermas, especially his *Strukturwandel der Öffentlichkeit: Untersuchungen zu einer Kategorie der bürgerlichen Gesellschaft,* 13th ed. (Darmstadt, 1982); and his *Legitimationsprobleme des Spätkapitalismus* (Frankfurt a.M., 1973).

19. Hans-Ulrich Wehler, *Gesellschaftsgeschichte,* vol. 2, *Von der Reformära bis zur industriellen und politischen "deutschen Doppelrevolution," 1815–1845/49* (Munich, 1987), p. 205.

20. Heinrich Heffter, *Die deutsche Selbstverwaltung im 19. Jahrhundert,* 2d ed. (Stuttgart, 1969), p. 350.

21. Hartmut Kaelble, "Wie feudal waren die deutschen Unternehmer im Kaiserreich? Ein Zwischenbericht," in Richard Tilly, ed., *Beiträge zur quantitativen vergleichenden Unternehmergeschichte* (Stuttgart, 1985), p. 149.

22. Zunkel, *Unternehmer,* pp. 251, 249.

23. Ibid., pp. 251, 106.

24. This interpretation differs little from the view of Engelberg, *Deutschland,* pp. 37–40.

25. Zunkel, *Unternehmer,* p. 249.

26. Ibid., p. 251.

27. The classic presentation of the "revolution from above" is Wolfgang Sauer's 1962 essay, "Das Problem des deutschen Nationalstaats," reprinted in Hans-Ulrich Wehler, ed., *Moderne deutsche Sozialgeschichte* (Cologne, 1966), pp. 407–36.

28. Wehler, introduction to Rochau's *Realpolitik,* p. 14.

29. Jürgen Kocka, *Unternehmensverwaltung und Angestelltenschaft am Beispiel Siemens 1847–1914: Zum Verhältnis von Kapitalismus und Bürokratie in der deutschen Industrialisierung* (Stuttgart, 1969), pp. 45–46; Böhme, *Deutschlands Weg zur Grossmacht;* Richard Tilly, "The Political Economy of Public Finance and the Industrialization of Prussia, 1815–1866," *Journal of Economic History* 26 (1966): 484–97; Heinrich August Winkler, *Liberalismus und Antiliberalismus* (Göttingen, 1979), pp. 21–22; Hans-Ulrich Wehler, introduction, *Realpolitik,* pp. 12, 14; Wehler, *Gesellschaftsgeschichte,* 2:206–7; Wehler, *Kaiserreich;* Wolfgang Mommsen, *Der autoritäre Nationalstaat: Verfassung, Gesellschaft und Kultur im deutschen Kaiserreich* (Frankfurt a.M., 1990), p. 261; Wolfgang Klee, *Preussiche Eisenbahngeschichte* (Stuttgart, 1982), p. 118; and Wolfram Siemann, *Die deutsche Revolution* (Frankfurt a.M., 1988), p. 228.

30. Böhme, *Deutschlands Weg zur Grossmacht,* pp. 29–49, 135 ff.

31. Ibid., pp. 91–134.

32. Ibid., p. 16.

33. Ibid., p. 60.

34. Otto Pflanze, "Another Crisis among German Historians? Helmut Böhme's

Deutschlands Weg zur Grossmacht," *Journal of Modern History* 40 (1968): 126–28; for two other informative discussions of Böhme's work, see Lothar Gall, "Staat und Wirtschaft in der Reichsgründungszeit," *Historische Zeitschrift* 209 (1969): 616–30; Hans-Ulrich Wehler, "Sozialökonomie und Geschichtswissenschaft," *Neue Politische Literatur* 14 (1969): 347–59.

35. Theodore S. Hamerow, *The Social Foundations of German Unification, 1858–1871: Ideas and Institutions* (Princeton, 1969), pp. 3–180; Hamerow, *The Social Foundations of German Unification: Struggles and Accomplishments* (Princeton, 1972), pp. 3–148. See, too, his *Restoration, Revolution, Reaction: Economics and Politics in Germany, 1815–1871* (Princeton, 1958), pp. 238–55.

36. Hamerow's wealth of information comes from printed sources and not from state or business archival repositories; Böhme consulted numerous state archives but centered his research on how trade policy was used as a tool of foreign policy.

37. See, for example, Hans Jaeger, *Geschichte der Wirtschaftsordnung in Deutschland* (Frankfurt a.M., 1988); Hubert Kiesewetter, *Industrielle Revolution in Deutschland, 1815–1914* (Frankfurt a.M., 1989); Wilhelm Treue, *Gebhardt Handbuch der deutschen Geschichte*, vol. 17, *Gesellschaft, Wirtschaft und Technik Deutschlands im 19. Jahrhundert* (Munich, 1986); W. O. Henderson, *The Rise of German Industrial Power, 1834–1914* (Berkeley, 1975); Wolfgang Mommsen, *Das Ringen um den nationalen Staat 1850–1890* (Berlin, 1993); James J. Sheehan, *German History, 1770–1866* (Oxford, 1989).

38. Hans Boldt presented a similar viewpoint in 1970: "Deutscher Konstitutionalismus und Bismarckreich," in Stürmer, ed., *Das kaiserliche Deutschland*, pp. 123–24; see also James Sheehan, *German Liberalism in the Nineteenth Century* (Chicago, 1983), pp. 115–16. For a judicious presentation of this segment of the constitutional crisis, see Otto Pflanze, *Bismarck and the Unification of Germany*, 2d ed. (Princeton, 1990), 1: chap. 8.

39. Michael Gugel, *Industrieller Aufstieg und bürgerlicher Herrschaft: Soziookonomischer Interessen und politische Ziele des liberalen Burgertums* (Cologne, 1975), pp. 230 ff.

40. Ibid., pp. 70–91, 230–31.

41. Ibid., p. 233.

42. Ibid., chap. 5.

43. Lothar Machtan and Dietrich Milles, *Die Klassensymbiose von Junkertum und Bourgeoisie: Zum Verhältnis von gesellschaftlicher und politischer Herrschaft in Preussen-Deutschland 1850–1878/79* (Frankfurt a.M., 1980), p. 10.

44. Ibid., p. 32.

45. Ibid., p. 31.

46. Ibid., p. 32.

47. Ibid.

48. Ibid., p. 40.

49. Gugel, *Industrieller Aufstieg*, p. 234.

50. Johann Jacoby and Franz Waldeck are examples of Prussian democrats who espoused genuine democratic beliefs. But the significance of such a democrat as

Jacoby in Prussian history is precisely his exceptional status. See Rolf Weber, *Das Unglück der Könige: Johann Jacoby 1805–1877* (Berlin, 1987).

51. Dieter Grimm, *Deutsche Verfassungsgeschichte 1776–1866* (Frankfurt a.M., 1988), chaps. 3–5.

52. Zunkel, *Unternehmer,* p. 134. Dumont's outlook could certainly be interpreted as opportunistic, as it was by the Düsseldorf Regierungspräsident von Spiegel in 1844. These men, von Spiegel wrote, gladly speak of politics, "but when one pursues their views closer, one finds out quickly that their judgments are based on either financial gain or personal prestige." Joseph Hansen, ed., *Rheinische Briefe und Akten zur Geschichte der politischen Bewegung* (Cologne, 1919; reprint 1969), 1:677; Zunkel, *Unternehmer,* p. 102.

53. Elisabeth Fehrenbach, "Rheinischer Liberalismus und gesellschaftlicher Verfassung," in Wolfgang Schieder, ed., *Liberalismus in der Gesellschaft des deutschen Vormärz* (Göttingen, 1983), pp. 272–95; Kurt Düwell, "David Hansemann als rheinpreussicher Liberaler in Heppenheim, 1847," in ibid., pp. 296–311; Wolfgang Kaschuba, "Zwischen Deutscher Nation und Deutscher Provinz: Politische Horizonte und soziale Milieus im frühen Liberalismus," in Dieter Langewiesche, ed., *Liberalismus im 19. Jahrhundert* (Göttingen, 1988), pp. 83–108; Toni Offermann, "Preussischer Liberalismus zwischen Revolution und Reichsgründung im regionalen Vergleich: Berliner und Kölner Fortschrittsliberalismus in der Konfliktszeit," in ibid., pp. 109–35, esp. pp. 109–12; Beate-Carola Padtberg, *Rheinischer Liberalismus in Köln während der politischen Reaktion in Preussen nach 1848/49* (Cologne, 1985), pp. 34–39; Sheehan, *German Liberalism,* pp. 35–48; Heinrich Best, *Die Männer von Bildung und Besitz: Struktur und Handeln parlamentarischer Führungsgruppen in Deutschland und Frankreich 1848/49* (Düsseldorf, 1990), pp. 373 ff.

54. Hamerow, *Social Foundations of German Unification: Struggles and Accomplishments,* pp. 15–17.

55. Heinrich Best, *Interessenpolitik und nationale Integration 1848/49* (Göttingen, 1980), pp. 121–273; Siemann, *Deutsche Revolution,* pp. 112–13.

56. Zunkel, *Unternehmer,* p. 134.

57. Joseph Hansen, *Gustav Mevissen: Ein Rheinisches Lebensbild 1815–1899,* 2 vols. (Berlin, 1906), 2:435.

58. Lothar Gall, "Liberalismus und bürgerliche Gesellschaft," pp. 162–86.

59. Padtberg, *Rheinischer Liberalismus,* pp. 232 ff.

60. Zunkel, *Unternehmer,* p. 100; Eugene N. Anderson, *The Social and Political Conflict in Prussia, 1858–1864* (Lincoln, Neb., 1954), p. 257.

61. Fehrenbach, "Rheinischer Liberalismus," p. 283. Similarly in 1830 he wrote that the middle class offered the crown greater stability against revolution than the landholding noble class:

Gerade der Mittelstand, weil dazu die angesehenen Kaufleute und Fabrikanten gehören, bietet dem Throne mehr Elemente der Stabilität und Ordnung dar, als der eigentliche Stand der Grundbesitzer. Der letztere läuft bei Krieg, bürgerlichen Unruhen und bei dem Wechsel der Regierung weit weniger Gefahr, als der Kaufmann und Fabrikant. Das Gewerbe der letzteren erleidet alsdann in den meisten

Fällen eine sehr empfindliche und häufig lang anhaltende Störung, während diejeni-
gen, deren Erwerb nur auf dem Grundbesitz beruht, mit Wahrscheinlichkeit darauf
zählen können, dass sie durch eine Veränderung der Regierung keinen Nachteil
erleiden, und dass der ihnen aus Krieg und Unruhen erwachsende Schade durch-
schnittlich reichlich durch die in der Regel mit einem solchen Zustande verbunde-
nen höheren Preise der Produkte des Ackerbaues kompensiert wird. ("Because respected merchants and manufacturers belong to the middle class, it offers the throne
more elements of stability and order than the rank of landed wealth. The latter runs
far fewer risks in war, civil unrest, and change of government than the merchant or
manufacturer. Their business suffers in these situations from pronounced and long-
lasting disturbances, while those whose livelihood derives from the land can with
probability rely on sustaining no disadvantages from a change in government. In the
case of war or civil disturbance, moreover, they would even be compensated with
higher agricultural prices, which as a rule accompany such conditions.")

David Hansemann, "Preussens Lage und Politik am Ende des Jahres 1830," in Joseph
Hansen, ed., *Rheinische Briefe,* 1:51.

62. Jeffry M. Diefendorf, *Businessmen and Politics in the Rhineland, 1789–1834*
(Princeton, 1980).

63. Ibid., p. 354.

64. Raymond Aron, "Social Class, Political Class, Ruling Class," in Reinhard
Bendix and Seymour M. Lipset, eds., *Class, Status, Power: Social Stratification in
Comparative Perspective,* 2d ed. (New York, 1966), p. 204.

65. Manteuffel served as agricultural minister from 1848 to 1850, but his influence in the cabinet extended beyond the sphere of farming.

66. Günther Grünthal, *Parlamentarismus in Preussen 1848/49–1857/58* (Düsseldorf, 1982), pp. 215–26. Manteuffel's middle course is perhaps best illustrated by
the fact that his government censored the extremely conservative *Neue Preussische
Zeitung (Kreuzzeitung)* in addition to liberal publications. In 1852, for example, the
government forbade the release of the newspaper three days in a row, July 13–15.
GStA Merseburg, Nachlass Ferdinand von Westphalen, Repository 92, nr. 3., p. 21.

67. Eric Dorn Brose, *The Politics of Technological Change in Prussia: Out of the
Shadow of Antiquity, 1809–1848* (Princeton, 1993). Brose's details on how formal and
informal webs of culture connected state and society in the 1830s and 1840s are com-
mendable.

68. David E. Barclay, *Frederick William IV and the Prussian Monarchy, 1840–
1861* (Oxford, 1995).

69. Barclay argues that after 1850 "it is, in fact, difficult to speak of a functioning Camarilla." Ibid., p. 223.

70. Kaelble, *Berliner Unternehmer,* p. 245.

71. Ibid.

72. Ibid., pp. 245, 276–77.

73. David Blackbourn, "Progess and Piety: Liberalism, Catholicism, and the
State in Imperial Germany," *History Workshop* 26 (1988): 57.

74. David Blackbourn and Geoff Eley, *Mythen deutscher Geschichtsschreibung:*

Die gescheiterte bürgerliche Revolution von 1848 (Frankfurt a.M., 1980). The essays were published later in English as *Peculiarities of German History: Bourgeois Society and Politics in Nineteenth-Century Germany* (New York, 1984). The latter is an expanded version of the original essays and addresses, among other things, the essays' initial criticism.

75. Geoff Eley, "The British Model and The German Road," in Blackbourn and Eley, eds., *Peculiarities*, pp. 79–80. In reference to this point, R. J. Evans points out "that there *was* a connection between liberalism and democracy. By supporting parliamentary rule, liberals in many countries helped willy-nilly to create the possibility of extending franchise by Act of Parliament, while such extensions could be more easily resisted in states without ministerial responsibility; and they contributed towards increasing the electoral pressures in favour of suffrage reform." "Missing Revolution," p. 88.

76. Eley, 58.

77. Ibid., pp. 59–60.

78. Ibid., pp. 144, 141.

79. Eley's claim of bourgeois dominance is, to my mind, overstated. His assertion that "in some ways—the sharpness of the rupture with the past, the definitive character of the legal settlement, the commanding strength of capital in the new national economy—German unification was more specifically 'bourgeois' in its content and more resoundingly 'bourgeois' in its effects than either the English or French Revolution had been" is stated with confidence because the aristocratic presence in unification is ignored. Given the pronounced dynastic element of the federated German union, it is hard to see a sharp "rupture with the past." The "definitive character" of Germany's legal structure is also misleading; it was in 1896 that parliament finally passed the basic civil code—the cultural symbol of bourgeois power—and only by an exceedingly narrow margin. The "commanding strength" of capital must also be qualified; the defensive posture of *Verbände* (lobbies and pressure groups) and the parliamentary stalemates over economic issues speak of compromise and not of dominance. It is true that we must better accent bourgeois agency, but in so doing we must also balance it with the "particular equilibrium of forces," which includes the aristocracy and the continuities of the neoabsolutist Prussian state.

The greatest problem with Eley's critique of the *Sonderweg* is his failure to address its core element: the influence of the state in culture, economy, and politics from 1648 to 1918. It is curious that Eley nods to the importance of Leonard Krieger, Georg Iggers, and Bernd Faulenbach yet does not refute their central theses: that early modern particularism and Hegelian idealism produced a unique perception of the state as a guarantor of civil society and liberty. This is, in fact, the kernel of the *Sonderweg* thesis, writes Jürgen Kocka, and a valid critique of it must recognize "the enormous significance of the fact that in Germany—as opposed to England or the United States—the erection of a public state bureaucracy preceded industrialization and parliamentarization and therefore stamped German society more distinctly than Anglo-American countries." Jürgen Kocka, "Der 'deutsche Sonderweg' in der Diskussion," *German Studies Review* 5 (1982): 375.

Finally, it is surely not unimportant to understand that Germans first posed the *Sonderweg* idea in the nineteenth and early twentieth centuries and not only believed in but celebrated their difference from the West. See the 1923 essay by Ernst Troeltsch, "The Ideas of Natural Law and Humanity in World Politics," reprinted in Otto Gierke, *Natural Law and the Theory of Society* (Cambridge, 1934), pp. 209–22; and the essay by Hajo Holborn, "Der deutsche Idealismus in sozialgeschichtlicher Beleuchtung," *Historische Zeitschrift* 174 (1952): 359–84.

80. David Blackbourn, "The Discreet Charm of the Bourgeoisie," in Blackbourn and Eley, eds., *Peculiarities,* pp. 287–88.

81. Ibid., pp. 262–63.

82. For an informative reading of Eley and Blackbourn's achievements, see Jane Caplan, "Myths, Models and Missing Revolutions: Comments on a Debate in German History," *Radical History Review* 34 (1986): 87–89.

83. Jürgen Kocka, ed., *Bürger und Bürgerlichkeit;* Kocka, ed., *Bürgertum im 19. Jahrhundert;* Langewiesche, ed., *Liberalismus im 19. Jahrhundert;* Niethammer et al., *Bürgerliche Gesellschaft in Deutschland;* David Blackbourn and Richard J. Evans, eds., *The German Bourgeoisie: Essays on the Social History for the German Middle Class from the Late Eighteenth to the Early Twentieth Century* (London, 1991).

84. Hartmut Kaelble, "Der Mythos von der rapiden Industrialisierung in Deutschland," *Geschichte und Gesellschaft* 9 (1983): 106–18.

85. Wolfram Fischer, "Wirtschafts- und sozialgeschichtliche Anmerkungen zum 'deutschen Sonderweg,' " *Tel Aviver Jahrbuch für deutsche Geschichte* 26 (1987): 96–116; here on pp. 102–5.

86. Ibid., p. 106; for the more pronounced autocratic behavior of French entrepreneurs see Patrick Fridenson, "Herrschaft im Wirtschaftsunternehmen: Deutschland und Frankreich 1880–1914," in Kocka, ed., *Bürgertum im 19. Jahrhundert,* 2:65–91; see also, Peter Stearns, *Paths to Authority: The Middle Class and the Industrial Labor Force in France, 1820–48* (Urbana, Ill., 1978), pp. 89–103.

87. Dolores Augustine-Perez, *Patricians and Parvenus: Wealth and High Society in Wilhelmine Germany* (Oxford, 1994); Dirk Schumann, *Bayerns Unternehmer in Gesellschaft und Staat 1834–1914* (Göttingen, 1992); see also Kaelble's "Wie feudal waren die deutschen Unternehmer?"

88. Thomas Nipperdey, *Deutsche Geschichte 1800–1866: Bürgerwelt und starker Staat* (Munich, 1983), p. 718.

89. Padtberg, *Rheinischer Liberalismus,* pp. 232–33.

90. Siemann, *Gesellschaft im Aufbruch: Deutschland 1849–1871* (Frankfurt a.M., 1990), p. 83.

91. Rürup, *Deutschland im 19. Jahrhundert,* p. 213.

92. Wehler, *Gesellschaftsgeschichte,* 3:92. In reference to the business class and its politics, one of the principal weaknesses to Wehler's otherwise impressive synthesis is discussing politics, economy, and social formations in separate sections. The effect of this organization is the absence of concrete linkage between economy and politics. The care taken to elucidate "structural conditions" and "developmental processes" is matched by a lack of attention paid to businessmen as their own political

agents. In this manner, the problems of banking, capital accumulation, and expansion of the infrastruture are handled as economic, but not political, problems. Ibid., 3:71–74. Furthermore, Wehler's overall reliance on Bismarck's "charismatic" leadership to explain how the Kaiserreich functioned is certainly questionable when examining how economic settlements were negotiated and brokered. In his essay "Wie 'bürgerlich' war das Deutsche Kaiserreich?" Wehler modified his overall perspective from that of *Das deutsche Kaiserreich* (1973), which had educated a generation of students on the crisis-ridden, oppressive structures of the German empire. His newer work concedes that a hetereogeneous bourgeois society with chances of social mobility did exist. See the above essay in Jürgen Kocka, ed., *Bürger und Bürgerlichkeit*, pp. 243–80; for his overall revision of the *Sonderweg* thesis, see *Gesellschaftsgeschichte*, 3:1284–95.

93. Rudolf Boch, *Grenzenloses Wachstum? Das rheinische Wirtschaftsbürgertum und seine Industrialisierungsdebatte 1814–1857* (Göttingen, 1993), p. 268.

94. Colleen A. Dunlavy, *Politics and Industrialization: Early Railroads in the United States and Prussia* (Princeton, 1994).

95. Ibid., p. 97.

96. Sheehan, *German Liberalism*, p. 109; Otto Pflanze, *Bismarck*, 1:111; Kitchen, *Political Economy*, p. 94.

97. Kaelble, *Berliner Untermehmer*, pp. 236–37.

98. Dieter Langewiesche, *Liberalismus in Deutschland* (Frankfurt a.M., 1988), p. 84.

99. W. W. Rostow, *The Stages of Economic Growth: A Non-Communist Manifesto* (Cambridge, Eng., 1961); Rainer Fremdling, *Eisenbahnen und deutsches Wirtschaftswachstum 1840–1879: Ein Beitrag zur Entwicklungstheorie und zur Theorie der Infrastruktur* (Dortmund, 1975); see also Fremdling's essay that compares Germany with Britain and the U.S., addressing Fishlow's and Fogel's criticisms of Rostow: "Railroads and German Economic Growth: A Leading Sector Analysis with a Comparison to the United States and Great Britain," *Journal of Economic History* 37 (1977): 583–604.

100. Frank Tipton, *Regional Variations in the Economic Development of Germany during the Nineteenth Century* (Middletown, Conn., 1976), p. 147.

101. This study will modify the claim by Bergengrün, Henderson, Tilly, Treue, Tipton, and others that Heydt represented the bridge that spanned the alliance between business and government.

102. Dahlmann quoted by Sheehan, *German Liberalism*, p. 39.

103. Hans-Ulrich Wehler, *Kaiserreich*, p. 14.

104. Fritz Redlich, *Der Unternehmer: Wirtschafts- und Sozialgeschichtliche Studien* (Göttingen, 1964); Toni Pierenkemper, *Die westfälischen Schwerindustriellen 1852–1913: Soziale Struktur und unternehmerischer Erfolg* (Göttingen, 1979).

105. Gerschenkron, *Economic Backwardness;* Walter G. Hoffmann, *Das Wachstum der deutschen Wirtschaft seit der Mitte des 19. Jahrhunderts* (Berlin, 1965); Rostow, *Stages of Economic Growth;* Knut Borchardt, "The Industrial Revolution in Germany, 1700–1914," in Carlo M. Cipolla, ed., *The Fontana Economic History of Europe*, vol. 1, *The Emergence of Industrial Societies* (Glasgow, 1973); Stanley Kuznets, *Modern Economic Growth* (New Haven, 1966); Fremdling, "Railroads and German Economic

Growth"; Reinhard Spree, *Wachstumstrends und Konjunkturzyklen in der deutschen Wirtschaft von 1820 bis 1913: Quantitativer Rahmen für eine Konjunkturgeschichte des 19. Jahrhunderts* (Göttingen, 1978).

106. W. O. Henderson, *The State and the Industrial Revolution in Prussia, 1740–1870* (Liverpool, 1958); Wolfram Fischer, "Das Verhältnis von Staat und Wirtschaft in Deutschland am Beginn der Industrialisierung," in *Wirtschaft und Gesellschaft im Zeitalter der Industrialisierung* (Göttingen, 1982); Richard Tilly, *Financial Institutions and Industrialization in the Rhineland* (Madison, 1966); Rainer Fremdling, *Eisenbahnen.*

Chapter Two

1. Heinrich Heine, 5 May 1843, *Lutezia II,* p. lvii, in Manfred Windfuhr, ed., *Heinrich Heine,* vol. 14/1, Düsseldorfer ed. (Hamburg, 1990), pp. 57–58.

2. For List's difficulties in realizing his vision of a German railway network see Heinrich Treitschke, *Deutsche Geschichte,* 3d ed. (Leipzig, 1890), 4:584 ff; Edwin Kech, *Geschichte der deutschen Eisenbahn-Politik* (Leipzig, 1911), pp. 36 ff; and Erwin V. Beckerath et al., eds., *Friedrich List: Schriften, Reden, Briefe* (Berlin, 1931). For List's problems with Prussia, see vol. 3, part 2, pp. 820 ff. See note 7 below for Harkort.

3. This upper bourgeoisie was one component of *Bürgertum,* identified by Jürgen Kocka as a "post-corporate supralocal social formation" made up of merchants, entrepreneurs and capitalists as well as professors, judges, journalists and high-ranking civil servants. This *Bürgertum* stressed "the principles of achievement and education, work and personality [and] the concept of a modern, secularized, post-corporate, self-regulating, enlightened 'civil society.' " Yet *Bürgertum* "cannot be seen as a 'class' in a Marxist or Weberian sense, since it included self-employed and salaried persons, and, more generally, persons with very different market positions." Kocka, "Bürgertum and Professions: Two Alternative Approaches," in Michael Burrage and Rolf Torstendahl, eds., *Professions in Theory and History* (London, 1990), pp. 63–64. For a more comparative perspective, see Kocka, "Stand-Klasse-Organisation: Strukturen sozialer Ungleichheit in Deutschland vom späten 18. bis zum frühen 20. Jahrhundert im Aufriss," in Hans-Ulrich Wehler, ed., *Klassen in der europäischen Sozialgeschichte* (Göttingen, 1979), pp. 137–65. For an excellent overview of the definitional and theoretical problems of *Bürgertum,* see Utz Haltern, *Bürgerliche Gesellschaft: Sozialtheoretische und sozialhistorische Aspekte* (Darmstadt, 1985). The commercial elite that emerged in Germany after 1830 was arguably the first German upper bourgeoisie that could be compared to the financially powerful merchant class that had arisen in England and France during the Atlantic Age, which redefined absolutism during the seventeenth and eighteenth centuries. For the absence of a commercial elite in early modern German history, see Hajo Holborn, "Deutscher Idealismus in sozialhistorische Beleuchtung," reprinted in Wehler, ed., *Moderne deutsche Sozialgeschichte,* p. 89.

4. Ludolf Camphausen, "Zur Eisenbahn von Köln nach Antwerpen" (Cologne, 1833), reprinted in Mathieu Schwann, *Ludolf Camphausen* (Essen, 1915), 1:288.

5. *Hermann,* 26. Stück, 30 Mar. 1825. See also Wolfgang Köllmann, *Friedrich Harkort,* vol. 1, *1793-1838* (Düsseldorf, 1964), pp. 91 ff.

6. This was the nucleus of the Steele-Vohwinkel, a thirty-three kilometer line renamed the Prince Wilhelm Railway in 1831. For discussions of early railroad building in Prussia, see Henderson, *Industrial Revolution,* chap. 8 and 9; Klee, *Preussische Eisenbahngeschichte,* chap. 1; Schreiber, *Die Preussischen Eisenbahnen und ihr Verhältnis zum Staat 1834-1874* (Berlin, 1874), pp. 1-17.

7. Harkort's biographer, Wolfgang Köllmann, notes that one should not underestimate his role in railroad development, but nor should one overestimate it. Indeed he is one of the original propagandists of railroads. But few of his projects were realized, and he lacked the patience and persistence to stick with the industry after 1835, when practical decisions were being made. Railroad construction was "only an episode in his life." Köllmann, *Harkort,* p. 110.

8. Alexander Bergengrün, *Staatsminister August Freiherr von der Heydt* (Leipzig, 1908), p. 41; Henderson, *Industrial Revolution,* p. 153, n. 1.

9. Bergengrün, *Heydt,* pp. 42-46.

10. Article 45 in the Treaty of Paris in 1815 called for the Rhine river to be toll-free "jusqu'à la mer." The Dutch exploited the vagueness of the French phrase to mean "near the sea" and not the intended "into the sea" and so continued to levy dues on ships and barges after 1815. Walter Steitz, *Die Entstehung der Köln-Mindener Eisenbahn* (Cologne, 1974), p. 39. The Rhenish-Westphalian antipathy toward the Dutch monopoly can be found in almost any chamber of commerce report or document regarding German commercial development in the 1820s or 1830s. For an example of a tirade against Holland, see Ludolf Camphausen's essays on a Rhenish-Belgian railway line, "Zur Eisenbahn von Köln nach Antwerpen" (Cologne, 1833, 1835), reprinted in Schwann, *Camphausen,* 1:296-97, 306-7.

11. Karl Kumpmann, *Die Entstehung der Rheinischen Eisenbahngesellschaft 1830-1844: Ein erster Beitrag zur Geschichte der Rheinischen Eisenbahn* (Essen, 1910), chaps. 3 and 4.

12. R. Tilly, *Financial Institutions,* p. 16.

13. These dates refer to the years the charters were issued according to Karl Bösselmann, *Die Entwicklung des deutschen Aktienwesens im 19. Jahrhundert* (Berlin, 1939), p. 201.

14. For mileage of rail, Hans Nordmann, *Die ältere preussische Eisenbahngeschichte* (Berlin, 1950), p. 9. That the most critical economic sector of early industrialization arose without state aid poses the question whether the state was the chief engine of German industrialization. See R. Tilly, "Political Economy of Public Finance"; R. Tilly, "Soll und Haben: Recent German Economic History and the Problem of Economic History," *Journal of Economic History* 29 (1969): 289-319; and R. Tilly, *Financial Institutions.* See especially Rainer Fremdling's *Eisenbahnen,* pp. 129-35, 165, 221-22.

15. Diefendorf, *Businessmen and Politics,* p. 227; Marion Gray, "Schroetter, Schön, and Society: Aristocratic Liberalism versus Middle-Class Liberalism in Prussia, 1808," *Central European History* 6 (1973): pp. 60-82; Wilhelm Treue, "Adam

Smith in Deutschland: Zum Problem des 'Politischen Professors' zwischen 1770 and 1810," in Werner Conze, ed., *Deutschland und Europa* (Düsseldorf, 1951).

16. Between 1826 and 1828 Harkort and other Westphalian notables proposed three projects, all of which failed because the government refused either to grant a charter or to supply a loan. These projects were Elberfeld-Heisingen (1826), Elberfeld-Düsseldorf-Krefeld-Venlo (1828), and Elberfeld-Barmen (1828). The latter received a charter (as opposed to the refusals of the first two) but was never built. The project needed a loan from the government, which it refused to do because it was only a "local" matter. Kumpmann, *Entstehung,* p. 24.

17. Bergengrün, *Heydt,* p. 41.

18. Steitz quoting Harkort, *Entstehung,* pp. 48–49.

19. Camphausen, "Eisenbahn Köln-Antwerpen" (Cologne, 1833), quoted by Steitz, *Entstehung,* p. 54.

20. See Camphausen's first railroad pamphlet in Schwann, *Camphausen,* 1:294.

21. Quoted in Alexander Bergengrün, *David Hansemann* (Berlin, 1901), pp. 166–67.

22. A. von der Leyen, "Die Durchführung des Staatsbahnsystems in Preussen," *Jahrbuch für Gesetzgebung, Verwaltung und Volkswirtschaft im Deutschen Reich (Schmollers Jahrbuch)* 7/2 (1883): 461–511.

23. E. Bülow-Cummerow, "Preussen, seine Verfassung, seine Verwaltung, sein Verhältnis zu Deutschland: Zweiter Teil" (Jena, 1843), quoted by Steitz, *Entstehung,* p. 59; see also Robert Berdahl, *The Politics of the Prussian Nobility: The Development of a Conservative Ideology, 1770–1848* (Princeton, 1988), p. 348.

24. A good introduction to the ideas of John Prince Smith is found in Donald Rohr, *The Origins of Social Liberalism in Germany* (Chicago, 1963), pp. 85–91. Another well-known laissez-faire publicist, Karl Heinrich Rau, was less doctrinaire than Smith and, like Prussian businessmen, saw a role for the state in economic planning.

25. Köllmann, *Harkort,* p. 108.

26. Ludolf Camphausen, "Zur Eisenbahn nach Antwerpen: Zweite Eisenbahnschrift" (Cologne, 1835), reprinted in Schwann, *Camphausen,* 1:308.

27. Steitz, *Entstehung,* pp. 42 ff.

28. Hansemann, *Die Eisenbahnen und deren Aktionäre in ihrem Verhältnis zum Staat* (Leipzig, 1837), p. 60. Hansemann believed that profits should gradually buy back shares, nullify the need to pay interest to investors, and thereby minimize shipping rates.

29. See Fremdling, *Eisenbahnen,* pp. 55–74, for tables and statistics on the continually reduced transport rates in the 1840s and 1850s. Fremdling argued that state railways, contrary to Hansemann's expectations, did not offer any more advantages in rate reduction than private railways.

30. Gustav Mevissen is one example of the blend between Hegel and St. Simon. See Joseph Hansen, *Mevissen,* 1:59–62, 122–26, 131 ff. For Saint-Simonianism, see Robert B. Carlisle, *The Proffered Crown: Saint-Simonianism and the Doctrine of Hope* (Baltimore, 1987), chaps. 6 and 13.

31. Padtberg, *Rheinischer Liberalismus,* pp. 32–33; Hansen, *Mevissen,* 1:246–51;

Hansen, ed., *Rheinische Briefe*, 1:296 ff; see also pp. 336–38. Camphausen used the *Rheinische Zeitung* to criticize government railroad policy.

32. The chief complaint among businessmen concerned money supply and investment capital. R. Tilly, *Financial Institutions*, chaps. 2 and 5.

33. Eric Dorn Brose, *Politics of Technological Change*, pp. 41–46.

34. For the social and political failures of the Reform Era, see Reinhart Koselleck, *Preussen zwischen Reform und Revolution*, 3d ed. (Stuttgart, 1967; paperback edition, 1989); Barbara Vogel, "Die preussischen Reformen als Gegenstand und Problem der Forschung," in Vogel, ed., *Preussische Reformen 1807–1820* (Königsberg, 1980), pp. 1–27.

35. For discussions on the first teams of railroad workers, see Jürgen Kocka, *Arbeitsverhältnisse und Arbeiterexistenzen: Grundlagen der Klassenbildung im 19. Jahrhundert* (Bonn, 1990), pp. 361–69; Klee, *Preussische Eisenbahngeschichte*, pp. 68–77.

36. For the Prussian government's regard for Rhenish law, see Diefendorf, *Businessmen and Politics*, pp. 213–41; also see the letter of Provincial Governor v. Pestel to Interior Minister von Brenn, 13 Sept. 1833, in Hansen, ed., *Rheinische Briefe*, p. 130. In 1825, the General Law Code (ALR) of Prussia was introduced into the Westphalian province. P. C. Martin, "Die Entstehung des preussischen Aktiengesetzes," *Vierteljahrsschrift für Sozial- und Wirtschaftsgeschichte* 56 (1969): 514.

37. Martin, "Entstehung," p. 514. The institutions that shaped Rhenish businessmen's relations to the state in the nineteenth century were instituted during the French occupation of the Rhine. This often overlooked period is clearly presented in Diefendorf's *Businessmen and Politics;* his argument that the formative period of entrepreneurial political attitudes lies between 1789 and 1830 is convincing. See, too, Padtberg's conclusion in *Rheinischer Liberalismus.*

38. Diefendorf, *Businessmen and Politics*, p. 256.

39. Ibid., pp. 332–33.

40. The government created a toll-free market within the Prussian provinces in 1817, a tariff policy that set the ground for the Zollverein in 1834.

41. Steitz, *Entstehung*, p. 35; Wehler, *Gesellschaftsgeschichte*, 2:120–21.

42. Ilya Mieck, *Preussische Gewerbepolitik in Berlin 1806–44: Staatshilfe und private Initiative zwischen Merkantilismus und Liberalismus* (Berlin, 1965), pp. 61–140, 164–200.

43. Klee, *Preussiche Eisenbahngeschichte*, p. 49; Mieck, *Gewerbepolitik*, pp. 89–90; Jonathan Sperber, "State and Civil Society in Prussia: Thoughts on a New Edition of Reinhart Koselleck's *Preussen zwischen Reform und Revolution*," *Journal of Modern History* 57 (1985): 278–96. See pp. 280–81 and n. 4 for his comments on Mieck's book, which casts doubt on the efficacy of the state as industrial promoter.

44. Koselleck, *Zwischen Reform und Revolution*, pp. 337 ff. My account only looks at industrial capitalism, but Hardenberg also saw agrarian capitalism as a necessary step for the survival of the state—in spite of fierce noble opposition. See Barbara Vogel, "Die 'allgemeine Gewerbefreiheit' als bürokratische Modernisierungsstrategie in Preussen," in Dirk Stegmann et al., eds., *Industrielle Gesellschaft und politisches System* (Bonn, 1978), pp. 59–78.

45. See, for example, Mevissen's "Gedanken über politische und soziale Entwicklung," and his 1843 essay, "Verhältnis des Staates zur fortschreitenden Geistesbildung," in Hansen, *Mevissen,* 2:87–91, 105–10. Rohr, *Social Liberalism,* chap. 5, shows that these men had different views on social liberalism, thus preventing any one generalization. Yet all incorporated the state into their sociopolitical outlook.

46. Henderson, *Industrial Revolution,* p. 152. Beuth and Schinckel's report can be found in the *Archiv für Bergbau und Hüttenwesen* 19 (1829).

47. David T. Murphy, "Prussian Aims for the Zollverein, 1828–1833," *The Historian* 53 (Fall 1991): 293.

48. Wolfgang Radtke, *Die preussische Seehandlung zwischen Staat und Wirtschaft in der Frühphase der Industrialisierung* (Berlin, 1981), p. 261; Wilhelm Treue, *Wirtschafts-, Finanz- und Technikgeschichte Preussens* (Berlin, 1984), p. 430.

49. Treitschke, *Deutsche Geschichte,* 4:582.

50. Henderson, *German Industrial Power,* p. 45.

51. Murphy, "Prussian Aims," p. 294.

52. Hamerow, *Restoration, Revolution, Reaction,* p. 8.

53. Klee, *Preussische Eisenbahngeschichte,* p. 98; for the king of Hannover quotation, see R. P. Sieferle, *Fortschrittsfeinde? Opposition gegen Technik und Industrie von der Romantik bis zur Gegenwart* (Munich, 1984), p. 112.

54. For a representative example of aristocratic technophobia, see the letter from Graf Brühle zu Potsdam to David Hansemann, 22 Feb. 1837, in Bergengrün, *Hansemann,* p. 199; and Sieferle, *Fortschrittsfeinde,* pp. 87–117.

55. Brose, *Politics of Technological Change,* p. 228.

56. For more information on this legacy fund, see chap. 6.

57. Charters had been granted to the Rhenish Railway, the Düsseldorf-Elberfeld Railway, and the Berlin-Potsdam Railway. Nordmann, *Eisenbahngeschichte,* p. 4.

58. Ervin V. Bekerath et al., eds., *Friedrich List: Schriften, Rede, Briefe,* vol. 3, part 2, *Schriften zum Verkehrswesen* (Berlin, 1931), pp. 820–25. Treitschke, *Deutsche Geschichte,* 4:590.

59. Steitz, *Entstehung,* p. 35.

60. Treitschke, *Deutsche Geschichte,* 4:590.

61. Radtke, *Seehandlung,* p. 265.

62. Rother's initial hostility to railroad building may stem in part from his role as estate owner. Later in 1838 he warned of the disastrous effect railroad labor, which paid high wages, would have on the agrarian labor market in the eastern provinces. Eichholtz, *Junker,* p. 95.

63. Treitschke, *Deutsche Geschichte,* 4:590; Nagler had, among other things, succeeded in increasing the daily postal ride from forty to seventy-five kilometers. Kumpmann, *Entstehung,* p. 16.

64. Brose, *Politics of Technological Change,* p. 218.

65. Opposing this group was the crown prince, a keen railroad enthusiast, Director General of Taxes Karl Georg von Maasen, Finance Minister Motz, and Minister of the Interior Schuckmann. This group, writes Wolfgang Radtke, lacked the influence to oppose the "mighty phalanx of king, Nagler, Vincke, Beuth, and Rother," and

"for the time being could do nothing against this powerful group." In 1837, owing to a heated dispute between the crown prince and Rother over the railroad law, the latter resigned from his position in the finance ministry and devoted his energy to the Seehandlung and the royal bank. Radtke, *Seehandlung,* pp. 261, 266.

66. Brose, *Politics of Technological Change,* p. 236.

67. Rudolph von Delbrück, *Lebenserinnerungen* (Leipzig, 1905), 1:135; for the attitude of king, see Treitschke, *Deutsche Geschichte,* 4:591–92.

68. Brose, *Politics of Technological Change,* pp. 231–34.

69. See Brose, *Politics of Technological Change,* pp. 231–33, for the significant role that the military played in shaping the Railroad Law of 1838 and, more successfully, in the Railroad Fund of 1842.

70. Steitz, *Entstehung,* p. 35.

71. Treitschke, *Deutsche Geschichte,* 5:501; Hajo Holborn, *A History of Modern Germany* (paperback edition, Princeton, 1982), 2:456.

72. Radtke, *Seehandlung,* p. 265.

73. Eichholtz, *Junker,* p. 89.

74. For these promises of a constitution, see E. R. Huber, *Dokumente zur deutschen Verfassungsgeschichte,* (Stuttgart, 1964), 2:41–43, 57–58. The act of promulgating a constitution stemmed partly from Hardenberg and Gneisenau's political vision, which, to quote Gneisenau, was to make Prussia a model state, "splendid in the three areas that alone enable a people to become great: military glory, a constitution and the rule of law, and the flowering of the arts and sciences." Friedrich Meinecke quoting Gneisenau, *The Age of German Liberation, 1795–1814* (Berkeley, 1977), p. 122. The king grudgingly accepted the constitution as a necessary measure to keep in step with time.

75. Diefendorf, *Businessmen and Politics,* p. 252.

76. For a succinct history of the United Diet, see E. R. Huber, *Deutsche Verfassungsgeschichte seit 1789* (Stuttgart, 1960), 2:491–98.

77. Holborn, *History of Modern Germany,* 2:457.

78. Huber, *Verfassungsgeschichte,* 2:484–85.

79. Certainly the Prussian state circumvented this law through questionable bookkeeping. By not recording all incomes flowing to the state and through the ability of the Seehandlung to camouflage loans on the international market for the government, the Prussian state could pay its old debts, create new ones, and still give the impression that the state was minimizing debt and keeping to the law. Wehler, *Gesellschaftsgeschichte,* 2:379–80; Ernst Klein, *Geschichte der öffentlichen Finanzen in Deutschland (1500–1870)* (Wiesbaden, 1974), pp. 120–21.

80. Steitz refers to the "hochpolitischen Charakter" of Camphausen's railroad essays. *Entstehung,* p. 54. See also Schwann, *Camphausen,* 1: chap. 1, for Camphausen's oppositional attitudes toward absolutism in the 1830s. Hansemann's political remarks are explicit in his 1841 essay—see n. 98. And Harkort, too, saw a political dimension to railroad building. He is reputed to have said, "Railroads are the hearse that will carry the German aristocracy to its grave."

81. *Gesetz-Sammlung für die königlichen preussischen Staaten,* 3 Nov. 1838, nr. 35, pp. 505–16.

82. *Gesetz-Sammlung,* 1838, nr. 35, par. 46, p. 515.

83. *Gesetz-Sammlung,* 1838, nr. 35, par. 42, p. 514.

84. There were only two dead letters in the law: par. 26, which foresaw the use of more than one company on the same railway line; and par. 32, which limited the profit of a railway company to 10 percent. These restrictions were never enforced. Treitschke called the law "one of the last memorable works of the old bureaucratic state." *Deutsche Geschichte,* 4:593. Kumpmann also praises the law. *Entstehung,* p. 38. For a balanced assessment, see Wehler, *Gesellschaftsgeshichte,* 2:618.

85. K. A. Varnhagen von Ense, 12 Apr. 1838, *Tagebücher* (Leipzig: Brockhaus, 1861), 1:87.

86. Radtke, *Seehandlung,* p. 271. The Rhenish Railway directors never accepted the legality of this paragraph and said so in their communications to the government.

87. Bergengrün, *Hansemann,* pp. 203–5.

88. Ibid., pp. 203–6.

89. Ludolf Camphausen, "Versuch eines Beitrages zur Eisenbahngesetzgebung" (Cologne, 1838), reprinted in Schwann, *Camphausen,* 1:420.

90. Bergengrün, *Hansemann,* p. 207.

91. Klee, *Preussische Eisenbahngeschichte,* p. 101.

92. Bergengrün, *Hansemann,* p. 198.

93. Ibid., p. 196.

94. Bergengrün quoting Hansemann, ibid., pp. 206–207.

95. Bergengrün quoting Hansemann, ibid., p. 207.

96. Ibid., p. 208.

97. Ibid., p. 207.

98. We see here how industrialism and the political and legal needs of business affected Hansemann's vision of a liberal constitutional state. In this respect, Hansemann's Rhenish liberalism does not correspond to Lothar Gall's otherwise useful generalization that German liberalism was "preindustrial."

99. Hansen, *Mevissen,* 1:417 n. 1.

100. For stock quotes in the 1830s and 1840s, see Julius Michealis, *Deutschlands Eisenbahnen* (Leipzig, 1859), appendix 1, pp. 1–67.

101. Bergengrün, *Hansemann,* pp. 210–17; see also Ammon (first president of the Rhenish Railway, 1839–44), *Erinnerungen an Fr.von Ammon* (unpublished manuscript, Cologne, 1878), pp. 154 ff. Only extant copy in HAStK. When the sale was made public, the government reacted with indignation, especially Ernst von Bodelschwingh, the provincial governor of Westphalia; the question whether a foreign state government could interfere in a business enterprise in the state of Prussia became an issue. Stockholders also railed against the arbitrary actions of the directors. The issue continued through the 1840s into the 1850s. See G. Heuser to Ammon, 6 Jan. 1844, HAStK, 1003, Akten Heuser, unpag.; see also the protocols of the Rhenish Railway directors, 1849–50, for their conflict with the Prussian government regarding the Belgian votes. HAStK 1028, nr. 7, pp. 42, 53.

102. In this respect the opposing binary categories of private- or state-induced growth of modern economic historians such as Rainer Fremdling and Richard Tilly are slightly misleading. It is true that private companies successfully established the

railroad industry in Germany, and this fact should indeed modify our notions of the role of the state in capitalist economy; but that should not lead us to believe that it was the wish of businessmen to build railroads independent of state help. Nor can we measure the effect of government props and incentives in the 1840s that allowed railroad stocks to soar. Hans-Ulrich Wehler, for example, speaks of the incredible ease with which private companies subscribed stock in the 1840s but fails to mention that this was only after the Railroad Fund was created in 1842. Thus Wehler notes that the Lower Silesian Mark Railway's first issue of stock was subscribed in one day, yet neglects to add that the Prussian government guaranteed a 3.5 percent return. *Gesellschaftsgeschichte,* 2:677. Indeed, many railroad companies prospered without any direct state help, but it is still impossible to gauge the indirect effect of committed governments like Saxony, Bavaria, or Prussia for overall railroad growth.

103. Compare stock notations from June 1840 and from June 1842: Berlin-Anhalt, 105:105.5; Berlin-Potsdam, 130:127.25; Berlin-Stettin, 100:96; Düsseldorf-Elberfeld, 96 (1841):84; Magdeburg-Leipzig, 101.25:117.25; Rhenish Railway, 88:93.5. The Magdeburg-Leipzig was the only clearly successful security. The Rhenish Railway showed improvement in this period but fell again to 71.75 in June of 1843. Compared to the stock's level of 117.5 in 1837, the year before the railroad law, this stock quotation was not good. Michealis, *Deutschlands Eisenbahnen,* appendix, pp. 1–67.

104. In the 1840s railroad equities yielded the best dividend on the stock market, exceeding both state paper and other joint-stock enterprises such as coal mines, textile mills, and machine factories. Wehler, *Gesellschaftsgeschichte,* 2:615; Fremdling, *Eisenbahnen,* p. 145.

105. Radtke, *Seehandlung,* p. 274; Henderson, *Industrial Revolution,* p. 164.

106. Schreiber, *Eisenbahnen,* p. 8; Radtke, *Seehandlung,* pp. 273 ff.

107. Alexander Bergengrün, *Staatsminister August Freiherr von der Heydt* (Leipzig, 1908), pp. 139–41.

108. Brose, *Politics of Technological Change,* pp. 223–24.

109. For a concise discussion of the army's early support of railroads, see ibid., chap. 7.

110. For the most incisive discussion of the king's reforms, see David E. Barclay, *Frederick William IV,* pp. 120–26, 130.

111. Eichholtz quoting King Friedrich Wilhelm IV, *Junker,* p. 105. The final composition of the Standing Committee was not 64 members but 98: 32 from the cities, 20 from the country, and 46 from the nobility. Treitschke, *Deutsche Geschichte,* 5:184.

112. Eichholtz quoting Friedrich Wilhelm IV, *Junker,* p. 105.

113. Veit Valentin, *Geschichte der deutschen Revolution von 1848–49* (Berlin, 1930), 1:41; Koselleck, *Zwischen Reform und Revolution,* pp. 363 ff; Treitschke, *Deutsche Geschichte,* 5:182.

114. In December 1841 the king decreed a law that prevented the Prussian censors from restricting any "serious and modest attempt at the truth." See the "Erlass der drei Zensurmeister an die Oberpräsidien betr. grössere Gleichförmigkeit und Erleichterung der Presszensur," in Hansen, ed., *Rheinische Briefe,* pp. 307–9.

115. Huber, *Verfassungsgeschichte,* 2:488.

116. Bergengrün, *Hansemann,* p. 112.

117. Eichholtz, *Junker,* p. 110.

118. Huber, *Verfassungsgeschichte,* 2:489; for the older issue of maintaining the customs and ways of the provinces or encouraging greater state coherence, see Huber, *Verfassungsgeschichte,* 1:164, 171.

119. Ludolf to Otto Camphausen, 30 Oct. 1842, *Rheinische Briefe,* p. 371.

120. Treitschke, *Deutsche Geschichte,* 5:185; Huber, *Verfassungsgeschichte,* 2:489–90.

121. Eichholtz, *Junker,* p. 109.

122. Ibid., p. 111.

123. Treitschke, *Deutsche Geschichte,* 5:186.

124. Eichholtz, *Junker,* p. 110.

125. Treitschke, *Deutsche Geschichte,* 5:186; Eichholtz, *Junker,* p. 110; Bergengrün, *Heydt,* p. 53.

126. The need for a thorough, critical political biography of Heydt is patently clear, but the dearth of materials largely prevents it. The repository of August von der Heydt's papers in the Prussian state archive (Rep. 92 von der Heydt) is thin and unhelpful in drawing a portrait of this complex man. His other papers, once stored in the Heydt-Kersten & Söhne bank archive in Elberfeld were allegedly destroyed in the Second World War. The sources that were available to Alexander Bergengrün that produced his insightful biography *Staatsminister August Freiherr von der Heydt* are apparently no longer extant, thus making a much-needed critical political biography extremely difficult. Although stamped with a statist, historicist method, Bergengrün remains the best single source on Heydt. See also Wolfgang Köllmann, "August von der Heydt," in *Wuppertaler Biographies* 1 (Elberfeld, 1958), and his entry on Heydt in *Neue Deutsche Biographie* (1972), 9:74–76; Marie Luise Baum, *Die von der Heydts aus Elberfeld* (Wuppertal, 1964); Treue, *Technikgeschichte Preussens.* The entry on Heydt in *Allgemeine Deutsche Biographie* (1880) borders on hagiography. The company's festschrift provides a cursory history of Heydt's bank: Hans Kurzrock, *200 Jahre von der Heydt-Kersten & Söhne 1754–1954* (Elberfeld, n.d.).

127. The committee for the Elberfeld-Witten Railroad was constituted in 1835 and dissolved in July 1836; in August 1837 the Rhine-Weser Railroad Company received a charter to build but dissolved after preliminary cost projections dampened optimism for attracting share-capital. The Düsseldorf-Elberfeld line, however, succeeded. It was constituted in June 1835, received its state charter to build in February 1837 (delayed because of the undetermined route of the Rhein-Weser project), and opened its first stretch in September 1837. It merged with the Berg-Mark railroad in 1856. See Julius Michaelis, *Deutschlands Eisenbahnen: Ein Handbuch für Geschäfts-leute, Capitalisten und Speculanten* (Leipzig, 1859), pp. 38, 103, 120.

128. Bergengrün, *Heydt,* pp. 46–49.

129. The company first established itself in July 1843. Bergengrün, *Heydt,* pp. 46–56; J. Michaelis, *Deutschlands Eisenbahnen,* p. 38.

130. *Allgemeine Deutsche Biographie,* 12:359. Heydt's bank became a leading

financial investor in this bank. Daniel von der Heydt represented the bank's interests as a director in the 1850s.

131. Henderson, *Industrial Revolution,* pp. 165–66.

132. Hansemann nonetheless criticized particular features of the Railroad Fund in his 1843 essay "Über die Ausführung des preussischen Eisenbahnsytems." Among other things, he criticized the unconditional interest guarantee, which he thought would encourage lazy management and imprudent decision making. To encourage intelligent and active direction in private companies, he believed the state should adjust its subsidies and pay less to companies using too much of their gross profits to cover overhead. Here Hansemann contradicts his earlier criticism of the state's "sense of fairness." The fixed legal settlement of 3.5 percent corresponded more to his earlier proposal of lawfulness and certitude. Camphausen, too, saw in the Railroad Fund a scheme that benefited mostly noble interests in the east. Of course neither was a dispassionate viewer. Their company, the Rhenish Railway, was not included among the subsidized companies, which greatly surprised them. Bergengrün, *Hansemann,* p. 239. For Camphausen's criticism of the Railroad Fund, see Eichholtz, *Junker,* p. 107.

133. Wehler, *Gesellschaftsgeschichte,* 2:615.

134. Bergengrün, *Hansemann,* p. 239.

135. Bösselmann, *Entwicklung des deutschen Aktienwesens,* p. 201. Common stock amounted to 60,087,00 of this sum.

136. For Germany's superiority over France, see G. Rütter's 1854 pamphlet in LHAK, Rep. 403, nr. 11893, p. 47. Whereas France had 504 "geographic miles," Germany possessed 1,097.

137. The law of May 1840, which prohibited buying foreign state paper on margin, and the Joint-Stock Company Law of 1843, which introduced rigorous conditions for starting up a company, are also important to mention, but these did not have the effect of the 1844 law. "Until 1844 one could speculate unhindered with railroad stock." Helmut Kubitschek, "Die Börsenverordnung vom 24. Mai 1844 und die Situation im Finanz- und Kreditwesen Preussens in den vierziger Jahren des 19. Jahrhunderts (1840 bis 1847)," *Jahrbuch für Wirtschaftsgeschichte* 4 (1962): 58–62; Martin, "Entstehung," pp. 526–27.

138. Eichholtz, *Junker,* pp. 90 ff.

139. Kubitschek, "Börsenverordnung," p. 67.

140. Wehler, *Gesellschaftsgeschichte,* 2:114.

141. Hamerow, *Restoration, Revolution, Reaction,* pp. 75–78.

142. For a brief summary of the history of the government's decision to revise the law, see Kühlwetter, Quadflieg, Mevissen, "Zusammenstellung von Gründsätze für ein neues Eisenbahn-Gesetz unter Berücksichtigung der bisherigen Erfahrungen," 1847, HAStK, 1073, nr. 81, unpag.

143. "Betreffend die Revision des Gesetzes über die Eisenbahn-Unternehmungen vom 3. Nov. 1838," 30 Dec. 1843, BLHA, Re. 3B IV, nr. 147, pp. 136 ff.

144. See the "Zusammenstellung von Gründsätzen für ein neues Eisenbahn-Gesetz unter Berücksichtigung der bisherigen Erfahrungen," Oct. 1847, HAStK 1073, nr. 81, pp. 1–19.

145. Hansen, *Mevissen,* 1:417.

146. Wehler, *Gesellschaftsgeschichte,* 2:621; Hansen, *Mevissen,* 1:417.

147. For the half-measure of the trade department, Rudolf Delbrück, *Erinnerungen,* 1:143–46; Rudolf Boch, *Grenzenloses Wachstum? Das rheinische Wirtschaftsbürgertum und seine Industrialisierungsdebatte 1814–1857* (Göttingen, 1991), p. 180; for the problems of the Royal Bank, see Radtke, *Preussische Seehandlung,* pp. 123 ff.

148. Kaelble, *Berliner Unternehmer,* p. 257.

149. Consider, for example, Friedrich Engels' opinion, which greatly influenced subsequent historiography: "Prussia, the most progressive German land, has lacked until now a bourgeoisie wealth, strong, united, and energetic enough to clear away absolute rule and destroy the remnants of feudal nobility." "Die preussische Verfassung," 6 Mar. 1847, *Marx-Engels Werke* 4 (Berlin, 1964), p. 30.

150. Kubitschek, "Börsenverordnung," p. 74.

151. Kaelble, *Berlin Unternehmer,* p. 255.

152. Ibid., pp. 260–61.

153. Bergengrün quoting Hansemann to Karl Deahna, 8 Apr. 1839, *Hansemann,* p. 219.

154. Delbrück, *Lebenserinnerungen,* 1:183.

155. Brose, *Politics of Technological Change,* p. 253.

156. Kubitschek, "Börsenverordnung," p. 69.

157. Eichholtz, *Junker,* p. 177; Eduard Kafka, *Eisenbahnangelegenheiten und Personalien in lexikalischer Form* (Leipzig, 1885), pp. 192, 206, 209; *NZ,* 19 Jan. 1860.

158. Eichholtz, *Junker,* pp. 172–75; Kafka, *Eisenbahnangelegenheiten,* pp. 268, 305.

159. Eichholtz, *Junker,* p. 176.

160. Martin, "Entstehung," p. 517.

161. Kubitschek, "Börsenverordnung," p. 61.

162. John Gillis, *The Prussian Bureaucracy in Crisis, 1840–1860: Origins of an Administrative Ethos* (Stanford, 1971), pp. 13–15; Lenore O'Boyle, "The Democratic Left in Germany, 1848," *Journal of Modern History* 33 (1961): 374–83.

163. Eichholtz, *Junker,* pp. 138–50.

164. Wehler, *Gesellschaftsgeschichte,* 2:677.

165. Of the six liberals cited by Huber as principal spokesmen, these four railroad entrepreneurs were included. The other two were August von der Heydt and Karl Wilhelm Kyllmann. Huber, *Verfassungsgeschichte,* 2:494.

166. Bergengrün, *Hansemann,* p. 357.

167. Friedrich Engels, "Germany: Revolution and Counter Revolution," in Leonard Krieger, ed., *The German Revolutions: The Peasant War in Germany and Germany: Revolution and Counter Revolution* (Chicago, 1967), p. 127.

168. Although it became clear by June 1846 that the securities upholding the finances of the state and nobility were not adversely affected by the speculation in railroads, Friedrich Wilhelm nonetheless ordered his ministers to refuse any petitions for railroad charters. This action of the king directly frustrated his own aim of attracting private capital to build a railroad between Berlin and Königsberg. Kubitschek, "Börsenverordnung," p. 70.

169. Radtke, *Seehandlung,* p. 298.

170. The final conference that decided to build at state cost was on 16 March 1847 (following a memorandum from Finance Minister Flottwell to the king on 13 March 1847), which followed the promulgation of the patent. However, the issue had been discussed for over a year. Radtke, *Seehandlung,* pp. 297–98.

171. Huber, *Verfassungsgeschichte,* 2:484–85; for the "Verordnung über die zu bildende Repräsentation des Volkes" from 15 May 1815, see Huber, *Dokumente,* I, nr. 19, pp. 56–57.

172. The Diet consisted of 613 representatives: 307 came from the noble and knight's estates; 306 came from property owners from towns and countryside (*Städte- und Landgemeinden*), thus giving the nobility a majority of one. Of these 307 aristocratic votes, 70 came from the noble estate, which made up the Lords' Curia (*Herrenkurie*). This body had the privilege of assembling separately and casting a "virile vote" (*Virilstimme*) on matters outside of finance and taxation. Huber, *Verfassungsgeschichte,* 2:492. For the peculiar aristocratic composition of the Curia, see Valentin, *Deutschen Revolution,* 1:63. An early draft of the king's patent, written by Joseph Maria Radowitz, stated bluntly, "We are not transforming German princely rule into constitutional sovereignty; royal authority will not be subordinated to the rule of the majority." Treitschke, *Deutsche Geschichte,* 5:183.

173. Bergengrün, *Hansemann,* p. 351 n. 1. Drafted by Camphausen the program demanded: (1) annual assemblies; (2) the authority to approve all loans, including loans using the collateral of state domains; (3) the authority to approve all loans for war; (4) the appointment of an eight-person deputation to express these grievances; (5) the authority to regulate and levy taxes; (6) the authority to advise on all laws pertaining to property and civil rights; (7) the right of petition for all affairs, not just domestic matters; and (8) recognition that it is invalid for any committee of provincial diets to replace the legislative functions of the United Diet.

174. Huber, *Verfassungsgeschichte,* 2:492–93; Bergengrün, *Heydt,* pp. 81–83; Valentin, *Deutschen Revolution,* pp. 62–67; Wehler, *Gesellschaftsgeschichte,* 2:677 ff.; Treitschke, *Deutsche Geschichte,* 5:606–13.

175. Criticism of the patent, the proposal of a Prussian naval fleet, the creation of a trade ministry, the advocacy of civil rights for Jews and dissidents, the demand for parliamentary immunity, and, of course, the discussion on finance, budgets, and the budgetary powers of the diet were some of the debated issues in the United Diet. It was within the context of the United Diet's claim for budgetary power that the Eastern Railway loan played such an important role.

176. Bergengrün quoting Heydt, *Heydt,* p. 87.

177. Karl Marx quoting Hansemann in *Marx-Engels Werke* 12 (Berlin, 1963), p. 637. The original: "Bei Geldsachen hört die Gemütlichkeit auf."

178. Wehler quoting Prussian government, *Gesellschaftsgeschichte,* 2:678.

179. For thorough treatments of the revolution, see Rudolf Stadelmann, *Soziale und politische Geschichte der Revolution von 1848* (Munich, 1848); Valentin, *Deutsche Revolution;* Wehler, *Gesellschaftsgeschichte,* 2:641–780; Manfred Botzenhart, *Deutschen Parlamentarismus in der Revolutionszeit 1848-1850* (Düsseldorf, 1977).

180. Bergengrün, *Hansemann,* pp 507 ff.

181. Ibid., 517.

182. "Denkschrift die Erwerbung und den Bau von Eisenbahnen betreffend," GStA Merseburg, Rep. 77, tit. 258, nr. 1, pp. 65–90; here, p. 65. This document was copied to be signed by both Milde and Hansemann, but there is little doubt that the author is Hansemann. (Hereafter this "Denkschrift" will be referred to as Hansemann 1848.)

183. The secondary literature is divided on this. Bergengrün believes that the fifty million was an "energetic beginning" for nationalization, while von der Leyen and Henderson believe that Hansemann sought complete ownership. Bergengrün's interpretation is, to my mind, more plausible. Bergengrün, *Hansemann,* p. 517; von der Leyen, "Preussische Eisenbahnpolitik," pp. 141–49; Henderson, *Industrial Revolution,* p. 172.

184. For Hansemann's criticism of bureaucracy, see Hansen, ed., *Rheinische Briefe:* for his 1830 essay to the king, pp. 20–23, 40: and his 1840 publication, pp. 207–12. Also Bergengrün, *Hansemann,* chap. 4, documents Hansemann's belief that only private railroad administration could ensure efficiency. Equally out of character is Hansemann's warning that private railway companies were beginning to "associate" and forming "large *common* transport institutes" and that therefore the state should monopolize before private railways did. Hansemann 1848, p. 67. Hansemann was most likely alluding to the Association of Prussian Railway Administrations, an association that did little more than arrange timetables and clock setting. Hansemann knew that private railway companies were far from building cartels and knew from experience that the government possessed the power to deny a company the charter or stock emission to effect such a goal. In the early 1840s he had tried to expand the Rhenish Railway to the right bank of the Rhine, which would have established a monopoly, and had been denied the charter. Moreover, Hansemann had staunchly defended the right of voluntary associations, especially in the commercial sphere, throughout his political career, thus making this argument in his 1848 memorandum appear as rhetoric to ingratiate himself with state bureaucrats.

185. Bergengrün, *Hansemann,* chap. 4.

186. This interpretation contrasts with the views of A. von der Leyen, Alexander Bergengrün, and W. O. Henderson, who claim that Hansemann was a consistent promoter of state ownership throughout his career. I see a more wavering, opportunistic attitude in Hansemann.

187. This electoral procedure would later be changed to the three-class voting system in 1850.

188. See, for example, the *Kölnische Zeitung,* nr. 327, 8 Dec. 1848: "The event has already influenced the bourse. The funds have appreciably climbed and each person who is in any way involved jumps with a self-pleasing joy for the new times, which one hopes will lead to even more profitable results."

189. König to Mevissen, 25 May 1849, HAStK, 1073, nr. 40.

Chapter Three

1. Karl Marx, "Statistische Betrachtungen über das Eisenbahnwesen" (23 Jan. 1862), *Marx-Engels Werke* 15 (Berlin, 1964), p. 447.
2. Klee, *Preussische Eisenbahngeschichte*, p. 224.
3. Borchardt, "Industrial Revolution in Germany," p. 120.
4. *VBMHGA* 1855–57, pp. 41–42; *VBMHGA* 1861–63, p. 26; *VBMHGA* 1864–66, pp. 28, 45.
5. For average costs of joint-stock mining companies, see the comparative costs in the trade ministry's files on company charters in GStA Merseburg, Rep. 120A XII 5, nrs. 1–6; for a discussion on Prussia's state debt, see *NZ* 3:95 (27 Feb. 1850). For other comparative references, such as per capita income estimates in Germany, see Hoffmann, *Wachstum*, p. 825.
6. The creation of the German locomotive industry can be aptly illustrated by the origin of locomotives in operation in Prussia between 1840 and 1853. Nineteen out of the 20 locomotives in operation came from London in 1841, but 99 out of 105 locomotives came from Germany by 1853. By 1855, German manufacturers had almost completely captured the market from foreign competitors. For the number and origin of locomotives in Germany, see Fremdling, *Eisenbahnen*, p. 76, table 26. For Borsig, see Hans Mottek, *Wirtschaftsgeschichte Deutschlands*, 2d ed. (Berlin, 1971), 2:173. There are unfortunately no comprehensive statistics on railway employment. For pre-1848 years, Dietrich Eichholtz refers to "many tens of thousands"; Karl Obermann states there were "way over one hundred thousand"; and Jürgen Kocka estimates between 90,000 and 171,000 railroad workers for the German Confederation in the years 1850–61. Hans-Ulrich Wehler states the figure 26,000 for 1850, which quadrupled by 1864. The Prussian trade minister Heydt gave 41,467 as the figure of people employed on Prussian railways in 1858, but this number might well have excluded the navvies currently working on railbed construction. See *VBMHGA* 1858–60, p. 54; Dietrich Eichholtz, "Bewegungen unter den preussischen Eisenbahnbauarbeiten in Vormärz," in *Beiträge zur deutschen Wirtschafts- und Sozialgeschichte des 18. und 19. Jahrhunderts* (Berlin, 1962), p. 256; Obermann, "Zur Rolle der Eisenbahnarbeiter im Prozess der Formierung der Arbeiterklasse in Deutschland," in *Jahrbuch für Wirtschaftsgeschichte* (1970/Teil II): 134; Jürgen Kocka, *Arbeitsverhältnisse und Arbeiterexistenzen*, pp. 361–68; Wehler, *Gesellschaftsgeschichte*, 3:71. For figures on coal consumption, see Wehler, *Bismarck und der Imperialismus*, p. 55. Between 1850 and 1860, raw iron production increased in the Customs Union territory from 214,560 tons to 530,290; steel production, from 196,950 tons in 1850 to 426,260 in 1860. By 1860 these two heavy-industry sectors employed over 48,790 workers. *Gesellschaftsgeschichte*, 3:73, 75.
7. *VBMHGA* 1852–54, pp. 31–32; *VBMHGA* 1855–57, pp. 41–42. Because the last set of figures for 1856 only refer to private companies, the total figures are actually higher.
8. W. W. Rostow, "The Take-Off into Self-Sustained Growth," *Economic Jour-*

nal 66 (1956): 25–48; *Stages of Economic Growth,* p. 55; see also, Rostow, ed., *The Economics of Take-Off into Sustained Growth* (London, 1963); Borchardt, "Industrial Revolution in Germany," p. 120; Reinhard Spree and Jürgen Bergmann, "Die konjunkturelle Entwicklung der deutsche Wirtschaft 1840 bis 1864," in Hans-Ulrich Wehler, ed., *Sozialgeschichte Heute: Kritische Studien zur Geschichtswissenschaft* (Göttingen, 1974), pp. 289–335. A "Kondratieff" business cycle is named after the Soviet economist N. D. Kondratieff who (using English wages, interest rates, and prices) first posed the theory of three long business cycles in Europe and North America between 1780 and 1920. The three cycles, each of which included shorter upward and downward cycles, were periodized: 1780–1844/51, 1844/51–1870/75, and 1870/75–1920. See N. D. Kondratieff, "Die langen Wellen der Konjunktur," *Archiv für Sozialwissenschaft und Sozialpolitik* 56 (1926): 573–609. Although research since the 1920s has found several problems with the model, its schema remains useful. For a stimulating discussion on stage and cycle theories in economic history see Wehler, *Gesellschaftsgeschichte,* 2:597–604. For the most recent literature on business cycles, see Knut Borchardt, "Konjunkturtheorie in der Konjunkturgeschichte," *Vierteljahrsheft für Sozial- und Wirtschaftsgeschichte* 72 (1985): 537–55.

9. Alexander Bergengrün, *Staatsminister August Freiherr von der Heydt* (Leipzig, 1908), p. 28.

10. Jonathan Sperber, *Rhineland Radicals: The Democratic Movement and the Revolution of 1848–49* (Princeton, 1991), p. 81.

11. In fact, August's brother Carl used the association's rooms in August 1848 to give a speech advocating absolute monarchy. Sperber, *Rhineland Radicals,* p. 329.

12. Bergengrün, *Heydt,* pp. 94–95.

13. *Allgemeine Deutsche Biographie,* 12:359.

14. Köllmann, *Neue Deutsche Biographie,* 9:75.

15. Sperber, *Rhineland Radicals,* p. 310.

16. Treue, *Technikgeschichte Preussens,* p. 258.

17. Ibid., p. 440; Bergengrün, *Heydt,* p. 54. Heydt (who joined his father's bank in 1824) orchestrated handsome profits for his bank with intitial stock offerings of private railroad companies in the 1840s. He also served as director for railroads. During the 1850s, he remained a silent partner with the bank, providing a direct conduit of superior financial intelligence from the trade ministry to his brother and bank partner, Daniel von der Heydt.

18. The formulation regarding bureaucracy and modernization comes from Sheehan, *German History,* pp. 725–26.

19. See chap. 6 for a fuller discussion of Bodelschwingh's and Patow's opposition to Heydt.

20. Abraham Oppenheim to Gustav Mevissen, 21 Apr. 1850, Archiv Oppenheim, Band 161N, nr. 5.

21. *VBMHGA* 1848–51. Because of these conditions both government and private circles considered these railways to be state entities. *VZ,* nr. 249, 16 Dec. 1849.

22. There were a number of lawsuits that protested the rate at which the state re-

deemed the stockholders of the Cöln-Minden-Thüringer Railway, but the courts eventually backed the government. See GStA Merseburg, Rep. 2.2.1., nr. 29535, unpag.; Rep. 93E, nr. 3742, unpag.

23. GStA Merseburg, Rep. 93E, nr. 821, unpag. The smooth administrative takeover can partially be ascribed to the relationship of the railway to Trade Minister von der Heydt, whose family member Daniel was a director. The Heydt's Elberfeld bank, Heydt-Kersten & Söhne, was also the company's bank.

24. Henderson, *Industrial Revolution*, p. 174.

25. R. Delbrück and J. Hegel, eds., *Handelsarchiv: Sammlung der neuen auf Handel und Schiffahrt bezüglichen Gesetze und Verordnung des In- und Auslandes und statistische Mittheilungen über den Zustand und die Entwicklung des Handels und der Industrie in der preussischen Monarchie* (Berlin, 1850-), p. 313.

26. The government-backed stocks also produced a long-term disadvantage: investors assessed the worth of a stock primarily according to whether the dividend was guaranteed by the state. This tended to create two basic groups of stocks, common and preferred, and altered a company's basic principle to attract capital on the bourse. Stockholders of railroad securities not having a guarantee complained that government interference devalued their stocks. This tradition of government-sponsored dividend guarantees, which began in the mid-1840s and continued after 1848, did indeed create a dilemma. Underwriting major issues of bonds and stocks could only be achieved with the government's aid. Investors became jaded with 3.5 or 4 percent minimum and thus endangered the attractiveness of competing railways. The Rhenish Railway stockholders, for example, complained that the government's support of the Aachen-Düsseldorfer and the Cologne-Crefeld endangered the worth of their stock. *VZ*, nr. 274 (23 Nov. 1849), nr. 276 (25 Nov. 1849), nr. 285 (6 Dec. 1849), and nr. 291 (13 Dec. 1849). See nr. 285 for a particularly stinging attack on Heydt.

27. Schreiber, *Eisenbahnen*, p. 37; *VBMHGA* 1848-51, p. 31. In actuality, the loan from the state chest was only for twenty-two million thalers; it was agreed that eleven million thalers would come from the Railroad Funds.

28. A. J. P. Taylor considered the Eastern Railway incident in United Diet to be a major factor in the starting of the 1848 revolution in Prussia. *The Course of German History*, 10th ed. (New York, 1979), pp. 67-68; for a more scholarly assessment of the Eastern Railway's place in the revolution, see Valentin, *Deutsche Revolution*, 1:79-80.

29. The Saarbrücken and Westphalian railways were originally private projects that had gone under in 1847 and 1848. Local infighting and money disputes halted the Saarbrücken's construction, whereas Westphalian railroad stockholders refused in 1848 to pay any more installments. The Westphalian Railway, originally called the Cologne-Minden-Thuringian Railway, linked Hessian and Hannoverian lines with the port of Emden via Rheine und Münster, which also connected with the lines of the Cologne-Minden Railway that led to Osnabrück and to the Dutch border on the Rhine. Enabling trains to travel from Cologne to Hamm, Cassel, Erfurt, and Leipzig and eventually on to Dresden, Görlitz, Breslau, and Cracow, this link was a vital traffic

artery that connected central Germany to the Rhineland and Westphalia. The Prussian government especially desired this line, for it was a corridor between the eastern and western provinces that was independent of Hannover, a state that traditionally enjoyed logistical leverage over Prussia. Similarly, the Saarbrücken Railway connected the Rhenish hinterland with Paris. Any delay in its construction threatened to bypass Prussia in the major traffic thoroughfares from Ostende, Antwerp, and Paris to central and southern Germany in favor of the line's new competitor, the Paris-Strasbourg line. Because the railway was situated on the border, the state ascribed major military value to the line.

30. See the report of the Second Chamber, "Die Ausführung der Ostbahn, der Westphälischen und der Saarbrücker Eisenbahn," GStA Merseburg, Rep. 169C, Abschnitt 19, nr. 1, vol. 1, p. 127: "Sie [die Kommission] geht jedoch von dem Gesichtspunkt aus, dass der Übergang aller Eisenbahnen in das Eigenthum des Staates stets das Ziel der Regierung bleiben müsse, niemals aus den Augen verloren werden dürfe, und auf dessen Erreichung durch jedes sich darbietende Mittel hinzustreben sei." ("The commission, however, takes the viewpoint that the transfer of all railways into the state's possession must always remain the government's goal. This aim must never be lost from view; the government must strive to reach it through every means available.") Schreiber, *Eisenbahnen,* p. 23; Henderson, *Industrial Revolution,* pp. 172 ff.; and Bergengrün, *Heydt,* p. 169.

31. Because of its significance, the story will be told in full in chap. 4.

32. For Heydt's frustration at having his directives on controlling workers disregarded by private railways, see GStA Merseburg, Rep. 77, tit. 260, nr. 3, vol. 1, p. 103; see the protocols of the board of directors for the Rhenish Railway for their insistence on more proof from the ministry, HAStK, Best. 1028, nr. 7, p. 196; for the resistance of the Magdeburg-Leipzig Railway, which refused to fire certain workers, GStA Merseburg, Rep. 77, tit. 260, nr. 6, vol. 1, pp. 13–14, 44. The same railway also refused to fire Hans Viktor von Unruh from its board of directors, in spite of Heydt's direct pressure, but Unruh resigned anyway in the best interests of the company. Hans Viktor von Unruh, *Erinnerungen aus dem Leben von Hans Viktor von Unruh,* ed. Heinrich von Poschinger (Stuttgart, 1895), pp. 170–73; see also Berlin Police Director Hinckeldey's monitoring of "democratic" railroad businessmen. "Die Überwachung der Demokraten und ehemaligen Eisenbahn-Direktors Theodor Olshausen," BLHA, 30 Berlin C, tit. 94, nr. 12055.

33. For the case of director Bloem, see GStA Merseburg, Rep. 77, tit. 260, nr. 3, vol. 1, p. 103.

34. For the ministerial documentation on the purge of railroad workers, see "Verfahren gegen Eisenbahn-Beamten, 1849–58," GStA Merseburg, Rep. 77, tit. 260, nr. 6, vols. 1 & 2. Wolfgang Klee notes that the order to purge democrat workers was especially directed at the Rhenish Railway. *Preussische Eisenbahngeschichte,* p. 119.

35. GStA Merseburg, Rep. 77, tit. 260, nr. 3, vol. 1, pp. 89 ff.

36. For documentation on the state takeover, see GStA Merseburg Rep. 93E, nr. 751, nr. 3414; 2.2.1., nr. 29558; 90a K. III. 3, nr. 12.

37. See the Railroad Commissioners' report to Heydt, the official protest of the directors to the trade ministry, and the minister's response to the director, GStA Merseburg, Rep. 93E, nr. 751, pp. 45–56; Unruh, *Erinnerungen,* p. 197.

38. Klee, *Preussische Eisenbahngeschichte,* p. 224.

39. For a complete discussion on the railroad tax, see chap. 6.

40. Combined with normal dividends, the state earned a total profit of 5,737,573 thalers in 1860, 7,208,989 thalers in 1863, and 14,888,950 thalers in 1866. *VBMHGA* 1858–60, p. 39; *VBMHGA* 1861–63, p. 46; *VBMHGA* 1864–66, p. 45. Between 1847 and 1860 the Upper Silesian paid 1,919,897 thalers and the Cologne-Minden 2,336,682 thalers, a total of 4,256,579 thalers.

41. *VBMHGA* 1852–54, p. 36. Bergengrün, *Heydt,* pp. 189 ff; Henderson, *Industrial Revolution,* pp. 179 ff.

42. Julius Jaeger, *Die Lehre von den Eisenbahnen auf Grundlage des Staates* (Munich, 1865), p. 93 n. 3; Heydt's discussion of reserve funds in his administrative report for the years 1855–57 avoids this point. *VBMHGA* 1855–57, pp. 37, 41.

43. For the conflict between the trade ministry and the Potsdam-Magdeburg Railway, see *EbZ* 9:42 (19 Oct. 1851), p. 165; for the ongoing years-long struggle between the government and the Rhenish Railway, see the company's protocols of October 1858, HAStK 1028, nr. 9, pp. 154, 165. The Magdeburg-Leipzig Railway and the Wilhelms Railway also had problems in this regard.

44. Heydt's 950 thaler fine on the Cologne-Minden directors in February 1857 for not submitting information on time appeared so unusually harsh and arbitrary that the king called on Heydt to justify his actions in writing. See Heydt's direct report (*Immediatbericht*) to Friedrich Wilhelm IV, 29 Apr. 1857, GStA Merseburg, Rep. 2.2.1., nr. 29629, p. 148.

45. See, for example, the protocols of the Rhenish Railway, 5 Nov. 1858, HAStK, Best. 1028, nr. 9, p. 180.

46. Heydt and Mevissen broke off in contact in the years 1848–55, partly because of railroad charters. Hansen, *Mevissen,* 1:687–88; For references to the competition between state and private railways, see Kleist-Retzow to Heydt, 28 Feb. 1852, LHAK, Best. 403, nr. 11721, p. 321. Any concession in the Rhineland was an exhaustive process. For a frank discussion of Heydt's suspicious attitude toward charter requests, see the report of the Rhenish Railway's general agent to the trade ministry, 17 Aug. 1858, HAStK, 1028, nr. 9, p. 128.

47. For rejections, see GStA Merseburg, Rep. 93E, nrs. 3271–72, (1844–66).

48. Mottek, *Wirtschaftsgeschichte,* 2:142; Horst Blumberg, "Die Finanzierung der Neugründungen von Industriebetrieben in Form der Aktiengesellschaften während der fünfziger Jahre des 19. Jahrhunderts in Deutschland, am Beispiel der preussichen Verhältnisse erläutert," in Hans Mottek, ed, *Studien zur Geschichte der industriellen Revolution in Deutschland* (Berlin, 1960), p. 185; see also Hans Rosenberg, *Die Weltwirtschaftskrise 1857–1859* (rpt., Göttingen, 1974), p. 65.

49. In the 1870s Bethel Henry Strousberg, although hardly a disinterested party, remarked that the Prussian trade minister was the "unquestioned master" who alone decided whether charters would be granted. During the tenure of Heydt, he wrote, "no

new private enterprise was possible." Bethel Henry Strousberg, *Dr. Strousberg und sein Wirken* (Berlin, 1876), pp. 241, 245. Regarding Heydt's policy of no new charters, railway directors of existing companies most likely held an ambivalent attitude, because the government's refusal to allow new companies also increased the chances for private companies to expand their networks. For instance, under the leadership of Gustav Mevissen, the Rhenish Railway clearly tried to establish a monopoly on the left bank of the Rhine, after absorbing the Bonn-Cologne and Cologne-Crefeld railways—despite Mevissen's public speech endorsing the merits of competition. For Mevissen's inconsistencies between what he practiced and what he preached, see Padtberg, *Rheinischer Liberalismus,* p. 81.

50. GStA Merseburg, Rep. 93E, nrs. 3846–47, "Die Übernahme der Münster-Hammer Eisenbahn betreffend," 1849–55, unpag; Michealis, *Deutschlands Eisenbahnen,* pp. 228–29.

51. For figures on capitalization and dividend returns, see J. Michaelis, *Deutschlands Eisenbahnen,* pp. xv–vii. The averages for state-run Berg-Mark, Aachen-Düsseldorfer, Cöln-Crefeld, Prinz Wilhelm, and the Ruhrort-Crefeld-Gladbacher were 1 7/8, 3 1/2, 3/10, 7/15, 3 17/24. The dividend for the Aachen-Düsseldorfer railway was guaranteed, thus making the average dividend rate of 1.37 artificially high.

52. Ibid., p. 345.

53. Ibid., p. 342.

54. Henderson, *Industrial Revolution,* p. 178.

55. Special Director Lewald to the Royal Railroad Commission, 12 July 1855, GStA Merseburg, Rep. 93E, nr. 765, unpag.

56. Railroad Commissioner Nostitz to Heydt, 7 May 1856, GStA Merseburg, Rep. 93E, nr. 765, unpag.

57. Trade Minister Heydt to Friedrich Wilhelm IV, 23 Sept. 1856, GStA Merseburg, Rep. 93E, nr. 3420, p. 231.

58. Railroad Commissioner Nostitz to Heydt, 7 May 1856, GStA Merseburg, Rep. 93E, nr. 765, unpag.

59. Railroad Commissioners Nostitz and Schwedler to Heydt, 10 August 1856, GStA Merseburg, Rep. 93E, nr. 3420, pp. 70–71.

60. See the protocol of the Verwaltungsrat of 22 Aug 1856 to note the dissent of the directors but the anguished realization that it was suicide for the company to allow competition into the Tarnowitz mines. GStA Merseburg, Rep. 93E, nr. 3420, pp. 81–84.

61. *Schlesische Zeitung,* 13 Aug. 1856, p. 1784.

62. Railroad Commissioner Nostitz to Heydt, 26 Aug. 1856, GStA Merseburg, Rep. 93E, nr. 3420, p. 98. In a personal letter to Heydt on 20 Aug. 1856, Nostitz noted that the directors' vote was 8 to 6 for the takeover. A state official (Maybach) then gave an oration against the consequences of a negative vote with the result that a second vote produced a vote of 11 to 3. p. 90.

63. W. O. Henderson, *The State and the Industrial Revolution in Prussia, 1740–1870* (Liverpool, 1958), p. 179.

64. In 1855 the Wilhelmsbahn yielded a 18.18 percent profit, paying a dividend

of 16 percent, which the *EbZ* called the best profit-dividend ratio in Germany. *EbZ* 15:34 (27 August 1857), p. 129.

65. Railroad Commissioners Nostitz and Schwedler to Heydt, 2 Jan. 1857, GStA Merseburg, Rep. 93E, nr. 3417, unpag.

66. Railroad Commissioners Nostitz and Schwedler to Heydt, 2 Jan. 1857, and Heydt to Railroad Commission/Breslau, 17 Jan. 1857, GStA Merseburg, Rep. 93E, nr. 3417, unpag.

67. These were the branch lines of the Kaiser-Ferdinands-Nordbahn between Oderberg and Oswiecim and the Austrian Staatsbahn between Oswiecim and Trzebinia. Michaelis, *Deutschlands Eisenbahnen,* p. 387.

68. See the concerns of the Railroad Commissioners Nostitz and Schwedler in their memorandum to Heydt, 14 March 1857, GStA Merseburg, Rep. 93E, nr. 3417, unpag.

69. *NZ,* 8 April 1857; note also the Railroad Commission's comment to the trade minister in which a written protest of prominent Berlin stockholders (among them the bankers Bleichröder, Hirschfeld, and Wolff) laid the blame more with the state railroad commission than with the company management. 14 March 1857, GStA Merseburg, Rep. 93E, nr. 3417.

70. See Heydt to king, 13 Sept. 1857, GStA Merseburg, Rep. 93E, nr. 3418, unpag.

71. Staatsanwalt v. Schelling to Handelsminister Holzbrieck, 8 Aug. 1862, GStA Merseburg, Rep. 93E, nr. 3419, unpag. The criticism was published in the Breslau *Börsenzeitung* on 4 July 1862 and Heydt sued for defamation of character. His acquittal was interpreted in a political light by Albrecht von Roon in a letter to Bismarck. Otto von Bismarck, *Gedanken und Erinnerungen* (Stuttgart, 1898), vol. 1, p. 243.

72. Eggert and Simon to Heydt, 26 August 1857, GStA Merseburg, Rep. 93E, nr. 3418, unpag.

73. Rudolf Delbrück, *Lebenserinnerungen* (Leipzig, 1905), I, p. 223.

74. *Der Aktionär* 5:224 (11 April 1858), p. 209.

75. Unruh, *Erinnerungen,* pp. 170, 197.

76. See the reports of Breslau's Polizei-Präsident von Kehler to the ministry of the interior, Sept. 29, Oct. 15, Nov. 24, and Dec. 10, 1855, GStA Merseburg, Rep. 77, tit. 359, nr. 1, Bd. 23, pp. 191, 202, 234, 254–56; see also the police report on the Silesian election of 1855 in StAP, Rep. 30 Berlin C, tit. 94, nr. 12880, p. 26.

77. 1855 Jahresbericht der Berliner Kaufmannschaft, Staatsarchiv Potsdam , Rep. 2A I HG, nr. 71 p. 3; 1853 Jahresbericht der Handelskammer Cöln, *Handelsarchiv* 1854, vol. 1, sec. III, p. 31; for its 1855 report, Hansen, *Mevissen,* II, pp. 533–37 and *Handelsarchiv* 1856, I, p. 485. 1853 Jahresbericht der Handelskammer Hagen, *Handelsarchiv* 1854, I, sec. III, p. 383; 1855 Jahresbericht der Handelskammer Crefeld, *Handelsarchiv* 1856, I, p. 329ff.; Jahresbericht der Handelskammer Elberfeld und Barmen, *Handelsarchiv* 1856, I, p. 389; see also Padtberg, *Rheinischer Liberalismus,* pp. 40–81.

78. Friedrich Zunkel, *Unternehmer,* p. 198.

79. Michael Gugel, *Industrieller Aufstieg und bürgerliche Herrschaft: Soziööko-*

nomische Interessen und politische Ziele des liberalen Bürgertums in Preussen zur Zeit des Verfassungskonflikts 1857–1867 (Cologne, 1975), p. 32 n. 11.

80. These incidents lend support to Thomas Nipperdey's statement that liberals did not "retreat" from politics after 1848; instead the nature of politics had changed. Nipperdey, *Deutsche Geschichte 1800–1866: Bürgerwelt und starker Staat* (Munich, 1983), p. 684.

81. *EbZ* 8:40 (6 Oct. 1850), p. 177. *EbZ* 10:36 (5 Sept. 1852), p. 153; *EbZ* 12:41 (9 Oct 1854), p. 162; *EbZ,* 28 May 1859, pp. 81–83; see also Hansen, *Mevissen,* II, pp. 537–44, for the Cologne Chamber of Commerce recommendations on how the government should amend the economic problems caused by the mobilization.

82. Heydt to Friedrich Wilhelm IV, 22 June 1857, GStA Merseburg, Rep. 2.2.1., nr. 29531, pp. 109–10.

83. James Sheehan, *German History, 1770–1866* (Oxford, 1990), p. 786.

84. Quoted in Sheehan, *German History,* p. 732.

85. For entrepreneurs' high regard for commercial courts, see Zunkel, *Unternehmer,* p. 153. For a representative sampling of how the courts and government behaved toward railway companies regarding disputes with farmers, merchants, and town governments, see Staatsarchiv Potsdam, 2A IV, nr. 1926, nr. 1937, nr. 2046, nr. 2148.

86. The 1850s are often regarded as a period when the independence of courts was seriously compromised and made the tool of government will. The government expected obedience to its programs and certainly affected the civic ethos of Prussian bureaucrats. But, as John Gillis notes, the "government found the administrative bureaucracy somewhat easier to control than the judiciary." John Gillis, *The Prussian Bureaucracy in Crisis, 1840–1860: Origins of an Administrative Ethos* (Stanford, 1971), p. 154.

87. See GStA Merseburg, Rep. 90a K. III 3, nr. 26; Rep. 90a K. III. 3. nr. 14, vol. 1; and 90a K. III. 3., nr. 11, vol. 2 for these incidents that pitted railway companies against the war ministry.

88. See the Rhenish Railway's protocols of director meetings in HAStK, Best. 1028, nr. 6–9.

89. For businessmen's interests in a better legal system, see E. N. Anderson, *The Social and Political Conflict in Prussia* (Lincoln, Neb., 1954), p. 293; For the Prussian-German liberal interest in making ministers responsible to the courts but not to parliament, see Otto Pflanze, "Judicial and Political Responsibility in Nineteenth-Century Germany," in Leonard Krieger and Fritz Stern, eds., *The Responsibility of Power* (New York, 1967), pp. 162–82.

90. See Heydt's circular letter of 21 Oct. 1853 to railroad officials in the trade ministry regarding the hierarchical system of decision making, GStA Merseburg, Rep. 93E, nr. 1, p. 26. See 93E, nr. 7, p. 2 for Mellin's letter to the Westphalian Royal Railroad Commission of 1 Oct. 1851 reminding them that the collegial system did not operate at their bureaucratic level and that commissioners were not to confer with other ministries—they were only to receive their orders from Heydt's pen.

91. See, for example, the relationship between the state commissioners in Cologne and the trade ministry, especially regarding the relationship between the Cologne-Crefeld Railway and the Rhenish Railway. GStA Merseburg, Rep. 93E, nr. 3753, 1853–59, unpag. Moeller's memorandum of 18 July 1859 to Undersecretary Pommer-Esche provides a good example of a provincial official criticizing Heydt.

92. See HAStK, Best. 1073, nr. 43d, 161 and HAStK, Best. 1028, nr. 43–50, for Moeller's cooperation with the Rhenish Railway.

93. See Witzleben's "Promemoria betreffend die Eisenbahn-Unternehmungen in der Provinz Sachsen," Nov. 1856, GStA Merseburg, Rep. 93E, nr. 3271, pp. 163–72 and subsequent correspondence, pp. 173–237.

94. *EbZ* 8:31 (4 Aug. 1850), pp. 142–43; *EbZ* 15:35 (3 Sept. 1857). pp. 133–34; *EbZ* 18:31 (4 Aug. 1860), pp. 122–23. In the period 1850–59, thirty-four businessmen from the Rhenish and Westphalian provinces applied to the state for the coveted title of "Commercial Councillor." Karin Kaudelka-Hanisch, "The Titled Businessman: Prussian Commercial Councillors in the Rhineland and Westphalia during the Nineteenth Century," in David Blackbourn and Richard Evans, eds., *The German Bourgeoisie,* p. 96.

95. In the unpopular and disputed takeovers of the board of directors of the Lower Silesian–Mark and the Upper Silesian, members of the board of directors bore honorary titles. This would also be true of the night trains affair, the subject of chap. 4.

96. The behavior of railroad businessmen from 1848 to 1866 confirms Hartmut Kaelble's statement: "When using the most important new criterion of judgement, the political behavior of businessmen, there is little to see of the attempt to feudalize businessmen." See his "Wie feudal waren die deutschen Unternehmer?" pp. 165–66; see also the conclusions of Karin Kaudelka-Hanisch in "The Titled Businessman," pp. 87–114.

97. Sheehan, *German History,* pp. 787–88; Zunkel, *Unternehmer,* p. 52.

98. Max Weber, *The Theory of Social and Economic Organization* (New York, 1964), pp. 136 ff, 228 ff; Weber, *From Max Weber: Essays in Sociology* (New York, 1974), pp. 180 ff; Jürgen Kocka, "Bürgertum und Bürgerlichkeit als Probleme der deutschen Geschichte vom späten 18. zum frühen 20. Jahrhundert," in Kocka, ed, *Bürger und Bürgerlichkeit,* pp. 21–54; see also Kocka's "Bürgertum und bürgerliche Gesellschaft im 19. Jahrhundert," 11–78; Otto Pflanze, *Bismarck,* 1:106.

99. Böhme, *Deutschlands Weg zur Grossmacht;* Lothar Machthan and Dietrich Milles, *Die Klassensymbiose von Junkertum und Bourgeoisie* (Frankfurt a.M., 1980).

100. *BBZ,* 10 Aug. 1959. Von Polski's epithets are largely lost in translation: "Du Spitzbube, Schuft, Lump, Betrüger, Menschenfresser, nimm auch dieses Packet zu Deinen gestohlenen Millionen." Roughly, this would be: "You thief, scoundrel, bum, swindler, cannibal—put this packet with your stolen millions."

101. *BBZ,* 31 Jan. 1859.

102. Anton von Polski to Fr. Wilhelm IV, 10 Oct. 1858, GStA Merseburg, Rep. 2.2.1., nr. 29519, p. 204.

103. J. Michaelis, *Deutschlands Eisenbahnen,* pp. xv–xvii. Given the importance of these structural changes in Germany's largest investment sector, it is curious that

this transitional period has not been integrated into the larger questions addressing both the role of the state in industrialization and the relationship of the entrepreneurial class to the postrevolutionary conservatism of the Prussian state.

104. Georg Simmel, "Conflict," in *Conflict and the Web of Group-Affiliations* (New York, 1964), pp. 88–123; Lewis A. Coser, *The Functions of Social Conflict* (New York, 1967), pp. 34 ff.

105. For a fuller presentation of the choices of the Prussian state economy, see Otto Pflanze, *Bismarck,* vol. 1, chap. 5.

Chapter Four

1. A small sampling demonstrates the deplorable state of railroad equities in 1848–49. Using stock quotes from January and December of 1848 and April of 1849, the index for the Berlin Hamburg Railway was 100 3/4, 63 1/2, 46 1/2; Lower Silesian-Mark Railway, 88 1/4, 69, 72; Cologne-Minden, 95, 77 1/2, 76 1/2; Rhenish Railway, 84, 51 3/4, 48; Bonn-Cologne, 122, 102 1/2, 103 1/4. Although some railways escaped major losses, for example, the Magdeburg-Halberstadt, the dominant trend is reflected in the quotes given. See J. Michaelis, "Verzeichniss der Curse aller Bahnen," an appendix to *Deutschlands Eisenbahnen,* pp. 1–67.

2. See chap. 3.

3. At the height of the night train conflict in 1852, there was a total of 3357.05 kilometers of rail in Prussia, of which 2,112.83 was private. The Berlin-Hamburg, Berlin-Stettin, Berlin-Anhalt, Bonn-Cologne, Cologne-Minden, Düsseldorf-Elberfeld, Lower Silesia-Mark, Magdeburg-Leipzig, Muenster-Hamm, Prinz Wilhelm, and the Rheinische railways, companies which protested to the government, managed 2,002.06 kilometers of rail, or 94.7 percent of all Prussian private rail. Data drawn from Klee, *Preussische Eisenbahngeschichte* (Bielefeld, 1982), p. 224; and J. Michaelis, *Deutschlands Eisenbahnen,* pp. xii–xxii, 1–416.

4. Henderson, *Industrial Revolution,* p. 181; *VZ,* 24 Nov. 1849, nr. 275.

5. See article 19 of the treaty in H. F. L. Augustin, *Das Preussische Handels-Ministerium in seinem Verhaeltnisse zu den Privat-Eisenbahn-Gesellschaften* (Potsdam, 1859), p. 21.

6. Alexander Bergengrün, *Staatsminister August Freiherr von der Heydt* (Leipzig, 1908), p. 179; Augustin, *Preussische Handels-Ministerium,* p. 22.

7. "Bericht des Ausschusses der Berlin-Hamburg Eisenbahngesellschaft 1854/55," BLHA, Rep. 2A IV, nr. 1938, p. 10; Augustin, *Preussische Handelsministerium,* p. 22.

8. Minutes of the Rhenish Railway Directors, 14 June 1850, HAStK, Best. 1028, nr. 7, p. 65.

9. Ibid.

10. *Preussische Gesetzsammlung,* 1838, p. 513.

11. Minutes of the Rhenish Railway Board of Directors, 14 June 1850, HAStK, Best. 1028, nr. 7, pp. 65–66.

12. Ibid., 5 July 1850, HAStK, Best. 1028, nr. 7, p. 68.

13. Ibid., 6 Dec. and 23 Dec. 1850, HAStK, Best. 1028, nr. 7, pp. 103, 109.

14. Ibid., 23 Dec. 1850, HAStK, Best. 1028, nr. 7, p. 109.

15. Ibid., 3 Apr. 1851, HAStK, Best. 1028, nr. 7, p. 136.

16. Letter of Wittgenstein to the Rhenish Railway Directory, 17 Apr. 1851, HAStK, Best. 1028, nr. 136, p. 1.

17. Ibid.

18. Copy of the protocol of the Rhenish railway (Mevissen, Compes, Hirte, Strebel), Prince Wilhelm railway (Hangohr, Schreiner), the Bonn-Cologne railway (Mülhens), the Münster-Hamm railway (von Forckenbeck), the Düsseldorf-Elberfeld railway (Dietze) and the Cologne-Mindener (Wittgenstein, Oppenheim, Kühlwetter und Leopold), 23 Apr. 1850, HAStK, Best. 1028, nr. 136, p. 3.

19. The directors of the Bonn-Cologne and the Cologne-Minden Railway to Trade Minister von der Heydt, 29 Apr. 1851, HAStK, Best. 1028, nr. 136, p. 5.

20. Ibid.

21. Ibid.

22. Ibid., p. 7.

23. Ibid.

24. Ibid., pp. 5-6.

25. Ibid., p. 6.

26. The company lost control of its management when the government exercised a clause in the contract of a bond issued from the Prussian treasury to the company that gave the government the right to take control of the administration of the railroad after three years of consecutive losses. The Lower Silesian–Mark Railway lost money in 1847 and 1848, as did many railways, and the night trains in 1849 brought their losses to such a magnitude as to prevent them from borrowing to stave off a government takeover. In December 1851, the government announced its intention not only to administer the railroad but own it. This incident, in combination with the failed bid by Heydt in 1849 to purchase the Rhenish Railway, had put companies on their guard.

27. Minutes, 7 and 18 May 1852, HAStK, Best. 1028, nr. 7, pp. 242, 249.

28. The correspondence on this issue between the company and the government, which began in May 1851, can be followed in a pamphlet published by the railway company for public consumption. See "Der Konflikt des Königlichen Handels-Ministeriums mit der Direktion der Bonn-Cölner Eisenbahn Gesellschaft, die Einrichtung eines Nachtzuges betreffend," undated, HAStK, Best. 1028, nr. 135, pp. 20–22. The Cologne-Minden company had taken a similar step earlier by publishing its correspondence with Heydt in the *Kölnische Zeitung,* 7 Dec. 1851. See also the Bonn-Cologne's response to the trade ministry regarding the administrative takeover, 23 July 1852, HAStK, Best. 1028, nr. 135, pp. 45–57.

29. Undersecretary Adolf von Pommer-Esche (for Heydt) to Provincial Governor Kleist-Restow, LHAK, Best. 403, nr. 11812, 24 June 1852, pp. 469–70.

30. Heydt to the Cologne Royal Railroad Commission, 6 and 17 July 1852, HAStK, Best. 1028, nr. 135, pp. 36, 43.

31. Ibid., 17 July 1852, HAStK, Best. 1028, nr. 135, p. 43.

32. Minutes of the Bonn-Cologne Railway, 2 Aug. 1852, HAStK, Best. 1028, nr.

135, p. 307. At this meeting Heydt repeated the settlement terms originally offered to the company on 17 July 1852. HAStK, Best. 1028, nr. 135, p. 43.

33. Minutes of the Bonn-Cologne Railway, 2 Aug. 1852, HAStK, Best. 1028, nr. 135, p. 307.

34. Jung, director of the Bonn-Cologne Railway, to the Royal Railroad Commission in Cologne, 3 Aug. 1852, HAStK, Best. 1028, nr. 135, p. 61; Bonn-Cologne protocol, 2 Aug. 1852, HAStK, Best. 1028, nr. 135, p. 307.

35. Maschinenmeister W. Nohl to Directors of Bonn-Cologne Railway, 6 July 1852, HAStK, Best. 1028, nr. 135, p. 32.

36. Heydt to Provincial Governor Kleist-Restow, 24 Aug. 1852, LHAK, Best. 403, nr. 11812; Heydt to the directors of the Bonn-Cologne Railway, 24 Aug. 1852, HAStK, Best. 1028, nr. 135, pp. 71–72.

37. The trade ministry chose to base its litigation on the government's right to police and supervise roads and railways and not on its right to move the mail with railroads as stipulated in the 1838 law. The court found little application between this claim and the case at hand.

38. Minutes, 2 Apr. 1852, HAStK, nr. 7, p. 234.

39. See, for example, *VBMHGA* 1849–51, p. 28.

40. Of the scant literature that exists on night trains, historians have always accepted Heydt's assertion. Bergengrün, *Heydt,* pp. 177–80; Henderson, *Industrial Revolution,* pp. 180–82.

41. See chap. 3 for discussion on railroad associations. Alfred Chandler places the movement for cooperation between American companies for better transshipment and conveyance of passengers as starting in the 1870s. Chandler, *The Visible Hand: The Managerial Revolution in American Business* (Cambridge, Mass., 1977), pp. 122 ff. In this respect, the efforts of this association are impressively early.

42. Augustin, *Preussische Handels-Ministerium,* p. 25.

43. Ibid.

44. See Heydt's pro memoria to the king, 22 June 1857, GStA Merseburg, Rep. 2.2.1., nr. 29531, pp. 105–12, regarding his actions to bar the North German Railway Association's new measures for ticket and luggage transfer. Heydt resented decisions affecting Prussian railway service not being made by the trade ministry and furthermore suspected that foreign governments, especially Hanover and Brunswick, would use such private associations as an economic lever against Prussia.

45. Augustin, *Preussische Handels-Minsterium,* p. 23.

46. *BBZ,* 22 Mar. 1859, nr. 135, p. 563.

47. Minutes of the Rhenish Railway, 6 May 1853, HAStK, Best. 1028, nr. 7, p. 346.

48. "Protokol der General Versammlung der Actionärs der Berlin-Hamburger Eisenbahngesellschaft nebst Bericht des Ausschusses an dieselben," Berlin, 1853. BLHA, Rep. 2A I V, nr. 1938, p. 8.

49. For the Hamburg-Berlin Railway, see the "Bericht des Ausschusses 1854–55," 31 May 1855, p. 6 of brochure, BLHA, Rep. 2A IV, nr. 1938, p. 18. This pamphlet noted that the third appeal was still in process but warned of the imminent defeat. For the Rhenish Railway, see its board minutes, 1 Dec. 1854, HAStK, Best. 1028, nr. 7,

p. 470; and 2 Nov. 1855, HAStK, Best. 1028, nr. 8, p. 130; see also Hansen, *Mevissen,* 1:680.

50. Augustin, *Preussische Handels-Ministerium,* p. 22.

51. Ibid., p. 27. Augustin was director of the Berlin-Potsdam-Magdeburg Railway.

52. Henderson, *Industrial Revolution,* p. 181.

53. *BBZ,* 1 Nov. 1858, p. 2283. In 1858–59, railroad companies also began to complain again of the lack of profit in night trains and petitioned again for either revising schedules or receiving compensation. See, for example, the minutes of the Rhenish Railway, Feb.–Nov. 1858, HAStK, Best. 1028, nr. 9, pp. 21, 33, 149–50; also see the *BBZ,* 22 Mar. 1859, p. 563.

54. *BBZ,* nr. 566, 9 Nov. 1858, p. 2343.

Chapter Five

1. Obermann quoting Jacob Riesser, former director of the Darmstädter Bank, in "Die Rolle der ersten deutschen Aktienbanken in den Jahren 1848 bis 1856," *Jahrbuch für Wirtschaftsgeschichte* 2 (1960): 51.

2. Alfred Krüger, *Das Kölner Bankiergewerbe vom Ende des 18. Jahrhunderts bis 1875* (Essen, 1925), pp. 30–32, 138–45; Karl Erich Born, *International Banking in Germany in the Nineteenth and Twentieth Centuries* (Warwickshire, 1983), pp. 82–92; Treue, *Technikgeschichte Preussens,* pp. 488–89; Henderson, *German Industrial Power,* chap. 9; R. Tilly, *Financial Institutions,* pp. 111 ff.; Fritz Seidenzahl, "Eine Denkschrift David Hansemanns vom Jahre 1856: Ein Beitrag zur Entstehungsgeschichte der deutschen Aktienbanken," in Karl Erich Born, ed., *Moderne deutsche Wirtschaftsgeschichte* (Cologne, 1966), pp. 214–25; Hans Jaeger, *Geschichte der Wirtschaftsordnung,* pp. 80 ff.; Kiesewetter, *Industrielle Revolution in Deutschland,* pp. 286 ff; Manfred Pohl, "Die Entwicklung des deutschen Bankwesens zwischen 1848 and 1870," in Hans and Manfred Pohl, *Deutsche Bankengeschichte,* vol. 2, *Das Deutsche Bankwesen (1806–1848); Die Entwicklung des deutschen Bankwesens zwischen 1848 und 1870; Festigung und Ausdehnung des deutschen Bankwesens zwischen 1870 und 1914* (Frankfurt a.M., 1982), pp. 171 ff.

3. Bertrand Gille, "Banking and Industrialisation in Europe, 1730–1914," in Carlo M. Cipolla, ed., *The Fontana Economic History of Europe,* vol. 3, *The Industrial Revolution* (Glasgow, 1973), pp. 272–75; Knut Borchardt, "Industrial Revolution in Germany," pp. 147–148; H. Aubin and Wolfgang Zorn, *Handbuch der deutschen Wirtschafts- und Sozialgeschichte,* vol. 2, *Das 19. und 20. Jahrhundert* (Stuttgart, 1976) pp. 411–20; Treue, *Gebhardt Handbuch,* 17:238 ff.; Wolfram Fischer, ed., *Europäische Wirtschafts- und Sozialgeschichte von der Mitte des 19. Jahrhunderts bis zum Ersten Weltkrieg* (Stuttgart, 1985); Hermann Kellenbenz, *Deutsche Wirtschaftsgeschichte,* vol. 2, *Vom Ausgang des 18. Jahrhunderts bis zum Ende des Zweiten Weltkriegs* (Munich, 1981) pp. 147 ff.; and Mottek, *Wirtschaftsgeschichte,* pp. 140 ff. Mottek, although not elaborating, states, "Die Gründung all dieser Aktienbanken war, ebenso wie bereits die Bildung des Schaaffhausenschen Bankvereins, ein gegen den Wider-

stand der absolutistisch-junkerlichen Elemente errungener Erfolg im Klassenkampf der Bourgeoisie" ("The founding of these joint-stock banks, as was the creation of the Schaafhausen'schen Bank, marked a decisive success of the bourgeoisie's class struggle against the resistance of absolutistic Junker elements.") (p. 140).

4. Obermann, "Der ersten deutschen Aktienbanken," pp. 47–75. For the alliance thesis, see ibid., pp. 49, 52, 56, 57.

5. Ibid., pp. 49, 52.

6. Helmut Böhme, "Preussische Bankpolitik 1848–1853," reprinted in Böhme, ed., *Probleme der Reichsgründungszeit,* (Cologne, 1968), pp. 117–58.

7. Ibid., p. 141.

8. Ibid., pp. 130–42.

9. Bergengrün, *Hansemann,* chap. 9; Walther Däbritz, *Gründung und Anfänge der Disconto-Gesellschaft Berlin* (Munich, 1931), pp. 43 ff.

10. For the sealed and signed copy of the law, see "Verordnung, die Betheiligung stiller Gesellschaften mit Aktien an Handels-Unternehmungen betreffend," GStA Merseburg, Rep. 2.2.1., nr. 30003, p. 120. The only historian to my knowledge who makes reference to this octroi is the East German historian Horst Thieme in his un- published dissertation, "Die ökonomischen und politischen Widersprüche bei der Er- teilung von Konzessionen zur Gründung von Aktiengesellschaften in Preussen von 1850–1857" (Leipzig, 1957). Although making reference to it, Thieme does not ex- plore the problem. The obscurity of the event is also explained in large part by its absence in Heinrich Poschinger's three-volume collection of government documents pertaining to banking history, *Bankwesen und Bankpolitik in Preussen* (Berlin, 1879). These volumes are by far the best published collection of documents on banking poli- tics, but Poschinger did not have access to all documents (and as a historian, he wrote in open admiration of the empire and its economic structure). On Poschinger's restric- tions of "amtliche Zensur," see Böhme, "Preussische Bankpolitik 1848–1853," p. 118 n. 10.

11. Most economic histories convey this impression, either glossing over the problem altogether or noting Prussia's reluctance to grant joint-stock privileges but tolerating commandite companies. See, for example, Treue, *Gebhardt Handbuch,* 17:238 ff.; Henderson, *German Industrial Power,* pp. 123–29; Kiesewetter, *Industri- elle Revolution in Deutschland,* pp. 286–87. Richard Tilly's excellent work on banking does discuss the formation of the commandite banks in 1856, and although he alludes to the "hostility of Berlin bankers and the government," he never mentions the actual tensions. See *Financial Institutions,* p. 116. Helmut Böhme's and Karl Obermann's articles are two exceptions.

12. State Ministry to King Friedrich Wilhelm IV, 1 July 1856. GStA Merseburg, Rep. 2.2.1., nr. 30003, p. 87; Blumberg, "Die Finanzierung der Neugründungen," p. 170.

13. J. H. Clapham notes that commandite companies were common by the turn of the century in the Rhineland. *The Economic Development of France and Germany, 1815–1914,* 4th ed. (London, 1966), pp. 130–31. Richard Tilly is probably more accu- rate in writing that commandite companies were "little known in Prussia until the

middle of the century." *Financial Institutions,* p. 115. The first manipulators with limited partnerships were the French, who employed the commandite principle widely after the French Commercial Code of 1807 did not grant commandites corporate status. From 1820 the use of commandite companies became widespread in France. Between 1840 and 1848, over 1,400 commandite companies were founded, an average of 175 a year. Some French commandite companies grew into large operations in the 1830s. Jacques Lafitte, the former French finance minister, expanded the use of commandite companies in 1837 to engage in investment banking, producing a spate of imitators as well as legislation in the same year to restrict their use. The large investment banks were initially successful, but most went bankrupt in the financial crisis of 1848. Clapham, *Economic Development,* pp. 130–31; Rondo E. Cameron, "Founding the Bank of Darmstadt," *Explorations in Entrepreneurial History* 8 (1955–56): 115; Fritz Redlich, "Jacques Lafitte and the Beginning of Investment Banking in France," *Bulletin of the Business Historical Society* 22 (1948): 137–60.

14. Däbritz, *Gründung und Anfänge,* p. 64.

15. Ibid.

16. Alexander Bergengrün, *Staatsminister August von der Heydt* (Leipzig, 1908), p. 223.

17. Richard Tilly has shown the resourcefulness with which Rhenish and German businessmen employed non-intermediated credit—bills of exchange and acceptance, running credit, promissory notes, etc.—to accommodate expanding business in the face of money scarcity and deficient financial institutions, thus foiling the long-term importance of government control in the industrial revolution. Tilly, *Financial Institutions,* pp. 129–33; Tilly, "Finanzielle Aspekte der preussischen Industrialisierung 1815–1870," in Wolfram Fischer, ed., *Wirtschafts- und sozialgeschichtliche Probleme der frühen Industrialisierung* (Berlin, 1968) pp. 477–91; see also Fremdling, *Eisenbahnen.* Viewed macroeconomically, the restrictive policy of the Royal Bank did not perhaps retard growth of trade and industry because of clever *comptoir* banking. These interpretations, although instructive, neglect the frustrations and political friction that developed out of Prussia's mercantilist policies and how this affected the political relations of the business class with the government.

18. Prussia's eminent state economist, Christian von Rother, the president of the Royal Bank and, from 1837 to 1848, the director of the Seehandlung, was saddled with the dual task of addressing the mercantilist needs of the Prussian state (generating revenues, sanitizing debts, cutting back on a swollen bureaucracy, restoring credibility to state paper, and propping up the sagging value of provincial *Pfandbriefe*) while ostensibly introducing greater economic freedoms after the reforms of 1806–7. The criticism that Rother's policy served state fiscal needs more than private business was justified, yet gains were made for the private sector. In 1837 he lowered the prime rate to 4 percent and kept it there until the panic of 1844. Between 1837 and 1846 the loan bureau expanded its volume from 6 to 23 million thalers, and the bank's overall business volume doubled from 117 to 254 million thalers. This, however, did not suffice. Radtke, *Seehandlung,* pp. 120–21. For the Seehandlung's "minimal role" in the industrial revolution see Wehler, *Gesellschaftsgeschichte,* 2:638–39.

19. Flottwell, the finance minister, and Theodor von Schön charged that Rother's overly cautious policy did not address the needs of the time. This lent support to the public demand from the Berliner Kaufmannschaft, Berlin's stockbrokers, and, initially, King Friedrich Wilhelm. Radtke, *Seehandlung,* p. 123. For a list of the first 171 shareholders in the Prussian Bank, see GStA Berlin, Rep. 90, nr. 3574, pp. 26–27.

20. The most prominent critic was Harkort, who complained that the 1.5 million people of Westphalia were serviced by three small bankers in Münster and Schwelm. His demand for a private bank was similar to those of merchants and industrialists from Silesia, Posen, and the Rhineland. For a discussion of refused bank concessions, especially that of the Dessau joint-stock bank, see Radtke, *Seehandlung,* pp. 126–29; Däbritz, *Gründung und Anfänge,* p. 4.

21. Manfred Pohl, *Deutsche Bankengeschichte,* pp. 173–78; Born, *International Banking,* p. 52.

22. Poschinger, *Bankwesen,* vol. 2, *Die Jahre 1846 bis 1857,* pp. 136–37; Bergengrün, *Heydt,* pp. 224–25; Hansen, *Mevissen,* 1:660–61. Restrictions on interest deposits and the requirement for three signatures on a discounted note were the most commonly cited criticisms.

23. Heydt, for example, used these reforms to fend off criticism in the Landtag in 1851 and 1856. Poschinger, *Bankwesen,* 2:138, 160.

24. Hans-Ulrich Wehler's discussion of railroad building ignores the difficulties among financiers in raising the necessary capital. His statement "No wonder that deficiency of capital remained an unknown phrase for boards of directors for railroad companies" does not accurately characterize the concern among directors for attracting share capital and the effect of money supply on money markets in the 1850s and early 1860s. Wehler, *Gesellschaftsgeschichte,* 3:72.

25. See Heydt's objections to private joint-stock banks in his written opinion (*Votum*) of 23 Apr. 1853, GStA Berlin, Rep. 90, nr. 1185, unpag.; Poschinger, *Bankwesen,* 2:203–4; R. E. Cameron, *France and the Economic Development of Europe, 1800-1914,* 2d ed. (Chicago, 1965); Cameron, "Bank of Darmstadt," pp. 116 ff.; David Landes, "The Old Bank and the New: The Financial Revolution of the Nineteenth Century," in F. Crouzet et al., *Essays in European Economic History, 1789-1914* (New York, 1969), pp. 112–27; Jacob Riesser, *The German Great Banks and Their Concentration* (Washington, 1911), pp. 49–51; Henderson, *German Industrial Power,* pp. 123–24.

26. Born, *International Banking,* p. 84.

27. Hansen, *Mevissen,* 1:658. In 1854 the government threatened to rescind the charter, because the bank was moving too slowly in raising the loan.

28. Cameron, "Bank of Darmstadt," pp. 120 ff.; see Mevissen's reports of the Darmstädter Bank in 1854 in Hansen, *Mevissen,* 2:523–32; Born, *International Banking,* p. 84. For the list of the Darmstädter's transactions, see Alfred D. Chandler, *Scale and Scope: The Dynamics of Industrial Capitalism* (Cambridge, Mass., 1990), pp. 417–18.

29. Friedrich Wilhelm IV to State Ministry, 20 Apr. 1853, GStA Berlin, Rep. 90, nr. 1185, unpag.

30. Heydt's written opinion (*Votum*), 23 Apr. 1853, GStA Berlin, Rep. 90, nr.

1185, unpag; "Conclusum des Staats-Ministeriums," 27 Apr. 1853, GStA Berlin, Rep. 90, nr. 1185, unpag.

31. Riesser, *German Great Banks,* p. 64.

32. Delbrück, *Lebenserinnerungen,* 2:34.

33. See the "Geheimprotocolle der Verwaltung der *Bank für Handel und Industrie,*" May 1853, HAStK, Best. 1073, nr. 101a, unpag. Delbrück, along with District Governor von Moeller, former minister von Rabe, and Provincial Governor Kühlwetter, had invested in a 5 percent ten-year bond. These officials and four other investors put together a sum of 20,000 gulden.

34. Poschinger, *Bankwesen,* 2:170–79.

35. Landes, "The Old Bank and the New," p. 114.

36. L. M. Niebuhr, adviser to the king, commented in a position paper to the cabinet that both companies represented international financial powers (Crédit Mobilier and the Rothschilds) that had been competing with one another throughout Europe. The battle had now moved to Berlin. 26 Feb. 1856, GStA Merseburg, Rep. 120A XI 2, nr. 6, p. 130.

37. For copies of the petitions, see GStA Merseburg, Rep. 120A XI 2, nr. 6, p. 190; GStA Berlin, Rep. 90, nr. 1185, unpag. Although Mevissen believed the enterprise was assured a charter because it combined "the best names of the Prussian aristocracy with notable financial powers" (Hansen, *Mevissen,* 1:667), it is doubtful whether the nobles' names on the petitions had its intended effect. Niebuhr advised the cabinet ministers "not to lay too much weight on the influence of the non-bankers. With business decisions these men will fall into the hands of the bankers. . . . Because they [aristocrats] are not in the position to be a decisive influence, the bankers can say, not incorrectly, 'we have paid the men well for their names.' " 26 Feb. 1856, GStA Merseburg, Rep. 120A XI, nr. 6, p. 131.

38. Heydt quoted by Poschinger, *Bankwesen,* 2:158. Poschinger is vague about the date of Heydt's memorandum, placing it somewhere "in the middle of the 1850s" and does not cite the situation or the party for which it was written.

39. L. M. Niebuhr, 26 Feb. 1856, GStA Merseburg, Rep. 120A XI, nr. 6, p. 130.

40. I thank David E. Barclay for this biographical information on Niebuhr.

41. Heydt to Bodelschwingh, 7 Mar. 1856, GStA Merseburg, Rep. 120A XI, nr. 6, pp. 32–36. Here, p. 34. For a contrary view of Heydt's position, compare Bergengrün, *Heydt,* pp. 233–34.

42. Westphalen and Karl von Manteuffel to Otto von Manteuffel, 20 Feb. 1856, GStA Merseburg, Rep. 120A XI 2, nr. 6, p. 16.

43. Königliches Preussisches Haupt Bank Direktorium to Heydt, 14 Mar. 1856, GStA Merseburg, Rep. 120A XI 2, nr. 6, pp. 142–50.

44. Karl von Manteuffel to Heydt, 18 Mar. 1856, Rep. 120A XI 2, nr. 6, pp. 132–34.

45. Ibid., p. 134.

46. Westphalen to Heydt, 24 Mar. 1856, GStA Merseburg, Rep. 120A XI 3, nr. 6, pp. 177–78.

47. Ibid., p. 180. As an example, Westphalen cited the stock quotes of the Aus-

trian Credit-Anstalt, whose stock rose from 180 to 200 in one day yet fell to 157 only days later.

48. Ibid., p. 179.

49. Born, *International Banking*, pp. 29–30.

50. Ibid., p. 183. Using Dieterici's statistics, Manteuffel showed that bonds rose from 103,339,223 thalers in 1845 to 109,674,923 in 1849 and reached a figure of 114,497,383 in 1852—an increase of six million in the first four years but only a five million thaler increase in the last three. In view of how much better these last three years were for business and the bourse, the slowed-down growth was worrisome. Westphalen did not consider the fact that such securities did well precisely because of bad times, for they represented a safe investment. Prosperous peaceful times invited riskier but more profitable ventures.

51. Ibid., p. 184.

52. Ibid., p. 182.

53. Westphalen to Heydt, 22 Mar. 1856, GStA Merseburg, Rep. 120A XI 2, nr. 6, pp. 186–87.

54. Ibid, 25 Mar. 1856, GStA Merseburg, Rep. 120A XI 2. nr. 6, p. 226.

55. Friedrich Wilhelm to Heydt, 11 Mar. 1856, GStA Merseburg, Rep. 120A XI 2, nr. 6, p. 93.

56. See the letter of Emil Haber, Gerson Bleichröder, von Broch, and Graf Taironowsky Ludwig Erbprinz zu Bentheim to Heydt, 23 Feb. 1856, GStA Merseburg, Rep. 120A XI 2, nr. 6, pp. 39–42, in which members of the Preussische Credit-Gesellschaft declared themselves willing to merge with the Preussische Credit-Institut under certain conditions (a raised capital base and the assurance that certain members of the other company would not be put on the board of directors). Heydt also wrote to the provincial governor of Brandenburg, Heinrich Eduard von Flottwell, on 23 Feb. 1856, that a charter would be granted to the Rothschild proposal but that the specifications had yet to be determined. GStA Merseburg, Rep. 120A XI 2, nr. 6, p. 10. Heydt wanted charters for both proposals, but the other proponents for a charter, namely, Justice Minister Simons, Privy Councilors Niebuhr and Geppert, and the king, strove for a fusion. Their letters to Heydt stressed the negative aspect of competition and the volatility it would cause. The king asked Heydt to work earnestly toward a fusion; if that did not work, he was inclined to grant a charter only to the Rothschild project. For all letters, see GStA Merseburg, Rep. 120A XI 2, nr. 6. Simons to Heydt, 18 Mar. 1856, pp. 156–66; Friedrich Wilhelm to Heydt, 11 Mar. 1856, p. 93; Geppert to Heydt, 9 Mar. 1856, pp. 82–86; Niebuhr's position (*Stellungnahme*), 26 Feb. 1856, pp. 130–31.

57. Report of the state ministry, 26 Mar. 1856, GStA Merseburg, Rep. 2.2.1., nr. 30003, pp. 79–81. For the official rejection, see the Order of King Friedrich Wilhelm, p. 85.

58. Heydt to Illaire, 2 July 1856, GStA Merseburg, Rep. 2.2.1., nr. 30003, pp. 95–96.

59. Conrad Carl, Paul Eduard Conrad, Johann Friedrich Ludwig Gelpcke, Gustav Mevissen, and A. Mendelssohn were, for example, backers in the original Crédit Mobilier project and the Berliner Handelsgesellschaft. Petitioners of "Preussisches

Credit-Institut" to state ministry, 14 Feb. 1856, GStA Berlin, Rep. 90, nr. 1185, unpag; Poschinger, *Bankwesen,* 2:230.

60. Hansen, *Mevissen,* 1:647 n. 2.

61. See Hansemann's letter to Karl Mathy, a future partner in the Diskonto Gesellschaft, on 13 May 1851, Bergengrün, *Hansemann,* pp. 665–66.

62. David Hansemann emphasized this point in his 1852 brochure, "Das Wesen der Disconto Gesellschaft in Berlin und ihre Bedeutung," in Däbritz, *Gründung,* p. 13.

63. Bergengrün, *Heydt,* p. 236; Poschinger, *Bankwesen,* 2:228, n. 2.

64. As a contemporary jurist commented in 1858, "It is not usually a normal need when large capital is compelled to form as a commandite. Rather, the chosen form is mostly an instrument for other purposes, namely, to circumvent the state authorization of joint-stock companies." G. Vogt's 1858 article in *Zeitschrift für Handelsrechts* quoted by Klaus J. Hopt, "Ideelle und wirtschaftliche Grundlagen der Actien-, Bank, und Börsenrechtsentwicklung im 19. Jahrhundert," in Helmut Coing and Walter Wilhelm, eds., *Wissenschaft und Kodifikation des Privatrechts im 19. Jahrhundert,* vol. 5, *Geld und Banken,* p. 139 n. 55.

65. Born, *International Banking,* p. 85.

66. Richard Tilly states that "because of the hostility of the Berlin bankers and the government the new shares could not be placed in Berlin." *Financial Institutions,* p. 116. This view conflicts with the report of the Prussian state ministry to the king on 1 July 1856, which noted the commandite's "advantageous reception" on the bourse. GStA Merseburg, Rep. 2.2.1., nr. 30003, p. 87. It also conflicts with the more personal note from Heydt to Illaire, 2 July 1856, GStA Merseburg, Rep. 2.2.1., p. 95. In fact, in the first year of its reorganization, the Disconto Gesellschaft paid a dividend of 10 percent—a high dividend—and was subscribed in Berlin as well as Cologne and Frankfurt. For a table of the bank's stock returns, see Riesser, *German Great Banks,* p. 68.

67. Bergengrün, *Heydt,* p. 236.

68. David Hansemann made note of the government's shift in policy toward his bank (which constituted a privileged exception to the general attitude in the cabinet) in a letter to his son Adolf on 3 June 1856. See Hermann Münch, *Adolf von Hansemann* (Munich, 1932), p. 15.

69. Heydt to Illaire, 2 July 1856, GStA Merseburg, Rep. 2.2.1., nr. 30003, p. 95.

70. Recommendation of state ministry, 1 July 1856, GStA Merseburg, Rep. 2.2.1., nr. 30003, pp. 86–92.

71. Ibid., pp. 92–93.

72. Ibid., p. 93.

73. Ibid.

74. Ibid., p. 94. Heydt's support of unconstitutional legislation is especially interesting; his opposition to any economic innovation that diminished state control characterizes well his political style and why he did not always enjoy a favorable relationship with businessmen.

75. Telegram of Minister-President Manteuffel to [in the Haag] to Civil-Cabinet Councillor Illaire in Marienbad, 8 July 1856, GStA Merseburg, Rep. 2.2.1., nr. 30003, p. 108.

76. Manteuffels telegram to Illaire, 13 July 1856, GStA Merseburg, Rep. 2.2.1., nr. 30003, p. 109.

77. Poschinger, *Bankwesen,* 2:135.

78. Although broad support existed for bank reform, agricultural interests— represented most vocally by the estate owner von Lavergne-Peguilhen—failed to back Harkort because his bill did not include provisions for easier agricultural credit. A. Sartorius von Waltershausen, *Deutsche Wirtschaftsgeschichte 1815–1914,* 2d ed. (Jena, 1923), p. 185.

79. Ibid., pp. 135–61.

80. On this point of Manteuffel's "mild absolutism," see Grünthal, *Parlamentarismus,* pp. 471, 474.

81. See the two telegrams from Civil-Cabinet Councillor (*Geheim-Cabinettrath* Illaire) to Civil-Account Councillor (*Geheim-Rechnungsrath*) Flender (Bureau des Staatsministeriums), 14 July 1856, GStA Merseburg, Rep. 2.2.1., nr. 30003, pp. 110–11.

82. Otto v. Manteuffel to king, 18 July 1856, GStA Merseburg, Rep. 2.2.1., nr. 30003, p. 113.

83. Westphalen to king, 21 July 1856, GStA Merseburg, Rep. 2.2.1., nr. 30003, pp. 114–16.

84. Delbrück, *Lebenserinnerungen,* 2:82–84.

85. Direct Report of the state ministry to the king, 19 Aug. 1856, GStA Merseburg, Rep. 2.2.1., nr. 30003, pp. 117–18.

86. Ibid., p. 118.

87. Hansen, *Mevissen,* 1:667 and n. 4.

88. Riesser, *German Great Banks,* pp. 64–67; in 1856 alone the Disconto Gesellschaft invested three million thalers in Ruhr industrial companies, whereas after 1857 the bank invested mostly in railroads and government securities. Tilly, *Financial Institutions,* p. 116.

89. The use of this either-or schema to explain the 1850s is a cornerstone of the standard explanatory framework.

90. With railroad construction, for instance, the Darmstädter, the Disconto Gesellschaft, and the Berliner Handelsgesellschaft, by evading government supervision, loosened the trade ministry's grip on railroad funding and was a factor that frustrated Heydt's plan to nationalize all Prussian rail.

91. Insofar as this incident was a social action that circumvented and appropriated a power from the government, it was politically oriented. For this definition of a "politically oriented" action, see Max Weber, *Social and Economic Organization,* p. 154.

92. The only serious parliamentary study of the 1850s is Günther Grünthal's *Parlamentarismus.* This work, because of its focus on constitutional issues, fails to address the economic and social issues brought to the parliamentary floor. Heinrich Volkmann's *Die Arbeiterfrage im preussischen Abgeordnetenhaus 1848–1869* (Berlin, 1968), although promising in title, also fails to link up economics, politics, and society.

93. Grünthal also suggests the latent power of parliament. *Parlamentarismus,* pp. 472–73.

94. See Weber's discussion of "Types of Order in Corporate Groups" in *Social and Economic Organization,* pp. 148–51.

Chapter Six

1. Ministers Heydt and Patow to prince-regent, 23 Dec. 1860, GStA Merseburg, Rep. 2.2.1., nr. 29519, pp. 205–6; *VBMHGA* 1864–66, pp. 42–43. Historians have subsequently assigned causal significance to Prussia's role in railroad construction in the rapid industrialization of Germany after the 1840s. The literature on the role of the state in the first industrial revolution is large, but for direct references to Prussia's state railroads see Alexander Bergengrün, *Staatsminister Freiherr von der Heydt* (Leipzig, 1908), chap. 7; Henderson, *Industrial Revolution,* chaps. 8 and 9; Knut Borchardt, *Wachstum, Krisen, Handlungsspielräume der Wirtschaftspolitik* (Göttingen, 1982), p. 26; Wolfram Fischer, "Verhältnis von Staat," pp. 60 ff. More recently, Rainer Fremdling has refuted the thesis that the state was instrumental for the development of early railways (and industrialization): *Eisenbahnen.* Many of Fremdling's quantitative findings are supported by the archival sources on the Railroad Fund. The Eastern Railway notwithstanding, almost every state railroad project was started or could have been started by private interests. By 1849, when the Prussian state began its state programs, the railroad industry had long been established (twenty-six railroad companies existed in Prussia), thus weakening the assertion that state building was the motor of railroad development (Borchardt, Fischer, Henderson). Fremdling's hypothesis that railroad construction would have proceeded at a similar rate without state involvement has sound counterfactual qualities. See also Wehler, *Gesellschaftsgeschichte,* 2:621–22, who writes, "The profitability of rail construction showed itself to be so high that state help, argued hypothetically, would presumably 'not have been at all necessary.' " Alfred D. Chandler deemed state involvement to be so minimal that it did not merit mention in his discussion of German railroads: *Scale and Scope,* pp. 411–19. These judgments support the accuracy of Werner Sombart's much earlier statement, in 1903, that railroads "were a work of capitalism. . . . The states were visibly reserved." Sombart, *Deutsche Volkwirtschaft im Neunzehnten Jahrhundert* (Berlin, 1903), p. 281. Nonetheless, it seems unhistorical to underestimate the importance of state involvement in the 1840s and in the boom of the 1850s. It is, to my mind, equally unhistorical to underestimate the attitude of business circles that sought supplemental aid from the state. It is a weakness of economic history not to factor in the cultural mentality of German businessmen, who assumed that the state should aid large-scale business enterprise.

2. Pflanze, *Bismarck,* 1:109. The Stein-Hardenberg reforms opened up space for greater economic activity, but this does not discount the fact that other political reforms, constrained by the conservative restoration after 1820, fell far short of their goals. See Koselleck, *Zwischen Reform und Revolution,* 2d ed. (Stuttgart, 1975), chap. 3.

3. Although welcoming the state's enthusiasm for the new capitalistic economy, Prussian businessmen nonetheless grew restless under the lingering state paternalism

and did not hesitate to criticize it. See Richard Tilly, *Financial Institutions,* chaps. 4 and 5; and Radtke, *Seehandlung,* chaps. 2 and 3.

4. See chap. 3 for parliamentary citations; see also *NZ* 3:357, 14 Oct. 1849, for noting the houses' enthusiasm for state ownership.

5. See the editorial that quotes the *Ostsee-Zeitung* at length in *NZ* 3:400 (8 Nov. 1849).

6. *NZ* 3:404 (10 Nov. 1849) quoting the 8 Nov. 1849 editorial of the *Kölnische-Zeitung.*

7. See L. M. Niebuhr's "Denkschrift betr. Contrahirung einer grossen Anleihe: Fundirung einer grossen Anleihe durch die bisherigen Eisenbahn-Fonds," 26 Nov. 1852, GStA Merseburg, Rep. 92, Nachlass v.d. Heydt, nr. 8, pp. 35–43, esp. pp. 38–40.

8. *NZ* 4:75 (15 Feb. 1850).

9. *NZ* 4:99 (1 Mar. 1850); see also 3:95 (27 Feb. 1850) for a general criticism of the rising state debt that reached 156,019,872 thalers in 1850; for a cursory overview of the German understanding of public finance from 1800 to 1870, see Klein, *Geschichte der öffentlichen Finanzen,* pp. 125–34.

10. *VZ* criticized dividend subsidies for the Aachen-Düsseldorfer Railway, claiming it was unfair for the stockholders of other railroads in the Rhineland. Nr. 274 (23 Nov. 1849), nr. 276 (25 Nov. 1849), nr. 285 (6 Dec. 1849), and nr. 291 (13 Dec. 1849).

11. For criticism of the dividend guarantees and the adverse effect they had on the Rhenish Railway, see the *VZ,* 8 and 13 Jan. 1850; see also the stenographic report of the 116th Session of the upper house, reprinted in *VZ,* 13 Feb. 1850.

12. Heydt to king, 7 July 1852, GStA Merseburg, Rep. 93E, nr. 146, p. 9; *VBMHGA* 1855–57, p. 35. In total, the Fund contributed thirteen million thalers to the construction of these lines.

13. The evidence of this proposed loan to fund state construction would amend the view of W. O. Henderson, who maintained that Heydt dropped any ambition for rapid state ownership after 1849. See *Industrial Revolution,* p. 172.

14. Memorandum of Heydt to Bodelschwingh, 16 June 1852, GStA Merseburg, Rep. 77, tit. 258, nr. 1, vol. 3, pp. 148–49. The Fund's running account accrued as follows:

1843	500,000	1848	1,342,000
1844	528,000	1849	1,663,900
1845	629,000	1850	1,481,000
1846	1,021,000	1851	1,471,000
1847	1,205,200	1852	1,513,000

Heydt calculated from this pattern that the Fund's account would rise 100,000 for the next three years. In 1857 the account reached the legal limit of two million thalers. *VBMHGA* 1855–57, p. 46.

15. *VBMHGA* 1849–51, p. 22.

16. Bodelschwingh to Heydt, 28 Sept. 1852, GStA Merseburg, Rep. 77, tit. 258, nr. 1, vol. 3, p. 162. The price tags on these projects were Sieg-Ruhr, 8,750,000;

Rheine-Osnabrück, 1,500,000; Münster-Rheine, 1,500,000; Saarbrücken-Trier-Luxemburg, 6,000,000; Cologne Rhine bridge, 1,400,000; Breslau-Posen, 7,000,000; Bromberg-Thorne, 1,700,000. This came to 27,850,000 thalers.

17. Memorandum of Heydt to Bodelschwingh, 16 June 1852, GStA Merseburg, Rep. 77, tit. 258, nr. 1, vol. 3, p. 150.

18. Memorandum of Heydt to Bodelschwingh, 16 Mar. 1852, GStA Merseburg, Rep. 77, tit. 258, nr. 1, vol. 3, pp. 150–51. Heydt often used the lame condition of private investment in combination with foreign competition to drum up support. His tactic of sketching a Prussia economically devastated if bypassed in international trade was especially effective in winning the support of the king. For this reason the king backed Heydt's proposal to build the Saarbrücken-Trier-Luxembourg line. This fear of trade being a zero-sum game—in which what one gained, the other lost—was prevalent in the 1850s. It confirms Rainer Fremdling's thoughts on the early motivation in German states, cities, and towns to build railroads. See his application of Albert O. Hirschman's model of "external market concepts" in *Eisenbahnen,* pp. 7–9, 131.

19. Memorandum of Heydt to Bodelschwingh, 16 June 1852, GStA Merseburg, Rep. 77, tit. 258, nr. 1, vol. 3, pp. 151–55. The lines deemed important for the state to build were the Dortmund-Soest (Witten-Bochum-Alten Railway), Oberhausen-Arnheimer, Deutz-Frankfurt, Ehrenbreitstein-Giessen via Wetzlar/Wetzlar-Dillenburg, Brackmere-Padersborn, Düren-Schleichen, Landsberg-Cüstrin-Berlin (Eastern Railway connection to Stargard Posen), Berlin-Stralsund, Halle-Weissenfels-Zeitz (to Saxon-Bavaria border), and Görlitz-Reichenberg via Seidenberg.

20. Heydt to Bodelschwingh, 16 June 1852, GStA Merseburg, Rep. 77, tit. 258, nr. 1, vol. 3, p. 141.

21. Ibid.

22. It was the overall selection that aroused the suspicion of Bodelschwingh. He questioned the choice and placement of Heydt's proposed state lines and criticized the fitful, unsystematic way Heydt put together his complex of state railway lines. Bodelschwingh to Heydt, 28 Sept. 1852, GStA Merseburg, Rep. 77, tit. 258, nr. 1, vol. 3, p. 171.

23. Otto von Bismarck, *Gedanken und Erinnerungen* (Stuttgart, 1898), 1:256. For a fuller discussion on the king's "effacement" style of rule, see David E. Barclay, *Frederick William IV.*

24. Before conglomerating seven railroad projects into one, Heydt had lobbied individually for the Saarbrücken-Trier-Luxemburg line and the Rhine bridge at Cologne. Although Bodelschwingh saw the usefulness of both projects, he did not see the need for the state to involve itself directly. For Bodelschwingh's rejection of state construction of the Saarbrücken-Trier-Luxembourg line, see his *Votum,* 10 July 1852, GStA Merseburg, Rep. 77, tit. 258, nr. 1, vol. 3, pp. 201–2; for Bodelschwingh's opposition to the Rhine bridge project see his reply to Heydt, 17 June 1852, GStA Merseburg, Rep. 77, tit. 258, nr. 1, vol. 3, pp. 194–95; see also Undersecretary Horn (ministry of finance) to Heydt, 6 Aug. 1852, GStA Merseburg, Rep. 77, tit. 258, nr. 1, vol. 3, p. 198.

25. In January 1850, the government had taken over the administration of the railroad, and in November 1851 Heydt sought to buy it. Bodelschwingh opposed the

plan on the grounds that the takeover would hinder private enterprise and burden the state with an additional twenty-million thaler obligation to stockholders. Heydt, however, persuaded Manteuffel to present the issue to the entire cabinet. With the exceptions of Minister of Culture von Raumer and Finance Minister Bodelschwingh, the cabinet accepted the idea (14 Jan. 1852). Although outvoted, Bodelschwingh refused to accept the decision and declared that he had the right to veto any bill affecting state expenditure. The king agreed that Bodelschwingh was in principle correct but that this instance constituted an exception. Not taking defeat gracefully, Bodelschwingh offered new obstacles in February and had to be told a second time by the king (via Manteuffel) that the matter was settled. Against the backdrop of this dispute, Heydt's bid for a thirty-four million thaler loan appears overly confident, especially when Bodelschwingh had won the battle "in principle." See Heinrich von Poschinger, *Unter Friedrich Wilhelm IV: Denkwürdigkeiten des Ministerpräsidenten Otto Freiherrn von Manteuffel,* vol. 2, *1851–54* (Berlin, 1901), pp. 156–59.

26. See Küpfer's speech in the lower house during the debate over the railway's purchase. *SBHA,* 30 Mar. 1852, p. 871.

27. Bodelschwingh to Heydt, 28 Sept. 1852, GStA Merseburg, Rep. 77, tit. 258, nr. 1, vol. 3, pp. 162–63.

28. Bodelschwingh refuted Heydt's claim that the fund after 1855 would have 1.5 million thalers at its disposal. In calculating the fund's new financial status, the trade ministry had entirely left out the obligation of the fund to pay back the interest and remaining debt on the 1849 loan (930,000 thalers) and had grossly underestimated the reserve needed for stock guarantees (1,299,750 vs. 200,000 thalers). When added to the interest and debt payments that would be incurred by the intended loan (1,700,000), the Fund's budget came to 3,929,750 thalers—an overdraft of nearly two million. Heydt responded to this charge, stating that "all budget calculations use averages" and his computation was "no exception." Bodelschwingh to Heydt, 28 Sept. 1852, GStA Merseburg, Rep. 77, tit. 258, nr. 1, vol. 3, p. 166; Heydt to Manteuffel, 21 Nov. 1852, GStA Merseburg, Rep. 77, tit. 258, nr. 1, vol. 3, pp. 215–218.

29. Bodelschwingh to Heydt, 28 Sept. 1852, GStA Merseburg, Rep. 77, tit. 258, nr. 1, vol. 3, p. 167.

30. Ibid., p. 170.

31. Ibid., p. 167.

32. Ibid. Bodelschwingh used "speculation" as a synonym for "investment." For him it did not have the negative connotation that it carries today.

33. Ibid., p. 168.

34. Ibid., p. 169. Certainly there was inconsistency in this stance, for although Bodelschwingh bemoaned the increasing reliance on the state, he (in agreement with Heydt and the rest of the cabinet) opposed any bank reforms that would decentralize finance and give the commercial world greater independence. See chap. 5 on the bank politics of the 1850s.

35. Ibid., pp. 172–73.

36. *NZ* 7:338 (23 July 1853).

37. Heydt to Manteuffel, 21 Nov. 1852, GStA Merseburg, Rep. 77, tit. 258, nr. 1, vol. 3, pp. 217–18.

38. The two lines in question were the Luxembourg-Trier-Saarbrückener and the Düren-Schleichen lines. See Bodelschwingh to Manteuffel, GStA Merseburg, Rep. 77, tit. 258, nr. 1, vol. 3, pp. 278–79 for his comment to Manteuffel that an attempt was never made to find a private firm for the Luxembourg-Trier-Saarbrückener line. The other line, Düren-Schleichen, found English investors in 1854, but Heydt refused them the charter on the grounds that the consortium was only interested in speculation.

39. For Heydt's original argument for state construction—disappearance of private investors—see Heydt to Bodelschwingh, 16 June 1852, GStA Merseburg, Rep. 77, tit, 258, nr. 1, vol. 3, pp. 151. This contradiction did not escape Bodelschwingh: Bodelschwingh to Manteuffel, GStA Merseburg, Rep. 77, tit. 258, nr. 1, vol. 3, pp. 278–79.

40. Schreiber, *Eisenbahnen,* p. 38, 46–47. The two companies were the Cologne-Crefeld (1853) and the Rhein-Nahe (1857) railways.

41. For Heydt's 23 Oct. 1852 plea to Manteuffel to bring the issue to a general vote, see GStA Merseburg, Rep. 77, tit. 258, nr. 1, vol. 3., pp. 217–18.

42. See written opinion (*Votum*) of Heydt, 17 June 1852, GStA Merseburg, Rep. 77, tit. 258, nr. 1, vol. 3, p. 199.

43. See Heydt's 21 Nov. 1852 memorandum to Manteuffel in GStA Merseburg, Rep. 77, tit. 258, nr. 1, vol. 3.

44. Bodelschwingh to Manteuffel, 30 Nov. 1852, GStA Merseburg, Rep. 77, tit. 258, nr. 1, vol. 3, pp. 278–79.

45. *VBMHGA* 1852–54, p. 27. A direct state loan, of course, meant state-owned railways.

46. See paragraphs 38 and 39 of the 1838 Railroad Law. After the loans' amortization, the law stated, the tax revenues could be used only for the purchase of common stock of Prussia's railways.

47. See *SBHH,* 51st Sitting, 7 May 1853, p. 1032, for Mollard's speech on this matter.

48. *SBHA,* 26 Apr. 1855, p. 847.

49. Bergengrün, *Heydt,* p. 189.

50. *SpN,* 30 Mar. 1853; For the principal debate in the upper house, see *SBHH,* 51st Sitting, 7 May 1853, pp. 1031–56; for the lower house see 44th sitting, 8 Apr. 1853, reprinted in *SpN,* 9 Apr. 1853.

51. Ludwig Samuel Bogislav Kühne, a deputy from Berlin, was general tax director in the Prussian bureaucracy until 1849 and worked in the finance ministry in 1848. Günther Grünthal places him in the liberal opposition of parliament. *Parlamentarismus,* p. 443. Gerhard Eisfeld, too, recognizes Kühne as an old liberal. *Die Entstehung der liberalen Parteien in Deutschland 1858–1870: Studie zu den Organisation und Programmen der Liberalen und Demokraten* (Hannover, 1969), pp. 112–13.

52. *SBHH,* 7 May 1853, pp. 1032–36.

53. *SpN,* 22 Feb. 1853; see *NZ* 5:166 (11 Apr. 1853) for the first house's questioning the legality of progressive taxes. The companies that signed the petition were the Berlin-Anhalt, Berlin-Potsdam-Magdeburg, Berlin-Stettin, Magdeburg-Halberstädter, and the Magdeburg-Köthen-Halle-Leipzig railways.

54. *NZ* 6:80 (17 Feb. 1853).

55. *Neue Preussische [Kreuz-] Zeitung,* 7 Apr. 1853.

56. *SpN,* 22 Feb., 30 Mar., and 31 Mar. 1853.

57. Ibid., 2 Apr. 1853.

58. *NZ* 6:151 (2 Apr. 1853).

59. Ibid.

60. *EbZ* 11:17 (24 Apr. 1853), p. 67.

61. *VBMHGA* 1855–57, p. 48. See also *EbZ* 11:17 (24 Apr. 1853), p. 67.

62. *SBHH,* 7 May 1853, p. 1047.

63. *VBMHGA* 1855–57, p. 48.

64. *BBZ,* 15 Mar. 1859. This appears to be an accurate generalization for the late 1850s; for the mid-1850s, the levies ranged between 63,750 and 129,333 thalers. *VBMHGA* 1855–57, p. 48.

65. *VBMHGA* 1855–57, p. 48.

66. Ibid.

67. Fremdling, *Eisenbahnen,* p. 144.

68. The Rhenish Railway protested the tax vigorously and did not pay until 1855. See HAStK, Best. 1028, nr. 8, July 1855-July 1856, pp. 58, 93, 76, 105, 252–53. The Berlin-Hamburg and Berlin-Anhalt railways also protested, mostly because their company's rail (and concomitant profit) outside Prussia were taxed. For the Berlin-Anhalt protest, see GStA Merseburg, Rep. 2.2.1, 9 Sept. 1854, nr. 29531, pp. 48–51; see p. 47 for the king's rejection of protest, despite Heydt's admission that stockholders were indeed taxed twice. For the Berlin-Hamburg protest, see "Hamburg-Berlin Eisenbahngesellschaft Bericht des Ausschusses des Jahres 1854," 31 May 1855, in BLHA, Rep. 2A IV, nr. 1938, p. 18.

69. *VBMHGA* 1855–57, p. 29.

70. *SBHA,* 26 April 1855, p. 846.

71. *VBMHGA* 1858–60, p. 39.

72. There is no exact figure given for the extra-dividends at the end of 1859. A reasonable estimate can be attained by taking the annual average from the total profits cited by Heydt in 1857, 2,788,947, and extending it two more years, to give us 4,183,420. *VBMHGA* 1855–57, p. 48. This would correspond to the figure of 3,969,251 cited by Heydt in 1861 for the 1859 totals of the fund's major earners. His sum, however, did not include all railways. *VBMHGA* 1858–60, p. 38.

73. *VBMHGA* 1864–66, pp. 44–46.

74. The economic importance of these lines was indisputable. (1) The Rhine bridge at Cologne was the first attempt to span the river since the Romans built one on the same site. The bridge integrated the railways of the left and right banks of the Rhine, and its completion made Cologne the railway center of western Germany. (2) The Oberhausen-Arnheim line would extend the Cologne-Minden line along the right bank of the Rhine to the Dutch border (Arnheim) and connect Cologne with Utrecht, Rotterdam, and Amsterdam. The mid-Rhine region obtained quick access to the North Sea's major ports without the customs and tolls of the river route. (3) The Deutz-Giessen-Frankfurt line extended this Rotterdam-Cologne route southward, connecting Frankfurt, the rail center of southern Germany, with the northern European rail network. (4) The Sieg-Ruhr line was an industrial necessity; the railway joined

the iron industry of the Siegerland with the coal seams of the Ruhr. (5) Finally, the Breslau-Posen-Glogau was the vital north-south corridor in eastern Prussia that integrated the Silesian and Posen provinces.

75. Heydt to General State Treasury, 16 July 1859, GStA Merseburg, Rep. 93E, nr. 3748, pp. 39 ff.

76. The Guarantee Fund was composed of a series of contracts between the government and the two railways: an undefined commitment to build the Cologne bridge and Oberhausen-Arneheimer line in 1852 was put in writing 24 May 1853 and 22 May 1854; the Deutz-Siegen-Giessen line, 18 Apr. 1855; the Sieg-Ruhr line, 30 Apr. 1856. The Breslau-Posen-Glogau line was financed in contracts on 20 Feb. 1854 and 13 May 1857. These contracts constituted the Guarantee Fund, which became law 18 Apr. 1855 (*Gesetzsammlung* 1855, p. 235). *VBMHGA* 1855–57, p. 30; GStA Merseburg, Rep. 93E, 16 July 1859, nr. 3748, p. 39; J. Michaelis, *Deutschlands Eisenbahnen* (Leipzig, 1859), p. 107.

77. *VBMHGA* 1855–57, p. 30; J. Michaelis, *Deutschlands Eisenbahnen,* 107. Cologne-Minden Railway, September 1853, 3,000,000 thalers at 4 percent: Oberhausen-Arnheimer; Upper-Silesian Railway, February 1854, 8,000,000 at 3.5 percent: Breslau-Posen-Glogau; Cologne-Minden Railway, April 1855, 20,000,000 at 3.5 percent: Rhine Bridge and Deutz-Giessen; Cologne-Minden Railway, 30 April 1856, 12,250,000 at 3.25 percent: Sieg-Ruhr; Upper-Silesian Railway, 13 May 1857, 4,250,000 at 3.5 percent: Breslau-Posen-Glogau; Cologne-Minden Railway, April 1858, 3,000,000 at 4.5 percent: Oberhausen-Arnheimer.

78. Heydt to Regierungspräsident E. Moeller, 4 July 1857, GStA Merseburg, Rep. 93E, nr. 3748, p. 89. In the lower house Kühne made note of the Guarantee Fund's purpose of accelerating the stock purchasing program on 26 March 1857: *NZ* 10:145 (27 Mar. 1857).

79. Heydt to Bodelschwingh, 24 Sept. 1858, GStA Merseburg, Rep. 93E, nr. 3748, unpag. On 3 November 1858, Heydt wrote Bodelschwingh, a letter that anticipated and sought to fend off Bodelschwingh's criticism that these additional funds exceeded the legal limit of the Railroad Fund.

80. For the acceptance by the Upper Silesian Railway, see Heydt to Bodelschwingh, 9 Oct. 1858, and Heydt to Eisenbahn-Commissariat Kölns, 22 Oct. 1858, GStA Merseburg, Rep. 93E, nr. 3748, unpag.; for the rejection by the Cologne-Minden Railway see Heydt to Finanzminister Patow, 2 Dec. 1858, and Moeller to Heydt, 12 Jan. 1859, GStA Merseburg, Rep. 93E, nr. 3748, unpag.

81. The money came from the *Chatoull Vermögen.*

82. The executor, Alvensleben, had waived the railway's obligation of paying interest for the years 1847–49, but Heydt demanded it. See the letter from Heydt to Alvensleben, 15 Apr. 1850, GStA Merseburg, Rep. 93E, nr. 554, unpag.

83. See notice of 7 Mar. 1853, GStA Merseburg, Rep. 93E, nr. 554, unpag.

84. GStA Merseburg, Rep. 93E, nr. 55, 11 Apr. 1857, "Final Abschluss der Kgl. General Staats-Kasse von dem Eisenbahn-Legaten-Fonds für das Jahr 1856." The exact sum came to 215,900 thalers; the securities purchased came from the Aachen-Düsseldorfer (bonds), the Lower Silesian–Mark, the Cologne-Minden (com-

mon stock), the Stargard-Posen (common stock), and the Ruhrort-Krefeld-Kreis Gladbacher (common stock) railways.

85. See the December 1849 protest of the Thuringian Railway lodged with the Hohenzollern house and the 21 Jan. 1850 written position (*Stellungnahme*) of the three princes in GStA Merseburg, Rep. 93E, nr. 554, unpag.

86. See Heydt's position in his memorandum to the king, 25 Mar. 1853, and the king's subsequent order in GStA Merseburg, Rep. 93E, nr. 554, unpag. In the same file is the 27 Apr. 1855 notice from the state treasury to Heydt that the 1854 Thuringian railroad dividends had been paid.

87. See GStA Merseburg, Rep. 93E, nr. 555, unpag., for: 7 June 1856 protest from princes Wilhelm, Carl, and Albrecht to king; 28 June 1856 notice from king to cabinet to review the issue; the 16 Sept. and 27 Sept. 1856 opinions of Justice Minister Simons and Finance Minister Bodelschwingh; the 19 Nov. 1856 recommendation from crown lawyer; the 25 Mar. 1857 decree from king; the 23 May 1857 draft of the cabinet petition to king (handed in 13 June 1857); the 3 July 1857 reply of king; and the 28 July 1857 memorandum from Minister of Hohenzollern Affairs Massow to Heydt acknowledging transfer of funds on 14 July 1857.

88. See GStA Merseburg, Rep. 93E, nr. 556, unpag., for: the 5 Nov. 1858 notice by the prince to review the matter; the 24 Dec. 1858 letter from Finance Minister Patow to Heydt; the 27 Dec. 1858 written opinion (*Votum*) of Justice Minister Simons; the 28 Jan. 1859 *Votum* of Hohenzollern Minister Ludwig von Massow to Heydt and 26 Mar. 1859 notice regarding the opposition to cabinet vote; and the 11 Nov. 1859 royal edict.

89. See the 23 Apr. 1861 letter from Heydt to the head of the Hohenzollern Fideicommission asking whether the interest on the 810,000 thalers, intended for stock subscriptions in a private company, could be used toward a state railway in the form of a subsidy. GStA Merseburg, Rep. 93E, nr. 556, unpag. The request reveals Heydt's attitude toward parliament, which had told him two years earlier that state railways were out of the question.

90. See GStA Merseburg, Rep. 93E, nr. 556, unpag., for Heydt's memoranda to king and finance minister in January 1860.

91. See GStA Merseburg, Rep. 93E, nr. 556, unpag., for 23 Apr. 1861 memorandum from Heydt to Fideicommissioner von Uhden and 10 June 1861 response from Uhden to Heydt. In this note, Uhden stated that it was the king's decision but nonetheless outlined his position on the matter.

92. See GStA Merseburg, Rep. 93E, nr. 557, unpag., for the 25 June 1862 contract between the state and Magdeburg-Leipzig Railway and the 3 June 1863 memorandum from Bodelschwingh to Trade Minister Heinrich von Itzenplitz regarding the illegality of using the state treasury to transfer funds.

93. For Bodelschwingh's tabular presentation of the trade ministry's excesses with the Railroad Fund, see the appendix to Bodelschwingh's memorandum to Heydt, 29 May 1856, GStA Merseburg, Rep. 93E, nr. 550, p. 108.

94. *VBMHGA* 1855–57, p. 36. When the government took over this railway in 1852, the contract stated that all profits would go to the Railroad Fund. Between 1853

and 1857, the railway earned profits of 952,950 thalers, a significant sum of unaccounted thalers. Heydt defended this action by stating that these profits were unforeseen by the 1843 law and thus should not be factored into the equation. Bodelschwingh countered that the amount of the salt monopoly's contribution was also unclear in the 1843 law, but its real meaning "had nonetheless never been doubted." Bodelschwingh to Heydt, 23 Sept. 1856, GStA Merseburg, Rep. 93E, nr. 550, pp. 118–22; quotation on p. 118.

95. Bodelschwingh to Heydt, 21 Sept. 1856, GStA Merseburg, Rep. 93E, nr. 550, pp. 119–22.

96. See the letters of Bodelschwingh to Heydt, 28 Mar. and 16 June 1855, GStA Merseburg, Rep. 93E, nr. 550, pp. 73, 80–81.

97. If we take 1856 as an example, Heydt exceeded his own official budget by 311,300, used 1,226,755 thalers of railroad profits to cover the additional costs of the Münster-Rheine-Osnabrück line, 50,000 to build a coal mine, another 145,002 from the Lower Silesian–Mark Railway's profits, and approximately 50,000 from the dividends from the Thuringian Railway. Hence Heydt nearly doubled his budget. If we count the one million thalers of the Berg-Mark sale as well as the construction made possible by the Guarantee Fund (from which the fund accrued stock), the fund's annual budget was over four million thalers.

98. Grünthal, *Parlamentarismus,* p. 457.

99. For the correspondence regarding the *Depôtgeschäft* (also called a *Vorschussgeschäft*), see GStA Merseburg, Rep. 93E, nr. 549: 28 Mar. 1854, Heydt to Bethmann, p. 96; 30 Mar. 1854, Bethmann to Heydt, p. 97; 4 Apr. 1854, M. A. v. Rothschild to Heydt, pp. 102–3; 7 Apr. 1854, Heydt to Rothschild, p. 105; 10 Apr. 1854, Rothschild to Heydt, pp. 106–7; 5 Apr. 1854, W. Bischoffsheim to Heydt, p. 108.

100. Because Heydt presented state ownership of railways as a political and military tool, the influential ministers of interior and war (Westphalen and Bonin) generally supported him; Heydt's staunchest supporter was Simons, who always found legality in Heydt's plans. In regard to parliamentary controls, until 1856 every budget submitted to the houses overran the approved incomes and had to be balanced with other revenues that the chambers had not approved. The chambers were thus reduced to approving retroactively where what incomes should go to balance the budget—and not whether such revenues should be part of state expenses. See Grünthal, *Parlamentarismus,* p. 464, n. 65.

101. See Ludwig von Gerlach's diary entry of 16 Jan. 1855, in Helmut Diwald, ed., *Von der Revolution zum Norddeutschen Bund: Politik und Ideengut der preussischen Hochkonservativen 1848–1866; Aus dem Nachlass von Ernst Ludwig von Gerlach* (Göttingen, 1970), 1:356 (henceforth referred to as *Gerlach*). Bodelschwingh later apologized for putting the two liberals on the committee, stating that he wished only Patow, not Kühne. He also came to regret the liberals' domination of the budget committee. 15 Dec. 1856, *Gerlach,* 1:381.

102. Although Bodelschwingh's pessimism about Heydt's railroad credits pervade almost all financial memoranda after 1853, the most conclusive evidence of his genuine concern for Prussia's fiscal health can be seen in his letter to Otto v. Manteuf-

fel of 15 Feb. 1854. Here worries about both the Crimean War and its effect on Prussia and the long-term ability of the state to meet the annual million-thaler loan payments on railroads come to the fore. See Bodelschwingh to Manteuffel, 15 Feb. 1854, GStA Merseburg, Rep. 92, Nachlass O. v. Manteuffel, II, 24, pp. 82–85.

103. See the memorandum from Bodelschwingh to Heydt, 27 Feb. 1855, GStA Merseburg, Rep. 93E, nr. 550, pp. 66–67. It refers to Heydt's letter of February 24, which stated his view of Bodelschwingh's effrontery.

104. *SBHA*, 26 April 1855, p. 846.

105. Ibid., pp. 841–42.

106. Ibid., p. 841.

107. Heydt to king, 29 Apr. 1855, GStA Merseburg, Rep. 92, Nachlass v.d. Heydt, Korrespondenz 1851–57, pp. 63–64.

108. See the amendment's formulation in *SBHA*, 26 Apr. 1855, p. 841.

109. Ibid., pp. 841–50.

110. Ibid., 26 April 1848, p. 850.

111. Gillis, *Prussian Bureaucracy in Crisis*, p. 166.

112. Grünthal, *Parlamentarismus*, p. 452.

113. *SBHA*, 22 Feb. 1856, p. 502.

114. Von Gerlach quoted by Grünthal, *Parlamentarismus*, pp. 452, 455.

115. Grünthal, *Parlamentarismus*, p. 452; Leopold to Ludwig von Gerlach, 9 Mar. 1856, *Gerlach*, 2:894–95. For an incisive comment on Ludwig von Gerlach's political tactics in parliament after the revolution, see Grünthal's "Bemerkungen zur Kamarilla Friedrich Wilhelms IV. im nachmärzlichen Preussen," in Otto Büsch, ed., *Friedrich Wilhelm IV. in seiner Zeit* (Berlin, 1987), pp. 46–47. An insightful commentary on the Gerlachs' politics is found in Helmut Diwald's introduction to *Gerlach,* 1:10–79. Other prominent conservatives, such as F. W. Stahl and Bismarck, also sought to couple more closely monarchical and representative institutions. Pflanze, *Bismarck,* vol. 1, 2d ed. (Princeton, 1990), p. 54. For a discussion of early nineteenth-century conservatism in Prussia and its ability to change with the times, see Berdahl, *Politics of the Prussian Nobility.*

116. *Gerlach,* 27 Feb. 1856, 1:370; In March Leopold suspected opposition from Bodelschwingh to Ludwig's new demarche. Leopold to Ludwig von Gerlach, 9 Mar. 1856, *Gerlach,* 2:894.

117. See the letter from Leopold to Ludwig von Gerlach, 1 Mar. 1856, which suggests why the conservatives, who after the 1855 elections had the majority, eventually supported the tax extension because of their unpreparedness to achieve a parliamentary victory for the monarchical cause. *Gerlach,* 2:894.

118. Grünthal, *Parlamentarismus,* pp. 455–57. The upper house's motion was especially challenging, for it sought to revise article 62 of the constitution, which specified that the lower house alone had the right to approve or reject the entire budget and create the right to modify the budget in specific areas. See article 62 of the 1850 constitution in Huber, *Dokumente,* 1:407.

119. See the "Bericht der Finanz-Commission des Herrnhauses, Sitzungsperiode 1856–57," GStA Merseburg, Rep. 93E, nr. 551, p. 29. Overall the budget was raised

from 111,828,000 to 118,864,000 thalers, an increase of 7,036,000 thalers. *SBHA,* 21 Jan. 1856, p. 129. The question of civil servant salaries had been raised in the previous session and rejected by the lower house, whose liberal side suspected the *"Dringlichkeit"* (urgency) of the salary hike. See the speech by Patow, *SBHA,* 17 Dec. 1855, pp. 68–70. This issue for more money brought up the question of a property tax for landed estates. See the speeches of Kühne, Harkort, and Reichensperger, *SBHA,* 21 Jan. 1856, pp. 134–37.

120. Grünthal, *Parlamentarismus,* p. 459.

121. *Gerlach,* 16 Mar. 1857, 1:388.

122. The lower house was abruptly adjourned on 4 Dec. 1850 and was therefore unable to discuss and pass the budget for 1851. It was unclear whether the budget could be used without the lower house's approval. The government, however, announced it could continue to use funds on the basis of article 109. Earlier, on 20 Oct. 1849, Ludwig Gerlach had defended such an action; his argument, however, employed article 98 as a defense. The liberal Eduard Simson declared the government's action illegal on 24 Feb. 1851, using article 99, which actually addressed budget legislation. It was in the subsequent debate that Kleist-Restow, Arnim-Boitzenberg, and Bismarck sketched out the rough edges of the *Lücketheorie;* when the crown and parliament failed to agree on a law to pass the budget, the state passed into an emergency situation that empowered the cabinet to use funds to keep the state in operation. By a narrow margin on 25 Mar. 1851, the house voted to endorse Falk's motion to pass over Simson's motion to charge the government with illegal activity. In 1862 Bismarck would draw on this earlier argument to develop a defense using the "gap theory." Grünthal, *Parlamentarismus,* pp. 129 ff, 452 ff.; Diwald, *Gerlach,* 2:891; Pflanze, *Bismarck,* 1:64, 202.

123. Kühne in the plenum debate, 26 Mar. 1857. See the stenographic reports printed in *NZ* 10:145 (27 Mar. 1857).

124. Grünthal, *Parlamentarismus,* p. 459; *BBZ,* 15 Mar. 1859, p. 518.

125. *BBZ,* 15 Mar. 1859, p. 518.

126. Bodelschwingh to Heydt, 3 Apr. 1857, GStA Merseburg, Rep. 93E, nr. 551. p. 20.

127. See the "Allerhöchste Kabinettordres vom 10., 24. und 27. August 1857 betreffend die Staatsraths-Kommission zur Begutachtung mehrerer Prinzipienfragen der Finanz-Verwaltung," GStA Merseburg, Rep. 92, Nachlass v.d. Heydt, Korrespondenzen 1857–1862, p. 95. The men chosen for the commission were Minister-President von Manteuffel; State Minister von Alvensleben; Obergerichts-President von Gerlach; and Privy Councilors Voss, von Meving, Mathis, Kühne, and Niebuhr. Additional members of the state council were to be added. Friedrich Wilhelm to State Cabinet, GStA Merseburg, Rep. 92, Nachlass v.d. Heydt, nr. 10–13, p. 102.

128. Leopold to Ludwig Gerlach, 23 Aug. 1857, *Gerlach,* 2:927.

129. King to cabinet, 6 June 1857, GStA Merseburg, Rep. 92, Nachlass v.d. Heydt, nr. 10–13, p. 12.

130. *Gerlach,* 7 Feb. 1857, 1:383; but see p. 390, when the king congratulated

such men as Hohenlohe (a moderate liberal of the Wochenblatt party) for passing the tax. Although this would apparently contradict Bismarck's observation, the fact that his advisers counseled him not to suggests the king was again affirming his independent position to the cabinet.

131. See Heydt's resignation to the king, 8 Sept. 1857, GStA Merseburg, Rep. 92 Nachlass Otto v. Manteuffel, II, Privat Korrespondenz, Rep. v.d. Heydt, pp. 36–38.

132. Heydt found it especially insulting that he only learned of the commission by reading the printed publication and not through his minister-president. See his resignation letter to king, p. 37.

133. *NZ* 9:181 (19 Apr. 1856).

134. *NZ* 7:503 (27 Oct. 1854).

135. See the article, "Die 'Selbstkosten' des Eisenbahntransports," in *NZ* 11:127 (17 Mar. 1858).

136. *NZ*, 27 Oct. 1854, 19 Apr. 1856.

137. *NZ*, 18 Mar. 1859. This article showed how the state expended its gross profit of 3,258,515 thalers from state railways. After paying the interest fees, payments on the principal, construction costs, renewal costs, and the administrative fees of its railways, the state was in debt 1,393,420 thalers.

138. *VBMHGA* 1855–57, p. 49; *BBZ*, 15 Mar. 1859, p. 518.

139. *NZ*, 13 Mar. 1858.

140. See the report of the state cabinet to the king, 1 May 1858, GStA Merseburg, Rep. 2.2.1, nr. 27421, pp. 117–18.

141. See GStA Merseburg, Rep. 2.2.1, 1 May 1858, nr. 27421, p. 123 for Heydt's defense of the Railroad Tax.

142. See Bodelschwingh's dissenting opinion in the cabinet report to the king, 1 May 1858, GStA Merseburg, Rep. 2.2.1., nr. 27421, pp. 131 ff.

143. *VBMHGA* 1855–57, p. 48.

144. For the majority opinion see state cabinet to king, 1 May 1858, GStA Merseburg, Rep. 2.2.1., nr. 27421, pp. 127–31.

145. Eisfeld, *Entstehung*, pp. 61–62; see also Karl Marx's "Das neue Ministerium," a newspaper analysis in November 1858 of the New Era cabinet, in *Marx-Engels Werke* 12, p. 632. Grünthal places Patow in the liberal left faction of parliament, originally a coalition of the Simson/Auerswald/Beckerath faction with the old liberals Georg v. Vincke and Patow. Together the coalition mustered 65 votes but split in 1854 over an extraordinary military appropriations bill. After 1855 Patow was the leader of the "linke Opposition," one of four oppositional factions in the second chamber. *Parlamentarismus*, pp. 403–4, 411, 463–69.

146. Grünthal, *Parlamentarismus*, p. 108.

147. Patow to Heydt, 21 Nov. 1858, GStA Merseburg, Rep. 93E, nr. 552, p. 61. In particular the argument centered on the profits of the Ruhrort–Krefeld–Kreis Gladbacher Railway, which in 1857 earned 10,609 thalers in extra-dividends. The trade ministry kept this money, which, according to a contract in 1849, it was allowed to do. Bodelschwingh and Patow claimed that the fund had no rights to revenues other than

500,000 thalers from the treasury, salt monopoly revenues, and super-dividends from the Lower–Silesian Mark Railway, whose combined total should not exceed two million thalers.

148. Patow to Heydt, 29 Dec. 1858; Heydt to Patow, 30 Dec. 1858; Heydt to Patow, 25 Jan. 1859, GStA Merseburg, Rep. 93E, nr. 552, unpag.

149. Heydt and Patow to king, 7 Feb. 1859, GStA Merseburg, Rep. 2.2.1, nr. 28574, pp. 269–70.

150. *BBZ*, 2 Mar. 1859.

151. Ibid., 15 Mar. 1859.

152. Ibid., 19 Mar. 1859.

153. Ibid.

154. Ibid., 5 May 1859.

155. Bergengrün and Henderson both place too much weight on foreign policy and on the importance of the mobilization by not discussing the various domestic sources of opposition that had built up over the years against the Fund.

156. Unlike the Habsburg monarchy, whose neoabsolutistic cabinet only gave up state ownership of railways in 1854 because of its disastrous financial situation, the Prussian state yielded its claim to further ownership as a result of persistent pressure from its legislature. For Austrian state railroad policy, see H. H. Brandt, *Der österreichische Neoabsolutismus: Staatsfinanzen und Politik 1848–1860* (Göttingen, 1978), 1:315–25. Although the Prussian parliament complained of irresponsible expenditures in order to strengthen their right to control the budget, the fact remains that Prussia's state finances were in relatively good shape. A good indication of this is the relative ease with which Prussia financed the 146 million thalers to mobilize for war against Austria: only 30 million thalers needed to be raised in a loan. Klein, *Geschichte der öffentlichen Finanzen*, p. 125.

Chapter Seven

1. Böhme, *Deutschlands Weg zur Grossmacht*, p. 81.

2. Hamerow, *Social Foundations: Ideas and Institutions*, p. 6. For a thorough treatment of the depression's effects, see Rosenberg, *Weltwirtschaftskrise*, chaps. 3–5.

3. Böhme, *Deutschlands Weg zur Grossmacht*, p. 82.

4. Otto to Ludolf Camphausen, 22 Jan. 1860, HAStK, Best. 1023, L575.

5. R. Schramm to F. W. König, 19 Apr. 1860, HAStK, Best. 1073, nr. 81.

6. See Heydt to Railroad Commissioners in Cologne and Breslau, 19 Apr. 1857, GStA Merseburg, Rep. 120A XII 5, nr. 1, vol. 3, p. 163. The ban on foreign currency remained an issue of importance in the New Era. See, for example, *BBZ*, 12 Feb. and 14 Feb. 1859, pp. 300, 317.

7. Hamerow, *Social Foundations: Ideas and Institutions*, p. 9.

8. For the state ministry's discussion of the loan, see the protocol of the state ministry, 3 May 1859, GStA Merseburg, Rep. 90a B. III. 2b, nr. 6, Bd. 71, p. 88.

9. Ludolf to Otto Camphausen, 3 May 1859, HAStK, Best. 1023, L521.

10. Otto to Ludolf Camphausen, 11 May, 1859, HAStK, Best. 1023, L525.

11. Otto to Ludolf Camphausen, 30 May and 6 June 1859, HAStK, Best. 1023, L531 and L534; *NZ,* 23 Nov. 1859. 11,265,000 thalers of the loan, reported the *NZ,* came from bankers, financiers, entrepreneurs, and manufacturers. For a table of the amount subscribed in Prussian government districts (led by Berlin, Cologne, Düsseldorf, and Breslau) see *NZ,* 25 Nov. 1859.

12. *VBMHGA* 1858–60, p. 30.

13. A. Oppenheim to G. Bleichröder, 16 Oct. 1859, Bleichröder Collection, Harvard University, Box XXIX, f. 2.

14. *VBMHGA* 1861–63, p. 45; *VBMHGA* 1864–66, p. 42.

15. *VBMHGA* 1861–63, pp. 45–48.

16. A. Oppenheim to G. Bleichröder, 23 Sept. 1858, Bleichröder Collection, Harvard University, Box XXIX, f. 2. Oppenheim complained in particular about the flotation of new foreign loans that would prevent recovery.

17. HAStK, Best. 1028, nrs. 8 and 9. The railway also had difficulty procuring loans from banks with which it shared directors. In March 1859, the *Darmstädter* refused the railway's request for a million thaler loan, offering instead 500,000 thalers. See nr. 9, pp. 290–91.

18. A. Oppenheim to G. Bleichröder, 16 Oct. 1859, Bleichröder Collection, Harvard University, Box XXIX, f. 2.

19. Hamerow, *Social Foundations: Struggles and Accomplishments,* p. 10.

20. Otto to Ludolf Camphausen, 30 Oct. 1858, HAStK, Best. 1023, L488a.

21 . Hans Rosenberg's two-volume work, *Die Nationpolitische Publizistik Deutschlands: Vom Eintritt der Neuen Aera in Pruessen bis zum Ausbruch des deutschen Krieges* (Munich, 1935), does not include commentary of businessmen and economic newspapers, giving the misleading impression that businessmen were silent during this period. As the historian of the 1857 depression and the 1873 crash, Rosenberg's omissions are surprising.

22. See, for example, *BBZ,* 7 Nov. 1858, # 562, p. 2327; 8 Nov. 1858, #564, p. 2333; 9 Nov. 1858, #566, p. 2343; 10 Nov. 1858, #568, p. 2351; 13 Nov. 1858, #573, p. 2371; 1 Dec. 1858, #606, p. 2507–8; 21 Dec. 1858, #643, p. 2663; Ludolf to Otto Camphausen, 3 and 5 Aug. 1858, HAStK, Best. 1023, L481, L482; D. Hansemann to G. Mevissen, 9 Nov. 1858, HAStK, Best. 1073, nr. 116, p. 78–79.

23. *BBZ,* 4 Nov. 1858.

24. *BBZ,* 4 Nov. 1858.

25. For petitions to discharge Heydt, see 12 Dec. 1858 letter of Geheim Justizrat Schmaling (Naumburg a/Salle) to Fürst Hohenzollern-Sigmaringen, regarding the 21 Oct. 1858 petition of the Upper Silesian Railway investors and directors to dismiss Heydt. GStA Merseburg, Rep. 90a K. III. 3, nr. 14, Bd. I, p. 304. For the request of Rhenish and Westphalian businessmen to urge the dismissal of Heydt, see *BBZ,* 13 Nov. 1858, p. 2371. A petition from Westphalian entrepreneurs supporting Heydt was also submitted, but the editors asserted that "these views do not find resonance in the wider majority of industrial and commercial circles."

26. Augustin, *Preussische Handels-Ministerium;* and Augustin, *Preussische Finanzfragen* (Potsdam, 1859). Augustin's attack on the trade ministry appeared in two

newspapers in 1859: *Preussische Zeitung,* nrs. 174, 176, 190, 192, 234, and 236; and the *Berliner Börsen-Zeitung,* nrs. 218, 220, 224. The latter gave glowing reviews of Augustin's essays: 25 Mar. 1859, nr. 142, p. 591; and 16 Apr. 1859, nr. 180, p. 745. The essays received a long reply from Heydt, which was published in the *Preussische Zeitung* in 1859, and can be found in GStA Merseburg, Rep. 93E, nr. 562, unpag.

27. Augustin, *Preussiche Handels-Ministerium,* p. 10. The *BBZ* also criticized the legal framework of Heydt's railroad commissions, whose authority overstepped regulatory procedures and was not checked by any judicial review. 4 June 1859, pp. 902–3.

28. Leonor Reichenheim, "Das preussische Handelsministeriuim und die Gewerbefreiheit" (Berlin, 1860); Reichenheim's views were heartily endorsed in the liberal press; see "Die Handelsminister und die Gewerbefreiheit," *NZ,* 17 and 20 Aug. 1860.

29. D. Hansemann to G. Mevissen, 9 Nov. 1858, HAStK, Best. 1073, nr. 116, p. 78.

30. See, for example, the interpretation by Rudolf Boch, *Grenzenloses Wachstum? Das Rheinische Wirtschaftsbürgertum und seine Industrialisierungsdebatte 1814–1857* (Göttingen, 1991), p. 268.

31. See, for example, *BBZ,* 7 Nov. 1858, nr. 562, p. 2327; 9 Nov. 1858, nr. 566, p. 2343; 10 Nov. 1858, nr. 568, p. 2351; 13 Nov. 1858, nr. 573, p. 2371; 1 Dec. 1858, nr. 606, p. 2507–8; 21 Dec. 1858, nr. 643, p. 2663. See also the correspondence between Ludolf and Otto Camphausen, 3 and 5 Aug. 1858, HAStK, Best. 1023, L481 & L482.

32. Otto to Ludolf Camphausen, 19 Mar. 1862, HAStK, Best. 1023, L 657.

33. Ibid., 12 May 1862, HAStK, Best. 1023, L 664.

34. Ibid.

35. "Der preussische Landtag von 1863," *Deutsche Vierteljahrsschrift* (1863), Heft 3, nr. 103, pp. 124 ff; Bergengrün, *Heydt,* p. 290.

36. Heydt to Mevissen, 30 Jan. 1863, HAStK, Best. 1073, nr. 157, unpag. The original: "Ich bin in der Politik verbraucht."

37. *SEG* 1865, 16 Jan., p. 155–56. The feudal party selected Heydt as candidate for chamber president. The chamber elected Grabow with 222 votes, while Heydt received 31.

38. Henderson, *Industrial Revolution,* p. 185.

39. D. Hansemann to G. Mevissen, 9 Nov. 1858, HAStK, Best. 1073, nr. 116, p. 78.

40. Delbrück, *Lebenserinnerungen,* vol. 1; see also the letters of Otto Camphausen to his brother Ludolf.

41. Delbrück, *Lebenserinnerungen,* vol. 1; Gillis, *Prussian Bureaucracy in Crisis;* see especially Brose, *Politics of Technological Change.*

42. Bismarck, *Gedanken und Erinnerungen,* p. 269.

43. For the laws reducing the coal excise tax and ending the *Direktionsprinzip,* see the *Preussische Gesetz-Sammlung,* 22 May 1861, pp. 225–26, and 10 June 1861, pp. 425–30. For an overview of the coal mining issue from 1850 to 1866, see "Besteuerung der Bergwerke," GStA Merseburg, Rep. 2.2.1, nr. 27423, unpag. For the initial difficulties in assembling enough votes for the 1861 laws, see the letter of Otto to Ludolf Camphausen, 16 Apr. 1861, HAStK, Best. 1023, L616.

44. "Der Herr Handelsminister v. d. Heydt und der Bergbau. I," *Zeitung für das deutsche Bergwerks- und Hüttenwesen* (Wochen Beilage der *BBZ*), 18 Nov. 1858.

45. Treue, *Gebhardt Handbuch,* 17:124.

46. Numerous chambers of commerce submitted suggestions for revising the railroad paragraphs. *BBZ,* 23 July 1859.

47. The commission consisted of directors from the Lower Silesian–Mark, Berlin-Anhalt, and the Austrian Kaiser Ferdinand Northern railways along with the Bavarian Traffic Agency, Saxon finance officials, and the Hannoverian general directory of railroads. *BBZ,* 23 Jan. 1860, p. 144.

48. "Die Eingabe der preussischen Eisenbahn-Verwaltungen an den Herrn Handelsminister von der Heydt, betreffend den Titel V. des Alleg. Deutschen Handels-Gesetzbuch," reprinted in *BBZ,* 7 Feb. 1860.

49. *NZ,* 18 Jan. 1861.

50. Otto Camphausen noted to Ludolf on 11 Nov. 1862 that the Prussian government was successful in selling the trade treaty at the 1862 Handelstag and in commercial regions outside of Prussia. HAStK, Best. 1023, L686a.

51. O. Michaelis, 25 July 1862, *SEG* 1862, pp. 152–54. Alongside the principal economic reasons, Michaelis also interpreted the treaty as a necessary "patriotic" response to Austria's challenge to dissolve the Customs Union.

52. There were, of course, setbacks; the attempt to suspend usury laws did not pass the House of Lords, and in 1861 a business tax was passed.

53. Its passage greatly affected the army reform bill and the preliminary phase of the constitutional conflict. Exceptions to the scholarly neglect of this issue are Anderson, *Social and Political Conflict,* pp. 110–18; and especially Thomas Kohut, "The Prussian Land Tax Reform of 1861" (master's thesis, Univ. of Minnesota, 1975).

54. Kohut, p. 9; August Meitzen, *Der Boden und die landwirtschaftlichen Verhältnisse des preussischen Staates* (Berlin, 1868), 1:19.

55. *Jahrbuch für amtliche Statistik des preussischen Staates 1863* (Berlin, 1864), 1:158; Kohut, "Land Tax," p. 7.

56. August Meitzen, *Der Boden,* 1:20; Kohut, "Land Tax," p. 10.

57. For popular demands against the property tax, see the "Immediate-Eingaben" from citizens petitioning for reform of the property tax in 1848–49. GStA Merseburg, Rep. 2.2.1, nr. 27417, pp. 51–61. On 21 July 1848 the Nationalversammlung presented a law to abolish exemptions from property tax, which was never passed; see the report of the State Ministry on the matter which requested a commission to study the matter. GStA Merseburg, Rep. 2.2.1., nr. 27417, pp. 67–70; Bergengrün, *Hansemann,* pp. 510–13.

58. Huber, *Dokumente,* 1:393, 412.

59. Because the bill provided for the *Kreistag* governments, all of which were controlled by Prussian nobles, in carrying out the assessment and administration of the tax, liberal factions refused to support the bill. Seeing the impossibility of drafting a law that would please both the Chamber of Deputies and the House of Lords, the finance minister recommended that all further attempts to pass the bill be withdrawn.

GStA Merseburg, Rep. 2.2.1., nr. 27414, pp. 78–107. In December 1856 the cabinet suggested re-presenting the bill, but Friedrich William IV found fault with the bill, because a clause exempting the *Reichsunmittelbaren*'s domains and buildings had not been included. The emendation was minor, yet the bill never surfaced. See pp. 108–20.

60. The importance of the property tax reform in the summer of 1858 is noteworthy, because it is before Solferino, the Prussian mobilization of 1859, and the concrete military reform plans that called for greater revenues. E. N. Anderson placed the military reform as the primary reason for William's support, a view that does not heed the longer history of the tax and the royal support for it, which predates the military-bill conflict. *Conflict,* pp. 9–10.

61. Otto to Ludolf Camphausen, 3 Nov. 1858, HAStK, Best. 1023, L491a. See also his missive of 5 Nov. 1858, HAStK, 1023, L493a. O. Camphausen was, however, not entirely happy with Patow's dilatory handling of the property tax reform bill.

62. Judging from his correspondence, it appears that O. Camphausen was the motor that drove the bill to the Landtag. Otto to Ludolf Camphausen, 28 Jan. 1859, HAStK, Best. 1023, L506.

63. *SEG,* 1861, pp. 33–40; Kohut, "Land Tax," p. 41, presents a slimmer margin of victory for the bill's passage.

64. Kohut, "Land Tax," p. 11.

65. Liberals, however, were not unaware of the dilemma. See, for example, the election program of the Constitutional Party, March 1862, in *SEG* 1862, pp. 130–31. This point is fully developed in Kohut's thesis.

66. This point is put forth by both Anderson and Kohut.

67. Pflanze, *Bismarck,* 1:278.

68. Otto to Ludolf Camphausen, 6 June 1861, HAStK, Best. 1023, L619.

69. Martin notes the *Vormärz* as the starting point; see "Entstehung"; Diefendorf's *Businessmen and Politics* locates the origins of this political style during the French occupation.

70. Its German name: *Central-Verein der Actien-Gesellschaften in Rheinland und Westphalen. BBZ,* 13 Oct. 1858, nr. 516, p. 2143; *Der Aktionär* 5:255 (14 Nov. 1858), p. 709.

71. F. Hammacher to G. Mevissen, 3 Nov. 1858, HAStK, Best. 1073, nr. 116, p. 45. The German title to the coal mining lobby was the *Specialverein für bergbauliche Interessen,* commonly known as the *Bergbauverein.*

72. *BBZ,* 24 Jan. 1859, p. 201. The association's name in German was the *Handels- und Gewerbeverein für Rheinland und Westphalen.*

73. *BBZ,* 19 Jan. 1859, p. 237.

74. Zunkel, *Unternehmer,* p. 201.

75. F. Hammacher to G. Mevissen, 3 Nov. 1858, HAStK, Best. 1073, nr. 116, p. 45.

76. Zunkel, *Unternehmer,* p. 202.

77. E. N. Anderson quoting *BBZ* in *Social and Political Conflict,* p. 320.

78. For the role of the chambers of commerce in postal reform, see GStA Merseburg, Rep. 90a B. III. 2b, nr. 6, Bd. 73, p. 202 (4 Dec. 1861); for the request of a chair for commercial law at Prussian university and the resulting report of Bethmann-

Hollweg to Heydt, 8 Nov. 1860, see GStA Merseburg, Rep. 120C VIII 1, nr. 25, vol. 3, p. 174; for Heydt's response to the Handelskammer, p. 180; see pp. 169, 184–86, 200–201 for issues of Wechselsteuer, Stempelsteuer, and railroad freights. Zunkel sees 1866 as the year when government relaxed its position toward the chambers of commerce, but ministry files at Merseburg reveal a much earlier rapprochement. Zunkel, *Unternehmer*, p. 199.

79. Ältesten der Kaufmannschaft von Berlin, "Bericht über den Handel und die Industrie von Berlin im Jahre 1859," BLHA, Rep. 2A, I HG, nr. 71; see also the protocols of the state ministry, 19 May 1859, GStA Merseburg, Rep. 90a B. III. 2b, nr. 6, Bd. 71, p. 94. The reform concerned reducing the legal requirements and simplifying the bureaucratic procedure to start up life and fire insurance agencies.

80. "Die Aufhebung der Durchfurzölle," *NZ,* 22 Dec. 1860.

81. D. Hansemann to Heydt, 2 Apr. 1860, GStA Merseburg, Rep. 120C VIII 1, nr. 25, vol. 3, pp. 133–34; for the reports and recommendations of the Handelskammer and Kaufmannschaften from Frankfurt a.O., Berlin, Erfurt, and Crefeld, pp. 135–65.

82. *NZ,* 30 Dec. 1859.

83. Hamerow, *Social Foundations: Ideas and Institutions,* pp. 349–50; Andreas Biefang, *Politisches Bürgertum in Deutschland 1857–68: Nationale Organisationen und Eliten* (Düsseldorf, 1994), pp. 209 ff.

84. Heinrich Kruse to G. Mevissen, undated (c. 1863), HAStK, Best. 1073, nr. 116 (emphasis original).

85. F. von Diergardt to G. Mevissen, 7 Mar. 1860, HAStK, 1073, nr. 116.

86. F. von Diergardt to G. Mevissen, 7 Mar. 1860, HAStK, 1073, nr. 116.

87. See, for instance, Diergardt's information from Undersecretary von der Reck on the best procedure for the Rhenish Railway to attain the right to absorb the Aachen-Düsseldorf Railway. Diergardt to Mevissen, 10 Feb. 1863, HAStK, Best. 1073, nr. 289.

88. Diergardt to Mevissen, 7 Mar. 1860, HAStK, Best. 1073, nr. 116.

89. Zunkel, *Unternehmer,* p. 118.

90. Protocols of the board of directors, 15 Oct. 1858, HAStK, Best. 1028, nr. 9, p. 154.

91. Protocol of the board of the directors, 7 Jan. 1859, HAStK, Best. 1028, nr. 9., p. 215.

92. Dept. of Interior (in Cologne) to Pommer-Esche (in Coblenz), 7 Apr. 1859, GStA Merseburg, Rep. 93E, nr. 3753, unpag; Regierungspräsident E. Möller to Pommer Esche, 8 Apr. 1859, GStA Merseburg, Rep. 93E, nr. 3753; *BBZ,* 25 May 1859, p. 989; minutes of Rhenish Railway directors, 11 Nov. 1859, HAStK, Best. 1028, nr. 9, p. 505; Decree of Prince Wilhelm and state ministry, 21 Aug. 1859, LHAK, Best. 403, nr. 11887, p. 61.

93. Von der Reck to Railroad Commission in Cologne, 4 Sept. 1860, LHAK, Best. 403, nr. 11801, pp. 405–6.

94. Heydt to Railroad Commission in Cologne, 26 Apr. 1860, LHAK, Best. 403, nr. 11887, p. 343.

95. The Upper Silesian company received permission from the trade ministry to cancel construction of a potentially unprofitable line on the right bank of the Oder

and further received the hitherto forbidden right to run its own coalmining operation. Heydt to Prince William, 7 Nov. 1859, GStA Merseburg, Rep. 2.2.1., nr. 29574, pp. 273–75; decree of Prince William, 14 Nov. 1859, GStA Merseburg, Rep. 2.2.1., nr. 29573, p. 19; Position paper of Heydt, 28 Jan. 1860, GStA Merserburg, Rep. 90a K III 3, nr. 14, Bd. 1, p. 306. The Cologne-Minden railroad also received advantageous concessions to fuse its operations in a central station with the Rhenish Railway and new stipulations for the construction of its lines to Giessen and Arnheim.

96. *BBZ,* 13 Sept. 1859.

97. Ibid., 27 Feb. 1860 and 12 Mar. 1860.

98. Ibid., 15 Mar. 1860.

99 . See, for example, *NZ,* 4 and 13 Feb. 1862 and 4 Apr. 1862.

100. Ibid., 29 July 1862.

101. Ibid., 20 Aug. 1862.

102. For the petition of Kaufmann Schierer, see Director Offerman of Upper Silesian to Finance Minister Heydt, 31 Mar. 1862, GStA Merseburg, Rep. 93E, nr. 3420, pp. 280–81.

103. *BBZ,* 1 Sept. 1859 and 13 Jan. 1860.

104. See the "Bericht der vereinigten Commissionen für Handel und Gerwerbe und für Finanzen und Zölle über Petionen," Chamber of Deputies, 7th legislative period, 2nd session, 1863, GStA Merseburg, Rep. 93E, nr. 3420, pp. 309–14; quotation on p. 310.

105. Maybach to Heydt, 1 Mar. 1861, GStA Merseburg, Rep. 93E, nr. 3884, unpag.

106. Manfred Ohlsen, *Der Eisenbahnkönig: Bethel Henry Strousberg: eine preussische Gründerkarriere,* 2d ed. (Berlin, 1987), p. 62.

107. Bismarck, *Gedanken und Erinnerungen,* pp. 269–70.

108. *VBMHGA* 1861–63, p. 35.

109. *VBMHGA* 1861–63, p. 48.

110. In 1862, the average stock quote on German markets rose ten points, followed by incremental rises of 3.7, 2.4 and 2.3 for the years 1863–65. Reinhard Spree, *Die Wachstumszyklen der deutschen Wirtschaft von 1840 bis 1880* (Berlin, 1977), p. 377.

111. *VBMHGA* 1861–63, p. 44.

112. *VBMHGA* 1855–57, p. 22; *VBMHGA* 1858–60, p. 28; *VBMHGA* 1861–63, p. 25; *VBMHGA* 1864–66, p. 26–27. The percentages are, respectively 40.8, 37.1, 33.7, and 32.1.

113. Henderson, *Industrial Revolution,* pp. 186–87.

114. *VBMHGA* 1855–57, p. 22; *VBMHGA* 1858–60, p. 28; *VBMHGA* 1861–63, p. 25.

115. Sheehan, *German Liberalism,* p. 85.

116. Otto Michaelis, *Das Monopol der Eisenbahnen* (Berlin, 1861), pp. 49–50; "Der volkswirtschaftliche Kongress," *NZ,* 28 Sept. 1861.

117. From 1857 to 1859, private railroads in Prussia yielded an average dividend

of 6.33, 5.68, and 5.66 percent, whereas state administered lines offered an average dividend of 5.72, 4.35, and 4.42 percent. *VBMHGA* 1858–60, p. 54. For a principled rejection of state-run railways from Berlin's leading liberal newspaper, see the editorial of 25 Nov. 1856 in *NZ* 9:554. For the hesitancy of industrialists to trust the trade ministry as the sole decider of contracts, see Unruh, *Erinnerungen,* p. 189–94.

118. Hamerow, *Social Foundations: Ideas and Institutions,* p. 26.

119. See, for example, the reaction against the Cologne-Minden's new freights in 1859 that pitted Ruhr industrialists against the railway. *BBZ,* 31 Mar. 1859.

120. "Das Monopol der Eisenbahnen, I & II" *NZ,* 20 Apr. and 17 May 1861. See also O. Michaelis, *Monopol.*

121. The decision enabled the Berg-Mark Railway to absorb the smaller railways, establishing a balance of commercial power between the Rhenish, Cologne-Minden, and the Berg-Mark railways in the Rhenish-Westphalian industrial region. See "Bericht [der Handelskammer Crefelds] betreffend die Fusion der Aachen-Düsseldorf-Ruhrorter Eisenbahn mit der Rheinischen resp. der Bergisch-Märkischen," 27 Apr. 1863, HAStK, Best. 1073, nr. 81, unpag. For the perceived threat of the political mobilization against the Rhenish Railway, see Fr. Diergardt to König, 6 Mar. 1861, HAStK, Best. 1073 III, nr. 1, unpag; and, in the same file, Itzenplitz to Rhenish Railway directors, 18 Apr. 1863. For earlier protests of railway mergers, see the Düsseldorf's chamber petition to Heydt, 10 Jan. 1857, LHAK, Best. 403, nr. 11895, pp. 179–191. See also Padtberg, *Rheinischer Liberalismus,* pp. 62–63.

122. See "Die politische Machtstellung der grossen Industrie," *NZ,* 30 July 1859.

123. Ohlsen, *Eisenbahnkönig,* pp. 253 ff; Strousberg, *Dr. Strousberg,* chap. 3; Henderson, *Industrial Revolution,* p. 186; see also Bismarck's characterization of Itzenplitz in *Gedanken und Erinnerungen* (Berlin, 1898), 1:269–71.

124. Pflanze, *Bismarck,* 1:278.

125. *VBMHGA* 1861–63, pp. 28–38; *VBMHGA* 1863–66, pp. 34–39.

126. *VBMHGA* 1861–63, pp. 46–47; *VBMHGA* 1864–66, p. 43. A fifth of this sum went to the Cologne-Minden Railway, whose Deutz-Giessen line in 1864–66 demanded subsidies amounting to 993,805 thalers.

127. See the cabinet votes of Itzenplitz and Bodelschwingh, 27 May 1863, GStA Merseburg, Rep. 90a K. III. 3, nr. 15, Bd. II, unpag.; *VBMHGA* 1861–63, p. 32.

128. For the Landtag's emendation of the charter for the Eifel line between Trier and Call (9 Dec. 1864), see the memorandum of Bodelschwingh and Itzenplitz to king, 28 Jan. 1865, and the state cabinet to king, 3 July 1866, GStA Merseburg, Rep. 90a K. III 3, nr. 2, pp. 45–48.

129. Ludolf to Otto Camphausen, 8 June 1865, HAStK, Best. 1023, L 796.

130. *SEG* 1865, 28–29 March, p. 161.

131. ARbdB, nr. 15394, unpag. The chamber rejected the bill on 1 Apr. 1865.

132. For the 1864 and 1866 agreements, see GStA Merseburg, Rep. 90a K. III. 3, nr. 15, Bd. II, unpag.; *Gesetzsammlung* 1866 (19 Feb.), p. 114.

133. Pflanze, *Bismarck,* 1:261–62, 280.

134. On the question of whether or not the Prussian state could finance a war,

see Otto Pflanze, *Bismarck,* 1:261–62; for the discussion that was raised in the Chamber, see Engelberg, *Bismarck: Urpreusse und Reichsgründer,* 3d ed. (Berlin, 1988), pp. 562–63.

135. Gerson Bleichröder to Bismarck, 20 Dec. 1862, GStA Merseburg, Rep. 90a K.III., nr. 11, Bd. 2, p. 359, and memorandum, pp. 360–67; Itzenplitz to Bismarck, 11 Feb. 1863, ibid.; the claim that Bleichröder's proposal was ten million too low was later emended in other estimates by the finance ministry. See the estimates in 1864 and 1865 that set the value between fifteen and seventeen million thalers, GStA Merseburg, Rep. 151 HB, nr. 1339, pp. 1–8.

136. Memorandum of D. Oppenheim, 15 May 1865, GStA Merseburg, Rep. 151 HB, nr. 1339, p. 9; for the value of the Guarantee Fund, see the printed protocol of the extraordinary general stockholder's meeting, 28 Aug. 1865, HAStK, Best. 1073, nr. 247, p. 4. The state was, however, required to retain two million thalers in the fund.

137. *SEG* 1865, 18 July, p. 174.

138. D. Oppenheim to Itzenplitz, 8 June 1865, GStA Merseburg, Rep. 151 HB, nr. 1339, p. 10; and Oppenheim's "Hingeworfene Gedanken über die im Cöln-Mindener Eisenbahn-Statuten vorgesehene Aktien-Amortisation," 26 June 1865, p. 12.

139. Memorandum of finance ministry to Itzenplitz, 13 July 1865, GStA Merseburg, Rep. 151 HB, nr. 1339, pp. 44–47.

140. For provisional contract, *SEG* 1865, p. 174; for 10 Aug. 1865 contract, GStA Merseburg, Rep. 151 HB, nr. 1339, pp. 49–57; for crown's acceptance, pp. 62–63; and for public notice of agreement, *Staatsanzeiger,* 26 Sept. 1865, p. 3087.

141. For the analysis of the transaction's legality, see the undated position paper (c. 1865), GStA Merseburg, Rep. 90a K. III. 3, nr. 11, Bd. III, pp. 31–37; the position paper of Wollny, 18 June 1865, Rep. 151 HB, nr. 1339, pp. 13–17; Itzenplitz's memorandum to Bodelschwingh, p. 30; and Wollny's reiteration of illegality, 21 Aug. 1865, p. 60.

142. See the note by Itzenplitz to higher authority, presumably Bismarck, on the political logic of the deal, 8 July 1865, GStA Merseburg, Rep. 90a K. III. 3, nr. 11, p. 17–18.

143. Memorandum of finance ministry to general state treasury, 26 Sept. 1865, GStA Merseburg, Rep. 151 HB, nr. 1339, p. 64.

144. Heydt to President of Chamber of Deputies Forckenbeck, 23 Nov. 1866, "Übersicht von den zur Deckung der Kriegskosten des Jahres 1866 bereits veräusserten und noch vorhandenen Effecten," GStA Merseburg, Rep. 151 HB, nr. 1339, p. 217.

145. See the printed protocol of the Cologne-Minden's extraordinary general stockholder's meeting, 28 Aug. 1865, HAStK, Best. 1073, nr. 247, p. 2.

146. Printed protocol, 28 Aug. 1865, HAStK, Best. 1073, nr. 247, p. 4.

147. Regarding the thirteen million thaler sale, the statement by Hasso von Wedel, Wittgenstein's biographer, that although Rhenish circles "despised" the upcoming Austro-Prussian war, the Cologne-Minden Railway "certainly did not suspect what it did" when buying the state option is hard to believe. See Hasso von Wedel,

Heinrich von Wittgenstein 1797-1869: Unternehmer und Politiker in Köln (Cologne, 1981), p. 143. Funding the imminent war with Austria had become an all important question in the cabinet and part of the reason why Bismarck requested Heydt's return to the Finance Ministry in June 1866 to replace Bodelschwingh, who had greater reservations than Heydt about spending money without parliamentary authorization.

148. See the protocol of the committee "für die Anlage des Schleswig-Holsteinschen Kanals," HAStK, Best. 1073, nr. 566, pp. 112 ff.

149. Engelberg, *Bismarck,* 1:562.

150. See the "Auszug aus dem Sitzungsprotokoll der Direktion von 17. October 1865," HAStK, Best. 1073, nr. 241.

151. Zunkel, *Unternehmer,* p. 221.

152. For the participation of businessmen and industrialists in the political process of the 1860s, see Kaelble, *Berliner Unternehmer,* p. 230; Sheehan, *German Liberalism,* p. 80–81; Anderson, *Social and Political Conflict,* pp. 293, 298, 303. Among the electors chosen in Berlin there were 550 merchants, 240 industrialists, 17 brewers, and 3 bankers. Such lists show "that in spite of the unwillingness of merchants and industrialists as a rule to take the time to serve as Landtag deputies, these groups devoted many hours of service to secure the election of liberals from their district and were actively concerned not merely with municipal affairs but with problems of state and national life" (p. 303). See also Anderson, Appendix C on p. 445 for the percentage of merchants who sat in the Landtag from 1848 to 1866.

153. Zunkel, *Unternehmer,* p. 193.

154. Kaelble, *Berliner Unternehmer,* p. 230. Unfortunately, Kaelble's analysis of businessmen's politics ends in 1862, thus preventing a clear long-term assessment of where and how political attitudes drifted.

155. "Constitutionelles Wahl-Programm," 1 Nov. 1861, Nachlass Hansemanns, GStA Merseburg, Rep. 92, nr. 38, pp. 115–16.

156. "Die Ansprüche und die demokratische Partei," *NZ,* 6 Dec. 1860.

157. Ludolf to Otto Camphausen, 5 Jan. 1859, HAStK, Best. 1023, L505.

158. Otto Pflanze, "Juridical and Political Responsibility in Nineteenth-Century Germany," in Leonard Krieger and Fritz Stern, eds., *The Responsibility of Power* (New York, 1967), chap. 9.

159. See Anderson for figures.

160. *NZ,* 30 July 1859.

161. For Hansemann's refusal of candidature, *BBZ,* 13 Nov. 1858, p. 2371; for quotation, Hansemann to Mevissen, 9 Nov. 1858, HAStK, Best. 1073, nr. 116, pp. 78–79.

162. F. Diergardt to Mevissen, HAStK, Rep. 1073, nr. 112 I, p. 178.

163. Ludolf to Otto Camphausen, 20 Oct. 1862, HAStK, Best. 1023, L685a.

164. The king, according to L. Camphausen, wished to come but refused because of his irritation that Cologne might appoint Bockum-Dolfs as lord mayor (*Oberbürgermeister*). Ludolf to Otto Camphausen, 19 Nov. 1862, HAStK, Best. 1023, L 687.

165. Hansen, *Mevissen,* 1:738.

166. Thomas Parent, *"Passiver Widerstand" im preussischer Verfassungskonflikt: Die Kölner Abgeordnetenfeste* (Cologne, 1982), p. 74.

167. For the invitation to the "pflegende Berathung," see HAStK, Best. 1073, nr. 116, p. 90.

168. "Der preussische Landtag von 1863," *Deutsche Vierteljahrsschrift* (1863), Heft 3, nr. 103, p. 124; Zunkel attributes the authorship to Beckerath: *Unternehmer,* p. 213.

169. Ludolf to Otto Camphausen, 3 Jan. 1863, HAStK, Best. 1023, L 695.

170. *SEG* 1863, pp. 114–15.

171. Ludolf to Otto Camphausen, 3 Jan. 1863, HAStK, Best. 1023, L 695.

172. Diergardt to Mevissen, 17 Jan. 1863, HAStK, Best. 1073, nr. 116, p. 212.

173. Hansen, *Mevissen,* 1:739.

174. Zunkel, *Unternehmer,* pp. 216–17; Parent, *Passiver Widerstand,* p. 68.

175. For the role of the Cologne deputy banquets in the constitutional conflict, see Thomas Parent, *Passiver Widerstand;* for quotation (F. Lasalle), see p. 180.

176. Ludolf to Otto Camphausen, 23 July 1863, HAStK, Best. 1023, L 718.

177. F. Diergardt to Simson, 28 Sept. 1863, HAStK, Best. 1073, nr. 112 I, p. 773.

178. Quoted in Zunkel, *Unternehmer,* p. 217–18.

179. Quoted in Zunkel, *Unternehmer,* p. 217, n. 42.

180. Unruh, *Erinnerungen,* pp. 241 ff.; Engelberg, *Bismarck,* pp. 484–91.

181. See Mevissen's "Promemoria über den preussischen Verfassungskonflikt, den deutschen Bundesstaat und das zukünftige deutsche Parlament," in Hansen, *Mevissen,* 2:575–84; quotation on p. 576.

182. Quoted in Engelberg, *Bismarck,* p. 562.

183. Quoted in Zunkel, *Unternehmer,* p. 195.

Chapter Eight

1. O. Michaelis, May 1864, "Eisenbahnaktionäre und Eisenbahninteressenten," in *Volkswirtschaftlichen Schriften* (Berlin, 1873), 1:111.

2. Thomas Nipperdey, *Deutsche Geschichte,* pp. 720–21.

3. There were an additional 1,429.92 kilometers of private railway in Prussia administered by the government. See Klee, *Preussische Eisenbahngeschichte,* p. 224.

4. "Beiträge zur Beurtheilung des Verhältnisses der Eisenbahnen zum Staate," *Mittheilungen des Vereins zur Wahrung der gemeinsamen wirtschaftlichen Interessen in Rheinland und Westfalen* (Jan. and Feb. 1876), BA Potsdam, Rep. 41.01, nr. 22, pp. 35 ff.

5. Pflanze, *Bismarck,* 2:457.

6. See file "Den Erwerb der Eisenbahnen Deutschlands für das Reich betreffend 1876–77," BA Potsdam, Rep. 41.01, nr. 22; for Bismarck's relationship to his ministers, see Pflanze, *Bismarck,* 2:333–36, 457–58.

7. For an overall incisive discussion of the 1873 crash and its subsequent downward business cycle, see Wehler, *Gesellschaftsgeschichte,* 3:1258–66.

8. See table 36 of Fremdling's *Eisenbahnen,* p. 144. The figures for Prussian railways are slightly higher but followed the same consistently downward trend: 1871, 8.1 percent; 1875, 5.7; 1879, 5.6. Prussian state paper yielded 4.1 percent in the late 1870s.

9. *SBHA,* 1878–79, 1:95–171, 505 ff.

10. For figures on freight traffic on railways, see B. R. Mitchell, *European Historical Statistics, 1750–1975,* 2d ed. (New York, 1980), p. 620. Whereas freight traffic had climbed from 5,300 millions of ton/kilometers in 1870 to 6,400 in 1871, 8,200 in 1872, and 9,900 in 1873, it leveled off thereafter with only minimal increases: 1874, 10,100; 1875, 10,400; 1876, 10,800; 1877, 11,000; 1878, 11,100.

11. Jeffry Diefendorf, *Businessmen and Politics in the Rhineland, 1789–1834* (Princeton, 1980), pp. 83 ff.

12. Jürgen Kocka has also noted that "the liberals faced particular difficulties because of the time of German modernization. The problems of nation building, conflict over political participation and the constitutional order, and the 'social question' brought about by capitalist industrialization . . . may confront a nation at different points in its history, perhaps one after the other, as was the case in most of Europe and North America. In contrast, Germany faced these issues or crises within the same quarter of a century, particularly in 1848 and in the 1860s." Kocka, "Problems of Working-Class Formation in Germany: The Early Years, 1800–1875," in Ira Katznelson and Aristide R. Zolberg, *Working-Class Formation: Nineteenth-Century Patterns in Western Europe and the United States* (Princeton, 1986), p. 348.

BIBLIOGRAPHY

Archival Sources

Geheimes Staatsarchiv preussischer Kulturbesitz Merseburg (GStA Merseburg, formerly Deutsches-Zentral Archiv, Dienststelle Merseburg)

Akten des Ministeriums für Handel, Gewerbe und öffentliche Arbeit (Reps. 93E, 120A).

Akten des Finanzministeriums (Rep. 151).

Akten des Ministeriums des Innern (Rep. 77).

Akten des Hauses der Abgeordnete (Rep. 169C).

Akten des Geheim-Zivilkabinetts (Rep. 2.2.1.).

Akten des Ministeriums der auswärtigen Angelegenheiten: Handelspolitische Abteilung (Rep. 2.4.1.).

Akten des Staatsministeriums, 1851–66 (Rep. 90A).

Nachlässe (Rep. 92):

August von der Heydt

Otto von Manteuffel

David Hansemann

Rudolf von Delbrück

Karl von Vincke

Rudolf von Auerswald

Brandenburgisches Landeshauptarchiv, Potsdam (BLHA, formerly Staatsarchiv Potsdam)

Akten des Polizei-Präsidiums der Stadt Berlin (Rep. 30 Berlin C).

Akten des Oberpräsidiums der Provinz Brandenburg (Rep. 1).

Akten der Bezirksregierung Potsdam (Rep. 2A).

Akten der Bezirksregierung Frankfurt a. O. (Rep. 3B).

Akten der Gewerbeaufsichtsämter (Rep. 55).

Bundesarchiv Potsdam (BA Potsdam, formerly Zentrales Staatsarchiv Potsdam)

Akten des Reichsbahnamtes (Rep. 41.01)

Geheimes Staatsarchiv preussischer Kulturbesitz Berlin-Dahlem (GStA)

Akten der Seehandlung (Rep. 109).

Akten des Ministeriums für öffentliche Arbeit (Rep. 93).

Landesarchiv Berlin

Nachlass Heinrich Wilhelm Krausnick (Rep. 200).

Nachlass Hermann Weise (Rep. 200).

247

Landeshauptarchiv Koblenz (LHAK)

Akten des Oberpräsidiums der Rheinprovinz (Rep. 403).
Akten der Bezirksregierung Koblenz (Rep. 441).
Akten der Bezirksregierung Trier (Rep. 442).

Historisches Archiv der Stadt Köln (HAStK)
Akten der rheinischen Eisenbahnen: Rheinische, Bonn-Köln und Köln-Krefeld
Eisenbahngesellschaften (Rep. 1028).
Nachlass Gustav Mevissens (Rep. 1073).
Nachlass Ludolf Camphausens (Rep. 1023L).

Rheinland-Westfälisches Wirtschaftsarchiv (RWWA)

Jahresberichte der Handelskammer Kölns

Hauptstaatsarchiv Düsseldorf

Akten der Bezirksregierung Düsseldorf (Rep. 1020).

Archiv des Bankhauses Oppenheim (Köln)

Akten betreffend der Rheinischen Eisenbahngesellschaft (Band 161).

Archiv der Reichsbahndirektion Berlins (ARbdB)
Akten betreffend Eisenbahnverwaltung, 1848–1866, nr. 13389–16417
Bleichröder Collection, Baker Library, Harvard University

Correspondence of 1848–1886 period

Newpapers and Periodicals

Der Aktionär
Berliner Börsen-Zeitung
Berlinische [Spener] Nachrichten
Constitutionelle Zeitung
Deutsche Vierteljahrsheft
Eisenbahn-Zeitung
Kölnische Zeitung
National-Zeitung
Neue Preussische [Kreuz] Zeitung
Preussische Zeitung
Urwähler Zeitung
Vossische Zeitung

Printed Sources

Ammon, Fritz. *Erinnerungen von Fr. von Ammon.* Cologne, 1878.
Bismarck, Otto von. *Gedanken und Erinnerungen.* Stuttgart, 1898.
Camphausen, Ludolf. *Zur Eisenbahn von Köln nach Antwerpen.* Cologne, 1833.

————. *Zur Eisenbahn nach Antwerpen.* Cologne, 1835.

————. *Versuch eines Beitrages zur Eisenbahngesetzgebung.* Cologne, 1838.

von Delbrück, Rudolph. *Lebenserinnerungen.* 2 vols. Leipzig, 1905.

von Delbrück, R., and J. Hegel, eds., *Handelsarchiv: Sammlung der neuen auf Handel und Schiffahrt bezüglichen Gesetze und Verordnung des In- und Auslandes und statistische Mittheilungen über den Zustand und die Entwicklung des Handels und der Industrie in der preussichen Monarchie.* Berlin, 1850–.

Diwald, Helmut, ed. *Von der Revolution zum Norddeutschen Bund: Politik und Ideengut der preussischen Hochkonservativen 1848–1866; aus dem Nachlass von Ernst Ludwig von Gerlach.* 2 vols. Göttingen, 1970.

Fenske, Hans, ed. *Der Weg zur Reichsgrundung 1850–1870.* Vol. 5, *Quellen zum politischen Denken der Deutschen.* Darmstadt, 1977.

Gesetz-Sammlung für die Königlichen Preussischen Staaten.

Hansemann, David. *Die Eisenbahnen und deren Aktionäre in ihrer Verhältniss zum Staat.* Leipzig, 1837.

Hansen, Joseph, ed., *Rheinische Briefe und Akten zur Geschichte der politischen Bewegung.* Vol. 1. Reprint. Cologne, 1969.

Huber, Ernst R. *Dokumente zur deutschen Verfassungsgeschichte.* 2 vols. Stuttgart, 1961, 1964.

Poschinger, Heinrich von, ed. *Bankwesen und Bankpolitik in Preussen.* 3 vols. Berlin, 1879.

————, ed. *Unter Friedrich Wilhelm IV.: Denkwürdigkeiten des Ministerpräsidenten Otto Freiherrn von Manteuffel.* 3 vols. Berlin, 1901.

Schulthess, Heinrich, ed. *Europäischer Geschichtskalender.* 81 vols. Munich, 1860–1940.

Stenographische Berichte über die Verhandlungen des Landtages: Haus der Abgeordneten. Berlin, 1849–66.

Stenographische Berichte über die Verhandlungen des Landtages: Herrenhaus. Berlin, 1849–66.

Unruh, Hans Viktor von. *Erinnerungen aus dem Leben von Hans Viktor von Unruh.* Edited by Heinrich von Poschinger. Stuttgart, 1895.

Verhandlungen des ersten deutschen Handelstages zu Heidelberg vom 13. bis 18. Mai 1861

Verwaltungs-Bericht des Ministeriums für Handel, Gewerbe und öffentliche Arbeit. Berlin, 1848–66.

Secondary Sources

Anderson, Eugene N. *The Social and Political Conflict in Prussia, 1858–1864.* Lincoln, Neb., 1954.

Armstrong, John A. *The European Administrative Elite.* Princeton, 1973.

Aron, Raymond. "Social Class, Political Class, Ruling Class." In Reinhard Bendix and Seymour M. Lipset, eds., *Class, Status, Power: Social Stratification in Comparative Perspective.* New York, 1966.

Aubin, H., and Wolfgang Zorn. *Handbuch der deutschen Wirtschafts- und Sozialgeschichte.* Vol. 2, *Das 19. und 20. Jahrhundert.* Stuttgart, 1976.

Augustin, H. F. L. *Preussische Finanzfragen.* Potsdam, 1859.

———. *Das Preussische Handels-Ministerium in seinem Verhältnisse zu den Privat-Eisenbahn-Gesellschaften.* Potsdam, 1859.

Augustine-Perez, Dolores. *Patricians and Parvenus: Wealth and High Society in Wilhelmine Germany.* Oxford, 1994.

———. "Very Wealthy Businessmen in Imperial Germany." *Journal of Social History* 22 (1988): 299–321.

Baar, L. *Die Berliner Industrie in der industriellen Revolution.* Berlin, 1966.

Bahne, Siegfried. "Vor dem Konflikt: Die Altliberalen in der Regentschaftsperiode der 'Neuen Aera.' " In Ulrich Engelhardt, ed., *Soziale Bewegung und politische Verfassung.* Stuttgart, 1976.

Barclay, David E. "The Court Camarilla and the Politics of Monarchical Restoration in Prussia, 1848–58." In Larry Eugene Jones and James N. Retallack, eds., *Between Reform, Reaction and Resistance: Studies in the History of German Conservatism from 1789 to 1945,* 123–56 (Providence, 1993).

———. *Frederick William IV and the Prussian Monarchy, 1840–1861.* Oxford, 1995.

Baum, Marie Luise. *Die von der Heydts aus Elberfeld.* Elberfeld, 1964.

Beau, Horst. *Das Leistungswissen des fruhindustriellen Unternehmens in Rheinland-Westfalen.* Cologne, 1969.

Becker, W. "Die Bedeutung der nichtagrarischen Wanderung für die Herausbildung des industriellen Proletariats in Deutschland, unter besonderer Berucksichtigung Preussens von 1850 bis 1870." In *Studien zur Geschichte der Industriellen Revolution in Deutschland.* Vol. 1. Berlin, 1960.

———. *Die Entwicklung der deutschen Maschinenbauindustrie von 1850 bis 1870.* Berlin, 1962.

Beckerath, Erwin V., et al., eds., *Friedrich List: Schriften, Reden, Briefe.* Berlin, 1931.

Behnen, Michael. *Das preussische Wochenblatt 1851–1861. Nationalkonservative Publizistik gegen Staendestaat und Polizeistaat.* Göttingen, 1971.

Bendix, Reinhard. *Nation Building and Citizenship.* New York, 1964.

———. *Work and Authority in Industry.* New York, 1963.

Berdahl, Robert. *The Politics of the Prussian Nobility: The Development of a Conservative Ideology, 1770–1848.* Princeton, 1988.

Bergengrün, Alexander. *David Hansemann.* Berlin, 1901.

———. *Staatsminister August Freiherr von der Heydt.* Leipzig, 1908.

Berger, Louis. *Der alte Harkort.* Leipzig, 1890.

Berghahn, Volker. *Germany and the Approach of War in 1914.* London, 1973.

Berndt, Helga. "Die höheren Beamten des Ministeriums für Handel in Preussen 1871–1932: Eine Analyse zu ihrer sozialen Zusammensetzung und Verflechtung." *Jahrbuch für Wirtschaftsgeschichte* (1981): 105–200.

Best, Heinrich. *Interessenpolitik und nationale Integration 1848/49.* Göttingen, 1980.

———. *Die Männer von Bildung und Besitz: Struktur und Handeln parlamentarischer Führungsgruppen in Deutschland und Frankreich 1848/49.* Düsseldorf, 1990.

Beutin, Ludwig. *Gesammelte Schriften zur Wirtschafts- und Sozialgeschichte.* Cologne, 1963.

Biefang, Andreas. *Politisches Bürgertum in Deutschland 1857–68: Nationale Organisationen und Eliten.* Düsseldorf, 1994.

Blackbourn, David. *Populists and Patricians: Essays in Modern German History.* London, 1987.

———. "Progress and Piety: Liberalism, Catholicism, and the State in Imperial Germany." *History Workshop* 26 (1988): 57–78.

Blackbourn, David, and Geoff Eley. *The Peculiarities of German History: Bourgeois Society and Politics in Nineteenth-Century Germany.* New York, 1984.

Blackbourn, David, and Richard J. Evans, eds. *The German Bourgeoisie: Essays on the Social History for the German Middle Class from the Late Eighteenth to the Early Twentieth Century.* London, 1991.

Bloemers, Kurt. "Der Eisenbahn-Tarif-Kampf." In K. E. Born, ed., *Moderne deutsche Wirtschaftsgeschichte.* Cologne, 1966.

Blumberg, Horst. "Die Finanzierung der Neugründungen von Industriebetrieben in Form der Aktiengesellschaften während der fünfziger Jahre des 19. Jahrhunderts in Deutschland, am Beispiel der preussichen Verhältnisse erläutert." In Hans Mottek, ed., *Studien zur Geschichte der industriellen Revolution in Deutschland.* Vol. 1. Berlin, 1960.

Boch, Rudolf. *Grenzenloses Wachstum? Das Rheinische Wirtschaftsbürgertum und seine Industrialisierungsdebatte 1814–1857.* Göttingen, 1991.

Boerner, Karl-Heinz. *Die Krise der preussischen Monarchie von 1858 bis 1862.* Berlin, 1976.

Böhme, Helmut. *Deutschlands Weg zur Grossmacht: Studien zum Verhältnis von Wirtschaft und Staat während der Reichsgründungszeit 1848–1881.* Cologne, 1966.

———. *An Introduction to the Social and Economic History of Germany.* New York, 1978.

———. "Preussische Bankpolitik 1848–1853." In Böhme, ed., *Probleme der Reichsgründungszeit 1848–1879.* Cologne, 1968.

Boldt, Hans. "Deutscher Konstitutionalismus und Bismarckreich." In Stürmer, ed., *Das kaiserliche Deutschland.* Düsseldorf, 1970.

Borchardt, Knut. "The Industrial Revolution in Germany, 1700–1914." In Carlo M. Cipolla, ed., *The Fontana Economic History of Europe.* Vol. 4, *The Emergence of Industrial Societies.* Glasgow, 1973.

———. *Die Industrielle Revolution in Deutschland.* Munich, 1976.

———. "Konjunkturtheorie in der Konjunkturgeschichte." *Vierteljahrsheft für Sozial- und Wirtschaftsgeschichte* 72 (1985): 537–55.

———. *Wachstum, Krisen, Handlungspielräume der Wirtschaftspolitik.* Göttingen, 1982.

Born, Karl Erich. *Moderne deutsche Wirtschaftsgeschichte.* Cologne, 1966.

———, ed. *International Banking in the Nineteenth and Twentieth Centuries.* Translated by Volker Berghahn. Warwickshire, 1983.

Botzenhart, Manfred. *Deutsche Parlamentarismus in der Revolutionszeit 1848–1850.* Düsseldorf, 1977.

Bösselmann, Karl. *Die Entwicklung des deutschen Aktienwesens im 19. Jahrhundert.* Berlin, 1939.

Bramstedt, E. K. *Aristocracy and the Middle Classes in Germany: Social Types in German Literature, 1830–1900.* 2d ed. Chicago, 1964.

Brandt, H. H. *Der österreichische Neoabsolutismus: Staatsfinanzen und Politik 1848–1860.* 2 vols. Göttingen, 1978.

Brose, Eric Dorn. *The Politics of Technological Change: Out of the Shadow of Antiquity, 1809–1848.* Princeton, 1993.

Büsch, Otto, ed., *Friedrich Wilhelm IV. in seiner Zeit.* Berlin, 1987.

———, ed. *Das Preussenbild in der Geschichte: Protokoll eines Symposiums.* Berlin, 1981.

Büsch, Otto, and Klaus Zernack, eds. "Friedrich Wilhelm IV. in seiner Zeit: Beiträge." *Jahrbuch für die Geschichte Mittel- und Ostdeutschlands* 36 (1987): 1–360.

Cameron, Rondo E. "Founding the Bank of Darmstadt." *Explorations in Entrepreneurial History* 8 (1955–56): 113–30.

———. *France and the Economic Development of Europe, 1800–1914.* 2d ed. Chicago, 1965.

Cameron, Rondo E., et al. *Banking in the Early Stages of Industrialization.* Columbus, Ohio, 1967.

Caplan, Jane. "Myths, Models and Missing Revolutions: Comments on a Debate in German History." *Radical History Review* 34 (1986): 87–99.

Carlisle, Robert B. *The Proffered Crown: Saint-Simonianism and the Doctrine of Hope.* Baltimore, 1987.

Cecil, Lamar. *Albert Ballin: Business and Politics in Imperial Germany, 1888–1914.* Princeton, 1967.

Chandler, Alfred D. "The Railroads: Pioneeers in Modern Corporate Management." *Business History Review* 9 (1965): 16–40.

———. *Scale and Scope: The Dynamics of Industrial Capitalism.* Cambridge, Mass., 1990.

———. *The Visible Hand: The Managerial Revolution in American Business.* Cambridge, Mass., 1977.

———, ed. *The Railroads: The Nation's First Big Business.* New York, 1965.

Clapham, J. H. *The Economic Development of France and Germany, 1815–1914.* 4th ed. London, 1966.

Coser, Lewis A. *The Functions of Social Conflict.* New York, 1967.

Däbritz, Walther. *Gründung und Anfänge der Disconto-Gesellschaft Berlin.* Munich, 1931.

Dahrendorf, Ralf. *Society and Democracy in Germany.* New York, 1967.

Davidoff, Lenore, and Catherine Hall. *Family Fortunes: Men and Women of the English Middle Class, 1780–1850.* Chicago, 1987.

Diefendorf, Jeffry. *Businessmen and Politics in the Rhineland, 1789–1834.* Princeton, 1980.

Düwell, Kurt. "David Hansemann als rheinpreussicher Liberaler in Heppenheim 1847." In Wolfgang Schieder, ed., *Liberalismus in der Gesellschaft des deutschen Vormärz.* Göttingen, 1983.

Dunlavy, Colleen A. *Politics and Industrialization: Early Railroads in the United States and Prussia.* Princeton, 1994.

Eichholtz, Dietrich. "Bewegungen unter den preussischen Eisenbahn-Bauarbeiten im Vormärz." In *Beiträge zur deutschen Wirtschafts- und Sozialgeschichte des 18. und 19. Jahrhunderts.* Berlin, 1962.

———. *Junker und Bourgeoisie vor 1848 in der preussischen Eisenbahngeschichte.* Berlin, 1962.

Eisfeld, Gerhard. *Die Entstehung der liberalen Parteien in Deutschland 1858–1870: Studie zu den Organisation und Programmen der Liberalen und Demokraten.* Hannover, 1969.

Eley, Geoff. *From Unification to Nazism: Reinterpreting the German Past.* Boston, 1986.

Engelberg, Ernst. *Bismarck: Urpreusse und Reichsgrunder.* 3d ed. Berlin, 1988.

———. *Deutschland von 1848 bis 1871: Von der Niederlage der bürgerlich-demokratischen Revolution bis zur Reichsgründung.* Berlin, 1962.

Engels, Friedrich. "Die preussiche Verfassung." *Marx-Engels Werke* 4. Berlin, 1964.

———. "Germany: Revolution and Counter Revolution." In Leonard Krieger, ed., *The German Revolutions: The Peasant War in Germany and Germany: Revolution and Counter Revolution.* Chicago, 1967.

Enkeling, Joseph. "Die Stellung des Staates zu den Privateisenbahnen in der Anfangszeit des preussischen Eisenbahnwesens." Dissertation. University of Cologne, 1935.

Erdmann, Manfred. *Die Verfassungspolitische Funktion der Wirtschaftsverbände in Deutschland 1815–1871.* Berlin, 1968.

Evans, Richard J. "The Myth of Germany's Missing Revolution." *New Left Review* 149–54 (1985): 67–94.

———. *Rethinking German History: Nineteenth-Century Germany and the Origins of the Third Reich.* London, 1987.

Eyll, Klara van, et al. *Kölner Unternehmer und die Frühindustrialisierung im Rheinland und in Westfalen (1835–1871): Ausstellung des Rheinischen-Westfälischen Wirtschaftsarchivs zu Köln.* Cologne, 1984.

Faulenbach, Bernd. *Ideologie des deutschen Weges.* Munich, 1980.

Fehrenbach, Elisabeth. "Rheinischer Liberalismus und gesellschaftlicher Verfassung." In Wolfgang Schieder, ed., *Liberalismus in der Gesellschaft des deutschen Vormärz.* Göttingen, 1983.

Fischer, Ferdinand. *Preussen am Abschlusse der ersten Hälfte des neunzehnten Jahrhunderts: Geschichtliche, culturhistorische, politische und statistische Rückblicke auf das Jahr 1849.* Berlin, 1876.

Fischer, Fritz. *From Kaiserreich to Third Reich: Elements of Continuity in German History, 1871–1945.* Boston, 1986.

————. *Griff nach der Weltmacht: Die Kriegszielpolitik des kaiserlichen Deutschlands 1914–1918*. Düsseldorf, 1961.

————. *War of Illusions: German Policies from 1911 to 1914*. New York, 1975.

Fischer, Wolfram. *Der Staat und die Anfänge der Industrialisierung in Baden 1800–1850*. Berlin, 1962.

————. *Unternehmerschaft, Selbstverwaltung und Staat: Die Handelskammern in der deutschen Wirtschafts-und Staatsverfassung des 19. Jahrhunderts*. Berlin, 1964.

————. "Das Verhältnis von Staat und Wirtschaft in Deutschland am Beginn der Industrialisierung." In *Wirtschaft und Gesellschaft im Zeitalter der Industrialisierung*. Göttingen, 1982.

————. "Wirtschafts- und sozialgeschichtliche Anmerkungen zum 'deutschen Sonderweg.' " *Tel Aviver Jahrbuch fur Deutsche Geschichte* 26 (1987): 96–116.

————, ed. *Europäische Wirtschafts- und Sozialgeschichte von der Mitte des 19. Jahrhunderts bis zum Ersten Weltkrieg*. Stuttgart, 1985.

————, ed. *Wirtschafts- und sozialgeschichtliche Probleme der frühen Industrializierung*. Berlin, 1968.

———— et al., eds. *Sozialgeschichtliches Arbeitsbuch I: Materialen zur Statistik des Deutschen Bundes 1815–1870*. Munich, 1982.

Fischer-Fabian, Siegfried. *Preussens Krieg und Frieden: Der Weg ins deutsche Reich*. Munich, 1984.

Foelkel, M. "Einigkeit und Freiheit: Die Eisenbahnen ein Mittel nationaler Politik?" In *Zug der Zeit—Zeit der Züge: Deutsche Eisenbahnen 1835–1985*. Vol. 1. Berlin, 1985.

Fremdling, Rainer. *Eisenbahnen und deutscher Wirtschaftswachstum 1840–1879: Ein Beitrag zur Entwicklungstheorie und zur Theorie der Infrastruktur*. 2d ed. Dortmund, 1985.

————. "Railroads and German Economic Growth: A Leading Sector Analysis with a Comparison to the United States and Great Britain." *Journal of Economic History* 37 (1977): 583–604.

Fremdling, Rainer, and Patrick O'Brien, eds. *Productivity in the Economies of Europe in the 19th and 20th Centuries*. Stuttgart, 1982.

Frevert, Ute. *Bürgerinnen und Bürger: Geschlechterverhältnisse im 19. Jahrhundert*. Göttingen, 1988.

————. "Bürgerliche Familie und Geschlechterrollen: Modell und Wirklichkeit." In Lutz Niethammer et al., *Bürgerliche Gesellschaft in Deutschland: Historische Einblicke, Fragen, Perspektiven*. Frankfurt a.M., 1990.

————. *Frauen-Geschichte zwischen bürgerlicher Verbesserung und neuer Weiblichkeit*. Frankfurt a.M., 1986.

Funk, Albrecht. *Polizei und Rechtsstaat: Die Entwicklung des staatlichen Monopols in Preussen 1848–1918*. Frankfurt a.M., 1986.

Gall, Lothar. *Bürgertum in Deutschland*. Berlin, 1989.

————. " '. . . ich wünschte ein Bürger zu sein': Zum Selbstverständnis des deutschen Bürgertums im 19. Jahrhundert." *Historische Zeitschrift* 245 (1987): 601–23.

————. "Liberalismus und 'burgerliche Gesellschaft': Zu Charakter und Entwicklung der liberalen Bewegung in Deutschland." *Historische Zeitschrift* 220 (1975): 324–56.

―――. "Liberalismus und bürgerliche Gesellschaft." In Gall, ed., *Liberalismus*. Cologne, 1976.

―――. "Staat und Wirtschaft in der Reichsgründungszeit." *Historische Zeitschrift* 209 (1969): 616–30.

Gerhard, Ute. "Die Rechtsstellung der Frau in der bürgerlichen Gesellschaft des 19. Jahrhunderts: Frankreich und Deutschland im Vergleich." In Kocka, ed., *Bürgertum im 19. Jahrhundert*. Vol. 1. Munich, 1988.

Gerschenkron, Alexander. *Economic Backwardness in Historical Perspective*. Cambridge, Mass., 1962.

Gille, Bertrand. "Banking and Industrialisation in Europe, 1730–1914." In Carlo M. Cipolla, ed., *The Fontana Economic History of Europe*. Vol. 3, *The Industrial Revolution*. Glasgow, 1973.

Gillis, John. *The Prussian Bureaucracy in Crisis, 1840–1860: Origins of an Administrative Ethos*. Stanford, 1971.

Gisevius, H.-F. *Zur Vorgeschichte des preussischen-sächsischen Eisenbahnkrieges: Verkehrspolitischen Differenzen zwischen Preussen und Sachsen im Deutschen Bund*. Berlin, 1971.

Goertz, Hartmann. *Preussens Gloria: 66 Jahre deutscher Politik 1848–1914 in zeitgenösischer Satire und Karikatur*. Munich, 1962.

Gray, Marion W. "Schroetter, Schön, and Society: Aristocratic Liberalism versus Middle-Class Liberalism in Prussia, 1808." *Central European History* 6 (1973): 60–82.

Grew, Raymond, ed., *Crises of Poltical Development in Europe and the United States*. Princeton, 1978.

Grimm, Dieter. *Deutsche Verfassungsgeschichte 1776–1866*. Frankfurt a.M., 1988.

Groh, Dieter. *Negative Integration und revolutionärer Attentismus*. Frankfurt a.M., 1974.

Grünthal, Günther. "Bemerkungen zur Kamarilla Friedrich Wilhelms IV. im nachmärzlichen Preussen." In O. Büsch, ed., *Friedrich Wilhelm IV. in seiner Zeit: Beiträge eines Colloquiums*, 39–47. Berlin, 1987.

―――. *Parlamentarismus in Preussen 1848/49–1857/58*. Düsseldorf, 1982.

―――. "Die Wahlen zum preussischen Abgeordnetenhaus von 1858." In Jürgen Kocka et al., eds., *Von der Arbeiterbewegung zum modernen Sozialstaat: Festschrift für Gerhard A. Ritter zum 65. Geburtstag*. Munich, 1994.

Grützner, Friedhelm. *Die Politik Bismarcks 1862 bis 1871 in der deutschen Geschichtsschreibung: Eine kritische historiographische Betrachtung*. Frankfurt a.M., 1986.

Gugel, Michael. *Industrieller Aufstieg und bürgerlicher Herrschaft: Soziookonomische Interessen und politische Ziele des liberalen Bürgertums*. Cologne, 1975.

Habermas, Jürgen. *Legitimationsprobleme des Spätkapitalismus*. Frankfurt a.M., 1973.

―――. *Strukturwandel der Öffentlichkeit: Untersuchungen zu einer Kategorie der bürgerlichen Gesellschaft*. 13th ed. Darmstadt, 1982.

Haltern, Utz. *Bürgerliche Gesellschaft: Sozialtheoretischen und sozialhistorische Aspekte.* Darmstadt, 1985.

Hamerow, Theodore S. *Restoration, Revolution, Reaction: Economics and Politics in Germany, 1815–1871.* Princeton, 1958.

———. *Social Foundations of German Unification, 1858–1871: Ideas and Institutions.* Princeton, 1969.

———. *The Social Foundations of German Unification, 1858–1871: Struggles and Accomplishments.* Princeton, 1972.

Hansen, Joseph. *Gustav Mevissen: Ein Rheinisches Lebensbild 1815–1899.* 2 vols. Berlin, 1906.

Harris, James F. "The Authorship of Political Tracts in Post-1848 Germany." *German Studies Review* 10 (1987): 411–41.

Hattenhauer, H. *Geschichte des Beamtentums.* Cologne, 1980.

Hauser, Oswald, ed. *Preussen: Problematik Reich—zur Problematik "Preussen und das Reich."* Cologne, 1984.

Heffter, Heinrich. *Die deutsche Selbstverwaltung im 19. Jahrhundert.* 2d ed. Stuttgart, 1969.

Henderson, William O. *The Rise of German Industrial Power, 1834–1914.* Berkeley, 1975.

———. *The State and the Industrial Revolution in Prussia, 1740–1870.* Liverpool, 1958.

———. *The Zollverein.* 2nd ed. Chicago, 1959.

Henning, Friedrich-Wilhelm. *Die Industrialisierung in Deutschland 1800–1914.* Paderborn, 1975.

Henning, Hans-Joachim. *Die deutsche Beamtenschaft im 19. Jahrhundert: Zwischen Stand und Beruf.* Stuttgart, 1984.

———. *Das westdeutsche Bürgertum in der Epoche der Hochindustrialisierung 1860–1914: Soziales Verhalten und soziale Strukturen.* Wiesbaden, 1972.

Hindess, Barry. "Class and Politics in Marxist Theory." In Gary Littlejohn et al., eds., *Power and the State.* London, 1978.

———. "Marxism and Parliamentary Democracy." In A. Hunt, ed., *Marxism and Democracy.* London, 1980.

Hobsbawm, E. J. *The Age of Capital, 1848–1875.* New York, 1975.

Hoffmann, Walther G. *Das Wachstum der deutschen Wirtschaft seit der Mitte des 19. Jahrhunderts.* Berlin, 1965.

Holborn, Hajo. "Deutscher Idealismus in sozialhistorische Beleuchtung." *Historische Zeitschrift.* 174 (1952): 359–84.

———. *A History of Modern Germany.* 3 vols. Reprint. Princeton, 1982.

Hoppstädter, Kurt. *Die Entstehung der saarländischen Eisenbahnen.* Saarbrücken, 1961.

Hopt, Klaus J. "Ideelle und wirtschaftliche Grundlagen der Actien-, Bank-, und Börsenrechtsentwicklung im 19. Jahrhundert." In Helmut Coing and Walter Wilhelm, eds., *Wissenschaft und Kodifikation des Privatrechts im 19. Jahrhundert.* Vol. 5, *Geld und Banken.* Frankfurt a.M., 1977.

Huber, Ernst R. *Deutsche Verfassungsgeschichte seit 1789.* Vol. 2. Stuttgart, 1960.

Iggers, Georg G. *The German Conception of History: The National Tradition of Historical Thought from Herder to the Present.* Middletown, Conn., 1968.

Jaeger, Hans. "Business History in Germany: A Survey of Recent Developments." *Business History* 48 (1974): 28–48.

————. *Geschichte der Wirtschaftsordnung in Deutschland.* Frankfurt a.M., 1988.

————. "Neue Wege der historischen Unternehmerforschung." *Geschichte und Gesellschaft* 8 (1982): 554–63.

————. *Unternehmer in der deutschen Politik (1890–1918).* Bonn, 1967.

Jaeger, Julius. *Die Lehre von den Eisenbahnen auf Grundlage des Staates.* Munich, 1865.

John, Michael. "The Peculiarities of the German State: Bourgeois Law and Society in the Imperial Era." *Past and Present* 119 (1988): 105–31.

————. *Politics and the Law in Late Nineteenth-Century Germany: The Origins of the Civil Code.* Oxford, 1989.

Kaelble, Hartmut. *Berliner Unternehmer während der Fruhindustrialisierung: Herkunft, sozialer Status und political Einfluss.* Berlin, 1972.

————. *Industrielle Interessenpolitik in der wilhelminischen Gesellschaft: Der Centralverband der deutschen Industriellen.* Berlin, 1970.

————. "Der Mythos der rapiden Industrialisierung in Deutschland." *Geschichte und Gesellschaft* 9 (1983): 106–18.

————. "Wie feudal waren die deutschen Unternehmer im Kaiserreich? Ein Zwischenbericht." In Richard Tilly, ed., *Beiträge zur quantitativen vergleichenden Unternehmergeschichte.* Stuttgart, 1985.

Kafka, Eduard. *Eisenbahnangelegenheiten und Personalien in lexikalischer Form.* Leipzig, 1885.

Kaschuba, Wolfgang. "Zwischen Deutscher Nation und Deutscher Provinz: Politische Horizonte und soziale Milieus im frühen Liberalismus." In Dieter Langewiesche, ed., *Liberalismus im 19. Jahrhundert.* Göttingen, 1988.

Katznelson, Ira, and Aristide R. Zolberg. *Working-Class Formation: Nineteenth-Century Patterns in Western Europe and the United States.* Princeton, 1986.

Kech, Edwin. *Geschichte der deutschen Eisenbahn-Politik.* Leipzig, 1911.

Kehr, Eckhart. *Der Primat der Innenpolitik: Gesammelte Aufsätze zur preussisch-deutschen Sozialgeschichte.* Edited by Hans-Ulrich Wehler. Berlin, 1965.

————. *Schlachtflottenbau und Parteipolitik.* Berlin, 1930.

Kellenbenz, Hermann. *Deutsche Wirtschaftsgeschichte.* Vol. 2, *Vom Ausgang des 18. Jahrhunderts bis zum Ende des Zweiten Weltkriegs.* Munich, 1981.

Kellenbenz, Hermann, and Klara van Eyll. *Die Geschichte der unternehmerischen Selbstverwaltung in Köln 1797–1914.* Cologne, 1972.

Keller, Gottfried. *Der Staatsbahngedanke bei den verschiedenen Voelkern.* Aarau, 1897.

Kiesewetter, Hubert. *Industrielle Revolution in Deutschland 1815–1914.* Frankfurt a.M., 1989.

Kitchen, Martin. *The Political Economy of Germany, 1815–1914.* London, 1978.

Klee, Wolfgang. *Preussiche Eisenbahngeschichte.* Bielefeld, 1982.

Klein, Ernst. *Geschichte der öffentlichen Finanzen in Deutschland (1500–1870)*. Wiesbaden, 1974.

Kocka, Jürgen. *Arbeitsverhältnisse und Arbeiterexistenzen: Grundlagen der Klassenbildung im 19. Jahrhundert*. Bonn, 1990.

———. "Bürgertum and Professions: Two Alternative Approaches." In Michael Burrage and Rolf Torstendahl, eds., *Professions in Theory and History*. London, 1990.

———. "Bürgertum und bürgerliche Gesellschaft im 19. Jahrhundert: Europäische Entwicklungen und deutsche Eigenarten." In Kocka, ed., *Bürgertum im 19. Jahrhundert: Deutschland im europäischen Vergleich*, Vol. 1. Munich, 1988.

———. "Bürgertum und Bürgerlichkeit als Probleme der deutschen Geschichte vom späten 18. zum frühen 20. Jahrhundert." In Kocka, ed., *Bürger und Bürgerlichkeit im 19. Jahrhundert*. Göttingen, 1987.

———. "Capitalism and Bureaucracy in German Industrialism before 1914." *Economic History Review*, 2nd Ser., 33 (1981): 253–468.

———. "Der 'deutsche Sonderweg' in der Diskussion." *German Studies Review* 5 (1982): 365–79.

———. "Eisenbahnverwaltung in der industriellen Revolution: Deutsch-Amerikanischische Vergleiche." In H. Kellenbenz and Hans Pohl, eds., *Historia Socialis et Economica*. Stuttgart, 1987.

———. "German History before Hitler: The Debate about the German *Sonderweg*," *Journal of Contemporary History* 23 (1988): 3–16.

———. "Industrielles Management: Konzeptionen und Modelle in Deutschland vor 1914." *Vierteljahrsschrift für Sozial- und Wirtschaftsgeschichte* 56 (1969): 332–72.

———. "Problems of Working-Class Formation in Germany: The Early Years, 1800–1875." In Ira Katznelson and Aristide R. Zolberg, *Working-Class Formation: Nineteenth-Century Patterns in Western Europe and the United States*. Princeton, 1986.

———. "Stand-Klasse-Organisation: Strukturen sozialer Ungleichheit in Deutschland vom späten 18. bis zum frühen 20. Jahrhundert im Aufriss." In Hans-Ulrich Wehler, *Klassen in der europäischen Socialgeschichte*. Göttingen, 1979.

———. "Theory and Social History: Recent Developments in West Germany." *Social Research* 47 (1980): 426–57.

———. *Unternehmensverwaltung und Angestelltenschaft am Beispiel Siemens 1847–1914: Zum Verhältnis von Kapitalismus und Bürokratie in der deutschen Industrialisierung*. Stuttgart, 1969.

———. "Zur Schichtung der preussischen Bevölkerung während der industriellen Revolution." In Wilhelm Treue, ed., *Geschichte als Aufgabe: Festschrift für Otto Busch zu seinem 60. Geburtstag* (Berlin, 1988): 357–90.

———, ed. *Bürger und Bürgerlichkeit im 19. Jahrhundert*. Göttingen, 1987.

Köllmann, Wolfgang. "August von der Heydt." In *Wuppertaler Biographien*, number 1. Elberfeld, 1958.

————. *Bevölkerung in der industriellen Revolution: Studien zur Bevölkerungsgeschichte Deutschlands.* Gottingen, 1974.

————. *Friedrich Harkort.* Vol. 1, *1793–1838.* Düsseldorf, 1964.

Kondratieff, N. D. "Die langen Wellen der Konjunktur." *Archiv für Sozialwissenschaft und Sozialpolitik* 56 (1926): 573–609.

Koselleck, Reinhart. *Preussen zwischen Reform und Revolution.* 3d ed. Stuttgart, 1989.

Krieger, Leonard. *The German Idea of Freedom: History of a Political Tradition.* Boston, 1957.

Krüger, Alfred. *Das Kölner Bankiergewerbe vom Ende des 18. Jahrhunderts bis 1875.* Essen, 1925.

Kubitschek, Helmut. "Die Börsenverordnung vom 24. Mai 1844 und die Situation im Finanz- und Kreditwesen Preussens in den vierziger Jahren des 19. Jahrhunderts (1840 bis 1847)." *Jahrbuch für Wirtschaftsgeschichte* 4 (1962): 57–78.

Kumpmann, Karl. *Die Entstehung der Rheinischen Eisenbahngesellschaft 1830–1844: Ein erster Beitrag zur Geschichte der Rheinishen Eisenbahn.* Essen, 1910.

Kuznets, Stanley. *Modern Economic Growth.* New Haven, 1966.

Landes, David. "The Old Bank and the New: The Financial Revolution of the Nineteenth Century." In F. Crouzet et al., *Essays in European Economic History, 1789–1914.* New York, 1969.

————. *The Unbound Prometheus: Technological Change and Industrial Development in Western Europe from 1750 to the Present.* Reprint. New York, 1982.

Langewiesche, Dieter, ed., *Liberalismus im 19. Jahrhundert.* Göttingen, 1988.

————. *Liberalismus in Deutschland.* Frankfurt a.M., 1988.

————. *Liberalismus und Demokratie in Württemberg zwischen Revolution und Reichsgründung.* Düsseldorf, 1974.

Langewiesche, Dieter, and Klaus Schonhoven, eds. *Arbeiter in Deutschland: Studien zur Lebensweise der Arbeiterschaft im Zeitalter der Industrialisierung.* Paderborn, 1981.

Lees, Andrew. *Revolution and Reflection: Intellectual Change in Germany during the 1850s.* The Hague, 1974.

Lepsius, M. Rainer. "Parteisystem und Sozialstruktur: Zum Problem der Demokratisierung der deutschen Gesellschaft." In Gerhart A. Ritter, ed., *Deutsche Parteien vor 1918.* Cologne, 1973.

Leyen, A. von der. "Die Durchführung des Staatsbahnsystems in Preussen." *Jahrbuch für Gesetzgebung, Verwaltung und Volkwirtschaft im Deutschen Reich (Schmollers Jahrbuch)* 7/2 (1883): 461–511.

————. "Die preussischen Eisenbahnpolitik des Jarhes 1848." *Archiv fuer Eisenbahnwesen* (1880): 141–49.

Lipset, Seymour M., and Reinhard Bendix. *Social Mobility in Industrial Society.* Berkeley, 1967.

Lowy, Michael. *The Politics of Combined and Uneven Development.* London, 1981.

Machtan, Lothar, and Dietrich Milles. *Die Klassensymbiose von Junkertum und Bourgeoisie: Zum Verhältnis von gesellschaftlicher und politischer Herrschaft in Preussen-Deutschland 1850–1878/79.* Frankfurt a.M., 1980.

Martin, P. C. "Die Entstehung des preussischen Aktiengesetzes." *Vierteljahrsschrift für Sozial- und Wirtschaftsgeschichte* 56 (1969): 499–542.

Marx, Karl. *Marx-Engels Werke* 12. Berlin, 1963.

———. *Marx-Engels Werke* 15. Berlin, 1964.

Matzerath, H. *Urbanisierung in Preussen 1815–1914.* Stuttgart, 1983.

Mayer, Arno. *The Persistence of the Old Regime.* New York, 1981.

Meinecke, Friedrich. *The Age of German Liberation, 1795–1814.* Berkeley, 1977.

Meyer, B. H. "The Administration of Prussian Railroads." *American Academy of Political and Social Sciences Annals* 10 (1897): 389–423.

Michaelis, Julius. *Deutschlands Eisenbahnen: Ein Handbuch für Geschäftsleute, Capitalisten und Speculanten.* Leipzig, 1859.

Michaelis, Otto. *Das Monopol der Eisenbahnen.* Berlin, 1861.

———. *Volkswirtschaftliche Schriften.* Vol. 1. Berlin, 1873.

Mieck, Ilya. *Preussische Geschichte in Berlin 1806–1844.* Berlin, 1967.

———. *Preussische Gewerbepolitik in Berlin 1806–44: Staatshilfe und private Initiative zwischen Merkantilismus und Liberalismus.* Berlin, 1965.

Mitchell, B. R., *European Historical Statistics, 1750–1975.* 2d ed. New York, 1980.

Moeller, Robert G. "The Kaiserreich Recast? Continuity and Change in Modern German Historiography." *Journal of Social History* 17 (1984): 655–84.

Moll, Georg. *"Preussischer Weg" und burgerlicher Umwaelzung in Deutschland.* Weimar, 1988.

Mommsen, Wilhelm. *Grösse und Versagen des deutschen Bürgertums: Ein Beitrag zur politischen Bewegung des 19. Jahrhunderts, insbesonders zur Revolution 1848/49.* 2d ed. Munich, 1964.

Mommsen, Wolfgang. *Das Ringen um den nationalen Staat 1850–1890.* Berlin, 1993.

———. *Der autoritäre Nationalstaat: Verfassung, Gesellschaft und Kultur im deutschen Kaiserreich.* Frankfurt a.M., 1990.

Moore, Barrington, Jr. *Social Origins of Dictatorship and Democracy.* London, 1967.

Mosse, W. E. *The German-Jewish Economic Elite, 1820–1935: A Socio-Cultural Profile.* Oxford, 1989.

Mottek, Hans. *Wirtschaftsgeschichte Deutschlands: Ein Grundriss.* Vol. 2, *Von der Zeit der französischen Revolution bis zur Zeit der Bismarckschen Reichsgründung.* Berlin, 1971.

Münch, Hermann. *Adolf von Hansemann.* Munich, 1932.

Muncy, Lysbeth W. *The Junker in the Prussian Administration under William II, 1888–1914.* New York, 1944.

———. "The Prussian Landräte in the Last Years of the Monarchy: A Case Study of Pomerania and the Rhineland, 1890–1918." *Central European History* 6 (1973): 299–338.

Murphy, David T. "Prussian Aims for the Zollverein, 1828–1833." *The Historian* 53 (Fall 1991): 285–302.

Na'aman, Shlomo. *Der deutsche Nationalverein: Die politische Konstituierung des deutschen Bürgertums 1859–1867.* Düsseldorf, 1987.

Niethammer, Lutz, et al., eds. *Bürgerliche Gesellschaft in Deutschland: Historische Einblicke, Fragen, Perspektiven.* Frankfurt a.M., 1990.

Nipperdey, Thomas. *Deutsche Geschichte 1800–1866: Bürgerwelt und starker Staat.* Munich, 1983.

—————. *Nachdenken über die deutsche Geschichte: Essays.* Munich, 1990.

—————. *Die Organisation der deutschen Parteien vor 1918.* Düsseldorf, 1961.

Nordmann, Hans. *Die ältere preussische Eisenbahngeschichte.* Berlin, 1950.

Noyes, Paul. *Organization and Revolt: Working Class Associations in the German Revolutions of 1848–49.* Princeton, 1966.

Obenaus, Herbert. *Anfänge der Parlamentarismus in Preussen bis 1848.* Düsseldorf, 1984.

Obermann, Karl. *Deutschland von 1815 bis 1849. Von der Gründung des Deutschen Bundes bis zur bürgerlich-demokratischen Revolution.* Berlin, 1961.

—————. "Ludolf Camphausen und die bourgeoise Konterrevolution." *Zeitschrift für Gescichtswissenschaft* 18 (1970): 1448–69.

—————. "Die Rolle der ersten deutschen Aktienbanken in den Jahren 1848 bis 1856." *Jahrbuch für Wirtschaftsgeschichte* 2 (1960): 47–75.

—————. "Zur Beschaffung des Eisenbahn-Kapitals in Deutschland in den Jahren 1835–1855." *Revue internationale d'histoire de la banque* 5 (1972): 315–52.

—————. "Zur Genesis der bürgerlichen Klasse in Deutschland von der Julirevolution 1830 bis zu Beginn der 40er Jahren des 19. Jahrhunderts." *Jahrbuch der Geschichte* 16 (1977): 33–66.

—————. "Zur Rolle der Eisenbahnarbeiter im Prozess der Formierung der Arbeiterklasse in Deutschland." *Jahrbuch für Wirtschaftsgeschichte* (1970).

Obermann, Karl, et al., eds. *Männer der Revolution von 1848.* 2 vols. Berlin, 1987–88.

O'Boyle, Lenore. "The Democratic Left in Germany, 1848." *Journal of Modern History* 33 (1961): 374–83.

O'Brien, Patrick. *The New Economic History of the Railways.* New York, 1977.

Obst, Erich. *Die Grundlagen der Verkehrsentwicklung Schlesiens und die Entstehung des schlesischen Eisenbahn-Netzes.* Breslau, 1942.

Offermann, Toni. *Arbeiterbewegung und liberales Bürgertum in Deutschland 1850–1863.* Bonn, 1979.

—————. "Preussischer Liberalismus zwischen Revolution und Reichsgründung im regionalen Vergleich: Berliner und Kölner Fortschrittsliberalismus in der Konfliktzeit." In Dieter Langewiesche, ed., *Liberalismus in der Gesellschaft des deutschen Vormärz.* Göttingen, 1983.

Ohlsen, Manfred. *Der Eisenbahnkönig: Bethel Henry Strousberg: eine preussische Gründerkarriere.* 2d ed. Berlin, 1987.

Padtberg, Beate-Carola. *Rheinischer Liberalismus in Köln während der politischen Reaktion in Preussen nach 1848/49.* Cologne, 1985.

Parent, Thomas. *"Passiver Widerstan" im preussischen Verfassungskonflikt: Die Kölner Abgeordnetenfeste.* Cologne, 1982.

Parsons, Talcott. "Democracy and Social Structure in Pre-Nazi Germany." In Parsons, ed., *Essays on Sociological Theory.* Glencoe, 1954.

Petersdorff, Hermann von. *Kleist-Retzow.* Stuttgart, 1907.

Pflanze, Otto. "Another Crisis among German Historians? Helmut Böhme's *Deutschlands Weg zur Grossmacht,*" *Journal of Modern History* 40 (1968): 118–29.

———. *Bismarck and the Unification of Germany.* Vol. 1, *The Period of Unification, 1815–1871.* 2d ed. Princeton, 1990.

———. *Bismarck and the Unification of Germany.* Vol. 2, *The Period of Consolidation, 1871–1880.* Princeton, 1990.

———. *Bismarck and the Unification of Germany.* Vol. 3, *The Period of Fortification, 1880–1898.* Princeton, 1990.

———. "Bismarcks Herrschaftstechnik als Problem der gegenwärtigen Historiographie." *Historische Zeitschrift* 234 (1982): 561–99.

———. "Judicial and Political Responsibility in Nineteenth-Century Germany." In Leonard Krieger and Fritz Stern, eds., *The Responsibility of Power.* New York, 1967.

———. " 'Sammlungspolitik' 1875–1886: Kritische Bemerkungen zu einem Modell." In Pflanze, ed., *Innenpolitische Probleme des Bismarck-Reiches.* Munich, 1983.

Pierenkemper, Toni. *Die westfälischen Schwerindustriellen 1852–1913: Soziale Struktur und unternehmerischer Erfolg.* Göttingen, 1979.

———. "Die Zusammensetzung des Fuhrungspersonals und die Lösung unternehmerischer Probleme in frühen Eisenbahngesellschaften." *Tradition: Zeitschrift für Firmengeschichten und Unternehmensbiographien* 21 (1976): 37–49.

Pohl, Hans, and Manfred Pohl. *Deutsche Bankengeschichte,* vol. 2, *Das Deutsche Bankwesen (1806–1848); Die Entwicklung des deutschen Bankwesens zwischen 1870 und 1914.* Frankfurt a.M., 1982.

Pollard, Sidney, ed. *Region und Industrialisierung: Studien zur Rolle der Region in der Wirtschaftsgeschichte der letzten zwei Jahrhunderte.* Göttingen, 1980.

Prevadovich, Nikolaus von. *Die Fuhrungsschichten in Preussen und Osterreich 1806–1918.* Wiesbaden, 1955.

Puhle, H.-J. *Agrarische Interessenpolitik und preussischer Konservatismus im wilhelminischen Kaiserreich 1893–1914.* Hanover, 1966.

———. *Von der Agrarkrise zum Präfaschismus.* Wiesbaden, 1972.

Radtke, Wolfgang. *Die preussiche Seehandlung zwischen Staat und Wirtschaft in der Frühphase der Industrialisierung.* Berlin, 1981.

Reddy, William. *Money and Liberty in Modern Europe.* New York, 1987.

———. *The Rise of Market Culture.* Cambridge, 1984.

Redlich, Fritz. "Jacques Lafitte and the Beginning of Investment Banking in France." *Bulletin of the Business Historical Society* 22 (1948): 137–60.

———. *Der Unternehmer: Wirtschafts- und Sozialgeschichtliche Studien.* Göttingen, 1964.

Riesser, Jacob. *The German Great Banks and Their Concentration.* Washington, 1911.

Rochau, August Ludwig von. *Grundsätze der Realpolitik angewendet auf die Zustände Deutschlands.* Edited by Hans-Ulrich Wehler. Frankfurt a.M., 1972.

Rohr, Donald. *The Origins of Social Liberalism in Germany.* Chicago, 1963.

Rosenberg, Hans. *Bureaucracy, Aristocracy, and Autocracy: The Prussian Experience, 1660–1815.* Reprint. Boston, 1968.

————. *Grosse Depression und Bismarckzeit.* Berlin, 1967.

————. *Die Nationalpolitische Publizistik Deutschlands: Vom Entritt der Neuen Aera in Preussen bis zum Ausbruch des deutschen Krieges.* 2 vols. Munich, 1935.

————. *Die Weltwirtschaftskrise 1857–1859.* Reprint. Göttingen, 1974.

Rostow, Walter W. *The Stages of Economic Growth: A Non-Communist Manifesto.* Cambridge, 1961.

————. "The Take-Off into Self-Sustained Growth." *Economic Journal* 66 (1956): 25–48.

————, ed. *The Economics of Take-Off into Sustained Growth.* London, 1963.

Rürup, Reinhard. *Deutschland im 19. Jahrhundert 1815–1871.* Göttingen, 1984.

Salsbury, S. *The State, the Investor, and the Railroad: Boston and Albany, 1825–1867.* Cambridge, Mass., 1967.

Sauer, Wolfgang. "Das Problem des deutschen Nationalstaats." Reprinted in H.-U. Wehler, ed., *Moderne deutsche Sozialgeschichte.* Cologne, 1966.

Sax, Emil. *Die Eisenbahnen.* Vienna, 1879.

Schieder, Theodor. *Staatensystem als Vormacht der Welt 1848–1918.* Frankfurt a.M., 1975.

Schivelbusch, Wolfgang. *Geschichte der Eisenbahnreise. Zur Industrialisierung von Raum und Zeit im 19. Jahrhundert.* Munich, 1977.

Schlumbohm, Jürgen. *Der Verfassungskonflikt in Preussen 1862–1866.* Göttingen, 1970.

Schoeps, Hans-Joachim. *Preussen: Geschichte eines Staates.* Frankfurt a.M., 1966.

Schreiber, *Die Preussischen Eisenbahnen und ihr Verhältniss zum Staat 1834–1874.* Berlin, 1874.

Schumann, Dirk. *Bayerns Unternehmen in Gesellschaft und Staat 1834–1914.* Göttingen, 1992.

Schwann, Mathieu. *Ludolf Camphausen.* 3 vols. Essen, 1915.

Schwartz, O., and G. Strutz. *Der Staatshaushalts und die Finanzen Preussens.* Vol. 1. Berlin, 1901.

Seidenfus, Stephan. "Eisenbahnwesen." In K. G. A. Jeserich, ed., *Deutsche Verwaltungsgeschichte.* Vol. 2, *Vom Reichsdeputationshauptschluss bis zur Aufloesung des Deutschen Reiches.* Stuttgart, 1983.

Seidenzahl, Fritz. "Eine Denkschrift David Hansemanns vom Jahre 1856: Ein Beitrag zur Entstehungsgeschichte der deutschen Aktienbanken." In Karl Erich Born, ed., *Moderne deutsche Wirtschaftsgeschichte.* Cologne, 1966.

Sell, F. C. *Die Tragödie des deutschen Liberalismus.* Stuttgart, 1953.

Sheehan, James J., ed. *Imperial Germany.* New York, 1976.

————. *German Liberalism in the Nineteenth Century.* Paperback edition. Chicago, 1983.

————. *German History, 1770–1866.* Oxford, 1990.

Sieferle, R. P. *Fortschrittsfeinde? Opposition gegen Technik und Industrie von der Romantik bis zur Gegenwart.* Munich, 1984.

Siemann, Wolfram. *Die deutsche Revolution.* Frankfurt a.M., 1988.

———. *"Deutschlands Ruhe, Sicherheit und Ordnung": Die Anfänge der politischen Polizei 1806–1866.* Tübingen, 1985.

———. *Gesellschaft im Aufbruch: Deutschland 1848–1871.* Frankfurt a.M., 1990.

Simmel, Georg. *Conflict and the Web of Group-Affiliations.* New York, 1964.

Simon, Walter M. *The Failure of the Prussian Reform Movement.* Ithaca, 1955.

Smith, Cecil O, Jr. "The Longest Run: Public Engineers and Planning in France." *American Historical Review* 95 (1990): 657–92.

Sombart, Werner. *Deutsche Volkwirtschaft im Neunzehnten Jahrhundert.* Berlin, 1903.

Sperber, Jonathan. *Political Catholicism in Nineteenth-Century Germany.* Princeton, 1984.

———. *Rhineland Radicals: The Democratic Movement and the Revolution of 1848–49.* Princeton, 1991.

———. "State and Civil Society in Prussia: Thoughts on a New Edition of Reinhart Koselleck's *Preussen zwischen Reform und Revolution.*" *Journal of Modern History* 57 (1985): 278–96.

Spree, Reinhard. *Wachstumstrends und Konjunkturzyklen in der deutschen Wirtschaft von 1820 bis 1913: Quantitativer Rahmen für eine Konjunkturgeschichte des 19. Jahrhunderts.* Göttingen, 1978.

———. *Die Wachstumszyklen der deutschen Wirtschaft von 1840 bis 1880.* Berlin, 1977.

Spree, Reinhard, and Jürgen Bergmann, "Die konjunkturelle Entwicklung der deutschen Wirtschaft 1840 bis 1864." In Hans-Ulrich Wehler, ed., *Sozialgeschichte Heute: Kritische Studien zur Geschichtswissenschaft.* Göttingen, 1974.

Stadelmann, Rudolf. *Soziale und politische Geschichte der Revolution von 1848.* Munich, 1948.

Stahl, Wilhelm. *Der Elitekreislauf in der Unternehmerschaft: Eine empirische Untersuchung für den deutschsprachigen Raum.* Frankfurt a.M., 1973.

Stearns, Peter. *Paths to Authority: The Middle Class and the Industrial Labor Force in France, 1820–48.* Urbana, Ill., 1978.

Stegmann, Dirk. *Die Erben Bismarcks: Parteien und Verbände in der Spätphase des wilhelminischen Deutschlands; Sammlungspolitik 1897–1918.* Cologne, 1970.

Steitz, Walther. *Die Entstehung der Köln-Mindener Eisenbahn.* Cologne, 1974.

Stern, Fritz. *Gold and Iron: Bismarck, Bleichröder, and the Building of the German Empire.* New York, 1977.

Streisand, Joachim. *Deutsche Geschichte in einem Blick.* 5th ed. Berlin, 1980.

Strousberg, Bethel Henry. *Dr. Strousberg und sein Wirken.* Berlin, 1876.

Stürmer, Michael, ed. *Das kaiserliche Deutschland: Politik und Gesellschaft 1870–1914.* Düsseldorf, 1970.

Teuteberg, H.-J. *Westfälische Textilunternehmer in der Industrialisierung: Sozialer Status und betriebliches Verhalten im 19. Jahrhundert.* Dortmund, 1980.

Thieme, Horst. "Die ökonomischen und politischen Widersprüche bei der Erteilung von Konzessionen zur Gründung von Aktiengesellschaften in Preussen von 1850–1857." Dissertation. University of Leipzig, 1957.

Thompson, E. P. *The Poverty of Theory and Other Essays.* London, 1978.

Tilly, Charles, ed. *The Formation of National States in Western Europe.* Princeton, 1975.

Tilly, Richard. *Financial Institutions and Industrialization in the Rhineland, 1815–1870.* Madison, 1966.

———. *Kapital, Staat und sozialer Protest in der deutschen Industrialisierung.* Gottingen, 1980.

———. "The Political Economy of Public Finance and the Industrialization of Prussia, 1815–66," *Journal of Economic History* 26 (1966): 484–97.

———. "Soll und Haben: Recent German Economic History and the Problem of Economic History." *Journal of Economic History* 29 (1969): 289–319.

———, ed. *Beiträge zur quantitativen vergleichenden Unternehmersgeschichte.* Stuttgart, 1985.

Tipton, Frank. *Regional Variations in the Economic Development of Germany during the Nineteenth Century.* Middletown, Conn., 1976.

Trebilcock, Clive. *The Industrialization of the Continental Powers, 1780–1914.* New York, 1981.

Treitschke, Heinrich. *Deutsche Geschichte.* 5 vols. 3d ed. Leipzig, 1890.

Treue, Wilhelm. "Adam Smith in Deutschland: Zum Problem des 'Politischen Professors' zwischen 1770 and 1810." In Werner Conze, ed., *Deutschland und Europa.* Düsseldorf, 1951.

———. *Gebhardt Handbuch der deutschen Geschichte.* Vol. 17, *Gesellschaft, Wirtschaft und Technik Deutschlands im 19. Jahrhundert.* 8th ed. Munich, 1986.

———, ed. *Geschichte als Aufgabe: Festschrift für Otto Büsch zu seinem 60. Geburtstag.* Berlin, 1988.

———. *Wirtschafts-, Finanz- und Technikgeschichte Preussens.* Berlin, 1984.

Valentin, Veit. *Geschichte der deutschen Revolution von 1848–49.* 2 vols. Berlin, 1930.

Vance, James E., Jr., *Capturing the Horizon: The Historical Geography of Transportation since the Sixteenth Century.* New York, 1986.

———. Transportation and the Geographical Expression of Capitalism." In Eugene D. Genovese and Leonard Hochberg, eds., *Geographical Perspectives on History.* Oxford, 1989.

Varnhagen von Ense, Karl A. *Tagebücher.* Vol. 1. Leipzig, 1861.

Veblen, Thorstein. *Imperial Germany and the Industrial Revolution.* New York, 1913.

Vogel, Barbara. "Die 'allgemeine Gewerbefreiheit' als bürokratische Modernisierungsstrategie in Preussen." In Dirk Stegmann et al., eds., *Industrielle Gesellschaft und politisches System.* Bonn, 1978.

———. "Die preussischen Reformen als Gegenstand und Problem der Forschung." In Vogel, ed., *Preussiche Reformen 1807–1820.* Königsberg, 1980.

Vogel, Ursula. "Patriarchale Herrschaft, bürgerliches Recht, bürgerliche Utopie: Eigentumsrechte der Frauen in Deutschland und England." In Kocka, ed., *Bürgertum im 19. Jahrhundert.* Vol. 1. Munich, 1988.

Volkmann, Heinrich. *Die Arbeiterfrage im preussischen Abgeordnetenhause 1848–1869.* Berlin, 1968.

Wagenblass, Horst. *Der Eisenbahnbau und das Wachstum der deutschen Eisen- und Maschinenbauindustrie 1835–1860.* Stuttgart, 1973.

Walter, Hans. *Die innere Politik des Ministers von Manteuffel und der Ursprung der Reaktion in Preussen.* Berlin, 1910.

Waltershausen, A. Sartorius von. *Deutsche Wirtschaftsgeschichte 1815–1914.* 2d ed. Jena, 1923.

Weber, Max. *From Max Weber: Essays in Sociology.* New York, 1974.

———. *The Theory of Social and Economic Organization.* New York, 1964.

Weber, Rolf. *Das Unglück der Könige: Johann Jacoby 1805–1877.* Berlin, 1987.

Wedel, Hasso von. *Heinrich von Wittgenstein 1797–1869: Unternehmer und Politiker in Köln.* Cologne, 1981.

Wegmann, Dietrich. *Die leitenden Verwaltungsbeamten der Provinz Westfalen 1815–1918.* Munster, 1969.

Wehler, Hans-Ulrich. *Bismarck und der Imperialismus.* Cologne, 1969.

———. *Deutsche Gesellschaftsgeschichte.* Vol. 2, *Von der Reformära bis zur industriellen und politischen "deutschen Doppelrevolution," 1815–1845/49.* Munich, 1987.

———. *Deutsche Gesellschaftsgeschichte.* Vol. 3, *Von der "deutschen Doppelrevolution" bis zum Beginn des Ersten Weltkrieges 1849–1914.* Munich, 1995.

———. *Das deutsche Kaiserreich.* Göttingen, 1973.

———. *Krisenherde des Kaiserreichs 1871–1918: Studien zur deutschen Sozial- und Wirtschaftsgeschichte.* 2d ed. Gottingen, 1979.

———. *Modernisierungstheorie und Geschichte.* Göttingen, 1975.

———. "Sozialökonomie und Geschichtswissenschaft." *Neue Politische Literatur* 14 (1969): 347–59.

Winkler, Heinrich August. *Liberalismus und Antiliberalismus.* Göttingen, 1979.

Witt, Peter-Christian. *Die Finanzpolitik des deutschen Reiches von 1903 bis 1913.* Lübeck, 1970.

Wortmann, W. *Eisenbahnbauarbeiter im Vormärz: Sozialgeschichtlicher Untersuchung der Bauarbeiter der Cöln-Mindener Eisenbahn in Minden-Ravensberg.* Cologne, 1972.

Wunder, Bernd. *Die Rekrutierung der Beamtenschaft in Deutschland—eine historische Betrachtung.* Konstanz, 1979.

Wuttmer, Heinz. "Die Herkunft der industriellen Bourgeoisie Preussens in den vierziger Jahren des 19. Jahrhunderts." In Hans Mottek et al., *Studien zur Geschichte der industriellen Revolution in Deutschland.* Berlin, 1960.

Zeise, Roland. "Die Rolle des Zollvereins in den politischen Konzeptionen der deutschen Bouurgeoisie von 1859/66." In Helmut Bleiber et al., eds., *Bourgeoisie und bürgerliche Umwälzung in Deutschland 1789–1871.* Berlin, 1977.

———. "Zur Genesis und Funktion der deutschen Handelskammern bis zur Reichsgrundung 1871." *Jahrbuch für Wirtschaftsgeschichte* (1976): 63–82.

Zunkel, Friedrich. "Beamtenschaft und Unternehmertum beim Aufbau der Ruhrindustrie 1849–1880." *Tradition* 9 (1964): 261–77.

————. *Der rheinisch-westfälische Unternehmer 1834–1879: Ein Beitrag zur Geschichte des deutschen Bürgertums im 19. Jahrhundert.* Cologne, 1962.

————. "Das Verhältnis des Unternehmertums zum Bildungsbürgertum zwischen Vormärz and Erstem Weltkrieg." In M. Rainer Lepsius, ed., *Bildungsbürgertum im 19. Jahrhundert* (Stuttgart, 1992).

INDEX